Writing Strategies

Plus Collaboration

Mary Sue Koeppel

Florida Community College at Jacksonville

Second Edition

SIMON & SCHUSTER CUSTOM PUBLISHING

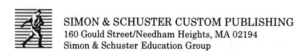
SIMON & SCHUSTER CUSTOM PUBLISHING
160 Gould Street/Needham Heights, MA 02194
Simon & Schuster Education Group

Copyright Acknowledgments

Contents

Writer's Decision Three—Who Will Listen to Me? Why? 95

Acknowledgments

Many people have contributed to the making of this text, both the first and second editions. First among them, I thank Robert B. Gentry of Florida Community College at Jacksonville for contributing his writings and for his insightful assistance, particularly with the argument and essay-test chapters.

Without the questions and responses of those who attended the National Institute for Teachers of Writing in Greenfield, Massachusetts, and in Portland, Maine, as well as my workshops in universities and colleges around the United States, this book would never have been written. Thank you!

My colleagues Professors Susan Slavicz, Sally Nielsen, William Strickland, Richard Green, Kathleen Ciez, Carol Grimes, and Belinda Smith each used the text and spent important time with me offering valuable suggestions and insights for this second edition. The new readings are offered, often at their suggestions. Susan Slavicz is to be singled out for her contribution of six peer editing worksheets. Nancy Smith made important suggestions for the cover. In addition, test questions were given by Reginald Touchton, Julie Aires, and Bill Vockell, and reactions to several specific chapters were offered by Lawton Green, Arnold Wood, Jean Shepherd, Jeff Olma, and Charles Feldstein. I thank all of my colleagues at Florida Community College at Jacksonville for their support, especially Betsy Griffey, Charles Smires, and Joan Hill.

I am grateful to other faculty from around the United States who read the manuscript and gave reactions to the first edition: Toby Fulwiler, University of Vermont; Louise Skilling, Miami Dade Community College, Florida; Mary Colgan McNamara, EXEL, Tampa, Florida; Nancy Hall, Suffolk Community College, New York; Patricia Hoff, Pewaukee High School, Wisconsin; Leigh Barker and Thomas Cheesebro, Waukesha County Technical College, Wisconsin; Willa Wolcott, University of Florida, Gainesville; Ann Fey, Rockland Community College, New York. Professors Katherine Adams, Marcia S. Curtis, Orian Green, George Hammerbacher, and Nancy Roediger reviewed the original manuscript and offered valuable perceptions.

Hal Hawkins and the entire group at Simon & Schuster made this second edition possible. Thank you!

Introduction

What will I write about?

What will I say about my topic?

Whom do I want to read my paper?

What do I want my readers to get from my essay?

What words should I use?

How should I organize my information so the audience is affected the way I want?

These are questions writers ask. Perhaps you ask some of these same questions, too. To answer such questions, writers (whether consciously or unconsciously) must make certain decisions. You can learn to make all these same decisions yourself. This text shows how.

In "The Writing Process" (Chapters 1–20), you learn to ask many questions and make the decisions writers must make: choose an idea; gather supporting information; decide upon an audience, purpose, and writing voice; organize and write the information to win your audience to your purpose; and plan appropriate sentence strategies. To summarize the first part of the book, I show in Chapter 20 how I made all these decisions as I wrote an essay called "Why I Love Where I Live".

So the first half of this book is about the writing process itself. The second half (Chapters 21–34) shows you how to create different kinds of essays which your instructors may ask you to write.

This text is designed so each chapter presents a different strategy for mastering the writing task. Each chapter contains explanations, examples, (created by students and professional writers), self-helps, collaborative learning materials, writing tasks, and checklists for you.

Each chapter offers you a variety of Collaborative Learning experiences and many different Writing Tasks. Choose those which you find most helpful. Because each short chapter is a self-contained unit, you can concentrate on certain chapters or skim others without losing continuity.

This text was born from my experiences as a teacher in many kinds of schools—the university, the community college, the technical institute, and the college prep school. I have also had the privilege of teaching teachers at the annual National Institute for Teachers of Writing, first in Portland, Maine, and then in Greenfield, Massachusetts. In all these experiences, I wished to make the teaching and learning easier, more under-standable, and even a bit more fun. I hope that this text fulfills these ambitions. But most important, I hope this book stimulates you to create your best work!

Part I

The Writing Process

writer's decision one

What Will I Write About?
Techniques for Choosing a Subject

Introduction

Are you always assigned specific subjects for each paper in every one of your courses? If your answer is yes, you may want to skip Chapters 1–5.

But if you sometimes choose your topics, or if teachers assign broad subjects that you must tackle to find a suitable smaller topic, Chapters 1–5 will help you. Each of these chapters demonstrates a different strategy for finding a subject about which you choose to write:

Chapter 1—Listing
Chapter 2—Tree Branching
Chapter 3—Clustering
Chapter 4—Free Writing
Chapter 5—Questioning

Try all five strategies because the strategy that works best in one situation may not fit another. Your writing occasions will vary and so will the strategies that work best for you.

These techniques work in composition courses. But their use goes further. With them, you can focus answers for essay tests, pinpoint topics for papers, or find subjects to research. In business, you can use these techniques any time you are unsure of exactly what you ought to write. Try them in your personal writing too.

Chapter One
Listing

Idea List—Your Safety Net
When You Can't Think of Anything to Write

This sounds easy enough: Just list thirty-five things (ideas, people, events, points of view) that interest you.

Even if you have ideas for your first paper or two, make this list anyway. It will save you time when you can't think of anything to write about.

How can you find thirty-five items that interest you? You might want to start by listing the following:

Your hobbies
Your personal interests
Topics in class discussions
Lectures that fascinated you

Also think of the magazines and newspapers you read. List

The kind of articles you like to read
Topics you like to read about

What do you think about

When you have nothing special you have to think about?
When you stay up late at night talking and discussing?
What puzzles you?
What frightens you?

What worries you?

What you would like to know more about?

If you spend half an hour trying to answer these questions, you will begin to create a fascinating index to your own personality. Over time, you'll be surprised at the items on your list that will change and those that will still be there five to fifteen years from now.

If you don't finish your quota of thirty-five ideas, let the assignment rest. But carry a piece of paper and a pen with you and, during the next few days, keep thinking about your interests. As an idea strikes you at work or while you're brushing your teeth or before you go to sleep, jot it down.

Another trick. Take some of your larger ideas and break them into separate parts. For example, suppose you think sometimes of death. What about death frightens you? Puzzles you? You might add to thoughts about death:

Life after death

Reincarnation

Sibling's death and how it affected your family

Whether life of the elderly should be prolonged by medical discoveries

Thinking of death could lead you to other thoughts:

Memory of the first time you saw a dead animal

Hunting—why people hunt or should not hunt

Industrial accidents

Do we need a national health program?

How do little children understand death?

Some of these thoughts may interest you enough to go on your list.

Here is one student's list of thirty-five topics:

1. Whether people with AIDS should be allowed to marry
2. Alcoholism in teenagers
3. Alcoholism in families
4. Teenage suicide by girls
5. Video games and their effects on children
6. Senior citizens in college
7. Television violence
8. TV for the hearing handicapped
9. The kind of person I should marry
10. Who should report child abuse?

11. Sailboat racing and its expense

12. American hostages

13. Sailing in the Great Lakes

14. Trout fishing

15. American theater on Broadway

16. Should government subsidize farmers?

17. Women's centers

18. Why teens run away

19. The effect of Japan on the U.S. housing industry

20. Inner-city schools

21. Newest kinds of music

22. Whose fault is it that kids have problems in school?

23. Parliamentary procedure—does it help or hinder?

24. South Africa and the moral issues for the United States

25. Is euthanasia murder?

26. The Vietnam War Memorial in Washington, D.C.

27. Which computer is best for college students?

28. Orwell's <u>1984</u>

29. Japanese cooking

30. Immigration laws

31. Central America compared to Vietnam

32. Decorating a room

33. Public college versus private college

34. Latchkey kids

35. Rights of bicyclists

Another student's list looks like this:

1. Stress and how to handle it

2. Herbs and spices that can be grown in this part of the country

3. Growing roses
4. Alzheimer's disease and its effect on the family
5. Fears
6. Step-parenting from the kid's point of view
7. Our shopping-mall culture
8. Friendships
9. How exercise builds bones
10. Should adopted children search for natural parents?
11. Forming a band
12. Services for runaways
13. How to get funding for college
14. How to improve memory
15. How to reduce the federal deficit
16. Pets helping sick people
17. Does the Weight-Watcher's diet work?
18. How today's Olympics compare with the ancient Olympics
19. Should the United States have a military draft?
20. Is eighteen the best legal drinking age?
21. What causes depression?
22. The kind of car insurance I should have
23. Should a person be hypnotized against smoking?
24. Are there ghosts?
25. Where would I live if I could live anywhere?
26. Is it better to grow up on a farm or in a city?
27. What do today's clothing styles mean?
28. Body contact in college basketball
29. How would I redesign the top music video?
30. The 911 phone emergency system
31. The best football player today

32. *Life in my grandmother's house when she was a teenager*
33. *Does faith healing work?*
34. *Should the driving age be lowered?*
35. *What is masculinity?*

Break up Large Topics

Your list will help you find subjects for papers only if you pinpoint specific areas of a subject that interest you. For example, you may be interested in the city of New York. But that subject is too large. So ask yourself exactly what you find interesting about that huge topic. What about New York is interesting to you? Your answers go on your list:

> The street people in New York
> The 1800s architecture in New York
> Subway graffiti in New York
> The kinds of art galleries in New York
> Restaurants where patrons were shot in New York

What to Avoid

- Avoid subjects you don't care about.
- Avoid topics so broad they can be broken into many topics.
  For example, *European history, classical music,* and *African travel* won't work because a library contains whole bookshelves on each subject. Such topics would be much more useful to you if you list the specific ideas about European history, classical music, or African travel that intrigue you. Do the costumes and pageantry of medieval knights interest you? If so, put that down instead of history. Does prison life during the Civil War or the Vietnam War fascinate you? Including specifics like these on your list will help you remember topics when you need them.
- Avoid topics you know nothing about. If you tackle such topics, you'll have to do a good deal of research before you can write about them.

COLLABORATIVE LEARNING

1. Work together in your group to practice narrowing subjects. To do this, one of you can name any topic. Then work together to break that topic into five to seven smaller topics. (Reread the discussion of death earlier in this chapter to see how death was broken into several topics.) Select at least six topics and break them down into smaller topics. Appoint one person in your group to record all your ideas.

2. After each of you in the group has written at least ten or more items on your own list, tell your group about two or three items from your list that most interests you. You may find some common interests among members of your group.

3. If you are having trouble finding enough topics, read an item on your list to your group and ask the group for ideas about how the topic might be divided into subtopics. Add the ideas from the group to your own list. For example, the group might suggest breaking major league baseball into the following smaller issues:

How to pitch a spitball	Best player	Salaries
Tobacco chewing	Best team	Drug testing

4. Exchange your completed list with several students in the course to find out what their interests may be. If their lists give you an idea, add it to your own list.

Name _____

Section _____

WRITING TASKS—LISTING _____

A. Make your own list of thirty-five things (ideas, people, opinions) that interest you. You don't have to write about specific items on your list, but save it to refer to whenever you don't know what to write about. As the course progresses, change your list or add to it when it seems appropriate.

1.

2.

3.

4.

5.

6.

7.

8.

9.

10.

11.

12.

13.

14.

15.

16.

17.

18.

19.

20.

21.

22.

23.

24.

25.

26.

27.

28.

29.

30.

31.

32.

33.

34.

35.

   B.   Put an asterisk (*) next to the two or three ideas that most fascinate you.

   C.   Ask two people not in your class to tell you about two or three ideas that each finds interesting. Write a short paper about what you find out from them.

Checklist for Your List of 35 Topics

Yes   **No**

_____ _____ 1. Is everything on your list interesting to you?

_____ _____ 2. Do you have at least thirty-five topics?

_____ _____ 3. Are the subjects specific? (Avoid general topics like *girls, college, football, hunting,* or *theology* because they are too vague.)

Chapter Two
Tree Branching

A Technique for Finding a Good Idea

Another way to think up ideas for writing is known as tree branching because, when you're finished, you will have a page of ideas that might look like a tree with many branches.

Tree branching is easy to do. On a blank piece of paper, make a tree with the ideas that come to mind. You can see an example of such a tree in the diagram on the next page. Draw lines from one idea to another to show how one idea led to another.

The student, whose tree appears here, chose stress from her list of thirty-five topics. She wrote stress in the middle of her paper and drew a tree trunk around the word. She immediately thought of some *effects of stress,* so she drew a line from the tree trunk and wrote *effects* on the first branch of her tree. She listed six effects of stress and connected each one to the tree branch. Then she thought of some reasons why people are stressed. So she drew another line from the tree trunk and named it *causes* of stress. She didn't list all of the causes because she began to think about ways people could *manage stress.* Because stress management was a new idea, she needed a third branch she called *control/management.* Suddenly she started to list all the ways college students could control their stress.

As she listed eight ways to control stress, she knew she could write a good paper about that topic. The student, however, might not have thought to write about *methods college students could use to manage their stress* if she hadn't done the tree-branching exercise.

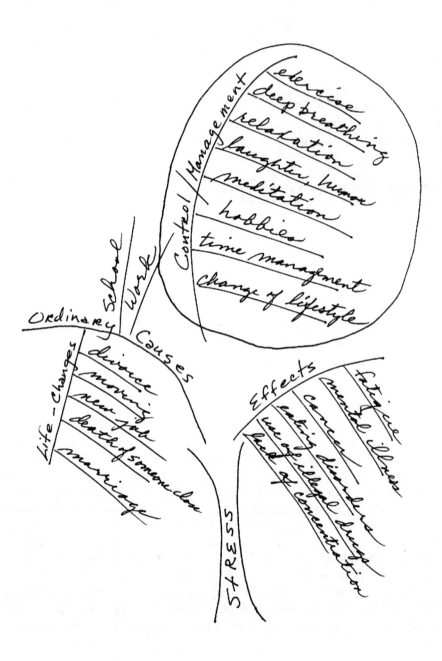

Another student started a tree about going to college. When he created his tree, which you can see below, he realized he was interested in writing about the costs of college.

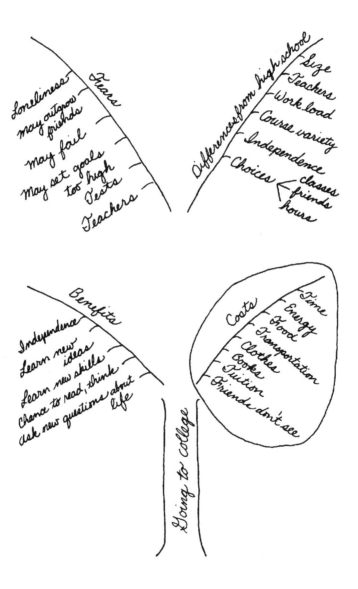

What to Avoid

- Avoid trying to force chronological events to fit on a tree because chronological events don't usually separate into trees.
- Avoid creating a skimpy tree. Build at least three or four main branches onto your trunk and at least five to fifteen twigs onto each main branch until you find a specific topic that excites you.
- Avoid putting unrelated ideas on the same tree. If you get a completely new idea, start another tree with that idea.

COLLABORATIVE LEARNING

1. Practice the tree-branching technique in your writing group. Have a volunteer draw a tree using the group's ideas. For the trunk, use an idea from one of the lists of thirty-five interesting ideas the members of your group created in Chapter 1 or work together as a group to choose a new idea. Then add related, smaller ideas as main tree branches. Finally, add related ideas as twigs on each tree branch. Work as a group so the tree shows all of your ideas. Do two or three trees together until you are satisfied that you know how to use the technique.

2. See how differently your trees can grow even though you each begin with the same idea. In your group, all begin drawing your trees using the same topic as the trunk. Then work separately to finish your trees. (Begin with one of these topics: *salespeople, tuition, crime on TV, spring break, crying, toys, videos, skiing, motherhood.*) After you finish, discuss how your trees differ.

Name _____

Section _____

WRITING TASKS—TREE BRANCHING _____

1. Use tree branching to find an idea for a paper. How? Take an idea (perhaps from the list of thirty-five topics you created in Chapter 1) and use it as the trunk of your tree. Break that topic into three to five related ideas. Attach these as tree branches. Then hang twigs (related smaller ideas) on each main branch. Good ideas for papers are usually found in branches with many twigs. When you find an idea that interests you, draw a ring around that part of the tree.

2. In writing, explain how you created your tree and found the idea.

3. Make several trees so you have several good ideas to use later.

Checklist for Your Tree Branching

Yes *No*

____ ____ 1. Do you have several main branches on your tree?

____ ____ 2. Did you work with a subject until you have at least three or four main branches with five to fifteen twigs (related ideas)?

____ ____ 3. Have you found an idea that interests you?

____ ____ 4. Did you circle the part of the tree that interests you?

Chapter Three

Clustering

Looking for an Idea? Try a Cluster.

Clustering is a good way to search for a topic because it helps you find out what is in your mind. It may remind you of tree branching, but it is a much more relaxed and less obviously organized method.

To begin, write a word or topic on a blank sheet and circle it. You could get this topic from your list of thirty-five topics (Chapter 1) or it might be something you've been thinking about lately or something that comes to you at the moment.

Then daydream; just let your mind drift and see what comes to you. You might think of other words, facts, colors, images, lines of songs, smells, people, opinions, situations, feelings, or bits of dialogue you've heard. Let one thought or image lead to another and write down whatever comes to you. Sometimes you'll be surprised by what lurks in your mind.

How Clustering Works

The writer whose clustering appears in the diagram on the next page started with the word *hunger*. During the first few seconds, she thought about her lunch that noon: a plastic-covered sandwich from a machine in a dirty cafeteria. She wrote:

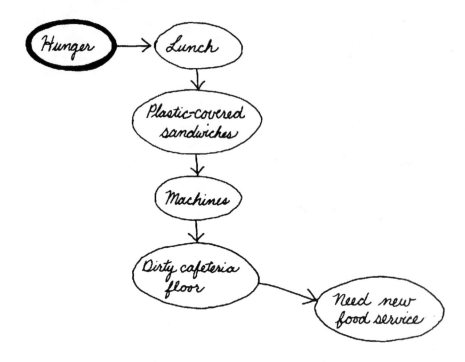

Other ideas about hunger also flashed into the writer's mind, so she wrote these words, too. Hunger led to thoughts of Ethiopia, then Africa, then South Africa and apartheid. Apartheid stopped her thoughts, so she returned to her word Africa and began writing again. She thought of the Band-Aid Concert, of trucks with food but no bridges for them to cross to deliver the food. That image reminded her of the pictures of starving children she'd seen on TV. At that second, she knew that she could write about these starving kids.

So she kept adding her images and feelings as she pictured those children—no laughing, flies on faces, flies in open eyes of children, milk and flour in bowls but no spoons, listless kids, her feeling of guilt, the sound of crying, but no talking; she felt sad.

Her finished cluster looked like this next diagram.

Cluster Words Turn up in Writing

Then the writer began to write. Notice the images from the cluster: *milk, flour, bowls, no spoons, flies.* She adds other images, too, that come into her mind as she writes.

First Draft from the Cluster

So sad. Baby fingers dipped into bowls of flour wet with milk. Flour and milk soggy enough to stick to little fingers. They raised their milk-flour fingers to their mouths and sucked. American kids their age sucked like that on pink and grape popsickles, licked vanilla ice-cream cones. All the while, flies crawled into starving children's open eyes.

Even this first draft lets you see the starving children eating soggy flour off their fingers. But the writer doesn't stop. She tells the reader how she feels by comparing the starving kids sucking their fingers with American kids sucking on Popsicles and ice cream. The comparison makes the reader cringe and perhaps share the writer's feelings of guilt.

Why Clustering Works

Some students use clustering more easily than other techniques because the writer jots down only the word or image that leads to the next image, which means that the pen can keep up with the speed of a writer's thoughts (most people think between 400 and 600 words a minute). By keeping up with the speed of daydreams, a writer using clustering can find a good idea in a couple of minutes, sometimes in just a few seconds.

The wonderful aspect of this searching technique is that it often frees the writer's subconscious so ideas and images from the subconscious go into the writing to make it more powerful.

The student whose cluster appears on the next page began with the word *running*. The student found his topic: his irritation with runners' monotonous conversations about *weight, races, diet, runner's high, marathons,* and *timings*.

What to Avoid

- Avoid staring at the page waiting for a good idea. Relax and start clustering. Let your mind run loose around any idea. Record all the images that come to you.
- Avoid trying to organize all your ideas. Just use arrows to show how one idea led to another.
- Avoid censoring thoughts that seem unrelated to your subject. Even unrelated images might lead you to a good topic.
- Avoid being vague. (This is the most important bit of advice you can get!) Instead, try to imagine specific sounds, feelings, colors, people, situations, movements, lines of songs or dialogue. Detail will help you find a topic and write the paper.

COLLABORATIVE LEARNING

1. Practice clustering in your writing group. One of you can draw the cluster, putting down what everyone says. Begin with one word or phrase from this list: *hunger, heat, jail, President of the United States, evening news, fast foods, stupid exercises, proms.*

    Then, as a group, add all the thoughts that come to you as you think about that word. Follow each other's words, and your cluster will go places one of you might never have taken the idea alone. Remember to add details—feelings,

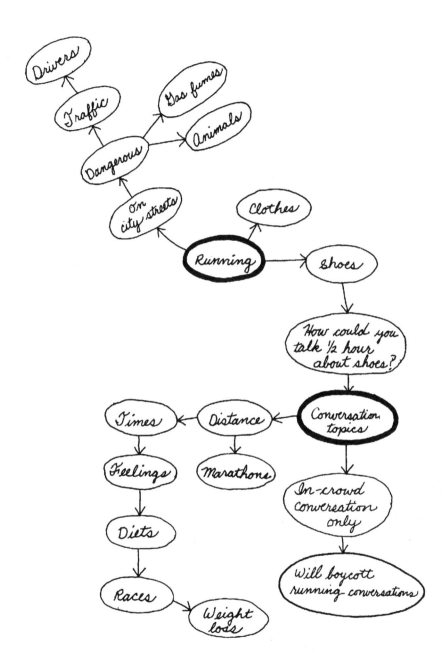

The student begins with the word "running" and discovers a topic for a paper: "Conversations of runners."

colors, images, lines of dialogue or songs, people, situations, facts. Add at least twenty circled words to your cluster. Then stop to check whether or not you used different kinds of details on your cluster. With colored pens or pencils, mark the different types of details your group used: lines of songs or lines of dialogue about the topic, sounds, smells, facts, images, tastes, feelings, colors, people, sights, movies or videos, and pictures. Keep adding to the cluster until you have left out none of these details. When the cluster is finished, discuss how you might use some of the ideas on the cluster.

Try a second cluster. (Begin with a word from the list in Collaborative Learning 1 or the Writing Task list.) Have one person in the group draw this cluster. Other group members call out the thoughts that come as they think about the words already on the cluster. (Nothing is right or wrong about any word. Just follow up on each other's words.) Again, after filling about twenty circles, check to see that you clustered different types of details. When the cluster is finished, each of you can sign your own name to the parts of the cluster that are most interesting to you.

2. Show each other several clusters you created alone. Explain how you moved from one idea to another. Tell about your "Ah-Ha" feeling, the feeling writers get when they know they've written something they can use.

Name _____

Section _____

WRITING TASKS—CLUSTERING _____

1. Use clustering to find ideas for a paper. How? Write one word (perhaps from the list of thirty-five topics you created in Chapter 1) on this paper and circle it. If you don't want to start clustering with your own topic, begin with one of the following words.

hunger	car wreck	peace	bills
fear	money	dad	MTV
guilt	woods	home	beginning

    Then let your mind relax. Write down the ideas, lines of songs, colors, smells, feelings, pieces of conversation associated with that word in your mind. At some point, perhaps a few minutes or a few seconds into the exercise, you'll hit on something that seems right for writing! That's your "Ah-Ha" feeling. When you find that feeling, stay with it and cluster around it.

2. Make several clusters about different words so you get the feel of clustering.

Checklist for Your Clusters

Yes   *No*

____   ____   1. Did you let your mind drift and relax while you clustered?

____   ____   2. Did you put color, people, lines of songs, facts, sounds, specific details and feelings into your cluster?

____   ____   3. Did you cluster until you got an "Ah-Ha" feeling that meant you knew you could write about a topic in the cluster?

Chapter Four

Free Writing

Looking for an Idea? Try Free Writing.

Another way to discover a topic is to write about anything that comes to mind until a good idea surfaces. Some professional writers call this free writing; others call it looping. Here are techniques to make free writing work for you.

How to Free Write

Begin with a blank sheet of paper. Instead of writing organized paragraphs with topic sentences and supporting details, do something very different. Record thoughts just as they come into your mind. Don't worry about grammar or sentence structure. Just record, for a whole page, all the ideas that come to mind. Try to keep writing. Don't stop. Even if you must describe the blank page, keep writing. Ideas will come.

Don't worry if you ramble because this is an exercise. You're trying to find an idea to write about; you're not writing a final paper.

Your ideas probably won't be in any logical order, and they may not even make much sense. Don't worry. Gradually you'll hit on something that interests you. At that point, you'll probably stick to that interesting topic and keep writing about it.

Don't expect to hit upon a topic in just one page of writing. You may have to write several pages before that idea comes.

Free Writing: Step One

To begin, choose any subject. (You may want to start with a topic from your list of thirty-five topics created in Chapter 1.) Write your topic at the top of the page, then think about that topic and write whatever comes into your head. Try not to put down your pen until you have filled the entire sheet.

One student had *lamps* on her list. *Antique lamps.* She couldn't imagine what she would say about them. So she started with antique lamps and wrote whatever came to her mind. It didn't matter that she got off the subject of lamps and on to something else. She wrote what she thought about, whatever sprang into her head. Here is her first page of free writing.

> Let's see. I'm trying to find a subject for my next paper. Antique lamps—what can I say about them? Blue glass—found in a flea market in Vienna—the old lady in the flea market, crippled, at least she had a cane, who kept clutching at my sleeve asking me to buy her little crocheted doilies—ugly, little, white, round circles. Finally, my husband felt sorry for her and bought all she had. Vienna—the garbage—the magnificent mile as in Chicago—Chicago's Michigan Ave. But that reminds me of Mary, my friend whom I hadn't seen in almost eight years and saw this summer. She lives in Chicago, on the second floor in a lovely apartment facing a park. When we rang the buzzer and entered the front hall of the building, she called down just as in the movies, "Up here, Sue!" There she stood, leaning over the banister, the same Mary, but with her husband. Talked all night.

Notice how the writer skipped from antique lamps, to Vienna, to the old lady, to garbage, to the magnificent mile in Vienna that reminded her of the magnificent mile in Chicago. That started her thinking of her friend Mary in Chicago whom she hadn't seen for a long time and their friendship.

That is what free writing is: going from thought to thought and staying with a thought as long as it interests you.

Free Writing: Step Two

Free writing, alone, may not lead to a good idea for a paper. So stop at the end of the first page and read it over. Ask yourself, "Is there an idea here I would like to explore? Which thought here is most interesting to me?"

For example, the student whose example you are reading here decided she was most interested in her friend Mary and their eight years of friendship, not in Vienna or garbage or the crippled old lady. So she began her next page of free writing with Mary and their friendship. Again she wrote whatever came to her mind.

> Here's my second page! Guess I'd like to talk about Mary and friendship. But what do I want to say? I have three really close friends (women). Mary and Sara went through high school with me, and we are still friends. Jane and I met when we were both eighteen and we are close. What is a close friend? What are the qualities of friends who stay one's whole life? Like the film *Four Seasons.* One of the actresses says of her friends: You get to know them—at first all you see is what you like. Then you spend more time and find out what you don't like so much. But you

have to decide if you're going to stay with them or if you are going to drop them and start with new friends. In the movie, she decides that she doesn't want to grow old and lonely because she kept picking new friends every time she found faults in her old friends. She decides to keep her friends even after she sees their problems.—I haven't seen many movies about friendship; lots of movies about love, but not so many about lasting friendships.

Notice that the writer stayed with *friendship* but didn't say much about Mary.

Free Writing: Step Three

Read over the page you just finished and choose the most interesting idea. Begin your third page with that idea. When the student whose example you're reading looked over her page, she found she wanted to write about Mary and what makes a friendship like theirs last. She began her third page with that idea.

> I think I have something here! Friendships that last. The question is, what makes a friendship last for as long as mine and Mary's? Well. (1) We met when we were young in grade school—and grew up together. She is one of the people who knows who I used to be and who I am now, and she likes the changes in me. I like her for that. Nothing about me will surprise her very much. (2) She was there in the exciting moments of life—high school—first jobs—first promotions—first car— first home. (3) I called her when my two brothers each of them was killed by a drunken driver—she let me talk and cry and get my anger out. (4) I was there when she needed me, too, like when she first went to Mexico to work. I went along until she was settled. (5) Guess these ideas boil down to some very specific information about human nature: trusting the friend, allowing for changes, making possible time together.

This student had found ideas that led to a good paper. Look how far she had come. She started this free-writing exercise by writing about antique lamps. And she came upon a totally different subject, one she could use in a longer paper. Some students find discovery through free writing to be helpful. Some even find it fun. Free writing lets you see what you're thinking.

What to Avoid

- Avoid rambling for five or six pages without focusing on any topic! If after that many pages you haven't found a good idea, try a different technique. (See Chapters 1, 2, 3, and 5.)

- Avoid going from page to page without first reading the page you've just finished and picking out the most interesting idea on it. Begin each new page with the best idea you've had.

- Avoid wondering what to say. Just keep writing. Don't stop.

COLLABORATIVE LEARNING

1. In your writing group, try free talking instead of free writing. Let one member of the group keep talking for an entire minute without pausing to wonder what to say next. The person may ramble but must keep talking for a whole minute. After a minute, the group's timekeeper should stop the speaker, and the group should tell the speaker the most interesting thing said. The same speaker should talk for another minute but begin with the idea the group identified as most interesting. After another minute, the group should again tell the speaker the most interesting thing said.

   Switch roles until *everyone* has a chance to free-talk. After you finish, discuss how free talking relates to free writing. What are the similarities and differences? What did you learn about discovering subjects? Write down a summary of your discussion.

2. Exchange your pages of free writing with other students in your group. Explain how you went from page to page and how you came up with your best idea. Seeing what others did may give you ideas for doing your own free writing.

Sample topics

Good writers	Affirmative action
Best sports team	Illegal activities of students
Favorite movie	Religious convictions
Favorite foods	Popular art
Student loans	Comic book art
Stylish dressing	Dressing for success
Inflated grades	American eating habits
Happiness	Women's sports

Name _____

Section _____

WRITING TASKS—FREE WRITING _____

1. Free-write for at least three pages. To begin, choose a subject and write whatever comes to mind. Just keep writing. After you complete a page, read what you've written to find your most interesting idea. Underline it. Begin the second page of free writing with that idea. Try to think about it while you write the second page. If you leave that topic for a new idea, though, that is fine. After you've completed the second page, read it over, look for your most promising idea for a paper and underline it. Use that idea to begin page three. By the end of this search, you ought to discover a subject.

    If you wish, use one of the following ideas to begin your free writing:

    > Once upon a time, I saw . . .
    > When I watch the rain, I . . .
    > Studying leads to . . .
    > The most frightening idea in today's world . . .
    > Whenever the TV . . .
    > Dancing . . .
    > Sometimes I wonder if . . .
    > The world would be a happier place if . . .
    > A dream . . .

Page 1:

Underline your most interesting idea on this page.

Begin this page by copying the most promising idea which you underlined on page 1.

When you reach the end of this page, stop writing. Reread your freewriting and underline the most promising line on this page.

Name _____

Section _____

Begin this page by copying what you underlined on the previous page as your most promising idea for a writing assignment. Continue free writing about that topic until you fill this page.

2. Write a letter to your teacher explaining why you do or do not enjoy free writing. Explain how you used it and why you think it did or did not work. End your letter by explaining the technique for finding a subject that seems to work best for you.

Checklist for Your Free Writing

Yes	No		
____	____	1.	Did you free-write for at least three pages?
____	____	2.	Did you read over each page before you began a new page?
____	____	3.	Did you use your most interesting idea from each finished page to start the new page?
____	____	4.	Did you discover a good topic for writing?

Chapter Five

Questioning

Questioning—Another Technique for Finding a Topic

Questioning works well when you have a general notion of a subject but have not decided on your specific angle. A writer can search any subject to limit or discover a part that might be appropriate for a required paper. This restricting can be done by asking three types of questions: informative questions, position questions, and personal questions. Each type of question generates a different kind of paper and a unique way of handling the subject. Suppose your sociology instructor assigned a paper on child abuse. Because entire books are written on the topic, your teacher could expect you to do a good job only if you wrote about some aspect of child abuse. The questioning technique explained here will help you choose which part of a large subject to study.

Why Questioning Works

To use questioning to help you find a particular slant or angle on a topic, ask specific questions about your topic. Keep asking questions until you find one that intrigues you.

Then in your paper, answer only one question or several related questions. See how easily questioning helps you limit a topic?

Guidelines for Questioning

When you begin to ask questions, you may be tempted to answer them. Don't. At this point, you just want to ask questions.

Don't worry if you don't know the answers to some questions. You can worry about learning the entire answer later, when you actually choose a particular question to answer in your paper.

Keep asking questions until you think to yourself, "Ah-Ha! I'd like to know the answer to that one!" or "I wouldn't mind spending some time thinking about that question." Even if you do not get that "Ah-Ha!" feeling, at least you'll discover that some questions are more provocative or meaningful than others.

Three Types of Questions

You can ask three different types of questions depending on the kind of paper you want to write.

If you want to write a paper that simply explains, ask *informative* questions.

If you prefer to write a paper that persuades or argues for or against something, ask *position* questions.

If you are interested in doing personal writing, ask *personal* questions that lead to an understanding of your own involvement in the topic.

HINTS FOR ASKING THE THREE TYPES OF QUESTIONS _____

Informative Questions

Before writing a hard news story, a reporter asks six very important questions to find out who, what, where, when, how, and why. You can make the same six questions work for you.

- *Who* questions ask who was involved. Who are the people, the agencies, groups?
- *What* questions ask what happened. What is it? What is it like? Unlike? You want to know what did or might happen or what something means. You might ask for a definition.
- *Where* questions ask where something happened or happens.
- *When* questions ask about time.
- *How* questions ask about a process, for directions, how something happened or happens, or how something works.
- *Why* questions ask for reasons, causes, explanations. They want to know why something occurs or does not occur.

How does this work? Here's an example. One student asked the six informative questions about the general topic *child abuse*. In just minutes, she wrote a long list of questions, many of which could lead to fine topics for papers.

Who?

1. Who abuses children?
2. Who is doing something about child abuse?
3. Who should be held responsible for reporting abuse?

What?

1. What is child abuse?
2. What is a legal definition of abuse?
3. What causes child abuse?
4. What are the punishments for child abuse?
5. What are treatments for abusers?
6. What can be done to prevent abuse?

Where?

1. Where does child abuse most frequently happen?
2. Where is it most frequently exposed?

When?

1. When does child abuse most often occur? Ages? Time of year? Times in parents' lives?
2. When does punishment for misbehavior become abuse?

How?

1. How do the courts deal with child abuse?
2. How does abuse affect children later in life?
3. How does abuse affect the family?

Why?

1. Why are children abused?
2. Why is child abuse receiving so much media attention?

Position Questions

Position questions go beyond a search for information. They force the writer to choose a side or take a position about something or someone. Here are examples of both informative and position questions so you can see the difference.

Informative question: Who killed Martin Luther King, Jr.?
Position question: Would Martin Luther King, Jr. have made a good president of the United States?

Informative question: What animals are used for scientific research at major universities?
Position question: Should animals be used for research?

Position questions force an answer that takes a stand. Here are some words that set up position questions:

Would	Will
Would not	Will not
Should	Does
Should not	Does not
Are	Is
Are not	Is not

To see how position questions work, read the questions listed here. If you answer any of these questions, you must take a stand on child abuse. (Certainly, only one of these issues could be treated completely in a short paper.)

1. Should corporal punishment of children be permitted?
2. Should children be taken from abusive homes?
3. Should children be forced to testify in open court against their abusers?
4. Should courts rely on the testimony of children under five years of age?
5. Are children today as abused as children who lived during the early days of the Industrial Revolution?

Personal Questions

Besides asking factual questions or position questions, you may sometimes ask personal questions. Personal questions seek knowledge about the topic from your own viewpoint or your own experience. Questions such as these would lead to personal information:

When did you first get interested in the topic?
Under what circumstances did you become interested?
Did something related to the topic happen to you or to someone else?
What motivated your interest in the topic?
Is your interest permanent or only temporary? Why?

The student considering child abuse asked herself the following personal questions to find out how she felt about child abuse:

1. When did I first become interested in child abuse? Why?
2. What circumstances surrounded my first interest?
3. Was I abused? Who else was abused?
4. What motivates my permanent interest in child abuse?

Be wary! Stating a personal reaction or involvement may not be appropriate for all topics or courses. Some instructors may not accept a personal point of view.

What to Avoid

- Avoid asking only one kind of question. Just for experience, ask all three types of questions about a subject.

- Avoid answering your questions while you search for a topic.

- Avoid guessing about the kind of paper you are expected to write for any course. Investigate so you can ask the appropriate type of questions. In other words, if you are expected to write a position paper, not a personal or informative paper, you must ask position questions.

COLLABORATIVE LEARNING

1. With your writing group, work out a set of informative, position, and personal questions on a topic the group chooses or on one of the topics listed in the "Writing Tasks" section of this chapter. After you finish, each person in the group should initial the questions that seem most interesting.

2. After you write your own set of questions about a subject, show your questions to several other students. Ask them to tell you other questions they would ask about your topic. (From them, you might learn a different approach to your subject.) Add their questions to your list and write their names next to their questions.

3. Take a short article (a page or less) from a magazine or newspaper to your writing group. After you all read the article, decide what questions the author answered in the article. Make a list of these questions to hand in with the article.

4. Have each person in your writing group write an answer to a different kind of question (informative, position, personal) about the same topic. (Choose your own topic or use one of those given in the "Writing Tasks" section of this chapter.) After all the papers are finished, read each others' papers. What differences do you find in the papers?

5. Read the following paragraph about tuberculosis (TB). The author packs factual information into each sentence. Together, study the first sentence to decide on the question(s) that the author had to ask in order to gather the information that was used in that sentence. Study each of the sentences in the paragraph in a similar way. Write out your list of questions.

> Tuberculosis, worldwide, still ranks among the top causes of death. In the U.S.A. there are hundreds of known cases of active TB and thousands of Americans may be infected without knowing it. Although tuberculosis can involve all body tissues and organs, the primary lesion almost always develops in the lungs. Bacilli entering a body by way of

the respiratory tract tend to attack the lungs before spreading to other parts of the body such as the bones and kidneys. Prompt treatment is therefore essential.

6. In the essays in *Seeds of Contemplation,* Thomas Merton writes about ideas which are not factual in the same way as are points about tuberculosis in the preceeding paragraph. For a challenge, read the following statement by Merton in his essay "What is Liberty?" Then write out at least four questions that Merton might have pondered as he wrote.

> Freedom therefore does not consist in an equal balance between good and evil choices but in the perfect love and acceptance of what is really good and the perfect hatred and rejection of what is evil, so that everything you do is good and makes you happy, and you refuse and deny and ignore every possibility that might lead to unhappiness and self-deception and grief . . . only the man who has rejected all evil so completely that he is unable to desire it at all, is truly free.

Name _____

Section _____

WRITING TASKS—QUESTIONING _____

1. Find an idea for a paper by asking all three kinds of questions: informative, position, and personal about a topic you select. After you have asked the questions, put an asterisk next to the two or three questions that most interest you. Use a topic of your own or select one of the following:

student government	crime	tuition	national park
fundamentalism	walking	dating games	computers
anorexia	smoking laws	zazen	bike trails
U.S. Bill of Rights	steroids	adoption	immigration
Martin Luther King, Jr.	heroes	caffeine	tutors

Subject_____

Informative Questions:

Who?

1.

2.

What?

1.

2.

Where?

1.

2.

When?

1.

2.

How?

1.

2.

Why?

1.

2.

Position Questions:
1.

2.

3.

4.

Personal Questions:
1.

2.

3.

4.

Name _____

Section _____

2. Write a short paper in which you give answers to a question you have asked.

Checklist for Your Questions

Yes   *No*

____ ____   1. Did you keep asking questions until you found a question that interested you?

____ ____   2. Did you ask all three kinds of questions?

____ ____   3. Did you avoid answering your questions while you searched for the topic?

____ ____   4. Is your final question pointed enough so you can answer it in a paper?

writer's decision two

How Will I Explain My Idea?
Techniques for Gathering Supporting Information

Introduction

Readers get bored easily. They want facts, explanations, examples, details, statistics, and any other information that proves a writer knows the subject and can make it interesting to readers. Chapters 6–9 explain important techniques for gathering such supporting information.

Chapter 6—Gathering Supporting Information from Yourself
> *Discover what you already know about your topic. Learn techniques to collect information from yourself.*

Chapter 7—Using General and Specific Information
> *Good writers use both kinds of information. If your teacher ever said to you, "too vague," you may find this chapter useful.*

Chapter 8—Interviewing
> *Learn how to get important information from other people.*

Chapter 9—Facts and Inferences
> *Can you tell the difference between facts and inferences? To make believers of your audience, you usually need both. You'll learn how to give credit to others for their ideas.*

Chapter Six
Gathering Supporting Information from Yourself

Often the difference between fine and poor writing lies in the amount of supporting information the writer provides about the topic. Good writers stack up details, proofs, examples, facts, quotes, statistics, instances. Mediocre writers, in contrast, give readers only a superficial look at a topic; they skimp on information.

Which of the following two speakers convinces you that the boss is wonderful?

Speaker 1: My boss is wonderful. You wouldn't believe what she did for me! She was there when I needed help.

Speaker 2: My boss is wonderful. When I needed a loan to buy a car because my old engine stopped working, I hadn't established any credit. So neither banks nor car dealerships wanted to risk a loan with me. But when I informed my boss I had to quit because of transportation problems, he loaned me five thousand dollars to buy a car. Interest to him is two percent lower than the bank's loan.

Although both speakers said they had wonderful bosses, only the second proved it. Good writers prove their points with supporting information.

Where to Find Supporting Information

Writers gather much of their specific information from an easily tapped source—themselves. They don't always go to the library or interview people to find facts, examples, specific quotes, interesting details, or images with which to explain their points. This chapter explains several strategies that will help you collect such information from yourself. (Chapters 8 and 9 deal with ways to collect information from others.)

Earlier chapters showed you various strategies for finding topics: listing, tree branching, clustering, free writing, and questioning. You might have already discovered that expanding and maneuvering these same strategies will help you uncover supporting information. If you have not made that discovery, this chapter will show you how to use these strategies to gather information.

Be aware of one huge difference between using a strategy for finding a subject and using the same one for gathering information about that subject. To collect information, you must limit your thinking to your topic. You cannot daydream about unrelated ideas.

What to Collect

Collect all the facts, statistics, examples, images, events, comparisons, contrasts, instances, events, quotes, lines of songs, commercials, feelings, steps, sense impressions, and dialogue that you know and can relate to the topic. You never know what you might use in a paper. An easy way to think of this part of writing is to imagine yourself taking inventory of what you know about the subject.

STRATEGIES FOR COLLECTING SUPPORTING INFORMATION

Listing

Making a list is a straightforward way to collect supporting information. You might simply list all the facts you know about your subject.

Or you could imagine yourself actually experiencing the situation about which you want to write. As you imagine it, list everything you mentally experience. Consider the following example.

A writer imagines what she would do to get ready for a hurricane. The list she creates could lead to a straightforward paper on how to prepare for one:

Fill car with gas.
Put fresh batteries in flashlights in case the electricity goes out.
Buy a week's supply of food that needs no cooking or refrigeration: bread, cereal, oranges, potato chips, tuna, sardines, apples, cookies, carrots.
Remove everything movable from yard.
Fill sterilized water containers with fresh water (1/2 gallon per person per day).
Clean bathtub and fill with fresh water.
Fill freezer's empty spaces with newspapers.
Board up large windows.
Tape windows.

Plan escape routes.
Pack suitcases in case of evacuation.

Hints: You can move beyond a simple list. Sometimes you might collect ideas from both sides of an argument. In such a case, you might make one list of all positive points and a second list of opposing points; or you might make one list of advantages and another list of disadvantages. If, for example, your topic were whether it's better to get a job or to attend college, you might make two lists: one with reasons for working and another with reasons for attending college. Or to clarify your thinking about a controversial issue, such as vegetarianism, you might make several lists, each list expressing a different viewpoint about the issue.

Tree Branching

Sometimes a subject breaks into several main points. In that case, a collection device like tree branching is helpful because it emphasizes major parts. Main points about your subject become main branches on your tree. Details that explain a main point become twigs. Build as many main branches as you need (perhaps 3 or 4) and place at least 5 to 15 twigs of specific information on each branch. A bushy tree loaded with specific information can lead to a well-developed paper. (For more information about tree branching, see Chapter 2.)

Making a tree may seem silly to you. But it is an excellent way to break your subject into logical parts and to be certain that you have collected enough supporting information about each part.

Hints: When collecting information on a tree, exhaust your topic. A tree looks lopsided or sick if it grows only one or two huge branches. So try to develop more than one or two main points about your subject. If you find you have too much information for one tree, you might have chosen a topic that is too large. In such a case, begin a new tree with a more focused subject. Add roots to your tree. Roots can explain the origins of your ideas.

Clustering

Clustering is another strategy that helps some writers find supporting information. Clustering helps you gather ideas fast when you are pressed for time. It also works well for writers who can relax and trust themselves to imagine or remember more than just the facts associated with a subject. If you are worried about letting go, remember that you can be logical later when you organize your ideas. (Review the discussion of clustering in Chapter 3 if you need a reminder of how to cluster.)

Hints: In your cluster, remember facts, feelings, colors, images, lines of songs, bits of dialogue, comparisons, examples, statistics, and sense impressions associated with the topic. You might wish to make several clusters about a topic before you are satisfied you've collected all you might use in your paper.

If they fit your topic, you might want to try special kinds of clusters.

- Create a journalist's cluster as you ask yourself who, what, where, when, why, and how about your topic.

- Or make several clusters around times related to your subject—past, present, future—or around specific dates.

- Or cluster around reasons or causes, or around why something happens or why something should or should not be done.

- Or propose solutions for a problem by creating clusters around each solution. Searching this way can lead to ideas you never imagined.

Free Writing

Some writers use this strategy to write down everything they might want to say about a subject. They write fast without worrying about punctuation, spelling, or the right wording. You can do the same. When you have finished a page of free writing, keep going until you have said everything you might want to say in the paper. If you become blocked but know you're not finished, reread a page. Choose the idea on that page that most interests you and write another page about that idea. Write until you are satisfied that you have recorded all the information you want to use in your paper. Because your purpose is to collect everything you know about the topic, don't stop to polish sentences. Get all your ideas down on paper. Organize later.

Hints: Stick to your topic. Be as detailed as possible. Comparisons, contrasts, examples, facts, statistics, your feelings, opinions, reactions—in fact, anything you know about the topic—can go into your free writing.

When you are finished, underline all your specific information to see how much you have. If your supply is limited to only three or four items per page, you probably need to free write more or try another strategy.

You may have problems if you use free writing to collect your supporting information: You may not find a structure for your paper which you would find using such strategies as tree branching. In addition, free writing may take longer than the other methods of information gathering. Finally, resist the temptation to use the free writing as your finished writing; during this process, you are only collecting information.

Question Grid

Using the question grid (that is, asking questions and answering them) works well if you have time. By asking questions and then answering them, you will collect supporting information. To be organized, you might ask and answer informative as well as position and personal questions. (Chapter 5 explains these kinds of questions.) The following is a question grid applied to the topic "Hospice Program."

The Hospice Program

Informative Questions and Answers

Who can participate in the hospice program?
—Families of terminally ill patients
—Terminally ill patients

Who works with parents and their families?
—Doctors
—Nurses
—Hospital staff
—Trained volunteers

What does the hospice program offer families?
—Emotional comfort
—Help in relating to the dying family member
—Help in coping after death

What do the families learn to do for the dying?
—Listen
—Encourage talking and sharing fears and hopes
—Help them live life as richly as possible to the end

When does the family use the hospice program?
—As soon as the family is aware of the terminal illness

How does one become a participant?
—Doctor's recommendation
—Request of family
—Acceptance by hospice staff

Why is the hospice program so beneficial?
—Provides emotional support for family and patient
—Allows freedom from physical pain for patient
—Supports freedom from invasive procedures
—Offers the opportunity to die with dignity in a homelike environment

Position Questions and Answers

Is the hospice program or the traditional hospital more helpful?
—The hospice offers more emotional support, greater freedom from pain and invasive
procedures, and homelike surroundings

Personal Questions and Answers

When did I first become interested?
—I had cancer myself

What were the circumstances?
—I had an operation and doctors discovered the cancer when I was twelve
—I'm fine now

How do I feel about the program?
—I admire it

HINTS: Be sure to ask and answer questions which fit your assignment. That is, if you ask and answer personal questions, be sure that your instructor will accept a personal approach to a subject.

Journal Keeping

Your journal is a wonderful place to look for supporting information. (If you have not started a journal, try journal keeping.)

What was it like to be a teen during World War II? How do we know what it was like to hide in an attic, afraid for one's life? We understand because a girl named Anne Frank wrote down what she thought and felt.

Was Christopher Columbus the first to discover America? Probably not! But we give him credit because he kept a record of what he and his ship went through.

How do we know what Socrates said? Plato, his student and friend, wrote it down, and we can read it thousands of years later.

You yourself might have a Baby Book that tells about the first year or so of your life. The book might include the name of the hospital where you were born, your first trip, when you got your first tooth, your first words, and other important notes about you as a baby. It may have one of your first curls! If you've never read your Baby Book, ask about it.

If you're lucky, somebody in your family kept a history. But most of us don't know what our ancestors were like. Wouldn't it be fun to hear a great-great-great-great-great grandmother tell about her husband, her marriage, her home, what she ate for dinner, and what she thought about the king?

Most people save something, a party invitation or marriage license. But how you might have felt and what you thought aren't stated in an invitation or the licence.

Why People Keep Journals

To be saved, thoughts have to be recorded. And that is how a journal is handy. In it, you save what you think and feel by recording your reactions, motives, insights, and important notions.

I once heard a writer give advice. She said we should write about love when we are in love because we won't remember what it was like ten year later. Pretty cynical stuff.

Your journal entries will give you many leads for topics, as well as supporting information, for papers you'll write later.

A journal is a good place to practice writing, to remember, and to think. In your journal you can react to ideas and information you learn in classes—English and others—to help make those ideas your own.

Students Talk About Their Journals

Students themselves have many points to make about keeping journals. Here are some quotes from students.

- "Many times I sit and think about things and suddenly get new insights. Unfortunately, however fine my thoughts seemed, by the next day I usually forget how I came to a particular conclusion. I'd like to record my thoughts in a journal for future reference."

- "I use my journal to react to things I learn in college, to relate new ideas to my own life."

- "I write about the feelings and thoughts I get from my job at the emergency room in the hospital. I see things there that make me wonder and be thankful."

- "Since our band has progressed so quickly . . . I include new songs, our travels, highlights, disappointments, and why I enjoy the lifestyle of a musician."

- "I keep a journal of the people and objects I see that might make interesting photographs."

- "I decided to write about the music I compose. I turn events that occur each day into songs."

- "I write about what I don't understand in my courses. Sometimes just writing about something helps me make sense of it."

- "I'm taking notes on how I and other people are pushed around in my new neighborhood."

Quick Suggestions for Journal Writing

- Jot down the date and the place you are making the journal entry. For example, "At Regency Mall, Wednesday, Aug. 31, 1996."

- Keep your journal in a notebook. You might want to buy a special book for your journal, but a simple spiral or looseleaf notebook will work just as well.

- Write with a pen. Pencil will fade and smudge.

- Write in your journal several times a week. People don't become great doctors or fine runners by practicing only once in a while. (Your teacher will probably have more specific instructions about how often you should write.)

- Think about your journal at odd times when you aren't busy. It can be fun to wonder what you'll say next.

- Don't worry about making your journal perfect. It is a place for you to think, keep records, and wonder. Nobody does that without a mistake.

- Write whenever you have a problem to solve, questions to ponder, decisions to make, papers to write, or something you do not understand in class.

Hints: Collect supporting information by rereading journal entries that relate to your subject. During the actual collecting, you might underline each related idea. Use the ideas to create a list, put the information on trees, or cluster. Sometimes, what you have already written may trigger many other ideas. Use those ideas, too.

What to Avoid

Avoid vague information. Instead collect different kinds of information that might be useful in your paper: facts, statistics, examples, instances, images, comparisons, contrasts, steps, events, quotes, bits of songs, or lines of dialogue you overheard. You never know what might be useful in a paper. But if you haven't collected something, you certainly won't be able to use it.

COLLABORATIVE LEARNING

1. Choose one strategy you would like to practice. Ask everyone in the group to collect information by using the same strategy on the same subject. Then use the chapter's hints and checklist to compare and discuss your results. What did you learn? Write up your conclusions for your teacher. You can assign topics or choose from those listed here:

superconductors	fast foods	drunken driving	AIDS
diet	athletic injuries	school spirit	prayer in schools
eliminating military	working mothers	crack	pit bulldogs
registration	censorship of	overexercising	suicide
political correctness	school books		

2. Take a newspaper or magazine article to your writing group. List all the supporting details the author used to explain the subject. Did the article offer a satisfying amount of supporting information? Summarize your conclusions for your instructor.

Additional Writing Tasks

If you'd like more practice collecting information so you will have enough support in a paper, try several of these tasks.

    a. List. What would you write in a complaint letter to the manufacturer of some product or service that did not measure up to your expectation? List facts that describe situations in which the product failed and the ways you'd like the manufacturer to resolve the problem. Write the letter and mail it to the manufacturer. Take a copy of your letter to class.

    b. Tree-branch. Make two trees: one that gathers supporting information for one side of an issue, the other with information for an opposing viewpoint. Use this supporting information to write a paper. To your finished paper, attach your trees along with your answer to this question: How did gathering information on the trees help you write the paper?

    c. Free write. You might prepare for an essay test, a paper, or a speech for another course by free writing all you might say about a subject appropriate to that course. When you finish free writing, underline all the specific information on your pages. If you do not have enough specific information to make your points believable, collect more. Show your work to someone in the course.

    d. Cluster under pressure. Choose a question that might appear on an essay test or quiz. Give yourself twenty minutes to answer the question. Start by clustering for three minutes or less; then write your paper in the remaining time. Clustering might help you gather information fast during essay tests or quizzes.

    e. Use questions and answers. Ask questions and give answers to collect information about an issue you are studying in another course. Explain how you might use that information in a paper.

Checklist for Supporting Information

Yes   *No*

____   ____   1. Is all your supporting information related to your topic?

____   ____   2. Did you use a strategy to help collect all your supporting information?

____   ____   3. Did you gather different types of information—facts, opinions, images, sayings, quotes, comparisons, contrasts, and statistics—about your topic?

____   ____   4. Did you collect enough information on your topic to convince or delight your reader?

Chapter Seven
Using General and Specific Information

Sometimes lack of specific information causes students' papers to be weak. Some poor papers sound like this:

> If I could vote for the re-election of the governor of our state, would I vote for him or her? Yes, I would vote to re-elect our governor because I think a good job has been done for the state. By this I mean that I think the job has been satisfactory, so l would surely say so in an election vote. For these reasons I think I would vote to re-elect the governor if I had the chance along with the rest of the state.

What is wrong with such a paragraph? It says nothing beyond the first statement that the governor has done a good job for the state and therefore should be re-elected. The writer offers no explanation of how the governor has been good for the state and deserves re-election. The paragraph lacks proof (facts, examples, or reasons) that the governor has done a creditable job. It is purely opinion and lacks support.

To be convincing, a writer must explain or offer proof for each point or position. A paper must contain explanations with suitable details, examples, statistics, facts, reasons.

Some papers have the opposite problem. What is wrong with the following paragraph?

> It is fourteen feet long and three feet wide. It is kept in the back yard chained to a tree. It needs a coat of paint or it will rust by next spring. Once we wanted to use it but found a rattlesnake curled up under one of the seats. Getting that snake out

without its biting us took an entire afternoon. By then it was too late to do what we had planned to do. It will hold at least 600 pounds, so three or four people can use it at once depending on their weight. We don't let little kids in because it could be too dangerous, and we don't want to take on that responsibility.

This paragraph offers details and facts but, unlike the previous paragraph, offers *no general statement* that ties the whole paragraph together. Is this a description of an old junker car? Is it a boat? Is it somebody's tree house? A writer needs to answer such questions somewhere in the piece of writing so the reader isn't left wondering.

A good piece of writing must have at least several levels of information: some general levels and others that become more and more specific.

Levels of Information

Working out various levels of information can be helpful when you find yourself being too general in a paper. It can help as well when you try to clarify any idea.

Suppose I say to you, "Imagine an animal." My direction is so general that you might picture a bird, or elephant, or dog, or lion, or monkey. If I get more specific about what to imagine, your images become clearer. A good writer is specific, thus clear.

I could ask you to get more specific if I said, "Picture only a four-legged animal." You couldn't picture a bird and still have the description fit, but you might picture an elephant or dog or lion or monkey.

Suppose I limit your image to a four-legged mammal. You still could imagine the elephant, dog, lion, or monkey.

Suppose you get even more specific so you see only an undomesticated, four-legged mammal. That would eliminate most dogs. But you still might picture an elephant, monkey, or lion.

If you get still more specific and imagine only an undomesticated, four-legged mammal that is less than four feet tall when fully grown, that description obviously eliminates the elephant, but you still could picture the lion and monkey.

If I ask you to picture only a black, undomesticated, four-legged mammal that is less than four feet tall, you have to eliminate the lion. So you have left the image of the monkey.

You can picture a specific kind of monkey, such as a chimp. You can get more specific and picture a specific chimp, for example, Tarzan's chimp called Cheeta.

But there were several Tarzan movies. So you would have to name a specific movie with a specific chimp named Cheeta who played with Tarzan. You could picture the chimp who played Cheeta in the 1958 Tarzan film. Only now have you identified a specific animal, an animal that could not be confused with any other.

The following chart shows how the thinking process turns from general (at the top) to specific (at the bottom).

The Thinking Process

1958	Tarzan's	Cheeta	Chimp	Monkey	Less than four-feet high	Four-legged	Undomesticated	Animal
								Animal
							Undomesticated	”
						Four-legged	”	”
					Less than four-feet high	”	”	”
				Monkey	”	”	”	”
			Chimp	”	”	”	”	”
		Cheeta	”	”	”	”	”	”
	Tarzan's	”	”	”	”	”	”	”
1958	”	”	”	”	”	”	”	”

Here is another simple example of movement from the general to the specific statement. A student walked into class complaining:

My finger hurts. (This is a general statement. We asked, ''Which one?'')
My *little* finger hurts. (''On which hand?'')
My *left* little finger hurts. (''Where?'')
My left little finger hurts between the last knuckle and the palm *under my ring.* (''On the skin or the flesh?'')
The *skin* on my left little finger hurts under my ring. (''How does it hurt?'')
The skin under the ring on my left little finger *itches.* (The student finally says what she means.)

Hints for Gathering Specific Information

Be as specific as you can when you gather supporting information. For example, note the problems in this *general,* vague cluster.

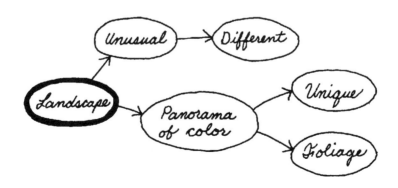

This vague cluster turned into the vague sentence: "The landscape is an unusual panorama of color." Readers see no clear picture of that landscape.

In a more specific cluster on the same topic, the student pictured a landscape and put images into the cluster. He pictured Greenland in the summer, the way he remembered it.

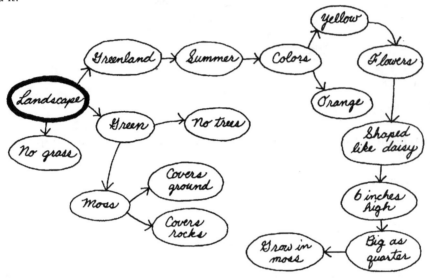

Now his cluster collected specific information. The student rewrote: "Greenland grows no trees, no grass. But in the summer, green moss covers the ground entirely, even the stones. Yellow and orange daisies, the size of quarters, peek up inches above the green moss. Yellow, orange, and green color the land."

Suppose you begin with the general statement: "That's an amazing car." Picture an amazing car and then list what you know about the car that separates it from other cars. For example,

> Turbo-charged
> Metallic-red exterior paint
> Tan leather interior
> Two-seater
> Digital dash
> Accelerates from 0 to 60 mph in 3.8 seconds
> Costs $150,000
> European Lamborghini

Then you might rewrite the general statement, "an amazing car" as "The metallic-red, turbo-charged, two-seater Lamborghini accelerates from O to 60 miles per hour in 3.8 seconds but costs $150,000."

COLLABORATIVE LEARNING

1. Working in your writing group, practice writing specific statements. Rewrite the following vague statements as specifically as you can. (Follow the examples of "an amazing car" and "panorama of color.")

> An awesome vehicle
> An awful accident
> An interesting place
> A likable guy
> An interesting assignment
> Birthday gifts that showed his friends' love
> Television's violence

2. Study a paper you have written. Underline all your vague words and then substitute specific words. Show the original and revised papers to your writing group. Ask the group for suggestions about other spots in the paper where you might be clearer, more specific.

3. Look through a magazine or textbook to find writing that uses specific wording. Take z qthe article to your group and read the parts that are so clear. Underline the specific words and show the article to your teacher.

WRITING TASKS

1. What specific information does the following paragraph lack? Cluster, list, tree branch, free write, or question until you create specific information to fill the lack. Then rewrite the paragraph so the reader knows exactly what the problems are and how they might be solved.

> At the college, we have problems which need to be handled. Only people in authority can do anything to solve the situation. Students have tried to change things but have had little success. But if nothing is done, there will be a worse and worse situation for all. Please do something to correct the problems as soon as possible. Students are getting impatient because they feel helpless to do anything.

2. What specific information would you use to describe one of the following?

Your grandmother or grandfather	Your closet
A party	Scene of a crime
A problem you must solve	Your foot
An experiment in a course	A date
A good class	A sore throat

After you have collected the details, write your description. Be as specific as possible so no other date or room or grandmother, or whatever, could be pictured but yours.

3. Collect specific information for a paper you are writing. Write the paper.

4. Revise one of your papers by substituting specific information wherever you are vague. Show both versions to your instructor.

5. Complete the work sheet at the end of the chapter.

Checklist for Specific Information

Yes	No		
____	____	1.	Did you use specific information in your writing?
____	____	2.	In each paragraph, did you offer several layers of information—some general, some specific?
____	____	3.	If you had problems being specific, did you create a ladder of information so you moved from the least to the most specific information?
____	____	4.	Did you avoid all vague description?
____	____	5.	Were you so specific that your words mean the same thing to each reader?

ask if have to do it

Name _____

Section _____

WORK SHEET—GENERAL AND SPECIFIC INFORMATION _____

1. Explain one of the following general statements. Cluster, list, tree branch, free write, or question to collect specific information. Then use the specific information you collected to write a detailed, clear, specific paragraph.

    a. When I was young, I suffered.

    b. Dreams often reveal suppressed feelings.

    c. It is difficult to learn a new language.

    d. The food in that restaurant needs upgrading.

    e. At night, sounds of the neighborhood indicate its mood.

Chapter Eight

Interviewing

Who tells a good story? Somebody in your family? A person you met on a plane or train? A teacher? People who have been in the military can sometimes fill up a whole afternoon with talk about Japan, the Mediterranean, or life aboard a ship. Have you listened to a vet from Vietnam talk about life? Sometimes older people's stories of life before you were born can help you understand life today.

You can find out almost anything if you ask the right people the right questions. So let's get more specific about interviewing.

Reasons for Interviewing

A simple reason for interviewing is to find enough supporting information to make your paper convincing.

When should you interview?

1. When you want to tap into the experience and background of experts

Often, by talking to experts, you can learn about angles on a topic you might never have discovered on your own. And if you are fortunate, the expert might guide you to other valuable sources.

Sometimes you need authorities when there are no accessible books or articles on your subject. Or if you can find reading material, you may wish to clarify certain points in a dialogue with an expert. Experts can also give you feedback. They can tell you if you are on the right track, answer your questions, and help you re-examine your inferences while they add to your store of facts and inferences.

2.   When no written records exist

Talking to the people involved is one way to investigate when no written records exist. For example, during an interview, you may discover peoples' feelings about rezoning in their neighborhood, or what it is like to be a foreign student in your part of the country. Your family history may not be recorded. Can you describe your parents' first date or their first car? Who was the first of your family to enter this country? What does your family name mean? What are the mysteries in your family? Unrecorded biographies are another kind of story. Who in your community has a biography of interest to others? Judges? Civil rights activists? Leaders? Sports people?

3.   When you want to keep up with a situation that is changing rapidly

For example, only someone at the state legislature may know up-to-date information about a new law about to be passed.

Kinds of Interviews

There are two approaches to interviewing: formal and informal.

Formal interviewing is carefully structured. You might make an appointment to see and talk with people, or hold a telephone interview. Sometimes you may write a letter or questionnaire and ask for responses to your questions.

Informal interviewing is more casual. You might ask questions of people on the street, drop in on people at their places of business or their organizational headquarters, converse with someone you know in his or her home or over lunch.

The approach you choose should depend on both your subject matter and the person to be interviewed. You would make an appointment to meet with the mayor, but you might drop in on your uncle.

Before the Interview

Let's follow a student, Katjin, through the process of gathering supporting information via the interview.

Decide on a topic. Katjin wants to study how terrorism affected an innocent person who lived in a country where terrorist acts happened.

Decide on the best people to interview. Katjin decides to interview one or two people who have actually lived in such a country to see how they were personally affected. Because she knows Lisa, a woman who survived problems in Ireland, she decides to interview her. If the interview does not offer enough information, Katjin knows she will interview other people.

Learn the backgrounds of the interviewee and your subject. Katjin needed to study background about terrorists' activities and philosophies before the interview, so she read several articles explaining the issues in Northern Ireland.

Create open (not closed) questions. Katjin wrote questions until she had more questions than she could ask. Certain considerations guided her while she made up her list. She was careful to write *open-ended questions,* questions that need more than a simple yes or no answer, because such questions provoke discussion. She avoided *closed questions,* questions that can be answered by a simple yes or no, because closed questions can stop discussion. Once the interviewee answered yes or no, she might offer no more information.

> *Closed question:* "Were you ever hurt by a terrorist's attack?" Yes or no may be the only answer the interviewee gives.
> *Open question:* "What kinds of terrorist attacks have you personally experienced?" This open question will let the interviewee tell about her own involvement, which is exactly what the interviewer wants.

Each of Katjin's questions, after much revision, is open-ended.

1. How has terrorism affected your country?
2. What terrorist's attacks have you personally experienced?
3. Were you ever hurt? What happened?
4. Some Americans are afraid to go to countries where terrorists are active. Based on your own experience, what would you say to those Americans?
5. Why did you live in Belfast even though terrorists frequently attacked in the city?
6. Why are the Irish terrorists fighting?
7. How will terrorism solve the problems in your homeland?
8. If you could talk to a terrorist, what would you like to say?
9. How has your country tried to deal with the terrorists?
10. What do you think motivates terrorism? How do you react to that kind of motivation?

Decide the best way to conduct the interview. There are three ways to conduct an interview: face-to-face, over the telephone, and in writing.

To set up a face-to-face interview, Katjin will ask to meet for an interview, make an appointment for a suitable time, and predict the length of time the interview will probably take. But she will be prepared to conduct the interview right on the spot if the interviewee wishes. (If the interviewee has a secretary, she may have to arrange a suitable time for the interview with the secretary.)

If Katjin decides to interview over the telephone, she would identify herself on the phone and request an opportunity to ask questions related to her purpose. If she should reach a secretary, she would identify herself, state her purpose, and ask for an interview.

The third method available to Katjin is to write asking for information. Follow a proper business letter format: identify the writer, the purpose, the reasons for choosing to contact this person, and specific questions. If a letter is directed to someone on a low budget, such as a church or a service organization, it is courteous to include a self-addressed, stamped envelope.

Set up the interview. Katjin asks Lisa for an interview and explains that her purpose is to find out what it was like to live in a country where terrorists worked. Before Lisa answers, Katjin assures her that the information is for a report about terrorism for a history course. Lisa agrees to an interview at 12:30 the same day, over lunch in the college cafeteria.

Organize your questions so you can refer to them easily. One method of organization is to write each question on a separate four-by-six-inch note card where you will have room left to write the interviewee's answer on the same card.

Alternatively, you can put all the questions on one sheet of paper, assigning each question a number. Then as each question comes up during the interview, record the number of the question with the answer on another sheet without rewriting the question.

Or you can write the questions down one side of a sheet of paper and leave the other side for answers.

Katjin decides to write each of her questions on a separate card.

Decide the first question to ask. The first questions should be fairly general so the interviewer can get an overall reaction and a feeling for the interviewee's responses and attitudes. Because it should set the mood and the tone for the rest of the interview, it must be chosen carefully.

Katjin chooses "Some Americans are afraid to go to countries where terrorists are active. Based on your own experience, what would you say to those Americans?"

"How" questions are good for beginnings, too. Katjin might have begun with "How has terrorism affected your country?"

Memorize the most important questions. Memorize because you don't want to sound as if you're reading questions from a list. Memorizing also helps bring questions to mind when they fit into the natural flow of the conversation.

Plan to take notes. Have at least two sharpened pencils and a pad of paper or set of cards for writing down responses to questions. Plan to record anything which occurs during the interview that might be useful to you as you write your paper.

Use a tape recorder. Be sure to get permission from the interviewee before you tape an interview. Have good batteries, bring twice as much tape as you think you may need, and know how to work your machine. Plan to use it inconspicuously. Once you start the tape, ignore it; don't even look at it. The interviewee may be inhibited by the machine, and you may decide not to use it. But a tape will give you a completely unbiased version of the interview and will be invaluable for getting exact quotes.

Although you record, still takes notes. If the machine were to malfunction, you would be without a record of the meeting.

Plan your introduction to the interview. Plan the way you will meet the interviewee, your first small talk, your introduction of yourself, and your explanation for doing the interview.

Katjin sees herself meeting Lisa in the college cafeteria, going through the food line with her, and eating before interviewing because she doesn't think she can eat and write answers at the same time.

Plan follow-up questions. Adhering to your preplanned list of questions may make the interview too rigid. So think of follow-up types of questions. If you want to hear more about some point before moving to a new question, expressions like these may be helpful:

I'd like to hear more about that.
That sounds so important, but I need a bit more explanation.
What do you mean by . . . ?

Practice repetition and paraphrasing. Sometimes you want to keep the person talking about a point, but a new question might spoil the mood or distract the speaker. Then you might use repetition, repeating the interviewee's last phrase with a question in your voice. Often that prompting will keep the interview going along the same topic. For example, suppose the last statement was, "I'll never forget that." You might question, "You'll never forget that?" (But be careful not to sound like a parrot!)

Paraphrasing, too, works wonderfully. Suppose the last statement was, "In my opinion, the worst effect of terrorism is that a terrorist is a hero to someone. It is very hard to sort out these values." You might paraphrase that in your own words: "If a terrorist might be somebody's hero, terrorism is really a moral issue, you think?" Such a paraphrase would surely give the interviewee a chance to explain.

Plan your ending. You might ask the interviewee for a summary or a concluding comment. Often you will find important new information in that last comment, especially if the subject feels relief that the interview is finished and is a bit more relaxed or off guard, or wants to add something that he or she feels has been left out.

After all this planning, you are ready for the interview.

During the Interview

Let the interviewee talk. Don't interrupt.

Listen. Don't tell the interviewee what you think or feel about the topic unless you are asked.

Don't argue if you think the speaker is wrong or incorrect.

Plan to be friendly, but not coy or buddy-buddy. Don't fawn or ooh and aah over your subject. Too much smiling, like fawning, makes you look silly.

Try to let the interviewee show up in the best light. People want to respect themselves and want respect from others.

Convince the interviewee that he or she will not be misquoted. You'll have to plan how you will do this. If you can tape the interview, you will have exact quotes. You may read back quotes during the interview, or you can call later and double check quotes, or you can let the subject read your paper before you hand it in. (Do the latter only if the person offers and you feel comfortable accepting.)

Write Up the Interview

Here are some suggestions.

- Begin your paper with a hook—an interesting quote or story which you learned during the interview.
- Use quotes so your readers get a feel for the type of person you interviewed.
- For variety, sometimes use indirect quotes, that is, sometimes say what the interviewee said in your own words.
- Attribute all the direct and indirect quotes to your interviewee.
- End the paper by referring again to the quote or story which you used in your introduction.

Here is Katjin's interview with Lisa. Study the way the first quote hooks the reader, the direct and indirect quotes, and the way Katjin ends her paper by returning to the beginning hook.

Katjin's Write-Up of Her Interview with Lisa

"I'm not afraid to live in Belfast because I have never seen any bombings or seen someone get killed, but there have been a couple of times when I have been really scared," says Lisa, a native of Belfast, Northern Ireland. She is eighteen years old and has lived all her life five miles outside Belfast.

During the last years, Belfast has made the news as the only city in Europe that has a "war" going on. This war, Lisa says, is due to strong religious opposition between Catholics and Protestants on the island. Lisa is a Protestant, and so is the majority of the population in Northern Ireland. The rest of Ireland, Eire, is Catholic, and contraventions have been going on between the two groups, Lisa says, ever since the island was divided.

"But," she says, "I think the serious trouble, like the bombings and the killings, started in 1970. I remember when it was 1977; then we used to say 'several more years to go.'

"The first time I was scared was when I was seven years old. I was in school when someone called the school and said that there was a bomb inside and that it would go off in five minutes. All of us had to go to the airraid shelter. Inside it, the teacher missed one pupil and had to go and get her. I remember all of us kids in the shelter watching our teacher who more or less had to drag the kid in with her. We were so afraid the bomb would explode before they got back.

"But nothing happened that time," Lisa adds.

"Another time," she continues, "I was in the supermarket. Suddenly they said on the speakers that all customers had to go to the airraid shelter. The IRA had called and threatened to blow the whole store in the air. I was so scared, but fortunately, they found the bomb before it went off.

"The worst time, though, was when the IRA placed a bomb in a car and put it in the street right outside my Grandma's hotel. Some parts of the hotel got destroyed but no one got injured. That is the only time I have known someone who suffered from the bombings.

"The IRA is a terrorist group," Lisa says, "and it scares me to see how they get young, unemployed people to join them. Then they [the IRA] scare them so much they are afraid to leave the organization.

"My family has never thought of moving because of the trouble," she says. "Despite the bombings and threats I am not afraid when I am walking around in Belfast. There are two streets I do avoid. One is Catholic. The other is Protestant. And where those meet, there is usually trouble."

About what will happen to Ireland in the future, Lisa says, "I know that the majority of the Northern Irish people want to remain British, but I think it will probably be United Ireland, because the Catholics are outgrowing us.

"No matter what happens in Northern Ireland," Lisa concludes, "it will always be my home. I could never move from Belfast. I just love it too much."

Writing an essay that weaves together material from several interviewees is more difficult. Kimberly Horner, the student writer of the next essay, hopes to become a nurse. To learn about her chosen career, Horner interviewed three nurses. She organized her essay around three major concepts which the women discussed.

(Names of interviewees have been changed.)

Thoughts to Consider Before Entering Nursing

by Kimberly Horner

"A person who wants to be an accomplished nurse must be interested in nursing, obtain an education, and have a strong desire for living a life of servanthood," said Beni Collan, a career nurse of seventeen years.

Collan's interest began as a child when she watched her aunt, a community health nurse in a small town of the Phillippines. "I loved the way she dressed in her whites and attended the sick who came to the dispensary. As I watched her make house calls, I knew that I wanted to share my love by helping, just as she had," said Collan.

Begg Efan, a nurse for ten years, became interested in a similar way: "I wanted to be a nurse because my mother was a nurse, and I liked the way she cared for the sick. I loved the idea of working with people and helping them feel better."

This same interest in helping and caring brought about the decision to be a nurse for Telle Esto, a legal nursing consultant and a nurse for ten years.

Education is important. Collan explained that in the Philippines the government required an individual, in return for an education, to give six months of time in service. "I was placed in a remote area of the Philippines where I attended the sick by making house calls and was ordered to deliver babies."

"We will always be educating ourselves," said Efan who has cared for many AIDS patients.

"Education on diseases like AIDS cannot be overlooked. AIDS patients need the same attention and understanding as anyone else. Safety precautions must be learned, and every nurse must adhere in order to protect from contraction," explained Collan.

"Above being interested and educated in nursing, though, a person must possess a strong desire to be a servant," stated Collan. "Nursing includes promoting health, preventing illness, caring for the sick, rehabilitating the injured, and caring for the dying. All these require a nurse to give of herself by serving others."

Efan indicated that sometimes the nurse is the only mediator between doctor and patient. This understanding allows the nurse to serve the patient's family as well as the patient.

Collan agreed, "The hardest part of serving is having to tell a family that a loved one has died. When this occurs, I am never able to separate work from emotion. I stand strong long enough to tell the family that a loved one is gone. Then I dismiss myself to the restroom for a good cry."

"For me, there have been many times when being a servant was not an easy task," said Efan. "I remember a time when HRS had come to our floor of the hospital to review patient records. I had gone to help a three-hundred pound patient who was confined to bed and required turning several times a day. I don't exactly recall all the details, but the next thing I knew, I was on the floor trapped under the patient. Just imagine the embarrassment I felt when only HRS workers heard my cries for help and came running to assist."

Esto stated that there will be many times when serving will cause a nurse to desire a new career. It is in these situations when the desire to serve must be strong.

Collan concurred by sharing a story. "I recall the time when a doctor gave me written orders to transfer a patient from the nursing home to the emergency room of a local hospital. I followed the orders and received a humiliating phone call from the doctor. He was cursing me and requesting that my paycheck be transferred to him to pay for his wait at the wrong hospital. As it turned out, the doctor called me the next day to apologize and to let me know that I had followed his request properly; it was he who had given an incorrect request for transfer. As you can see, without a strong desire to serve, nursing can be a difficult career and probably short lived."

All three nurses had advice for someone interested in the nursing profession. "If you are entering a nursing career for the money, go somewhere else. We are a profession of caring individuals; teamwork is vitally important," said Efan.

"I believe that a person who is interested in nursing, should first work as a nurses' aid to see if he or she likes the hospital atmosphere. Working in a hospital will open a person's eyes to many aspects of the nursing profession. If after working, you are still very interested, go for it!" said Esto.

Collan said, "Go for it! Nursing is very fulfilling for me, and it can be for you. It is very rewarding to be of service to the sick, the aged, the crippled, and the lonely. Prepare yourself, and you will enjoy it for a lifetime."

Sources Cited

Collan, Beni. Personal interview. 20 Mar. 1995.
Efan, Begg. Personal interview. 18 Mar. 1995.
Esto, Telle. Personal interview. 19 Mar. 1995.

To credit your sources informally, just name the sources and give their credentials within the paper. If you need to acknowledge your sources more formally, use the MLA (Modern Language Association) format as in the nursing paper. That is, name the interviewees in the paper and list them again in a Sources Cited page like the one given here.

COLLABORATIVE LEARNING

1. In your group, discuss *Katjin's Write-Up of Her Interview with Lisa*.

    a. For each paragraph, decide which questions Katjin must have asked in order to get the information she put in that paragraph. Make a list of those questions.

    b. What other questions would you have asked Lisa?

    c. What was the main point of Katjin's paper? Try to say it in just one sentence.

2. As a writing group, plan a formal interview of someone on your campus. Together, work out all the decisions that must be made before conducting the interview and have one person record all your plans. You will need to make the

following decisions: (a) topic, (b) person or people to interview, (c) questions to ask, (d) the best way to conduct the interview, (e) preparations that must be made, (f) an introduction to the interview, (g) follow-up questions, and (h) ways to end the interview.

If you cannot decide on a subject, choose one of these:

Ways living in the United States affected a foreign student
Ways freshmen adjust to college
Why faculty teach
How people choose their careers
How students study best
Security guards
Grounds and maintenance crew
Bookstore clerk
Sports hero

Actually have one person in the group hold the interview and tape it. Then, as a group, write up the interview using information on the tape. Hand in both the taped interview and your group's write-up. (You might use Katjin's write-up, earlier in this chapter, as an example.)

3. Investigate something by holding interviews. After you all agree on the subject to investigate, each of you should interview at least one person to discover what you can. (For example, you might interview foreign students about academic standards in their countries or older students about problems adjusting to college.) Follow the guidelines in this chapter. When each of you has completed interviews, share the information you gathered and combine it into one report written by your group.

WRITING TASKS

1. Watch an interview on television. In a paragraph, report how well the interviewer followed the guidelines in this chapter. Gather examples from the interview to prove your points.

2. Choose someone involved in something you find fascinating. Complete the worksheet at the end of this chapter. Hold an interview with that person. (If you can afford it, don't be afraid to telephone.) After the interview, write a paper in which you share information you gathered. Hand in your list of questions with your paper.

3. Write an evaluation of your interview. What worked well? What unexpected things happened? How did you handle the unexpected? What would you change if you had the chance to do the interview again?

4. Who is the one living person you would most like to interview if money, time, and your background were no problem? Write out all the questions you would ask on the worksheet at the end of the chapter. Then write out the answers you think the person might give.

5. Choose two or three people who are already in the career or profession which you would like to enter. Write out the questions you would like to ask on the worksheet at the end of the chapter. Then hold the interviews. Write up your findings in an essay.

Checklist for Your Interview

Yes	*No*		
____	____	1.	Did you choose the best person to interview for the information you wanted to collect?
____	____	2.	Did you choose the best way to conduct the interview—face-to-face, telephone, or letter?
____	____	3.	Did you prepare for the interview by writing out your main questions?
____	____	4.	Are all your questions open-ended?
____	____	5.	Did you memorize your most important questions?
____	____	6.	Did you plan your introduction? Your first question? Your follow-up questions? Your ending?
____	____	7.	Did you plan ways to make your interviewee comfortable?

Name _____

Section _____

INTERVIEWING WORKSHEET _____

Prepare to interview by composing *open-ended* questions which should get your interviewee talking. Write out at least ten *open-ended* questions which you might ask during the interviews.

My topic is _____

Questions for the interview:

1.

2.

3.

4.

5.

6.

7.

8.

9.

10.

Writing Task

List the names and addresses or phone numbers of people whom you would like to interview.

1.

2.

3.

4.

Chapter Nine

Using Facts and Inferences

You make inferences all day long about everything in your world. As you read this book,

> You infer that the chair you sit in will hold you up.
> You infer that the floor is strong enough to support you; it won't cave in.
> If you are outside, you infer that the neighbors will not shoot you.
> If you are in a car or on a bus, you expect that other drivers will stop for red lights.

Yet, you cannot be totally sure of any of these expectations. Why? There is the slightest chance that you might be wrong. You are guessing about other people and the future. Expectations and guesses are inferences. You can observe that the chair or bed or floor has supported you until now. You can see that the ceiling has not fallen in yet. The neighbors have not attacked you. Because you could observe these things in the past and can observe them in the present, you consider them facts. These facts might lead you to the logical inference that the setting in which you are reading is safe.

Good writers use many facts and inferences, but they must know the difference between the two.

Check Your Knowledge of Facts and Inferences

Try the following quiz to check your knowledge of the difference between facts and inferences. If a statement contains an inference, mark it with an I. If a statement is entirely factual, mark it with an F.

_____I_____ a. It is going to be a nice day today!

_____I_____ b. Peter deliberately avoided discussing his grades.

_F_   c. The person behind the counter gave two quarters and a dime to the person on the other side of the counter.

_I_   d. The bike rider cut to the left to avoid the pothole.

_I_   e. In anger, Doug hit the table with his shoe.

_I_   f. People who disagree often have good reasons.

_I_   g. Since Bill stopped dating his girlfriend, he is unhappy.

_I_   h. The teacher was delighted when the entire class passed.

_I_   i. He is an untrustworthy babysitter, but the children love him.

Working Definitions of Facts and Inferences

Facts must be clear, specific statements of what was observed. Facts describe only what *has happened in the past* or *is happening now.* (Example of a fact: I received a 92 on my first humanities exam.)

- Because facts must be verifiable, they cannot predict the future. (Example of a fact: I know the grade I received on the last humanities exam.)

- Facts answer questions like who, what, where, when, and how much by describing what is *observed by the five senses,* or *measured,* or *mathematically calculated.* (Example of a fact: The pig weighs forty pounds on this scale.)

- Only a *witness can state what was observed* as a fact; otherwise, the *source of the fact must be reported.* (Example of a fact: The podiatrist said I have a hammertoe.)

- A writer uses *facts* to explain or *support inferences.*

Inferences are opinions, judgments, guesses, beliefs, predictions, conclusions, suppositions, implications, evaluations, assumptions, or any other term that implies. (Example of an inference: Any president should be allowed to serve a third term.)

- An inference *cannot be verified;* only a fact can be verified. (You cannot verify the opinion, but you can offer facts to support the opinion that a president deserved a third term.)

- *Anyone can infer,* but only a witness can offer factual information. (So you need to collect facts from others and give sources for your facts.)

- Inferences *raise the questions* that are answered by the facts.

- In good writing, inferences *must be explained or supported with facts* or the inference is just an unsupported opinion.

Why Know the Difference between Facts and Inferences?

Acting on inferences information as if they were facts causes accidents, injury, and sometimes even fatalities. Auto accidents are usually caused by drivers who act upon an inference as if it were a fact. If you were ever in a car accident, think about the inference(s) that might have been made by the driver:

that there were no cars in the path of your car?
that the car ahead would stop?
that the other driver saw your car?
that the ice wasn't very slippery or the turn not as sharp?
that the other car's turn signal meant it was safe to pull out?

Knowing the difference between facts and inferences is important to defensive drivers, to good relationships between people, to health, and to good writing.

Answers to "Check Your Knowledge"

Go back to the section "Check Your Knowledge of Facts and Inferences" at the beginning of this chapter. Here are answers to the quiz.

_I_ a. It is *going to be a nice* day today!

Because this statement predicts the future, it is an inference. Also, it uses the word nice. Ask several people, "What is a nice day?" and you will probably get a variety of interpretations: 96 degrees and sunny, 82 degrees and not a cloud in the sky, raining and 72 degrees to name a few. Because "nice" is a judgment, the statement is an inference.

_I_ b. Peter *deliberately* avoided discussing his grades.

The word *deliberately* cannot be observed. Peter's motivation is unknown so the statement must be an inference.

_F_ c. The person behind the counter gave two quarters and a dime to the person on the other side of the counter.

You could observe a person giving two quarters and a dime to someone on the other side of a counter.

_I_ d. The bike rider cut to the right *to avoid the pothole.*

You might observe a bike rider, but you can only guess why the rider swerved. There could be other reasons for swerving that only the bicyclist knows.

_I_ e. *In anger,* Doug hit the table with his shoe.

You can observe Doug hitting the table with a shoe, but you can only assume that he did it because he was angry. Anger is an emotion that must be interpreted. Doug may have just wanted attention.

_I_ f. People who disagree *often have good reasons.*

This a general statement that cannot be observed. Can you observe a good reason? No. How many times does something occur if it occurs often?

_I_ g. Since Bill stopped dating his girlfriend, he is *unhappy.*

You cannot observe Bill's unhappiness. You can only observe his actions and interpret them as showing unhappiness. If he hasn't eaten, he may be unhappy or have an upset stomach or be on a diet.

___|___ h. The teacher was *delighted* when the entire class passed.

You cannot observe delight; you can only observe the teacher's words and actions, which you then interpret as delight.

___|___ i. He is an *untrustworthy* babysitter, but the children *love* him.

Here are two judgments: He is untrustworthy and the children love. Both are guesses. A factual statement would be limited to his and the children's observable behavior.

Gathering Supporting Information

Good writers use an abundance of facts. They want supporting information, explanations, proof details to validate main points. Much of your supporting information should be factual. Here are two lists of supporting information gathered by two students. Which list do you think will create a better paper?

Topic: Problems of the First Day of College

List of Supporting Information by Student A

Library is huge (inference)
Too much homework (inference)
Bookstore manager got mad at me (inference)
People think I'm a stupid freshman (inference)
Cafeteria staff could care less (inference)
Parking facilities are bad (inference)
Teachers don't care (inference)
Place is dirty (inference)

List of Supporting Information by Student B

Got to English ten minutes late; had to sit in only empty desk which was in front of the teacher (fact)
Books cost $214.57 (fact)
Took three hours to get through bookstore's lines (fact)
Only one upperclassman introduced himself and offered to help me (fact)
Homework the first night took me six hours (fact)
Cafeteria manager said I was too late for lunch (fact)
Didn't recognize one person all day (fact)
Lumpy dorm mattress (fact)
Roommate snores (fact)
History teacher said one out of three of his students passes (fact)
Cockroach in shower first morning (fact)

I hope you said that the second student listed much more convincing and interesting information. That student offered factual proof of problems on the first day of college, whereas the first student only hinted at these problems. A "cockroach in the shower" is a more startling fact than the inference that the "place was dirty."

Reported Facts and Inferences

By now you've realized how little you know for certain. Amazing, isn't it? There is, though, another kind of fact, reported fact. There are reported inferences as well.

Reported facts are observed by others and reported to us. We, in turn, report these facts to our readers. For example, perhaps your father or mother can tell you when you first learned to walk or who your first neighbors were. Your parents, who actually saw and heard and remembered the events, can report them to you. They can tell you what the world was like before you were born. Books, articles, and reports can tell you about events you could not experience. Because there is relatively little that each of us can experience, we are dependent on these reports. But it is important to acknowledge the source of reported facts when we, in turn, relay the facts to others.

> *Reported inference:* A report called "Estimates of Public Costs for Teenage Childbearing" says that offspring born of adolescents in 1985 will cost $6 billion in welfare benefits by the time the offspring are twenty years of age.
>
> *Reported inference:* The Center for Statistics judges that, if the population keeps expanding at its present rate, the earth will not be able to feed all of its people in the year 2500.

To report your source, simply state that information came from someone other than yourself: Name a magazine, like *Newsweek* or *Time,* or a specific person or organization or a specific book. Make statements like the following:

> "According to my grandmother who lived through World War II . . ." (This way the information comes from your grandmother via you.)
> "*Time* Magazine in August 1988 said . . ."
> "Professor Yyyitt at California College believes that . . ."

Reported facts and inferences are usually indicated by words like *said, believed, told, explained, reported, claimed, revealed, stated, contended, according to,* or *commented.* alledge

(If your professor wants you to use the documentation format of research paper, you will have to go another step. A good handbook will explain such documentation.)

Relationship of Facts and Inferences in Good Writing

Good writers need to know the difference between facts and inferences in several types of writing situations:

1. Main ideas (topic sentences for paragraphs and the thesis in an essay) should be inferences because inferences can be debated, argued, explained. Because facts cannot be debated, they should not substitute for a thesis and topic sentences.

2. Inferences (the topic sentences and the thesis) must be supported by facts. A paper with mostly inferences and few facts will be unconvincing. That is why it is so important to know the differences between the two and to use both facts and inferences in good writing. Facts are supportive when they answer the questions who, what, where, when, how, and sometimes why. If readers are to believe the opinions and judgments (thesis and topic sentences) in a paper, they must learn the facts that support the inferences. So writers collect and use many specific facts in their supporting information.

3. Reported information must be credited to its sources. You can simply and informally report the sources of your facts and inferences inside the paper. Or you can provide formal documentation as is done in a research paper.

In the following paragraphs, notice how all three points just mentioned work for the writer.

> According to the study released by the Center for Population Options [source], teenage pregnancies cost the taxpayers a great deal of money [topic sentence—inference]. The study notes that a teenager's baby born this year will cost the government $15,620 in welfare and other payments before the child reaches the age of twenty [inference about the future]. Taken as a group, the babies born this year to teen mothers will cost the taxpayers $6 billion in Aid to Dependent Children, adjusted for inflation, by the time the babies reach twenty [inference about the future]. To support these projections, the center cites today's statistics: This year the government spent $16.5 billion in welfare to support families begun by teenage mothers [fact]. About 1.1 million teenage girls become pregnant each year, and of this number, health statistics report about 513,000 births [facts]. The center releasing these statistics states that it is devoted to preventing unwanted pregnancies through family planning and education for teens [fact].

Sometimes you will need several layers of facts (proof details) and inferences in your writing. Several layers exist in this simple paragraph:

> Women's clothing is too expensive for my budget this season. [The topic sentence—inference—needs to be followed by supporting facts.] A simple white blouse costs $55, and a cotton skirt costs $75 at Macy's. [These are facts. You could add another minor inference, as in the next sentence.] Even sport clothes are too expensive. [You then have to prove that inference with more facts.] A pair of poplin shorts is $45 and a new swimsuit at $65 is not unusual [facts]. Because I work only fifteen hours a week for minimum wage while attending college [facts], I cannot buy these clothes [conclusion].

COLLABORATIVE LEARNING

1. In the sentences that follow, mark a statement F if the sentence is entirely factual. If there is any inference in the sentence, mark it I. Check your answers in your writing group. (Then find the answers at the end of this chapter.)

   I a. Combat troops should be made up of women as well as men, since women are equal to men under the law.

   I b. You don't love me anymore; you never bring me flowers or sweet surprises the way you did when we first met.

   I c. The reason people are fat is that they overeat.

   I d. Susan enjoys her work now that she has freedom from kids.

   F e. Harry hates pork, especially when it's covered with barbeque sauce seasoned with vinegar, but he eats it to please his girl.

   I f. Men should expect problems with female supervisors.

   I g. Jim should pass this course because he studies daily.

   I h. Vice presidents of the United States ought to be more than symbols.

   I i. Even though a mechanical heart keeps my dad alive, he has a negative attitude toward his cardiologist.

   ____ j. The manager quietly said, "I want you to get out of here!"

2. In your writing group, make up five inferences that could be drawn from the following facts. You do not have to use all the facts to explain each of your inferences.

American War Dead	
Civil War	497,000
World War II	406,000
World War I	116,000
Vietnam War	58,000
Korean War	54,000
Mexican War	13,000
Revolutionary War	4,000
Spanish-American War	2,400
War of 1812	2,000
Indian Wars	1,000
Persian Gulf War	141

Source: Department of Defense and Veterans Affairs.

3. Choose one of the inferences that follows and collect at least five or six facts to support or disagree with it. As a group, write a paper in which you use your facts to explain the inference.

   a. The person now president of the United States deserves to be the nation's leader.

   b. Our society treats the family farmer badly.

   c. Children often have the same attitudes as their parents.

   d. A degree in business is less valuable than a degree in the liberal arts.

   e. Music videos need to have warning labels if they contain sex, violence or obscene language.

4. Study a letter to the editor in a magazine or newspaper. Underline all the facts that support the writer's general points. Does the letter contain enough facts to convince you? As a group, write your own letter to the author of that letter. State your conclusions about the supporting information and, if necessary, offer advice.

WRITING TASKS

1. Underline all the facts and circle all the inferences in a paper you have written for one of your classes. Do you have facts to support each inference? How could you use facts to improve this paper? Write a letter to yourself reminding yourself of what you have discovered about your use of facts and inferences. Attach your letter to the paper to hand in.

2. For a topic of your choice, use any of the techniques to gather information (listing, clustering, tree branching, free writing, questioning) explained in the previous chapter. When you are finished collecting information, use a different colored pen to underline all of your facts. Do you have more facts than inferences? If the answer is yes, good! If the answer is no, add facts until the facts outnumber the inferences by about five to one.

Sample Topics

Olympic sports	Pizza
Thefts	Spirituality
Cultural customs	Comedians
Budgets	Drive-by shootings
Landfill	Aggressive behaviors
Speeders	Themes of sitcoms
Flat tax	Leadership
Netscape	Genes
Plagerism	Famous writer

3. Repeat Writing Task 2. Then write a paper using the information—facts and inferences—you collected. Before you turn in the paper, circle all the inferences and underline all the facts. Use the checklist at the end of this chapter to evaluate your paper.

4. Describe a situation in which a person acted on an inference as if it were a fact and the results were not the ones the person expected. Think about traffic accidents, surprises, court cases, jokes, comedy shows. Make up a story if you cannot remember one. Be sure to give your source credit if you heard the story from someone else.

Checklist for the Facts and Inferences in Your Paper

Yes	No	
____	____	1. Are your facts about only the past or present?
____	____	2. If you are reporting information as a fact, did you observe the fact?
____	____	3. If you did not observe a fact, did you name a reliable source and give that source the credit?
____	____	4. Do you have enough facts to convince your audience of your points?
____	____	5. Do you use many more facts than inferences?
____	____	6. If you guess, judge, decide, or conclude, do you offer facts to support these inferences?
____	____	7. If you use someone else's inference, do you report your source?

A note on Collaborative Learning exercise 1: All statements are inferences.

writer's decision three

Who Will Listen to Me? Why?
What Do I Want My Audience to Get from My Paper?
What Writing Personality Should I Use?
Techniques for Finding an Audience, a Purpose, and a Voice

Introduction

You'll be amazed at how three simple decisions—choosing a specific audience, defining your purpose, and determining your writing voice—improve your writing.

> *Chapter 10—Choosing an Audience*
>> *Want to make your writing better? Here is a sure way. Ask yourself: To whom am I writing? Pick a specific audience and then write your entire paper only for the people in that audience. This chapter shows you how.*
>
> *Chapter 11—Choosing a Purpose*
>> *Want another shortcut to good writing? Ask yourself: What do I want my audience to get from my paper? Choose a reason for writing to your audience and then make everything in your paper fit that reason.*
>
> *Chapter 12—Choosing a Writing Voice*
>> *Want to keep your audience interested? Pick a writing personality to match your audience and purpose.*

Have fun experimenting.

Chapter Ten

Choosing an Audience

Learning to make this decision may improve your writing more than any other writing decision you learn to make.

You knew about different audiences even as a child. Mothers and fathers often had to be approached differently. What worked to get permission from Dad wasn't always the same tactic that worked on Mom or Grandmother.

On job application forms people emphasize characteristics or traits about themselves to appeal to the employer they are trying to impress. Would you say the same things about yourself to a science professor needing a lab assistant and to a pizza cook needing a dish washer?

Do you tell all the same jokes to your minister or priest and your best friend? Why not?

Look at the number of magazines published for special audiences. Although a few—like *Time, Newsweek,* and *People*—appeal to Americans in general, most magazines are so specialized that a reader may choose a particular kind of magazine on almost any given subject: downhill, cross-country, or water skiing, for example. There are magazines for the person who crochets and different magazines for the knitter. A new Ford buyer gets one magazine, the new Chevy buyer another. There are magazines for architects, body builders, home builders, turkey hunters, golfers, and teenage girls. Magazine publishers have discovered audiences and created separate magazines to fit almost any person or hobby.

What Is an Audience?

Simply, an *audience* is the special group of people the author wants to read a paper. It may be as varied as a scholarship committee, a car repair dealer, the local film board, persons interested in collecting carnival glass, or adults at risk from AIDS. The audience is the people to whom the author writes.

Students sometimes ignore or forget about their audiences when they write. Ask yourself about your audience.

Who is your audience? If you said, "Anybody" or "Whoever wants to read my paper," you are missing an important way to improve your papers because most papers written for just anybody are so general or vague that no one wants to read them.

Create an Audience Profile

Making a profile of the people you want to read your paper will help you determine what you ought to emphasize, as well as what to play down, what to add, and what to leave out altogether. If you write without thinking of your audience, you may choose inappropriate information or vocabulary or structure in your paper. So find out all you can about your audience.

Know the Background of Your Audience

Each time you write you need to know these points about your audience:

Age	Values
Openness to new ideas	Social status
Education	Curiosity about the subject
Prejudices (likes and dislikes)	Sex
Interests	Experience
Background in the subject	Level of knowledge about the subject

Know the Motivation of Your Audience

Writers should know each audience well enough to predict what would influence it. Some possibilities follow; you may discover others as you think about your audience. What motivates your audience?

Anger	Fear
Facts	Statistics
Data	Stories
Examples	Humor
Curiosity	Awe
Money	Power
Goodness	Opinions of other people

Sample Audience Profile: Scholarship Committee for the College

Here is a sample audience profile. It describes the faculty members of a committee which awards academic scholarships. [Students might well create a profile similar to the one presented here before filling out scholarship applications.]

- Ages of scholarship committee members: 30–65

- Education of committee members: All have advanced degrees (masters or doctorate)

- Background: All are educators; some have families; some put themselves through college; some had financial advantages; one was raised in India; all have sat on the committee for at least two years

- Values: Learning, grade point average, determination, motivation to do well, creativity, desire for knowledge, ingenuity

- Prejudices: Against lack of interest in learning

- Interests: Future of college; awarding scholarships to deserving candidates; degrees are in theater, nursing, biology, finance, and psychology

- Openness to new ideas: One has received awards for developing new methods in his field; two have the reputation of being quite conservative

- Social status: Middle class

- Experiences: Teaching at this college for periods of four to thirty-six years

- Level of familiarity with student: One committee member taught applicant in three courses and encouraged student to apply; rest of committee does not know applicant

- Motivated by: records of past performance, GPA, courses taken, extracurriculars, references, and goals

Knowing the Audience Helps You Improve Your Paper

If you know your audience, you can decide what to leave out, what to emphasize, what to explain. Knowing the personality traits, values, and interests of your audience will help you choose supporting information that fits. Knowledge of your audience will help you decide how to begin and end, the kind of vocabulary to use, and even the slant to take. You will be able to judge what your audience will find interesting or boring.

As a writer, your job is to help your particular audience see things the way you do. If you don't know the people you want to reach, or if you are trying to make everybody or anybody see things your way, you have an impossible task. But if you choose a special audience, and if you've analyzed that audience, you will know what to say to make them see the way you do or at least to understand your position.

The following is a paragraph written by someone who forgot about audience. Who do you think would want to read it?

Why Should People Put in Small Home Gardens?

A great source of pleasure in today's home environment is a small home garden. Besides the aesthetic beauty of flowering vegetation, it is a source of seasonal color. Gardening has long been established as a source of emotional and physical therapy. How wonderful to watch something grow from seed to a healthy, mature botanical specimen! As our personal environments become smaller, the use of patio gardening becomes more popular. One of man's basic instincts is to reproduce foodstuffs. Whether growing food or ornamentals, gardening gives man the sense of being part of the earth. And of course, if you grow food products, you can control the chemical balance of your garden. And this balance is a major concern to many of us today because our environments are chemically polluted. Why should people have a small garden? It is fun!

This paragraph seems to be written to no one in particular. It gives a list of reasons why people might plant small gardens, but we don't know whom the author wants to read the paper. Is the author talking to people making seasonal color with a garden, or to people in need of emotional and physical therapy, or to people who want to watch botanical specimens mature, or to patio gardeners, or to people going back to nature, or to gardeners who fear additives in their foods, or to those who garden for pleasure? If the author is speaking to all these people, the paper doesn't offer enough information to fully interest any of them.

Notice that in the last third of the paragraph, the writer starts talking directly to you. But which person on the long list of gardeners is this *you*?

Here is how the paragraph could be rewritten for one group of gardeners:

Patio and Windowsill Gardening

You can be a gardener even if you live in a dorm or an apartment. You don't need a plot of land; all you need is a windowsill or a patio. In a one-gallon jug (just cut off the top of a milk container) you can grow a tomato plant, pepper, cucumber, or squash plant, or you can grow a grand bunch of marigolds or cosmos or mums. Before you plant, poke three or four holes about the size of a nickel in the bottom of the jug so if you water too much it can escape. Then for more drainage, line the bottom of the jug with little rocks or pieces of bricks. Next, fill the pot with soil to within an inch or so of the top. Then plant your seeds, but be sure to follow the directions on the seed package. Put a plate under the jug to catch the draining water and set it in your window or out on your patio. Keep the soil moist, not soaked. In a couple of days, you'll have sprouts. And voila! You'll be a gardener.

The revised "Patio and Windowsill Gardening" might interest would-be gardeners who have no access to traditional garden plots. These potential gardeners are the author's clear, recognizable audience. Choosing that audience helped the writer decide on her main points and her supporting information. Another benefit—the writer took much less time to decide what to say.

The following set of paragraphs shows how writer Ruth Ware revised her essay "The Creek" for a specific audience.

The Creek

by Ruth Ware

Draft 1

The creek's stagnant water appeared to be cursed by mother nature, who denied her winds the chance to travel down the steep embankments to ruffle the brackish surface. The only obvious life within the murky water was darting in and out of rusted cans that once carried the Coca-Cola logo. Broken tree branches from the overlying cypress trees and the jagged soda-pop bottles carelessly tossed aside by unthinking juveniles poked out of the putrid mud to provide the perfect obstacle course for the miniature fish. The soil along the banks was enriched with nutrients, and the foliage grew thick and green. Ferns, grasses, Cat's Ear, and other weeds of that sort choked each other as they belligerently battled for survival. Pampas grass drooped its sun-beaten leaves into the gloomy water's edge, perhaps a way to escape the late afternoon heat.

Draft 2: Revised for a Specific Audience

One doesn't need to be a well-educated ecologist or the president of Greenpeace to see the first stages of a serious problem of pollution in the small creek along Greenfid Road. Although steep banks along the infected water may grow an abundance of ferns, grasses, Cat's Ear, and an assortment of weeds, the creek itself is a definite eyesore. Rusted, faded Coca-Cola cans sit in the murky water. Broken tree branches and jagged pieces of soda-pop bottles carelessly tossed aside by thoughtless juveniles poke out of the putrid mud. Green clumps of slime and oil slicks float on the brackish water. One ought to consider the hazards of the situation. Mosquitoes lay their eggs on the stagnant surface. Rats and other smaller rodents overrun the creek like a junk yard. Where this disgusting tributary runs through a backyard, it can almost certainly cause a drop in property value. Property owners need to clean up their creek and stop the destruction, the pollution.

Certainly the first version of "The Creek" is a description of a polluted creek. But when the student was asked who her audience was, she wasn't sure. When she rewrote the paragraph, she chose as her audience the people who let the creek run wild through their property. And she gave those property owners reasons for focusing on the creek: In its present polluted state it could lower the property value and cause hazards, such as mosquitoes and rats. She kept the description of the pollution, but she focused it.

Study the essay "Freshman Frenzy: Major Anxiety" which Lisa Jervis wrote for *Seventeen*'s off-to-college, September issue. Her audience is the young reader of *Seventeen*. Notice how Lisa establishes her own credibility and talks to students about stress in college.

Freshman Frenzy: Major Anxiety

Lisa Jervis

Choosing a major? Easy. At the end of my first semester in college I marched into Professor Peterson's office, and when I marched out again about three minutes later, I was an official English major with a concentration in creative writing. I didn't have family members breathing down my neck telling me to be premed or anything. I didn't have professors discouraging me from pursuing my chosen field. I've never changed my major; I've never wanted to. No problem.

Not for me, anyway. A lot of people I know had just the opposite experience. Take my roommate, Rachel. Like most freshmen, she arrived on campus with absolutely no idea what she wanted to major in. She took classes in lots of different departments, figuring she'd probably hit on something she liked. She did—every day. She'd come home saying, "I think I want to major in art history," or "French was great today; maybe I'll major in French."

At the end of the first semester of our sophomore year, the Office of Academic Affairs started sending her threatening notes. They told her she wouldn't be able to enroll for the spring semester unless she picked a major. The pressure was on. She stayed up nights making complicated lists of what her schedule would be like if she were a religion major, a politics major, a psychology major.

"Look," I told her, "just pick something. You can always change it later." If I had known the lengths to which she would take my advice, I never would have opened my big mouth.

The next day she picked up the forms, filled them out, and declared a major in environmental studies. And then she proceeded to department-hop from environmental studies to religion to English to voice performance and back to English again—in the course of one semester. This last decision is final. So far.

Now granted, our experiences were sort of extreme. But even if you find the whole ordeal both more challenging than I did and less tortuous than Rachel did, you should be warned that choosing a major is only the warm-up for a much more grueling event: real life.

When I told my parents I had declared a major, I thought they'd be thrilled that I was so directed. Ha!

"What are you going to do with an English major?" asked my mother.

"Read books," I replied.

"No, I mean after that," she said. "You know, what kind of job?"

When I heard this, I flipped—it was my freshman year, and any job other than waiting tables or folding clothes was outside my concept of reality. I had a vague notion that I wanted to write—poetry, short stories, maybe a novel or two. But I also had the not-so-vague notion that writing isn't exactly a solid career choice.

My mother's little comment sent me straight to Panic Land. Should I go to graduate school? Should I study English or creative writing? More to the point, where could I get in? Should I get a job that could lead to a career? In what field? Or should I pump gas so that I would have time and energy to write? But what would I do with all my knowledge of literary theory if I were squeegeeing windshields? The questions were so overwhelming that I managed to put them out of my head for a while, but I knew they would come back to haunt me someday.

Unfortunately, someday is now. It's the beginning of my senior year, and I'm not much closer to a decision about what I'm going to do with my life than I was two and a half years ago. Periodically I go into a list-making frenzy: places I could live, skills I have, jobs I might want. Mostly, though, I try to stay pretty calm—until someone brings up the dreaded subject of postgraduate life.

At a party a few weeks ago some guy asked me what my major was. "English with a concentration in creative writing," I told him.

"Oh, so you're looking for a career in the food-service industry," he replied, no doubt thinking he was being funny. If I hadn't fled in terror, I probably would've hit him.

Because, really, where does he get off telling me how to run my personal business? And why is choosing a major—choosing a life—the enormous headache we all turn it into? The thing is, life is nothing but one big decision-making process, and there's no way around it. The trick is realizing that each decision, on its own, is really pretty small. Most important, you can always change your mind. Tons of people end up in fields that have absolutely nothing to do with their college majors. I know someone with a master's degree in medieval history who loves her job as a middle school science teacher. A psychology-major friend of mine is going to culinary school. Rachel, the English major, is going to Europe to sing. Maybe. And me, well, graduation is a mere eight months away, and all I know for sure is that I still want to be a writer. But that's okay. Right now that's all I need.

Practice Knowing Various Audiences

To become more aware of the power of the audience on your papers, think about how a writer must treat the same subject differently for different audiences.

Take a simple subject—a hometown. It will illustrate how different audiences will be interested in different points about the same general subject. Students chose twenty-five different audiences who might want to learn more about their hometown, Jacksonville, Florida. In square miles, it is one of the largest cities in the United States, so it provides many ideas. Here is one list of possible audiences:

Tourists
College students looking for beaches on spring break
Environmental Protection Agency
People in surrounding rural counties
Entrepreneurs searching for markets
Businesses in Jacksonville
Retirees from the North
Retirees in South Florida
The mayor
Townies (people who live in town, not along the beach)
Transportation Authority
Surfers
Local Arts Assembly
Golfers
Foreigners who enter through the port
Out-of-town developers
Shark fishermen
Tennis players
Marathon runners
Sailors about to retire from the military
City employees
People seeking to relocate for job opportunities
Sign companies
Beach bums

Writers would be silly to say the same information about their hometown to each group on this list. Beach bums and the mayor are not fascinated by the same things. Retirees in South Florida probably don't want to know the job market in the same depth as job relocaters. Golfers and developers don't ask the same questions. A general paper on Jacksonville risks boring them all.

Let's take another look at audience. This time the topic is selling a used car. Suppose a person wanted to sell a used car. Here is the general information that describes it:

Toyota Corolla	54 miles per gallon
One owner	1994
5-speed	AM-FM stereo
Blue	2-door
Sunroof	New steel-belted radial tires
12,000 miles	

The seller would have to decide who might buy such a used car. College students, families, and car buffs might want a good deal. How could the seller reach those three audiences? Here are some possibilities.

College kids   Advertise in the college newspaper.

Families   Advertise on the bulletin board of the local supermarket and in the classified ads of the local paper.

Car buffs   Advertise in the *Auto Trader* [magazine with car ads for car buffs].

The following are three different ads for the Toyota. Which ad is created for which of these three-audiences: college kids, families, car buffs? Why?

Ad 1: Totally awesome! '94 5-speed, sunroof, Toyota Corolla, metallic blue, 2- door, AM-FM stereo, triaxial speakers, plush black interior, tinted windows, 54 mpg, only 12,000 miles, great! Prime time buy for summer cruising. Call 241-COOL.

Ad 2: For Sale 1994 blue Toyota Corolla, one owner, dependable transportation, 12,000 miles, four new steel-belted radials, 54 mpg, 5-speed, AM-FM stereo. 241-2665.

Ad 3: 1994 Toyota Corolla, blue, 2dr, PS, PB, elect. windows, A/C, six-cyl., only 12,000 miles, 5-sp, AM-FM cass, new SB radials, ext. warn., orig own., ex. cond., 54 mpg. 241-2665.

When to Choose an Audience

Some writers know their audience and topic before they collect all their supporting information. This knowledge saves time because they can look for supporting information precisely suited to that audience.

Other writers choose an audience to fit their information. First they know what they will say; then they decide who might be interested.

Writers can choose, then discard, then choose another audience at any time in the writing process. The point is, finally, to decide on a specific audience and to make sure that everything in the paper fits that audience.

College Audiences

A few college instructors will ask that all papers be written for a general college audience. It is then the student's task to identify the interests and background of the audience and appeal to it. Writers should do an audience analysis, asking the same questions they would ask for any other audiences. Those instructors are unlikely to object to your limiting your audience to a specific part of the college population.

What to Avoid

- Avoid writing to "anybody" or "whoever is interested." Instead, choose a specific group or person to be your audience.

- Avoid a general audience like students or most Americans. Such audiences are too vague to be pleased. If you're addressing students, you will do best if you identify the students: College freshmen? College freshmen living in dorms? Seniors with jobs lined up after graduation? If you're addressing Americans, identify them: Politicians campaigning for the next election? Farmers? People making less than $10,000 a year? Women going to college after raising a family?

- Avoid putting off the choice of an audience. Make your decision as early as possible so it can help you shape your piece.

- Avoid ignoring your audience after you choose it. Instead make every word, every sentence, every paragraph, every idea fit the interests and the motivation of the people you want to listen to you. After you finish the paper, check it as if you were your intended audience. Then revise anything that detracts from the reaction you want.

COLLABORATIVE LEARNING

1. Become more conscious of audiences by doing an audience analysis of yourself. Using the points in the Audience Analysis as a guide, create an audience profile of yourself. Get to know yourself as an audience. (Use the worksheet "Audience Profile.")

   Compare your own profile with profiles of other students in your writing group. How are the profiles similar? How are they different? What conclusions can you draw about writing to people in your group? Draw up a composite audience profile for your group.

2. Pretend that you are on the committee sponsoring a walk to benefit Alzheimer's research. The walk is to be next weekend and will be part of a statewide benefit. How would you appeal to each person in your writing group so that each person will be motivated to participate in raising money by walking? Be specific for each person. (One group member, for example, may participate if he knows everyone else in the class will participate because he doesn't want to be left out. Another group member may be motivated to help because someone he or she knows has the dreaded Alzheimer's Disease for which there is no cure.) Share your ideas with other groups. See how many different motives you can discover in your audience.

Red or Punik color to remember something
— Bring wih Ad

3. You can all learn much about audience by choosing a magazine ad and answering these questions:

   a. What is the ad selling? Who is the intended audience? How did you determine the intended audience?
   b. In which magazine did the ad appear?
   c. Who or what is pictured in the ad? (The answer to the question seems obvious, but look closely to see images in ice cubes or other unexpected areas.)
   d. To whom would the picture, paper quality of the ad, color, and wording appeal? (What might be the reader's age, sex, background, job, social status, income? What are the reader's interests, values, hobbies, relationships?)
   e. Does everyone in the group react to the ad the same way? What do their reactions reveal about audiences? Write a summary of your findings.

4. Use parts a through e of question 3 to analyze a half or full page newspaper ad.

5. Find two articles about the same subject that are written for different audiences. For example, the same subject is sometimes treated in several newspapers; a sport topic may be discussed in several sports magazines. What is left out? What is emphasized? What is the same? How did the different audiences affect the news coverage? Share your conclusions with your writing group. Write a report on your findings.

WRITING TASKS

1. Become conscious of audience by doing an audience profile of yourself. Fill out the worksheet at the end of this chapter.

2. Create audience profiles so you can differentiate your letters to different audiences. To do this task, first write an audience analysis for each audience on the following list. Then write a separate letter to each audience asking for complete financial aid for the coming college term. (You may want to make up some of the information you use in the audience profiles and requests.)

   a. Your parent(s)
   b. College's financial aid officer
   c. Bank loan officer
   d. A childless neighbor who has known you since you were a youngster
   e. Community group offering financial aid to needy students
   f. Scholarship committee that awards full financial aid on the basis of grade point average

Before you write the letters, decide how you will change each letter to suit each audience. What will you leave out? What will you add? What will you emphasize? How will you try to convince each audience? How will you change your vocabulary? How will you change your sentence structure? Would you actually mail any of these letters? Why?

3. To make yourself more aware of audience, study titles of magazines on display in a bookstore, the magazine racks in a supermarket, or your college library. From speculating on the audiences for these magazines, what can you tell about the customers of the store, the area, and the management? Write a report of your findings.

4. Choose a specific audience for *every* paper you write. Even if you write for a course in which the instructor does not ask you to identify your audience, help yourself become a clearer writer by knowing your audience exactly.

Checklist for the Audience of Your Paper

Yes   *No*

____ ____ 1. Have you decided on a specific audience for your paper?

____ ____ 2. Have you created an audience profile for the audience of your paper?

____ ____ 3. Does every point in your paper appeal to your audience? Check all your supporting information, your beginning, your ending, the organization of your ideas, your main points.

____ ____ 4. Will your audience recognize that the paper is written for them? How?

Chapter Eleven

Choosing a Purpose

Suppose that in the first year I owned my new car, I   to take it to   dealer thirty-
nine times for servicing and repairs not covered by   Lemon Law.   ould certainly
feel better if I could complain about the car to som   e important.

But to whom should I send a letter?

I might write to the owner of the car dealersh   or to the Better Bu   ss Bureau, or
to the editor of the local newspaper; or I might   . send a letter to the   ad of Chrysler
Corporation. Any one of these four might be   itable audience.

If I decided to write those letters, I would   e to answer another   stion: What is
my purpose for writing to those people? O   urpose is obvious: I'm   gry and I want
satisfaction. But as I became more specific   ould ask for a different   of satisfaction
from each of these four people. In other   rds, I would have a diffe   purpose (reason) for writing each letter.

Audiences	Purposes	
Owner of car dealership	To appeal for a refund for the co car	39 repairs to my
Better Business Bureau	To blacklist the service departm ship	the local dealer-
Readers of "Letters to Editor"	To warn consumers to boycot model car or to boycott the car	certain make and rship
Chairman of Chrysler Corpor	To inform him of problems wi ship and beg him to use his pe	cal car dealer- ut

Well, I'm basically a nice person, so after looking at these four options, I decided to write to only the owner of the car dealership and ask for satisfaction. The other three letters, which would indict the dealer publicly, could be sent later if I did not get satisfaction.

Purpose and Audience Work Together

- Why am I writing to this particular audience?
- Why should my audience read this paper?
- What do I want my audience to get from the paper?

From these questions, you can see that audience and purpose work together in effective writing. Audience answers the writer's question: To *whom* am I writing? Purpose answers the question: *Why* am I writing this? Answers to both questions profoundly affect the paper.

Different audiences look at topics from different perspectives. Twenty-five different audiences might have as many as twenty-five different purposes for reading about the same topic. It is the writer's task to choose a purpose that fits the audience. This task of fitting audience and purpose can be clearly illustrated by the following examples.

Examples of Audiences and Purposes

Students can easily find audiences to tell about their hometowns. The following chart illustrates eighteen audiences with eighteen different reasons for learning about one town, Jacksonville, Florida. Thus, one subject may appeal to many audiences and imply as many purposes for writing.

Audiences	Purpose
Tourists	To inform about local tourist attractions: beaches, museums, sports, restaurants, hotels, theaters, historical forts, parks, campgrounds, ocean
Environmental Protection Agency	To ask about landfill problems and contamination
U.S. college students	To inform of universities and colleges open to out-of-state students
High-tech businesses outside the state	To inform of the opportunities available to new business and persuade them to locate here
Retirees from the North	To explain the advantages of retiring in the South
Retirees from South Florida	To persuade them to relocate away from problem areas
The mayor	To explain problems the mayor or mayor's office can probably solve
High school seniors	To explain advantages of having a high school diploma in the local job market

Golfers	To encourage use of beautiful golf courses and participation in tournaments
Foreigners who enter the port	To explain ethnic communities in the area
Commercial developers	To beg them to stop developing strip shopping centers
Shark fishermen	To explain the shark fishing opportunities
Tennis players	To inform about tournaments and professional instruction
National Historical Society	To request more funding
Runners	To praise numerous track clubs and meets
People needing job relocation	To inform about job opportunities available
Military personnel	To persuade them to stay in town after their tours
Beach bums	To compare beaches around Jacksonville to beaches of Daytona and Fort Lauderdale

After reading this list, some students could add other audiences and purposes. Relating to audiences and purposes like these can stretch the imagination and make the writer more conscious of choosing a specific audience and purpose.

How Purpose Affects a Paper

Here are three separate pieces written to roughly the same audience: readers of a local newspaper. Yet the purposes are different. As you read, you will see that purpose affects the way each piece is written.

Jacksonville is changing, developing an atmosphere of its own

by Ann Hyman

Atmosphere. It's how we know where we are.

Airports don't have it. They all feel the same. Some are just bigger than others.

But most other places have it. Cities and towns have it. With some, you'd hardly notice, but others knock you out. Cable cars? Hills and a bay? Obviously, it's San Francisco. Sidewalk cafes? It must be Paris. Double-decker buses and taxis that look like old Rolls-Royces? London. Wrought iron, jazz, and Creole cooking? New Orleans.

What about the atmosphere in Jacksonville? Come on, get serious. Skip the smart remark about the drive to the airport through the bottom of an inversion layer. That's not the kind of atmosphere we're talking about.

We're talking about how the city *feels*.

Way back before the downtown hotels disappeared one by one and the city fathers cleaned up the honky-tonks on Bay Street, Jacksonville had atmosphere.

It was a kind of a tough, anything-goes, anything-can-be-arranged atmosphere and it was heady stuff. You knew when you were in downtown Jacksonville. You could hear the guy hawking papers on the street outside the George Washington Hotel, and if you kept walking a few blocks, you could hear the music leaking out of the riverfront dives. You could have a beer at Benny the Bum's and watch sailors on liberty play the pinballs at the amusement arcades.

Granted, that's probably not the kind of atmosphere you want your hometown to have, and it certainly was not a wholesome family atmosphere, but it was the genuine article.

It disappeared with urban renewal and, for a lot of years Jacksonville has had the kind of atmosphere you'd hardly notice. It was a nice place to live, but you really wouldn't want to visit. Think back. A few years ago, when you had company from out of town, what did you do with them? You probably took them to St. Augustine.

We knew we had something good here, but we had not figured out what it was or how to present it. Marketing studies were done. It was discovered that people loved living in Jacksonville, but they didn't know why. It just felt good.

Whoever decides such things decided that Jacksonville needed an image. Remember the Gateway City? The Florida Crown? The Bold New City? How about Capture the Spirit? Florida's First Coast?

The problem with sitting down at an ad agency workbench and grinding out an image is that, catchy as the slogan and the theme song may be, they never quite ring true. It's the difference between Velveeta and aged Cheddar. It's the difference between "L.A. Is My Lady" and "New York, New York." One is a catchy tune. The other catches the mood, the atmosphere of the Big Apple.

Atmosphere, the real thing, has less to do with image than it has to do with imagination. You can close your eyes and remember what you love about the place, feel how it feels to be there. Jacksonville is getting there. Proof is the Riverwalk.

If you haven't been yet, go. Today, if possible. Forget any political quarrels you may have with it, and just look at it. It hands the city to you like a treasure.

From the Riverwalk, it looks like the Independent Life Building, the whole skyline, the river and all of the boats on their errands and the ships hauled up in dry dock at the shipyards and the big, blue bridge are mere components in a wonderful tableau arranged for your amusement.

One day last week, a man selling hotdogs from a pushcart tore up a couple of buns and offered them to the gulls. In less than a minute, he had a little congregation of them hovering at the edge of the dock, crying like squeaky hinges, diving, performing pirouettes midair to grab a free lunch. A duck waddled up to the hotdog cart like a matron out for an afternoon stroll, pausing for tea.

All kinds of people wandered along the dock. A sailor and his girl. A couple of kids—brother and sister by the look of them—on spring break, or sprung from school for some reason, walking with their mother. A young woman in a wheelchair. Three friends walking off lunch. Old people. Young people. Black people. White people.

There is an Italian saying that is translated: "How sweet it is to do nothing." The people on the Riverwalk were doing nothing. Sweetly. Creatively.

There's a knack to that, an art.

We're talking about savoring time—not wasting time. We're talking real leisure time.

Maybe there are exceptions but I think that all places with great atmosphere have a sense of leisure, and they have public places specifically designed for leisure, places to sit and watch the world go by.

Europeans always have understood this.

The uncomplicated joy of savoring time is one of the things most trans-Atlantic travelers bring home along with the souvenirs. It is not simply that we have been on vacation and so have had, by definition, time to spare. Rather, we have seen and understood that plazas and fountains and tree-lined boulevards are more than fancy and expensive icing on the urban cake.

They are more like bread and butter in a city that truly nurtures its citizens.

We are beginning to have some of that bread and butter for ourselves.

The Riverwalk is done, and it is wonderful. Friendship Fountain is back up to speed. Someday, Hemming Plaza may be done. The area surrounding the New Florida National Bank Building is taking shape as a little gem. In neighborhoods and at the Beaches, restaurants that invite savoring the place, watching the people, lingering over a second cup of coffee are not unknown.

Think about it. The city is changing before our eyes. It is becoming a wonderful place to visit, a place that feels good. That's not image. That's atmosphere.

Hyman's purpose is to entice people to savor a new atmosphere in the town. She wants people to feel good about that "wonderful" ambiance of their hometown where thousands of tourists visit yearly. In this essay, Ann Hyman talks about the rough, raw atmosphere before city renewal; the lack of atmosphere after urban renewal; and finally, the changes in the city that make it "feel good" today. These examples and images fit her purpose.

Here is another piece about the same city, but note the different purpose.

City passes growth milestone: It's now a 'top 50' metropolis

The Jacksonville metropolitan area has passed a population milestone since the 1980 census. The U.S. Census Bureau now classifies the consolidated city/county of Jacksonville plus the counties of Nassau, St. Johns and Clay as the 50th largest in the nation.

In becoming one of the top 50 cities in the nation, metro Jacksonville joined three other Florida cities at the top of the heap of 276 officially defined metropolitan areas in the country. The other Florida places: Miami (2,799,300), Tampa (1,810,900) and Orlando (824,100). . . .

While other Florida metro areas have bounded upward in the population ranks, Jacksonville has crept, comparatively speaking, into major-metropolis status. But that isn't necessarily bad.

Metro Jacksonville is confronting problems aplenty with its moderate growth rate. If we can't, or won't, meet the challenge, how can faster-growing cities dare even to hope that they can, or will?

The "City passes growth milestone" presents statistics. Its purpose is different from that of Hyman's essay. The editorial tells what the population used to be, how it has grown, how it compares to other cites. All this comparing leads the writers to their purpose: to subtly plead for growth management in a city facing "problems aplenty."

Notice how different the purpose is in the following ad. It tries to persuade readers to shop at a supermarket in the same area. Here, too, are statistics. But they are used for a totally different effect.

400,000 Customers a Week Cannot Be Wrong

The 400,000 area shoppers who come to Winn-Dixie every week come for a lot of reasons. They buy 152,724 pounds of the best W-D Brand U.S.D.A. Choice Beef available. They buy 15,077 heads of lettuce. . . . They don't have to waste time and money driving miles out of their way because our 39 locations put a WINN-DIXIE right in everyone's neighborhood!

The ad attempts to convince shoppers in several ways. It says that 400,000 people shop and save at the Winn-Dixie stores *every* week, and they cannot all be wrong. The ad overwhelms the reader—imagine 15,077 heads of lettuce and 152,724 pounds of beef. Thirty-nine locations offer convenience. Statistics serve a purpose: to convince the audience that Winn-Dixie is a great place to shop.

All three pieces of writing "Jacksonville is changing, developing an atmosphere of its own," "City passes growth milestone: It's now a 'top 50' metropolis," and "400,000 Customers a Week Cannot Be Wrong"—work for different purposes: the first, to get readers to notice and delight in the town's new atmosphere; the second, to encourage the town to manage growth; and the third, to woo shoppers to a certain supermarket chain.

State Your Specific Audience and Purpose for Each Paper You Write

Decide your audience and purpose for *every* paper because writers who are extremely clear about their audiences and purposes almost always improve their papers. A good writer motivates and interests an audience. The purpose gives direction to the paper so the writer knows exactly what to accomplish.

Authors who write to vague, general audiences for vague reasons often create uninteresting pieces because they do not know what is important or unimportant to everyone. It is hard to convince everyone of something especially if writers themselves are unsure of their purposes.

Attach statements of audience and purpose to all your papers so readers in the class and your instructor will know your intent and can respond to your paper accordingly.

You might write, for example, "My audience is _____ _____ . My purpose for writing is _____ ."

Examples of students' audience and purpose statements follow.

a. My audience is the financial aid officer. My purpose is to convince her that my loan application must be processed before January 2, or I will not be able to continue schooling here.

b. I want to show my father [audience] that the same character problems that caused Macbeth's downfall are destroying the company where he works [purpose].

c. Audience: teachers, parents of gradeschool children. Purpose: to show how nonverbal messages can harm learning.

What to Avoid

- Avoid writing without a purpose or reason. Instead, always know what you want your audience to get from your piece.

- Avoid a general purpose such as "so I'll get a good grade," or "so I will prove that I know the topic." Such reasons are not specific enough to help you shape your writing.

- Avoid ignoring your purpose when you do a final check of your finished paper. Instead, ask yourself, "Did I do what I wanted to do? Does each paragraph, sentence and word help the audience see my purpose?"

COLLABORATIVE LEARNING

1. In a group, practice thinking about audiences and purposes. (You will need a person to keep notes.) First, name a subject, for example, backpacking. Then work together to list six or so audiences for that topic (the recorder keeps a list). Audiences for backpacking might include the following:

   People who have never backpacked but would like to
   People who want to learn how to pack a backpack correctly
   Seasoned backpackers
   Winter campers
   Backpackers in bear country
   Backpackers where no fires are allowed
   Potential backpack buyers

   After the group names audiences, work together to brainstorm at least five reasons for writing to each audience. To do this, the recorder reads the first audience on the list. Then the group brainstorms reasons for writing to that audience. For example, for the first audience on the list, "People who have never backpacked but would like to," you might give these reasons for writing:

   To explain what backpacking is
   To explain the different kinds of backpacks
   To persuade readers to try backpacking
   To explain backpacking in military history
   To explain how early backpackers helped settle North America

   Use this exercise to stretch your imagination. You'll discover much more to write about than you ever imagined!

2. Read several magazine articles. Identify the audience and the purpose of each article. Then decide how the writer kept that audience and purpose in mind throughout the entire article. Share the articles and your conclusions with your writing group. Write your group's conclusions.

WRITING TASKS

1. Stretch your skill by imagining different purposes and audiences for the same topic. Fill out the worksheet at the end of the chapter.
2. Decide on an audience for your paper. Decide why you want that audience to read the paper. Then write so everything in the paper fits that audience and your reason for getting that audience to pay attention. When you are finished, explain to your instructor how your paper fits your specific audience and purpose.

3. Decide on a specific audience and purpose for a paper you have already written. Then revise that paper for that audience and purpose. Show both versions to your instructor.

Checklist for the Purpose of Your Paper

Yes	*No*		
____	____	1.	Have you a purpose for writing to your audience?
____	____	2.	Is your purpose appropriate for your audience?
____	____	3.	Will your audience know your purpose? How?
____	____	4.	Do you keep your purpose in mind throughout the paper?
____	____	5.	Do all parts of your paper keep to your purpose? Check your title, beginning, ending, organization, facts, and supporting information.

Name _____

Section _____

WORKSHEET—PLAYING WITH PURPOSES _____

Stretch your skill by imagining different purposes and audiences for the same topic. Choose a topic. List five different audiences who might be interested in that topic. Then list several different reasons for writing to each audience. This work will stretch your imagination! Different purposes can lead to different papers! A sample exercise begins here for you to follow.

Topic   **Audiences**   **Purposes**

TV evangelism

1. People who listen to TV evangelists
2. Preachers not on TV
3. Faith healers
4. People who do not attend religious services
5. TV evangelists themselves

a. Persuade them to contribute money
b. Ask them to question evangelist's motives
c. Explain benefits of religion

a. Congratulate them for avoiding TV
b. Encourage them to use TV and explain why
c. Explain why you do (or do not) respect TV evangelism

Chapter Twelve

Choosing a Writing Voice

Jazz, progressive, classical, rock, country! Each type of music has its own sound. can tell them apart. Some you like; some you may not like. Why?

Which of these sounds do you enjoy? A preacher on the radio? A love song? Fin nails scratching a blackboard? Rain on the window? Melting snow plopping from tre Snores? Sneezes? Burps?

We react to sounds and voices. We might praise a baby for burping. But what you think of someone who burps aloud in a fancy restaurant? Different voices, differe occasions cause different reactions.

Your Voice

In writing, your voice is the way you sound to your reader. You may sound like th anchor person on the evening news, a game show host, your dad, a favorite teacher, o a pedantic old maid.

From your voice, readers draw many inferences:

- Your feelings (for example, sad, sarcastic, enthusiastic)
- Your attitude toward ideas or people (such as like or dislike, respect or disrespect)
- Your mood (for example, upbeat, mixed-up, weary)

Whether you are being formal or informal, you have many voices. Each voice fits different situations and audiences. Writers call their voices their personae or their writing personalities.

It is your job as a writer to discover your own voice for a piece of writing and to use it!

Formal and Informal Voices

The *formal voice* uses the third person (he, she, it, they, them). It is impersonal, factual, serious. It uses a large vocabulary with no contractions. Often its sentences and paragraphs are long and sometimes complicated. A formal voice reveals the writer's feelings, attitudes, and moods quite indirectly and impersonally. (Many college teachers expect this voice in formal papers from students.)

Do you recognize the formal voice of the U.S. Declaration of Independence?

> When in the Course of human events it becomes necessary for one people to dissolve the political bonds which have connected them with another, and to assume among the powers of the earth, the separate and equal station to which the Laws of Nature and of Nature's God entitle them, a decent respect to the opinions of mankind requires that they should declare the causes which impel them to the separation. —We hold these truths to be self-evident, that all men are created equal, that they are endowed by their Creator with certain unalienable Rights, that among these are Life, Liberty and the Pursuit of Happiness.

An *informal voice* uses the first person (I, we, me, us) or second person (you). It is personal, conversational, even chatty. This voice uses short sentences, contractions, a simple but fitting vocabulary, and personal pronouns. It may use direct address and even question the reader. The informal voice reveals the writer's feelings, attitudes, and moods much more directly than the formal voice.

Listen to the difference between the informal voice in the next paragraph and the voice in the Declaration of Independence.

> Women of the '80s experienced so much discrimination—some discrimination at work, some in the home, some women couldn't begin to understand. But a few women kept fighting for equality until women today seem better off. Was the suffering worth it, or would the women be better off in America's kitchens?

How to Choose a Voice

To choose a writing voice, you must decide on the writer's personality you want to show in your writing. Here are some decisions you must make.

- Will you treat your topic formally or conversationally?
- What attitude will your voice take? Will you be positive, negative, neutral? Will you be fair? Will you respect your reader's background and point of view? Will you be factual, informative? Will you treat the subject as if it is trivial or important? Your reader will be able to tell whether you like or dislike your subject.
- What mood do you want to set? Here are some of your choices. You can be upbeat, serious, sarcastic, tongue-in-cheek, humorous, witty, melodramatic, conversational, or formal. Each of these moods will affect your readers, too, so you need to choose among

them carefully. If you are sarcastic, for example, will your readers think you are clever or disgusting?

- What feelings do you want your voice to reveal? Will you be enthusiastic or not? Will you be sad, delighted, moody, pondering, suspicious, angry, accepting, doubting? You can choose many other feelings toward your subject and your audience.

Types of Voices

The following statements contain different voices writing about tattoos. Picture the person and the attitude, mood, and feelings of each voice. Read each statement aloud so you can emphasize the difference in the voices.

Speaker 1: No person ornamented with tattoos lives a life worthy of emulation. Tattoos represent lowerclass elements because those who bear such markings are usually crude and crass.

Speaker 2: When I think of tattoos, I picture muggings, sleazy bars, beer bottles breaking over heads, venereal disease, riots, military police.

Speaker 3: Designs for tattoos are so simple I bet they're from Cracker Jack boxes!

Speaker 4: Walked around, had a few beers. Was I homesick! Didn't have money to call my girl long-distance. Saw a tattoo parlor and thought and thought about her. She'd have to know I loved her if I got one. Rolled up my sleeve. They painted a nice red heart with Cindy Lou in blue smack dab in the middle. Glad I did it. Cindy Lou is too. That tattoo lasted longer than any old phone call or postcard.

Speaker 5: To determine reasons why people are tattooed, a 1988 sociological study done in North and South America reports findings from interviews with 175 female and 175 male tattooed subjects. Each was asked, "At the time of its occurrence, what motivated you to subject yourself to tattooing?" Of the males, 25 percent responded that the tattoo was a symbol of variant behavior by which they could be distinguished from others; 42 percent reported reasons of affection; the remaining 33 percent could not remember their motivation, although they surmised that the cause was drug related. Of the females, 43 percent were tattooed in response to directives by important others in their lives; 48 percent expressed aesthetic pleasure in the design of the tattoos; the remaining 9 percent expressed no quantifiably similar motivations.

The first voice is pompous, prejudiced, formal and critical. The second voice is imaginative, less formal, less condemning; it doesn't judge as harshly as the first voice. Although the third voice is more casual in its homey comparison to Cracker Jack, it still is negative. You can hear all three negative, derogatory attitudes, but the mood and feelings of each voice are less harsh than the voice just preceding it.

A tattoo wearer speaks next. Can you hear affection for Cindy Lou and subtle amazement that anyone would question the reason for the red heart and the name inside? This voice is less sophisticated than the first three. The short sentences, simple vocabulary, contractions, and first person speak informally.

The fifth voice is formal, academic, factual, and seems to express neither like nor dislike for tattoos. The writer's emotion, attitudes and mood are hidden by the formal voice. Yet, you can find some words like *subject yourself* that reveal the writer's feelings. What other words give clues to the author's attitudes?

Finding Your Voice

Many freshman papers sound much alike. Except for unique grammatical problems and the name on the top, many papers could have been written by any of several people in a class.

However, if no one in the class could mistake your paper for someone else's paper, maybe you've discovered your own voice.

Each time you write a paper, choose a specific writer's voice. Use that voice to guide you through the paper. Make it determine your vocabulary, sentence structure, what you put in or omit, the ways you arrange your ideas. Describe the voice you use just as you describe your audience and purpose. You might say something like this: "I am writing to my state representative about the lack of funds for college athletics in the formal voice of a concerned, literate, varsity, basketball player."

Suggestions for Finding Your Voice

Write naturally. That means, don't try to sound like someone you are not. Don't try to use five-syllable words when a single-syllable word would do better. Don't try to imitate a teacher or a textbook.

Write from your own experience, your own background. Use your own examples. If you understand something well, you'll be able to write about it in ways that other people won't. Give examples or details that only you would know. Tell what you see; say what you mean. No one else sees as you do, nor has anyone had the exact experiences you've had.

Ask yourself often, "What do I mean? Can I say this sentence more clearly? Will my audience believe me?" Answer these questions and rewrite your paper until you like your answers.

Use yourself. If people tell you you are funny, use your sense of humor. Be dramatic, if it fits. If you're a good storyteller, use anecdotes or build to a climax to involve your readers. If you can play a musical instrument or dance well, put those rhythms into your writing.

Be honest. Don't try to write a paper in favor of an issue if you are against it. Your paper will probably sound phony if you do.

You have to want to say something to someone else. If you don't want to talk about your topic, or if you aren't excited about it, you will sound dull, bored, weak.

Professional Voices

Some of the great writers of the world use unmistakable voices. Anyone who has carefully read Shakespeare's great tragedies will often recognize his voice, even in a short passage from a play. Biblical words and cadences can be unmistakable for many readers. Who are some of the other easily recognized voices?

Below are two voices describing a town. One voice is a city's Downtown Development Agency, the other is Gerald Johnson Jr. who works at an advertising agency. One describes positive, factual information; the other gives "tips for visitors, offbeat advice that isn't likely to be found in travel guides." After reading both writers, describe each of the two voices in five or six words. What makes the voices so different? (Find examples of differences in vocabulary, humor, tone, clarity, statistics, information, purpose.)

Downtown We're Building Business

by the Downtown Development Agency

*The 17th largest city in the country and the fastest growing of all 17;

*The largest city in the United States in area, covering 840 square miles;

*Among Century 21 Real Estate Corporation's "21 best markets of opportunity in America";

*The insurance capital of the South with headquarters for 32 insurance companies;

*Home to 119 high-tech industries;

*Home to Mayo Clinic's first satellite diagnostic and treatment center;

*The nation's leading importer of foreign automobiles and trucks through the port;

*Home to a United States Navy complex of four installations with more than 40,000 personnel. . . .

*Similar to its sister projects (Harborplace in Baltimore and Faneuil Hall in Boston, for example), The Jacksonville Landing offers an extraordinary riverfront entertainment center with 100 shops, specialty food establishments, restaurants and cafes, and a market of fresh produce, meats, and seafood.

City Made Up of Three Parts

by Gerald Johnson Jr.

Jacksonville is a city in three parts, really. You got your Westsiders, your Southsiders and your Northsiders. There's no such thing as an Eastsider in Jacksonville.

The Westsiders are your rowdy bunch.

Football is BIG over here. Gators. Bulls. Tractor pulls. Fistfights. Anything you can get loud about.

Oh yeah, you got your silk-stocking crowd there on the river. They got their own schools for the kids and all. They pretty much keep to themselves. The women sit at Kaldi's, look at each other and clench their teeth.

You can get into a lot of trouble on the Westside. You can cruise Beaver Street, hit the sleazy joints and get a beer bottle smashed over your head. You don't really grow up on the Westside, but you do get older and you do need money, so you become a realtor (pronounced "rill-uh-ter"). You wear a leisure suit, unbutton maybe three buttons so folks can see your chest hair, and roll back your sleeves so people can see your tattoo.

On the Southside you got your hip crowd.

On Friday they go to "in" places, wear plastic-framed sunglasses with strings on them and look at each other. You never really meet anybody you didn't already know. You just see people from work and act like you just met them. This impresses the people around you; they figure everyone wants to meet you.

Men at these spots usually roll up their long sleeves (two turns only), stand with their legs spread, put their right hand in their right pocket with the thumb still out, put on their plastic sunglasses and look out at the water. It is not known why they do this.

The folks on the Southside who do have money know where they came from. They do not hold it over anyone because they know they could lose it quick. So they're spending it fast while they've still got it.

The Northsider is kind of like your gentleman farmer. You could see some guys with red necks on the Northside, but that wouldn't tell you anything. They could be real smart guys who just have to work outside, or they could be real stupid. You just never know.

The main road on the Northside is Dunn Avenue. This is a long, paved road where you can stop at a traffic light, look over and see a large tire. Usually there is a vehicle above the tire.

If you could boil all the guys in Northside down into one guy, you would have a used car salesman who gets off work early and has a vegetable garden he waters by hand with a hose in the afternoon.

Next, listen to the voice of one of today's most respected scientists, Lewis Thomas. Notice how simply he makes a profound scientific point. Let your imagination see what Thomas describes.

> There are said to be a billion billion insects on the earth at any moment, most of them with very short life expectancies by our standards. Someone has estimated that there are 25 million assorted insects hanging in the air over every temperate

square mile, in a column extending upward for thousands of feet, drifting through the layers of the atmosphere like plankton. They are dying steadily, some by being eaten, some just dropping in their tracks, tons of them around the earth, disintegrating as they die, invisibly.

Fine writers say exactly what they mean. Probably one of the most famous voices in English is that of Thoreau. Listen to his voice from his famous book, *Walden*. How would you say what he has said?

> I went to the woods because I wished to live deliberately, to front only the essential facts of life and see if I could not learn what it had to teach, and not, when I came to die, discover that I had not lived. I did not wish to live what was not life, living is so dear; nor did I wish to practice resignation, unless it was quite necessary. I wanted to live deep and suck out all the marrow of life, to live so sturdily and Spartan-like as to put to rout all that was not life, to cut a broad swath and shave close, to drive life into a corner, and reduce it to its lowest terms and, if it proved to be mean, why then to get the whole and genuine meanness of it, and publish its meanness to the world; or if it were sublime, to know it by experience, and be able to give a true account of it.

What to Avoid When Developing Your Voice

- Avoid trying to sound like someone else. Instead, study your own feeling, attitude, mood, and experience with the subject and then write honestly from these.

- Avoid a voice that ignores or angers your audience; that is, don't talk down to them or use an unfamiliar vocabulary without explaining it.

- Avoid sounding the same in all your writing. Instead, experiment so you fit your voice to each of your subjects, audiences, and purposes.

COLLABORATIVE LEARNING

1. What is your reaction to tattoos or tattoo wearers? Write it. In your group, read your statement about tattoos or their wearers. Ask the group to describe the voice they heard in your statement. After they finish, describe your voice as you thought to write it. Did you and your audience hear the same voice? Why?

2. Experiment with different voices in your writing group. Imagine that one of you just bought a new tire. Imagine that the first time the tire was on a car, the tire blew out and caused the driver to lose control and to slam into another car. Imagine how you would describe what happened to each of the following audiences:

    a. The salesperson who sold you the tire

    b. Your parents

    c. Your car insurance agent

    d. The friend you were to drive to a job interview

    e. Your composition instructor

    f. The driver of the car you hit

    g. The police officer at the scene of the accident

Certainly you would not give the same information to each person; nor would you use the same words or tone to each person. You'd change what you say and alter the sequence, feelings, and vocabulary to fit each situation.

Have one person in your group pretend to be the driver of the car with the bad tire. That person begins to describe what happened to the salesperson who sold the tire. At any point in the story, someone in the group can interrupt by calling out the name of someone else on the list: salesperson, officer, parents, whomever. The story teller then immediately pretends to tell the story to that new audience. Watch how the vocabulary and story change.

After a bit, the group should call out someone else on the list. The story teller should continue the story but as if to the new person. If the storyteller is stuck, the group might help by asking questions so the story will continue.

When you have finished, summarize the speaker's changes in vocabulary, details included or omitted, the sequence of the story, tone, feelings, parts emphasized or underplayed. What seemed appropriate? Effective?

3. Exchange papers with someone else in your class. Rewrite the other student's paper in your own voice. Then read your version and the other student's version of the paper to your writing group without telling them which one is yours. See if the group can name the paper you wrote. Have the group tell you how they knew.

WRITING TASK

1. Read exercise 2 of Collaborative Learning. Then, instead of telling the story of the car accident, write out what you would say to each of the people involved. Does writing change your voice? Should it?

2. Examine some of the texts you are using this semester. How would you describe the voices of the writers? Write a letter to one textbook's author or authors and explain why you react to the voice in that book the way you do.

3. Find an ad for some product you use. Read both the ad and the product information on the actual container. Are the voices different in the ad and on the label? How? Why? Summarize your findings in a paper; be sure to quote the ad

and container.

4. Write a paper about a subject of your own choice in an informal voice appropriate for some college work. Then rewrite that same paper in a formal, academic voice. Possible topics:

Crimes on campus	College costs
Falling in love the first time	Pleasant smells
Someone you admire	A good book
The best car buy today	Choosing a mate
Chocolate	The circus
Wood stoves	Prom night
Problems of spring break	Necessary worrying

5. Choose a topic for a short paper. Before you write your drafts, decide on your audience, purpose, and voice so they guide you through the paper. After you finish the draft, check the following elements to determine how well your voice fits your audience and your reasons for writing to that audience:

The way you get the audience's attention in the title
The way you grab the audience in the first sentences
The way you end your paper
Points you make
Each piece of supporting information you select
The way you treat the topic
The vocabulary and sentence structure you choose
Formal or informal voice

Checklist for the Writer's Voice in Your Paper

Yes   *No*

____   ____   1. Have you decided on a specific formal or informal voice for your paper?

____   ____   2. Have you described your voice for the paper?

____   ____   3. Do your points, examples, and other supporting information fit your voice?

____   ____   4. Does your vocabulary match your voice?

____   ____   5. Do your sentence structures match your voice?

____   ____   6. Does your writing voice sound different from other freshman voices?

____   ____   7. Have you experimented with different voices for your paper?

____   ____   8. Does your voice become apparent in the title and first sentences?

____   ____   9. Does your voice fit the way you begin and end the piece?

writer's decision four

What Is the Best Way to Organize My Ideas for This Audience and Purpose?
Techniques for Organizing and Drafting

Good writers arrange their information so it makes an impression on the audience. Is that easy? No. But Chapters 13 through 17 offer you help so you will achieve the effect you want.

Chapter 13—Arranging Information
> *What are some interesting ways to organize your supporting information?*

Chapter 14—Thesis Statements
> *How might you write main-idea sentences so they control the ideas and structure of your writing?*

Chapter 15—Organizing Ideas into a Paragraph
> *How do you put a paragraph together?*

Chapter 16—Understanding the Essay
> *What makes an essay? (Chapters 23 through 34 offer more specific instructions for writing all kinds of essays)*

Chapter 17—Titles, Beginnings, and Endings
> *What are some techniques for writing interesting titles, beginnings, and conclusions?*

Chapter Thirteen

Arranging Information

You know the importance of arranging ideas when you tell a good joke. Have you ever told the punch line too soon or left out a detail that made the joke fall flat? Some people tell jokes and even mix up the punch line. Their jokes obviously flop.

Good writing, like good joke-telling, demands attention to the arrangement of both main ideas and supporting information. People do not want to read jumbled ideas, hunt for important points or fit information together for themselves. They expect a logical, orderly presentation of information.

Ways to Arrange Your Supporting Information

This chapter shows you several effective ways to arrange ideas. Other orders are explained in Chapters 24–34 of this text.

1. *Time order* (also called chronological order)—Arrange your events in the order in which they happen. Tell the first event that happens; then explain each of the next events in chronological order until you end with the last event.

2. *Spatial order*—Arrange your points so you describe an object, or person, or scene in an easy-to-follow order and focus: from top to bottom, or left to right, or inside to outside, for example. You want your reader to see, hear, taste, smell, or feel what you describe in a logical, easy-to-follow order.

3. *Climactic order*—Arrange your information so the least important idea comes first, the second least important idea comes next, and so on, until you end with your most important idea. Save the best for last.

4. *Question and answer order*—Arrange your information so you ask a question and then offer the answer or answers.

5. *Problem and solution order*—Arrange your ideas so you first present the problem and then offer the solution to the problem.

1. Time Order

Time order, called chronological order, tells of events in the order in which they happen. Begin writing about the first thing that occurs and tell each of the next events in chronological order until you end with the last event.

Arrangement of supporting information in chronological order is absolutely essential when you give instructions on how to do something. Have you ever tried to follow the directions of someone who says halfway through the explanation, "Whoops, I forgot to tell you to . . ."? Leaving out some step or mixing up the order can spoil a recipe or project or, at the least, waste a good deal of money, energy, and time.

Some occupations require one to be skilled at this kind of time-ordering: teaching, technical report-writing, police work, narrating history, story-telling, training, supervising, coaching, and managing. But in fact, anyone who wants to tell someone how to do something, or how something was done, or the order in which events occurred can use time order. The following is an example of one student's use of time order in his writing.

Going Home

by James W. Koontz

I stood in front of the window looking at the runway. Where was the plane? Why wasn't it here? Could it have crashed? I was supposed to have left an hour ago; what happened to the plane? I was getting worried. I had had bad dreams before. Then suddenly, out of the bottom of the low-hanging, grey clouds emerged a silver airliner. There it was, the freedom flight, the aircraft that would take me to paradise. I was really leaving Vietnam today.

The plane landed and moved rapidly toward the terminal. For a brief moment, I thought that it might take off again! When the plane finally stopped, men were suddenly all over it like ants on a disturbed anthill. The faster they could get the plane ready for take-off, the safer it would be. Airliners were favorite targets for snipers. Nothing would be as bad for the morale of the Americans as the destruction of one of these planes. For that reason, the plane would stay on the ground for the shortest time possible.

The letters on the plane spelled American Airlines. To me they said, "I told you I would be back; come on aboard and let's go home." I was standing in line before the arriving passengers had even disembarked. Like everyone else, I did not want to be the last one in line and take the chance of not getting a seat. I watched the new arrivals coming down the steps; they all looked so young, so pale, so scared. I wondered if I had looked like that when I arrived a year ago. I could not remember. I nodded when a few said, "Hello," but my mind was not on them any more.

Standing in the door was a stewardess, the first American woman I had seen in a year. The line started to move, and as I got closer, I started to think of something I could say to her. As I slowly ascended the steps, my eyes started to tear. I was so happy to be going home I started to cry, and when I finally got to the door, I could barely manage a weak nod when she said, "Welcome aboard."

I found my seat, sat down, buckled up, and waited for the takeoff. There was no power on earth that would have been able to move me from that seat. I did not move. I did not blink. I stared straight ahead, frozen in place.

When at last the plane lifted off the runway, it went immediately into a combat climb. The pilot must have set a record for gaining as much altitude as possible in the shortest amount of time. I was thrown back, pinned against my seat. I grabbed the armrest so tightly that my knuckles turned white. I could hear the engines laboring for power and then scream as the demand on them continued to increase.

I was not scared. I felt that I would not be cheated out of life now. For almost a year, three hundred and forty-two days to be exact, I had dreamed of this day. I had faced death and I had walked away. Finally I was leaving Vietnam.

Suddenly, everything was quiet; without any warning the engine noise stopped, and the plane started to level out. It had finally reached a safe altitude, and now I could relax. I looked out the window; from the air Vietnam was a beautiful country; the landscape was occasionally marred by bomb craters, but other than that, it was green and looked like a country at peace. For me the war was over, and I was going home.

When the pilot finally announced that we had left Vietnamese air space and were now over the South China Sea, a loud cheer went up in the cabin. For the first time since boarding, everyone smiled, shook hands, slapped each other on the back. We knew at that moment, "This was for real." The stewardesses started serving drinks, and from one end of the plane to the other, men toasted one another, not for being in Vietnam, but rather for coming out alive.

Slowly the excitement subsided, and after a few minutes I became sleepy. I asked the stewardess for a pillow and blanket; the other men were doing the same. Eventually I fell into a deep, sound sleep. I know that I slept with a smile on my face because I slept in peace, not fear. When I did wake up I would be closer to home, and home was where I needed to be.

Key Words

Certain words, such as those listed here, help link supporting information in chronological order.

to begin	again	before
first	later	as
second	after	finally
then	in the past	now
soon	yesterday	at last
next	tomorrow	eventually
meanwhile	in the future	to end

2. Space Order

Use space order to describe an object, person, or scene in an easy-to-follow order and focus: from top to bottom or bottom to top, from left to right or right to left, from inside to outside or the reverse, from far away to close up.

Space order helps to describe clearly. Instead of jumping from detail to detail, you show how each detail relates to the other. If someone describes a room, like a den, and doesn't establish a focus to show things in relationship to each other, you may learn that a stereo system, video camera, stuffed deer head, and leather couch are in the room, but you wouldn't know where.

People in certain occupations are expected to write clear descriptions. Police must accurately describe crime or accident scenes, victims, and suspects. A style show must describe clothing; mechanical designers and drafters must, with precision, describe their drawings in words. One quality of good realtors, salespeople, waiters and waitresses is that they explain their products so well that customers buy.

Anytime you care enough to say, "I found the outfit, or computer, or apartment, or job I want!" you'll want to be able to describe it so your reader or listener can understand you've found specifically what you want.

Notice how the following paragraph by Emma Marx uses spatial order to create a general impression of a happy, working man.

> I remember one endearing photograph of my grandfather which I cherish. It is only a three-inch by four-inch black-and-white. In it, he stands dressed in a completely white outfit against some dark background I cannot make out. He is at least six feet tall, and on his head is a fluffy white hat shaped like a cream puff. On the huge, front brim is a Texaco emblem. His face under the hat is somewhat dark, but his teeth gleam in an obvious grin. His shirt is pure white, open at the neck, long-sleeved, and tucked into loose, white bib overalls. The two buckles on the overalls' suspenders glint, either from the sun or, more probably, from the flash bulb on the camera. Below the baggy pants, he wears white shoes with white laces. My mother told me that he wore this

white outfit, cleaned each night, to his gas station where he pumped gas, mended tires, and fixed cars. The small photograph captured Grandad as I remember him— proud of his work and happy with his life.

The following paragraph, written by Mary Landry, is an example of a student's use of space order.

My husband refers to our son's beat-up 1987 car as the junker, and I know it deserves the title. While moving it off the driveway, my hands stick to the steering wheel from the candy, cookies, and other foods he eats while he drives. Looking to the right side of the car, I view empty candy wrappers, soda cans, and pieces of scrap paper strewn on the seat, while down on the floor is enough dirt to make me wonder if he ever vacuums the carpet. Turning around to look into the back seat, I see more of the same mess as well as several sweat shirts, a couple of crumpled neck ties that he is required to wear to work, grubby tennis shoes, school books, and papers—all thrown about the seat and floor. Looking through the dirty windows is almost impossible, and while I try to get out of the car, the door handle falls off into my hand. The outside of his car has various bumps and scratches from front to back and hasn't been washed in months. The left rear wheel hub cap is missing, and the right tail light is broken. What I find most interesting, though, is how he can't understand why I won't let him use my car.

Key Words

Certain key words, such as the following, help a writer organize descriptions.

in front	above	to the left
behind	below	in the middle
beyond	nearby	to the right
far away	lower	next to
furthest away	at the bottom	across

3. Climactic Order

Climactic order arranges ideas so the least important supporting information is given first, the second least important information next, and so on, until you end with the most important information. You might arrange your supporting information in climactic order from

Least important to most important
Least effective to most effective
Least exciting to most exciting
Cheapest to most expensive
Good to better to best
Least convincing to most convincing
Least useful to most useful

Reasons, examples, statistics, facts, events, and opinions can all be arranged in climactic order. Climactic order is a teaser that holds the reader's attention until the end of the piece because the most important ideas are saved until last. It is especially effective for winning an argument or persuading. Usually in an argument, people try out their weaker arguments first and save their best for later. If they give away their best arguments first, their advantage dwindles by the end. People often expect the best reason in an argument to be the last, the clincher!

Mastering climactic order also enables you to answer essay test questions. For example, think of the following:

Explain why acid rain is a threat to our environment. (The essay answer could name and explain the reasons from the weakest to the gravest reason.)

What caused apartheid in South Africa? (The answer would give causes that range from least significant to most significant.)

How does the advertising in a culture reflect that culture's values? (The answer would arrange the ways beginning with the least important and ending with the most important.)

The following paragraph uses climactic order because the most tragic realization is last. A student Aubrey Payne, reflects in "The Dilemma of Third and North":

Through the hardware store door, all summer long, come skinny, scarred-up kids searching for bicycle tire patches or transistor batteries. A boy leaps skyward and grabs a can of paint from the window display. A child runs his hand along the counter and takes something. Someone shouts at the kid. Someone spits. Someone breaks a window. The kid is caught, threatened, and his undaunted reply is, "My mother doesn't care what I do!" You cannot mother the kid because you, too, are the enemy.

Notice that the activities mentioned in this next paragraph move from least to most important—entertainments, to knowledge, to salvation.

Standing on one side of the market place, the Gothic cathedral was the physical and spiritual focus of town life. People met there daily for worship and for other purposes. Mystery plays were performed before it; wandering preachers gave their sermons within its shadow—these were the *entertainments* of the middle ages. In its sculptures and stained glass the *knowledge* of the age was summarized for an illiterate public. In the church also, people were baptized, confirmed, married; from this point there still came the power for *salvation*. (from *Art and Civilization* by Bernard S. Meyers ©1967 by Hamlyn Publishing, London, England)

Key Words

Certain words, such as those listed here are useful in setting climactic order.

least	more	most
another	next	furthermore
most of all	most important	

Using Anticlimax

Sometimes you might reverse the order of climax. That is, you might arrange your reasons, facts, statistics, proofs, and examples beginning with your most important and gradually winding down to your least important. Do this if the most important reason, example, or statistic is one everyone already knows. It may be too well known to convincingly end an argument.

Using Humor

Sometimes climactic order can be funny or surprising. If you make your points increasingly important and then suddenly end with the unexpected, you may jolt a grin from your reader. "The student studied hard the days before the exam: he reviewed his old tests, he typed and memorized his notes, he reread the entire textbook, but he stayed in bed right through the test."

4. Question and Answer Order

Question and answer order is easy to understand. Simply ask a question and then answer it in the rest of the paragraph or essay. The question tells readers what to expect. The following two pieces make use of question and answer order. First, a high school student gives a profound answer to the question, "What, then, is education?"

Education

by Virginia Small

What, then, is education? Ideally, it is a person's continual discovery of his own uniqueness, his ability to understand and shape forces of life outside himself and cope with those he cannot shape. To do this, he must question constantly the pattern of life of which he is a part. Emphasis should be placed on discovery, rather than instruction.

Beginning

by Donna Sherrill

One of the most important questions in American society today is this: When does life begin? The question has much prominence because of the controversy over the legalization of most abortion methods since the 1973 Roe v. Wade decision of the Supreme Court. Most people with a conservative view believe that life begins at conception, while those with a liberal view believe life begins at birth. People in the center of the debate—the moderates—believe life begins with fetal movement, called quickening, at some point in the second trimester.

These three views raise a continuous war over the morality of abortion. Each group draws a line and says where life begins, thereby establishing their morality. But no one really knows when life does begin.

---

5. Problem/Solution Order

Organizing ideas into a problem/solution format often helps you separate your ideas into easily understood parts. Present or explain a problem to the reader and then offer a solution or solutions to the problem. Depending on your topic, you may choose to emphasize either the problem or the solution in your paper. If you have several solutions, arrange them in climactic or chronological order. Often, essay questions will ask for solutions to problems. In the business world, you will find yourself frequently using this order.

In the following paragraph, the problem is presented in the first three sentences; the solution is offered in the last four.

> Too many athletes are passing classes and graduating without learning anything but new plays. Many schools allow students to participate in sports even though they are failing their classes. These athletes may average twenty-five points a game, but may average a mere six hundred on their SAT scores. The solution is to make a mandatory rule that all athletes shall maintain at least a "C" average in all classes. A mandatory "C" will help athletes in the future as well as the present because, without skills, what happens to an athlete when he or she experiences a career-ending injury? If the colleges would toughen enough to require the "C" grade average for students wishing to participate in sports, there would be fewer illiterate people and more well-rounded athletes.

Key Words

Certain words help establish a problem/solution order.

problem	difficulty	puzzle
solution	resolution	answer

Don't do

1. COLLABORATIVE LEARNING FOR CHRONOLOGICAL ORDER _____

1. How is "Going Home" a chronological arrangement of events? Which key words does the author use? Which emotions does the speaker feel? Are these the same emotions you feel as you read the essay? Explain.

2. Decide how each of the following sentences could be developed in an essay that uses chronological order. Write down your explanations.

   a. By hard work, I earned my grade in the class.

   b. To hold a well-planned party, one needs to do several steps beforehand.

   c. Getting a student loan took an entire day.

2. COLLABORATIVE LEARNING FOR SPACE ORDER _____

1. How did the author organize the description of the grandfather? What other way might the same information have been organized? Rewrite the paragraph using a different organization.

2. In what way did the author organize the description of the 1987 junker? What other ways might the same information have been organized? The writer emphasized what we might see. Rewrite the junker's paragraph by adding smells and textures.

3. How could each of the following sentences be developed in a paper using spatial order? Decide what you might do, as a group, but do not write the paper. Give your teacher the decisions you make.

   a. The new shopping mall parking lot seems tastefully designed.

   b. The grounds surrounding the school need to be cleaned up.

   c. The testing room was set up so no one could cheat.

3. COLLABORATIVE LEARNING FOR CLIMACTIC ORDER _____

1. Arrange these sentences in climactic order, that is, from the least to the most important. Then rearrange them in anticlimactic order.

    a. The latchkey kids caused trouble!

        _____ They dripped catsup over the rug in front of the TV.

        _____ They flushed a shoe down the toilet.

        _____ They discovered where their father kept his pistol and shot the mail-carrier.

        _____ They burned down the garage by playing with matches.

    b. Thieves broke into the car and stole some expensive items:

        _____ The engine

        _____ Three half- eaten apples

        _____ Sixteen bottles of Coke

        _____ An IBM Personal Computer

        _____ The car radio

2. How could each of the following topics be treated with climactic order? Write out your answers together.

    a. There are reasons why students might go to college.

    b. The government should provide a free college education to all students who maintain a C average or better.

    c. During their sophomore year, all high school students should be required to live in a foreign country.

4. COLLABORATIVE LEARNING FOR QUESTION/ANSWER _____

1. In your group, choose a topic. Then together, write five questions that you might ask about the topic. Brainstorm how each question might be answered. Together, write your answers to one question in a paragraph or essay.

2. Find examples of the question/answer arrangement in your texts for other courses. Take these to your writing group to share.

5. COLLABORATIVE LEARNING FOR PROBLEM/SOLUTION ORDER _____

1. How might one of these topics be treated as a problem/solution? Summarize your discussion in a problem/solution format.

Drugs available in schools	Drug testing
Teenage runaways	Mandatory education until 16

2. Together write a paper using the problem/solution method. One of you chooses the problem. Others collect the supporting information for the solution and arrange it for the paper. The one who chose the topic writes the paper. Together, revise the rough draft.

3. Read an issue of a newspaper and together make a list of all the problems mentioned in the paper.

WRITING TASKS

1. In your texts and readings for other courses, locate an example of each of these five ways to organize supporting information. Make a copy of each example and then write a short paragraph explaining how the authors arranged the information. Might a more suitable method have been used by any author?

2. Look over your papers. Decide how you could improve one paper by using an order or orders explained in this chapter. Revise the paper. Turn in both the original and revised papers.

3. Write a paper using one or more of the orders explained in this chapter. Use key words which are appropriate for that kind of order.

Checklist for the Structure of Your Paper

Yes   *No*

____ ____   1. In your paper, did you use a method rather than a haphazard arrangement of your information?

____ ____   2. Can you give meaningful reasons for choosing your order or orders?

____ ____   3. Do your key words offer clues to your arrangement?

____ ____   4. Are all your key words unobtrusive?

Chapter Fourteen

Thesis Statements

A thesis works like street signs or a road map for the reader. True, most of us could get from one city to another without a road map or street signs if we knew beforehand where we were going, or if we took the time along the way to ask knowledgeable persons about how to get where we wanted to go. Yet, for most of us, a map and road signs save time and energy.

A thesis is often the most important sentence in a piece of writing because it tells the reader what the entire piece is about in just one sentence.

Many writers use such a sentence to shape ideas for their readers. However, some fine paragraphs or essays are so well designed they do not require a main-idea sentence; their writers imply their main ideas. But until students establish a firm control over the shape of their writing, main-idea sentences are usually helpful because they guide the writers and their readers through the compositions. Such sentences predict what will be said or illuminate what has already been said.

Characteristics of a Thesis

To write an effective thesis, you should know its characteristics. Then you can easily apply your knowledge to writing the thesis statement of an essay. Good main-idea sentences do these things.

- *Name the topic.* This is easy because you simply tell the reader the subject of the writing. For example—Beauty Queens
- *State an inference* (opinion, belief, judgment, prediction, conclusion) about the topic. Your statement is an inference if it can be denied, opposed, agreed with, argued. For

example, "Beauty queens must have the stamina of a stallion, the grace of a ballerina, the beauty of a rose, the personality of a wholesome girl, and the intelligence of Edison."

In the rest of your paper, give facts, examples or other supporting information to explain your inference. Many times, student writers think they have created a thesis but then don't know what else to say. One reason for this trouble is that they have written a statement of fact instead of an inference. Once writers state a fact, they can say little to explain it. (See the discussion of facts and inferences if you have questions.) As main-idea sentences, inferences work better than facts because inferences have to be defended or explained; therefore, they provide direction to the paper.

- *Predict or explain the structure* of the paragraph or essay. Predict the main ideas you will use and the arrangement of these ideas in your paper. For example, you may indicate that you will give background, or use comparison or description, or that you will study the effects of something or give reasons. This way, the reader is prepared for the way you will organize the paper and will know what to expect.

Notice how the following two examples of a thesis name the topic, state an opinion about the topic, and explain the structure of the paper.

EXAMPLE 1: A woman can dress well on a limited budget if she shops at discount stores, garage sales, factory outlets, and consignment shops.

Topic: A woman dressing well on a limited budget

Opinion: A woman can dress well on a limited budget if she shops at discount stores, garage sales, factory outlets, and consignment shops. (Some people might not believe that it is possible to dress well by shopping at such places, so the sentence gives an opinion.)

Structure: Because the author mentioned discount stores, garage sales, factory outlets, and finally consignment shops, she will need to discuss shopping in all those places. If she discusses each kind of store separately, beginning with discount stores, then she should discuss the garage sales next and so on.

EXAMPLE 2: Federal standards allow financial aid to be unfairly distributed to some students who do not need it while deserving students cannot get it.

Topic: Federal standards for financial aid.

Opinion: Federal standards allow unfair distribution of finanical aid. (People could surely argue whether or not this statement is true, so the sentence expresses an opinon.)

Structure: The paper shows that federal standards allow unfair financial aid to be given to undeserving students while needy students receive none. The main-idea sentence does not predict any other approach such as how to apply for financial aid, or a history of financial aid; nor will it discuss how federal aid can be supplemented by private loans. The reader should expect to learn only the federal standards that allow aid to be distributed unfairly.

Ten Hints for Writing a Good Thesis and Avoiding Problems

The following specific hints for writing good main-idea sentences address some common problems of student writers. After each hint, you will find examples of main-idea sentences written by students. The students first demonstrate the problem and then show how the sentence can be fittingly revised. Here are the ten hints.

1. *Name the specific topic of the paper in the main-idea sentence.* Readers usually want to know what you are writing about; they resent having to guess because the writing is vague.

> Faulty: This is a situation all of the people of the world must face sometime or other. (Readers must guess the situation; the sentence is vague.)
>
> Better: People face death with fear, with quiet resignation, or with hope. (Readers no longer must guess.)

* * *

> Faulty: Sometimes even city hall cannot handle what comes to it. (Reader must guess what city hall cannot handle.)
>
> Better: Growth can be so rapid that city hall will not have the tax dollars or the budget to provide city services to all the new subdivisions. (Readers now know that the paper will deal with rapid growth, taxes, and services to the subdivisions, all problems of city hall.)

2. *Make the topic small enough to be treated completely in the essay. Name only one position or issue in a thesis or topic sentence.* If you name two or more totally separate topics, or choose a large topic, you will have a very difficult time writing a unified paper.

> Faulty: Fast food is easy to find, but I love the subtle tastes of home cooking. (There are two topics: (a) It's easy to find fast foods and (b) the writer loves the subtle tastes of home cooking.)
>
> Better: The college cafeteria food offers the subtle tastes of home-cooked meals. (Now the only topic is obvious.)

* * *

> Faulty: A surprise party can be easily planned but dangerous if kids drive to and from it intoxicated. (There are two topics: (a) Surprise parties can be easily planned and (b) the dangers of driving if intoxicated.)
>
> Better: A well-planned surprise party involves four planning stages. (Now the only topic is the planning for the party.)

3. *Predict the specific supporting ideas or the way you'll arrange supporting information.* Help your reader know how you are going to develop the paper and make it much easier to follow.

Faulty: Nowhere but in the United States has junk food become a dietary problem. (This sounds as if the writer will stress that only the United States has this dietary problem. The reader could not guess that the paper would go on to explain that junk food causes malnutrition.)

Better: Eating only junk food can cause malnutrition because junk food lacks required vitamins. (Now this sentence predicts a paper about junk food causing malnutrition.)

* * *

Faulty: The American family farmer needs help. (The writer could be much more specific about the kinds of help or reasons for needing help.)

Better: An increase in consumption by consumers would provide American farmers the financial help they need. (Now the readers know the kind of help the writer thinks the farmer needs.)

4. *Use a sentence to state your main idea rather than a question.* A sentence makes a clearer statement of your position than a question. Questions arouse your reader's curiosity. But they should not be used in place of a main-idea sentence because they do not present inferences.

Faulty: Is drinking a national problem? (The writer gives no hint as to how the topic will be developed in the paper.)

Better: Because drinking affects military readiness, business production, and family happiness, excessive drinking is a national problem. (This sentence explains why the writer thinks drinking is a national problem so the reader expects that approach in the paper.)

* * *

Faulty: Why do Americans allow catastrophic illnesses to bankrupt people? (Writer is vague. The reader does not know what to expect.)

Better: Americans should vote for a national insurance so that catastrophic illnesses will not bankrupt people. (Now the reader expects an argument for a national insurance to cover the costs of catastrophic illnesses.)

5. *Use a complete sentence for your main-idea sentence.* A fragment or title will not state a clear inference.

Faulty: The Super Bowl winners over the last twenty years (The writer needs to state an inference about the superbowl and make the inference a complete sentence.)

Better: Super Bowl winners over the last twenty years reflect the rise and demise of brute strength.

* * *

Faulty: Jazz journalism (The writer needs to add the inference and make this a complete sentence.)

Better: Jazz journalism in the 1920s was a form of yellow journalism.

6. *Give an opinion,* not a fact. It is very difficult to build an entire paper on a simple fact that needs little explanation. You can explain or prove or develop an inference.

Faulty: The Great Lakes border the United States and Canada. (Once the writer gives this fact, what else is left to say?)

Better: Because the Great Lakes separate the United States and Canada, both countries have had to cooperate. (Now the statement is arguable.)

* * *

Faulty: In 1927, Babe Ruth hit sixty home runs. (If your fact is correct, what else is there to say?)

Better: Even though Babe Ruth's home run record has been surpassed, conditions in his day were so different from those today that he still deserves to hold the rank of baseball's best home run hitter.

7. *Use a vocabulary which fits your age, your level of education, and your audience.* Avoid expressing ideas the way you might have expressed them as a child.

Faulty: Skiing is fun and exciting. (Fun is a kid's word.)

Better: Downhill skiing reminds me of the first traumatic sled ride I took alone.

* * *

Faulty: My dog is a good pet. (The writer sounds like a child. Try to tell about your pet in a more adult, sophisticated way.)

Better: Since I've been living on my own, I understand why pets help lonely people cope with life.

8. *Avoid clichés (trite expressions).* People get tired of reading worn out, over-used descriptors.

Faulty: Single parenting is a long, hard row to hoe. (Eliminate the cliché: *long, hard row to hoe.*)

Better: Single parenting can be easier if the parent makes use of local public resources. (Now the reader understands the way the paper will develop.)

* * *

Faulty: New York is truly the Big Apple. (Eliminate the cliché.)

Better: To become a major actor in live theater, one must perform in New York City. (Now the writer says what the point is.)

If you want more information on clichés, see Writer's Decision Six.

9. *Use specific vocabulary to describe exactly what you intend to say.* You will have problems if your wording is so general that other words could be substituted and the main-idea sentence would still make sense. (See the discussion of general and specific information in Chapter 9.)

Faulty: Skiing is costly but very enjoyable. (You could substitute other words for the topic, skiing. For example, polo is costly but enjoyable. Rock concerts are costly but enjoyable. Adopting a handicapped child is costly but enjoyable. A new car is costly but enjoyable.)

Better: Although the clothing and equipment necessary for downhill skiing cost me at least $500, my enjoyment makes my investment worthwhile. (Here the writer is specific.)

* * *

Faulty: A friend is a very special person. (So is a parent, grandparent, teacher, mentor.)

Better: In times of tragedy, friends who have known each other since grade school are often more understanding than family or spouses. (This sentence is specific.)

10. *Avoid saying what everyone already knows.* The problem with stating only common knowledge is that there is nothing new to say to your reader.

Faulty: The equipment used in tennis includes racquets, shoes, and clothing. (This factual statement tells what almost everyone already knows about tennis. The reader will be bored. Also, the statement uses no inference.)

Better: By following the careers of major tennis stars, a good tennis player can learn how to act on the court. (All would not agree with this inference; the statement goes beyond common knowledge.)

* * *

Faulty: People are restoring old houses. (Common fact.)

Better: Restoration of old houses can be profitable if one carefully considers the neighborhood and the existing peculiarities of the structure. (Inference is no longer general knowledge.)

COLLABORATIVE LEARNING

1. Practice writing a thesis. To do this, one person in the group needs to keep a record.

   a. Name five or six topics and give an opinion about each.

   b. Work together to collect supporting information for each topic. (Use clusters, tree branching, or lists.)

   c. Condense your information into main-idea sentences for each topic.

   d. Use the checklist at the end of this chapter to evaluate your sentences.

2. In your writing group, rewrite each of the following sentences until it is a successful thesis for an essay. Use the chapter's "Ten Hints for Writing a Good Thesis" to guide you. (Hint: Not all are poor sentences.)

   a. The new technologies in our world are a good show.

   b. Due to its high purchase price and its fast depreciation, the worst investment today is the new automobile.

   c. Because a roommate pays half the bills, does she have the right to invite friends anytime, eat the food, and play the radio as loudly as she wishes?

   d. College students and time management skills.

   e. To reduce the death rates on the streets and highways of this county, drivers need to stop for yellow lights, keep the speed limits, maintain a distance of one car length for *every* ten miles of traveling speed, use turn signals, and obey all signs.

   f. No pain, no gain in exercise and in business.

   g. Pineapple is a name of a fruit grown in Hawaii.

3. Before joining your writing group, each of you should pick out the thesis sentence in one of your papers. Then in the writing group, one student reads only that sentence to the others. After hearing the sentence, the others write what they each expect to hear in the rest of the paper. Then the student reads the entire paper to the group. After the reading, the group compares their expectations with what they actually heard. If the main thesis needs to be rewritten, the group will help rewrite it.

4. Together build paragraphs. Choose the subject. Offer an opinion about the subject—the controlling idea. Together, gather supporting information that could fit into a paragraph. Then each person, alone, writes a paragraph using the same supporting information. Be sure to use a main-idea sentence. When you finish, compare your paragraphs. What do you learn?

WRITING TASKS

1. Study the thesis in essays which you've written for this course or other courses. Evaluate and improve them using the "Ten Hints for Writing a Good Thesis" offered earlier in this chapter.

2. If you need more practice on writing a thesis, complete the worksheet at the end of the chapter.

Checklist for Your Main-Idea Sentences

Yes	No		
____	____	1.	Did you identify the subject and make an inference?
____	____	2.	Did you use a statement rather than a question?
____	____	3.	Did you write a sentence rather than a fragment?
____	____	4.	If you used a thesis in your introduction, does it predict the ideas and the order of the paper?
____	____	5.	Did you use specific and clear wording?
____	____	6.	Did you state an inference, not just a fact?
____	____	7.	Does the vocabulary fit your audience?
____	____	8.	Did you avoid stating what everyone already knows?
____	____	9.	Did you omit clichés and trite sayings?

Chapter Fifteen
Organizing Ideas
into a Paragraph

Kinds of Paragraphs

There are several different kinds of paragraphs: those which must stand alone, those part of a larger work, those linking paragraphs, and those which begin and end essays.

- Sometimes a paragraph must be complete and stand alone. Use such a paragraph in short pieces and on tests that require a short answer, a discussion of only one main point. Such a paragraph must communicate without help from other paragraphs.

- Other times, paragraphs are parts of a large piece, for example, in essays, letters, tests. In these longer pieces, each paragraph should discuss only one major point, one inference. All paragraphs must relate to the main inference of the large piece.

- Some paragraphs link one set of paragraphs to another set. These are a special type; they are known as coherence paragraphs.

- Paragraphs that introduce and conclude essays are also different. (See Chapter 17 of this book for a detailed explanation of introductions and conclusions.)

This chapter will concentrate on the first two types of paragraphs.

Decisions Writers Must Make in Order to Write Paragraphs

To write a paragraph that can stand alone, you must make all the decisions which writers make. If you have worked your way through this book, you know that, at some point in the writing process, the writer must decide what to write about, what supporting information to use to explain ideas, who the audience is, what the reasons for writing to that audience are, what voice or personality to use, and how best to arrange information. All this makes the writing process sound quite complicated. But as you improve as a writer, you will realize that all writers make these decisions. They will not make these decisions in the same way or order you might; yet, each writer somehow has to decide what exactly to say, to whom, why, and how.

The following is a student's answer to the test question "Name and explain why a person working today might be considered a success." It is a good example to use to talk about the paragraph to see how the writer made all the decisions.

Today's Success

At the top of two professions—cartoonist and political commentator—sits Gary Trudeau. Trudeau became the first comic strip artist to receive the Pulitzer Prize for editorial cartooning. That award honors Trudeau for his two interests: political commentary through cartoon making. His role as political commentator received high praise from ex-president Gerald Ford, "There are only three major vehicles to keep us informed as to what is going on in Washington—the electronic media, the print media, and 'Doonesbury' and not necessarily in that order." *Time Magazine* notes, "In 'Doonesbury' the real and fictive combine, and actually blend into commentary. The results are often closer to truth than mere news reports." But "Doonesbury" is popular in more places than Washington. More than 60 million readers in over 450 newspapers in both the United States and Canada read "Doonesbury" daily. Book collections of the comic strip have sold over three-quarters of a million copies. People not in the political world read "Doonesbury" for the same reason they read "Bloom Country" or other editorial cartoons. They read because they want to laugh at the shenanigans of those in high office or because they want a commentary on the philosophy and thinking in their own world. Financial success through this vast readership and the national acceptance of his political statements put Trudeau at the top of two professions— funny paper illustrator and political commentator.

Let's examine how the writer created the paragraph.

DECIDING ON A TOPIC. To answer the test question, the writer decided to use Gary Trudeau as an example of success.

DECIDING ON APPROPRIATE SUPPORTING INFORMATION. The writer collected information that could prove Trudeau's success:

Trudeau won the Pulitzer Prize for editorial cartooning
60 million readers

"Doonesbury" appeared in over 450 newspapers in the United States and Canada

Book collections sold over three-quarters of a million copies

Ex-President Gerald Ford's quote on the cartoon's power

Time magazine talked favorably of "Doonesbury"

People read it for entertainment and political commentary

DECIDING ABOUT AUDIENCE, PURPOSE, AND VOICE. The audience is the teacher who asked the quiz question. The purpose for answering is a good grade. The voice is formal for academic writing.

DECIDING ABOUT ORGANIZATION. The writer decided to explain Trudeau's success with examples and arranged them in the order of least to most well known:

- The Pulitzer award Trudeau received proved that he was successful (least-known idea).

- Ford's quote on the fame Trudeau had achieved with Washington politicians (a better-known idea).

- *Time's* quote points up his fame and his recognition by the news media.

- His fame with the general public as seen in the numbers of books and newspapers sold (the best known idea).

The writer needed to bring all of this information together in a topic sentence that would immediately answer the test question. So the writer said, "At the top of two professions—cartoonist and political commentator—sits Gary Trudeau." The rest of the paper would use examples to explain why this statement was true.

The concluding statement wrapped up the ideas by returning to the point made in the beginning so the reader would go full circle back to the beginning and feel a sense of completeness. "Financial success through this vast readership and the national acceptance of his political statements put Trudeau at the top of two professions—funny paper illustrator and political commentator."

The student writer knew how to make these many decisions. A good writer must also consider other matters. The writer must make sure that everything is related to the main idea—*unity*. Then all the parts must fit together smoothly—*coherence*. The writer must also give importance—*emphasis*—to whatever needs it.

PARAGRAPH UNITY—MAKING SURE EVERYTHING RELATES TO THE SAME IDEA

In a good paragraph, all details must relate to the topic sentence. The writer must leave out anything irrelevant which might distract from the main point of the paragraph. Sometimes in writing you will find that unity requires you to cross out your favorite sentence or even your favorite, but unfortunately unrelated, point.

The following paragraph has problems in unity; problem sentences are underlined.

Is It Worth It?

Standing near the stage at rock concerts has its drawbacks. First of all, I usually end up standing next to someone who smokes, and smoke disturbs my breathing and waters my eyes. Then someone taller than I always stands in my direct view. <u>I am six foot, but even taller people than I are usually there.</u> Also, it is impossible to avoid those graceful individuals who are intent on bumping, shoving, and stepping on my feet as they try to get closer. Then there is the noise level. Standing next to an amplification system designed to fill a structure packed with a hundred thousand or so people hurts my ears and produces a tremendous after-the-concert headache. <u>I am allergic to aspirin, so the headache is even harder to get rid of than it should be.</u> I stand up close, but I cannot hear the separation of instruments because the acoustics there are distorted. And finally, I do not get the full effect of the stage design and lighting because I see only a part of the total stage. <u>What I do get for all this discomfort is a close look at some of the performers and the stage equipment.</u>

All the underlined parts of the paragraph are irrelevant. The reader doesn't care that the writer is six feet tall or allergic to aspirin. Neither of these facts has much to do with the drawbacks of listening to a rock concert near the stage, so those two ideas should be dropped.

The ending of the paragraph is more of a problem. The writer begins a new topic when he explains why he tolerates all the discomforts near the stage. If the writer held strictly to the promise he made his reader in the first part of the paragraph, he would present only the discomforts. The reasons for enduring the discomforts break the unity; reasons belong in another paragraph. One way to solve the problem with this ending would be to revise the topic sentence. Rewritten, the topic sentence could prepare the reader to expect a list of the discomforts and the reasons the writer endures them.

PARAGRAPH COHERENCE—CONNECTING EVERYTHING LOGICALLY _____

In a good paragraph, every inference, and all details, will connect smoothly and logically. Readers will understand you because your transitions easily lead them from detail to detail, from sentence to sentence, or from one paragraph to the next. Transitions tell the reader when you have ended one point and gone to another. They also tell the reader how various details relate: transitions may indicate that details contrast, that you will present another example or additional facts, that you are adding supporting statistics, or that you are summarizing.

Four Ways to Achieve Smooth Connections

Here are four ways to achieve these smooth connections: Use transitional words to connect ideas, arrange supporting information in logical order, repeat important words, and create parallel structure. An explanation of each follows.

1. USE TRANSITIONAL WORDS TO CONNECT IDEAS. In any writing, special words or phrases predict the arrangement of supporting information. Keep a long list of transitional words near where you work, and use those words in the ways specified here. For example, if you wish to add an idea or example or statistic to your paper, you might choose one of the words listed for *addition*.

Type of transition	Transitional words to use
Addition	and, also, in addition, in addition to, another, too, further, furthermore, of more interest, in fact, likewise, next, moreover, then, in the first place, in the second place
Comparison or similarity	like, as, similarly, likewise, just the same as, by comparison, in the same way, both
Contrast or difference	however, different from, in contrast, yet, on the other hand, but, on the contrary, not only . . . but also
Chronological order	to begin, first, second, third, one, two, three, again, later, now, soon, as, then, next, meanwhile, after, in the past, yesterday, tomorrow, in the future, finally, last, at last, to end
Climax	most of all, more, most important, most significant
Conclusion	to finish, to end, to draw together, to conclude
Concession	even though, still, yet, nevertheless, despite
Consequence	as a result, because, therefore, thus, consequently, since
Emphasis	yes, in fact, in truth, certainly, surely, as a matter of fact, emphatically, decidedly, obviously, without doubt
Example	for example, for instance, in one case, in this instance, in this case, another, as evidence
Purpose	for this end, to this end, for this reason, with this purpose, because, therefore
Repetition	to say it again, to repeat, to restate, to summarize, to draw together, to reiterate, what this means is
Spatial relationships	in front, behind, beyond; across, furthest away, in the background, above, below, nearby, lower, at the bottom, to the left, opposite, in the middle, next to
Summary	to summarize, to sum up, to draw together, in short

Transitional words can sometimes change or expand meaning. These next sentences, for example, use few transitions, so you aren't exactly sure of the writer's point:

> I enjoy a good film. I like a brooding, dark tragedy which will haunt me for days. The movie should make me understand something about human beings or living that I didn't know before watching the picture. I want to be touched by the emotions, the plot, the characters, and the meaning of the film.

But suppose the writer added a transition to show consequences. Then the paragraph might be revised like this:

> For me to enjoy it, a movie must be a brooding, dark tragedy whose emotions, plot, characters, and meaning I will remember *because* they helped me understand something significant about human beings that I didn't know before I saw the movie.

2. **ARRANGE SUPORTING INFORMATION IN LOGICAL ORDER.** Use the orders of climax, space, time, problem-solution, question-answer, etc. to make your paper coherent. Everything you learned about arranging your ideas in Chapter 13 can help you unify your paper. Look back over that chapter.

3. **REPEAT IMPORTANT WORDS.** A third way to create coherence is to repeat words from main-idea sentences later in the paragraph so readers see connections between the main idea and points discussed later. Look over the paragraph on "Doonesbury" and Trudeau and notice that the writer kept you thinking about Trudeau and "Doonesbury" by mentioning their names several times in the paragraph. Also study the paragraph about the rock concerts for repeated words.

4. **CREATE PARALLEL STRUCTURE.** These next sentences are parallel because they repeat similar words or grammatical patterns to show similar ideas.

> I came. I saw. I conquered. (Each sentence has the subject *I* and a verb in the past tense.)
> Eating is necessary and enjoyable. (*Necessary* and *enjoyable* are two parallel adjectives describing eating.)
> The beauty queen sang an opera, danced the tango, and rode the bucking mule. (*Sang, danced,* and *rode* are all verbs in the past tense; *opera, tango,* and *mule* are all objects of the verbs.)

Single words or whole sentences can be parallel. Parallel words must be in the same grammatical form—all verbs in the same tense, all adjectives, or all independent or dependent clauses. (See Decision VI for more work with parallel structure.)

Another Look at "Is It Worth It?"

Look again at the revised paragraph on the rock concerts. Here the most obvious transitions are underlined.

Standing near the stage at rock concerts has its drawbacks. First of all, I usually end up standing next to someone who smokes; smoking disturbs my breathing and waters my eyes. Then it never fails that someone taller than I stands in my direct view of the stage. Also, it is impossible to avoid those graceful individuals who are intent on bumping, shoving, and stepping on my feet as they try to get closer. Besides, I put up with the noise level. Standing next to an amplification system designed to fill a structure packed with a hundred thousand or so people tends to hurt my ears and produce a tremendous after the-concert headache. Worse still, being close makes it very difficult for me to hear the separation of instruments because the acoustics near the stage are distorted. And a final problem is that I do not get the full effect of the set design and lighting because I see only a part of the whole stage. If I cannot hear the sound and cannot see the full effects of the production, I guess I am a fool for standing so close to the stage. Well, it is my intention from now on to stay in a seat and enjoy the whole show without all the discomforts of the near view.

In this paragraph, *transitional words* like *first of all, then, also, finally,* and *worse still* introduce new supporting information to help the reader see that examples prove the author's point.

The *logical arrangement* of the first part of the paragraph is in simple climactic order; the paper moves from the least significant problem to the most significant problem faced by the writer at rock concerts. In fact, the worst problems, the inability to hear the sound and see the full effect of the production are such serious matters that the author reaches the conclusion that he will stay in his seat at the next rock concert.

A second kind of arrangement is also used. Because a solution is offered at the end of the list of problems, this paragraph uses the problem-solution arrangement. Both arrangements effectively structure the piece.

Repeated words and phrases emphasize the importance of details. Notice how the ending repeats the most convincing ideas: "cannot hear the sound," and "cannot see the full effects of the production," "standing close to the stage"; and "discomforts of the near view." With this wording, the reader sees how all the problems lead to the writer's conclusion: He will stay in his seat at the next rock concert and avoid all these problems.

Parallel structure emphasizes important ideas: "If I cannot hear the sound and cannot see the full effects of the production. . . ." This repetition of words and the structure of the phrases emphasize the importance of these facts.

PARAGRAPH EMPHASIS

The fine writer writes with emphasis. Emphasis places important points at special spots in the writing; it is created when a certain idea, word, sentence, or paragraph stands out.

The strongest spot is usually the end. The second strongest spot is usually the beginning. The weakest is often in the middle, the place where ideas are sometimes buried. These same three positions apply to sentences, paragraphs, and essays.

The middle is the point of least emphasis. This is where the reader sometimes skims, where examples or statistics that prove the inferences are often found—material of interest, but material that can be read quite fast. Think of the middle as a burying ground. As a kid, if you had to tell your mom and dad something that you really didn't want them to hear, you probably said it in the middle of much information. You hoped they wouldn't pay attention. And sometimes they didn't! The middle of a paragraph or memo or essay may be the point of least emphasis.

More important is the beginning of a sentence or piece of longer writing. People pay attention to beginnings. For example, personnel interviewers often decide to hire someone in the first thirty seconds of the interview. In the same way, the beginning of any work initially impresses readers and tempts them to read on. For that reason, writers may place their gripping information in the beginning.

The ending of the sentences, paragraphs, and entire essays is the most important. It is the writer's chance for a final, and sometimes lasting, impression.

In these next sentences, notice how easily the date can become either the focal point or unimportant.

- In 1492, Columbus sailed to the New World, the Americas. (1492 stands out.)
- Columbus sailed into the New World in 1492 and found the Americas. (1492 is buried.)
- When Columbus sailed into the New World, the Americas, it was 1492. (1492 stands out as the dramatic climax to the sentence.)

Another way to emphasize ideas is to place important points in independent clauses and the less important points in dependent clauses. For example, in a business letter, the writer must reference a phone call or letter to which he or she is responding, but that reference is not the major piece of information. Thus, the opening sentence of a letter might read, "As we discussed yesterday on the phone, the price for _____ is _____." The dependent clause contains less important information; the independent clause contains the price, which is the important point.

Beginning, middle, and end—the aware writer will use these positions wisely to shape emphasis in paragraphs, essays, memos, tests, letters, reports—in fact, in all writing, no matter how small or large. Emphasis is a powerful writer's tool; it is subtle but effective. When you make decisions about the information important to you and you present it in positions that convey that importance, you are helping your reader think and understand as you intend. You will never again merely hope the reader catches your intent because now you have a stylistic tool that ensures the reader's understanding.

COLLABORATIVE LEARNING

1. Study the following paragraph "Road Pizza" by student Ed Ashenden. What makes this an interesting piece? Together revise it, following the guidelines for unity.

Road Pizza

The sight of a dead dog or cat on the road is painful. To come across a dead animal on the way to work can ruin a morning; in fact, an entire busy day may be rudely interrupted with vivid images of the morning's encounter. On the return trip home, one is preoccupied that the dead bird, raccoon, possum, or whatever, may still be on the road, looking much, much worse. A person tells himself that accidents do happen; they are nature's way of thinning out the herd, survival of the fittest and all that ecological balance stuff. But why must the dead animals remain on the road? Can't the driver who hit the animal just remove it to the roadside brush? Or should it stay on the road as a memorial to remind drivers to slow down? Sometimes I'll stop my car, walk back, grab the dog or cat by the leg or tail, drag it to the roadside brush, and drive off feeling much better.

2. Find an example of your writing. Explain why it is or is not unified. Work with the members of your group to unify it.

3. The day began with a long, rumbling thunderstorm. It came close to the place where I had to work. Lightning struck the giant oak and it caught fire. Pouring rain put out all but a smoldering deep within the tree's trunk. One day later, smoke from the oak still gagged us.

   Rewrite the preceding paragraph four times, each time with different transitions to show (a) contrast, (b) chronology, (c) special relationships, and (d) consequences. After you try each of these four kinds of transitions, decide which of your revisions works best.

4. The women's movement has lost some of its momentum. The women's movement is making some gains. States are now deciding on equal pay for equal worth. A secretary (usually a woman) gets as much pay as a garbage collector (usually a man). Women still are not getting equal pay for equal work. Women make only about 69 percent of the pay men make, according to a *60 Minutes* report. Women make up 51 percent of the society. Few major corporations in the United States are headed by women.

   Rewrite the preceding paragraph three times. Use transitions to (a) predict examples, (b) emphasize contrast, (c) show problem/solution. Why does the paragraph need transitions?

5. As a group, rewrite the following paragraph either in climactic order or a problem/solution order.

Because of the increase in crime, people in the United States are protecting themselves. One of every three females will be sexually assaulted. One out of every two persons will experience a robbery of some belongings. People are buying protection. Home security systems are no longer the property of the wealthy. Watch dogs protect homes. Shooting ranges now offer courses for the untrained gun owner. People take courses to learn how to defend themselves against kidnapping. Long-distance travellers sometimes drive instead of taking the public transportation. Airports search baggage and passengers for weapons or bombs.

6. My new outfit cost me $175, but I don't have to worry about paying for it because my dad told me to choose anything I liked and he would pay the bill as my birthday gift from him.

    a. Reword this sentence to stress that the most important point is the cost. Hide the least important information in a dependent clause.

    b. Rewrite the sentence to emphasize that the buyer is dad.

    c. Finally rearrange the sentence to stress that dad promised to pay for anything.

7. In the late 1990s, a generation of older consumers, aged fifty-five to seventy, will control the marketplace and demand quality for their money.

    a. Arrange the sentence to emphasize the group's age.

    b. Arrange the words to stress control.

    c. Add your own ideas about these consumers, but bury your ideas in a dependent clause so they are unobtrusive.

8. Study an article in a popular magazine to see ways it emphasizes its points. Write a report to the class.

WRITING TASKS

1. Revise two or more of your paragraphs until they are unified, coherent, and emphatic. Use the hints given in this chapter to guide you. After your revisions of the paragraphs are finished, show your instructor your original papers and your revisions.

2. Write a paragraph for which you make all the decisions writers must make. Use other chapters in this text, if necessary, to help you decide on a topic, supporting information, audience, purpose, voice, and organization. (Use *Part II* of this text if you want to write a specific kind of paragraph.) Check your finished paragraph to make certain that the paragraph is unified, that is, all the details in your paragraph relate to your topic sentence. Use nothing unrelated to your main points in your paragraph. Secondly, check that *every* inference and all details connect smoothly and logically because you used transitional words, logical order, repetition of important words, and parallel structure. Finally, check for emphasis by making certain that your most important points stand out for your readers.

Checklist for your paragraphs

Yes   *No*

____   ____   1. Did you read the chapters on finding a topic if you had trouble finding a subject?

____   ____   2. Did you use the chapters on supporting information if you needed help finding enough ideas?

____   ____   3. Did you use the chapters on audience, purpose, and voice if you needed help to decide on your audience, purpose, or voice?

____   ____   4. Did you use the chapter on arranging information to help you organize your paragraph?

Unity

____   ____   5. Is every inference and detail in the paragraph related to your main-idea sentence?

____   ____   6. Did you leave out everything that distracts from your main inference?

Coherence

____   ____   7. Did you use transitional words to connect points?

____   ____   8. Did you arrange your ideas in a specific order?

____   ____   9. Did you repeat important words from the main-idea sentence so your reader remembers their importance?

____   ____   10. Did you use parallel structure to show similar ideas?

Emphasis

____   ____   11. Did you emphasize important ideas?

Chapter Sixteen

Understanding the Essay

An essay is
not a novel
not a short story
not a poem
not a song
not a play
not a movie script.

Some authors, like superstars, receive millions of dollars for creating best-selling novels. Some write plays that famous directors snatch for spectacular movies. But even famous authors cannot do every kind of writing equally well. Some writers can create great novels, but absolutely no one would buy their movie scripts. Others write fine how-to books but couldn't compose a song. In this book, you will not be asked to write a novel, a short story, a poem, or a play. Most people do not write such pieces, just as most people do not design skyscrapers or pitch major league baseball. You will write essays.

Here are some ways writers talk about essays: An essay is a set of paragraphs about one main idea or one inference. An essay expresses an attitude about an idea or about some aspect of life. An essay creates a unified point of view. An essay has to offer insight! An essay can be written for many reasons: to explain something, to argue something so your reader will agree, or to persuade someone to do something.

Some Sample Essays

The essays that follow are examples of different types of essays. They include

A letter to a young girl, Virginia
A famous essay by a master essayist, E. B. White
An answer to an essay test question

As you read these three pieces, keep in mind the decisions each writer must have made to create the piece. Mentally compare the pieces as you read. What does each essay have in common with the others? At the end of each essay you will find questions that will point out areas to consider.

Dear Virginia

Your little friends are wrong. They have been affected by the skepticism of a skeptical age. They do not believe except what they see. They think that nothing can be which is not comprehensible by their little minds. All minds, Virginia, whether they be men's or children's, are little.

In this great universe of ours, man is a mere insect, an ant, in his intellect, as compared with the boundless world about him, as measured by the intelligence capable of grasping the whole of truth and knowledge.

Yes, Virginia, there is a Santa Claus. He exists as certainly as love and generosity and devotion exist, and you know that they abound and give to your life its highest beauty and joy. Alas! How dreary would be the world if there were no Santa Claus. It would be as dreary as if there were no Virginias.

There would be no childlike faith then, no poetry, no romance to make tolerable this existence. We should have no enjoyment, except in sense and sight. The eternal light with which childhood fills the world would be extinguished.

Not believe in Santa Claus! You might as well not believe in fairies! You might get your papa to hire men to watch in all the chimneys on Christmas Eve to catch Santa Claus, but even if they did not see Santa Claus coming down, what would that prove? Nobody sees Santa Claus, but that is no sign that there is no Santa Claus.

The most real things in the world are those that neither children nor men can see. Did you ever see fairies dancing on the lawn? Of course not, but that's no proof that they are not there. Nobody can conceive or imagine all the wonders that are unseen and unseeable in this world.

You tear apart the baby's rattle and see what makes the noise inside, but there is a veil covering the unseen world which not the strongest man, nor even the united strength of all the strongest men that ever lived, could tear apart.

Only faith, fancy, poetry, love, romance, can push aside that curtain and view and picture the supernatural beauty and glory beyond. Is it all real? Ah, Virginia, in all this world there is nothing else real and abiding.

No Santa Claus! Thank God he lives, and he lives forever. A thousand years from now, Virginia, nay 10 times 10,000 years from now, he will continue to make glad the heart of childhood.

Questions

1. Is this letter only about Santa Claus? Why? Why not?
2. Why do you think that this letter, even though it is about 100 years old, is still often reprinted?
3. How did the writer show a sensitivity to the young girl's question and still speak to adults?
4. Find several well-worded sentences in the essay.

Once More to the Lake

E. B. White

One summer, along about 1904, my father rented a camp on a lake in Maine and took us all there for the month of August. We all got ringworm from some kittens and had to rub Pond's Extract on our arms and legs night and morning, and my father rolled over in a canoe with all his clothes on; but outside of that the vacation was a success and from then on none of us ever thought there was any place in the world like that lake in Maine. We resumed summer after summer—always on August 1st for one month. I have since become a salt-water man, but sometimes in summer there are days when the restlessness of the tides and the fearful cold of the sea water and the incessant wind which blows across the afternoon and into the evening make me wish for the placidity of a lake in the woods. A few weeks ago this feeling got so strong I bought myself a couple of bass hooks and a spinner and resumed to the lake where we used to go, for a week's fishing and to revisit old haunts.

I took along my son, who had never had any fresh water up his nose and who had seen lily pads only from train windows. On the journey over to the lake I began to wonder what it would be like. I wondered how time would have marred this unique, this holy spot—the coves and streams, the hills that the sun set behind, the camps and the paths behind the camps. I was sure that the tarred road would have found it out and I wondered in what other ways it would be desolated. It is strange how much you can remember about places like that once you allow your mind to return into the grooves which lead back. You remember one thing, and that suddenly reminds you of another thing. I guess I remembered clearest of all the early mornings, when the lake was cool and motionless, re-membered how the bedroom smelled of the lumber it was made of and of the wet woods whose scent entered through the screen. The partitions in the camp were thin and did not extend clear to the top of the rooms, and as I was always the first up I would dress softly so as not to wake the others, and sneak out into the sweet outdoors and start out in the canoe, keeping close along the shore in the long shadows of the pines. I remembered being very careful never to rub my paddle against the gunwale for fear of disturbing the stillness of the cathedral.

The lake had never been what you would call a wild lake. There were cottages sprinkled around the shores, and it was in farming country although the shores of the lake were quite heavily wooded. Some of the cottages were owned by nearby farmers, and you would live at the shore and eat your meals at the farmhouse. That's what our family did. But although it wasn't wild, it was a fairly large and undisturbed lake and there were places in it which, to a child at least, seemed infinitely remote and primeval.

I was right about the tar: it led to within half a mile of the shore. But when I got back there, with my boy, and we settled into a camp near a farmhouse and into the kind of summertime I had known, I could tell that it was going to be pretty much the same as it had been before—I knew it, lying in bed the first morning, smelling the bedroom, and hearing the boy sneak quietly out and go off along the shore in a boat. I began to sustain the illusion that he was I, and there-fore, by simple transposition, that I was my father. This sensation persisted, kept cropping up all the time we were there. It was not an entirely new feeling, but in this setting it grew much stronger. I seemed to be living a dual existence. I would be in the middle of some simple act, I would be picking up a bait box or laying down a table fork, or I would be saying something, and suddenly it would be not I but my father who was saying the words or making the gesture. It gave me a creepy sensation.

We went fishing the first morning. I felt the same damp moss covering the worms in the bait can, and saw the dragonfly alight on the tip of my rod as it hovered a few inches from the surface of the water. It was the arrival of this fly that convinced me beyond any doubt that everything was as it always had been, that the years were a mirage and there had been no years. The small waves were the same, chucking the rowboat under the chin as we fished at anchor, and the boat was the same boat, the same color green and the ribs broken in the same places, and under the floor-boards the same fresh-water leavings and debris—the dead helgramite, the wisps of moss, the rusty discarded fishhook, the dried blood from yesterday's catch. We stared silently at the tips of our rods, at the dragon-flies that came and went. I lowered the tip of mine into the water, tentatively, pensively dislodging the fly, which darted two feet away, poised, darted two feet back, and came to rest again a little farther up the rod. There had been no years between the ducking of this dragonfly and the other one—the one that was part of memory. I looked at the boy, who was silently watching his fly, and it was my hands that held his rod, my eyes watching. I felt dizzy and didn't know which rod I was at the end of.

We caught two bass, hauling them in briskly as though they were mackerel, pulling them over the side of the boat in a businesslike manner without any landing net, and stunning them with a blow on the back of the head. When we got back for a swim before lunch, the lake was exactly where we had left it, the same number of inches from the dock, and there was only the merest suggestion of a breeze. This seemed an utterly enchanted sea, this lake you could leave to its own devices for a few hours and come back to, and find that it had not stirred, this constant and trustworthy body of water. In the shallows, the dark, water-soaked sticks and twigs, smooth and old, were undulating in clusters on the bottom against the clean ribbed sand, and the track of the mussel was plain. A school of minnows swam by, each minnow with its small individual shadow, doubling the attendance, so clear and sharp in the sunlight. Some of the other campers were in swimming, along the shore, one of them with a cake of soap, and the water felt thin and clear and unsubstantial. Over the years there had been this person with the cake of soap, this cultist, and here he was. There had been no years.

Up to the farmhouse to dinner through the teeming, dusty field, the road under our sneakers was only a two-track road. The middle track was missing, the one with the marks of the hooves and the splotches of dried, flaky manure. There had always been three tracks to choose from in choosing which track to walk in; now the choice was narrowed down to two. For a moment I missed terribly the middle alternative. But the way led past the tennis court, and something about the way it lay there in the sun reassured me; the tape had loosened along the backline, the alleys were green with plantains and other weeds, and the net (installed in June and removed in September) sagged in the dry noon, and the whole place steamed with midday heat and hunger and emptiness. There was a choice of pie for dessert, and one was blueberry and one was apple, and the waitresses were the same country girls, there having been no passage of time, only the illusion of it as in a dropped curtain—the waitresses were still fifteen; their hair had been washed, that was the only difference—they had been to the movies and seen the pretty girls with the clean hair.

Summertime, oh summertime, pattern of life indelible, the fadeproof lake, the woods unshatterable, the pasture with the sweetfern and the juniper forever and ever, summer without end; this was the background, and the life along the shore was the design, the cottagers with their innocent and tranquil design, their tiny docks with the flagpole and the American flag floating against the white clouds in the blue sky, the little paths over the roots of trees leading from camp to camp and the paths leading back to outhouses and the can of lime for sprinkling, and at the souvenir counters at the store the miniature birch-bark canoes and the post cards that showed things looking a little better than they looked. This was the American family at play, escaping the city heat, wondering whether the newcomers in the camp at the head of the cove were "common" or "nice," wondering whether it was true that the people who drove up for Sunday dinner at the farmhouse were turned away because there wasn't enough chicken.

It seemed to me, as I kept remembering all this, that those times and those summers had been infinitely precious and worth saving. There had been jollity and peace and goodness. The arriving (at the beginning of August) had been so big a business in itself, at the railway station the farm wagon drawn up, the first smell of the pine-laden air, the first glimpse of the smiling farmer, and the great importance of the trunks and your father's enormous authority in such matters, and the feel of the wagon under you for the long ten-mile haul, and at the top of the last long hill catching the first view of the lake after eleven months of not seeing this cherished body of water. The shouts and cries of the other campers when they saw you, and the trunks to be unpacked, to give up their rich burden. (Arriving was less exciting nowadays, when you sneaked up in your car and parked it under a tree near the camp and took out the bags and in five minutes it was all over, no fuss, no loud wonderful fuss about trunks.)

Peace and goodness and jollity. The only thing that was wrong now, really, was the sound of the place, an unfamiliar nervous sound of the outboard motors. This was the note that jarred, the one thing that would sometimes break the illusion and set the years moving. In those other summertimes all motors were inboard; and when they were at a little distance, the noise they made was a sedative, an ingredient of summer sleep. They were one-cylinder and two-cylinder engines, and some were make-and-break and some were jump-spark, but they all made a sleepy sound across the lake. The one-lungers throbbed and fluttered, and the twin-cylinder ones purred and purred, and that was a quiet sound too. But now the campers all had outboards. In the daytime, in the hot mornings, these motors made a petulant, irritable sound; at night, in the still evening when the afterglow lit the water, they whined about one's ears like mosquitoes. My boy loved our rented outboard, and his great desire was to achieve singlehanded mastery over it, and authority, and he soon learned the trick of choking it a little (but not too much), and the adjustment of the needle valve. Watching him I would remember the things you could do with the old one-cylinder engine with the heavy flywheel, how you could have it eating out of your hand if you got really close to it spiritually. Motor boats in those days didn't have clutches, and you would make a landing by shutting off the motor at the proper time and coasting in with a dead rudder. But there was a way of reversing them, if you learned the trick, by cutting the switch and putting it on again exactly on the final dying revolution of the flywheel, so that it would kick back against compression and begin reversing. Approaching a dock in a strong following breeze, it was difficult to slow up sufficiently by the ordinary coasting method, and if a boy felt he had complete mastery over his motor, he was tempted to keep it running beyond its time and then reverse it a few feet from the dock. It took a cool nerve, because if you threw the switch a twentieth of a second too soon you would catch the flywheel when it still had speed enough to go up past center, and the boat would leap ahead, charging bull-fashion at the dock.

We had a good week at the camp. The bass were biting well and the sun shone endlessly, day after day. We would be tired at night and lie down in the accumulated heat of the little bedrooms after the long hot day and the breeze would stir almost imperceptibly outside and the smell of the swamp drift in through the rusty screens. Sleep would come easily and in the morning the red squirrel would be on the roof, tapping out his gay routine. I kept remembering everything, lying in bed in the mornings—the small steamboat that had a long rounded stern like the lip of a Ubangi, and how quietly she ran on the moonlight sails, when the older boys played their mandolins and the girls sang and we ate doughnuts dipped in sugar, and how sweet the music was on the water in the shining night, and what it had felt like to think about girls then. After breakfast we would go up to the store and the things were in the same place—the minnows in a bottle, the plugs and spinners disarranged and pawed over by the youngsters from the boys' camp, the Fig Newtons and the Beeman's gum. Outside, the road was tarred and cars stood in front of the store. Inside, all was just as it had always been, except there was more Coca Cola and not so much Moxie and root beer and birch beer and sarsaparilla. We would walk out with a bottle of pop apiece and sometimes the pop would backfire up our noses and hurt. We explored the streams, quietly, where the turtles slid off the sunny logs and dug their way into the soft bottom; and we lay on the town wharf and fed worms to the tame bass. Everywhere we went I had trouble making out which was I, the one walking at my side, the one walking in my pants.

One afternoon while we were there at that lake a thunderstorm came up. It was like the revival of an old melodrama that I had seen long ago with childish awe. The second-act climax of the drama of the electrical disturbance over a lake in America had not changed in any important respect. This was the big scene, still the big scene. The whole thing was so familiar, the first feeling of oppression and heat and a general air around camp of not wanting to go very far away. In midafternoon (it was all the same) a curious darkening of the sky, and a lull in everything that had made life tick; and then the way the boats suddenly swung the other way at their moorings with the coming of a breeze out of the new quarter, and the premonitory rumble. Then the kettle drum, then the snare, then the bass drum and cymbals, then crackling light against the dark, and the gods grinning and licking their chops in the bath. Afterward the calm, the rain steadily rustling in the calm lake, the return of light and hope and spirits, and the campers running out in joy and relief to go swimming in the rain, their bright cries perpetuating the deathless joke about how they were getting simply drenched, and the children screaming with delight at the new sensation of bathing in the rain, and the joke about getting drenched linking the generations in a strong indestructible chain. And the comedian who waded in carrying an umbrella.

When the others went swimming my son said he was going in too. He pulled his dripping trunks from the line where they had hung all through the shower, and wrung them out. Languidly, and with no thought of going in, I watched him, his hard little body, skinny and bare, saw him wince slightly as he pulled up around his vitals the small, soggy, icy garment. As he buckled the swollen belt suddenly my groin felt the chill of death.

Questions:

1. This essay, "Once More to the Lake," is one of the most frequently reprinted essays in English. The reason might be the way E. B. White talks about the relationship of father and son and the "creepy sensation." What is the "creepy sensation"?

2. Find words in the essay that tell sensory details of what White sees, hears, smells, touches, tastes. These details help readers feel as if they are with him.

3. What insight does White reach in the last sentence of the essay?

4. How does the entire essay lead to the insight of the last sentence? Give lines from the essay which support your idea.

An Answer to an Essay Test Question

Test question: "What is hypothermia, and how can it be prevented? Use an example to explain your points."

The All-Points Bulletin read: "Two mountain climbers, ages nineteen and twenty-one, are missing since Tuesday. Due to the unexpected snowstorm on Mount Olympia, they are presumed victims of hypothermia." But when they were found burrowed in a snow cave three days later, the victims were not suffering from hypothermia. They had known what hypothermia was and how to prevent it.

Hypothermia is caused by abnormally low body temperature which decreases the pulse rate and lessens the volume of circulating blood. When hypothermia moves in on its victims, it leaves them almost helpless. One of its common symptoms is drowsiness. Hypothermia causes its victims to lose the will to survive. Often they will simply lie down to rest and never awaken again.

To avoid the dangers of hypothermia, the mountain climbers had dressed warmly in several layers of clothing. Each wore thermal underwear, two loose wool shirts and two pairs of loose pants, three pairs of socks inside their boots, ski masks that covered their faces, wool caps with ear flaps, hooded parkas that reached to their knees, and insulated gloves. When the storm began, the climbers knew they had to keep dry. But because they were near no shelter on the mountainside, they set up their tent and built up pine branches around it to keep off the heavy snow. After doing all they could to keep out the snowstorm, they went inside the tent and changed into dry clothes from their backpacks. They knew that if either began to suffer from hypothermia, they had to crawl into the same sleeping bag and keep each other warm until the storm let up and they were rescued.

Because these climbers knew hypothermia's dangers and the techniques to prevent it, they were cold but safe when rescuers found them in their makeshift shelter three days after the all-points bulletin was issued.

Questions

1. How did the author weave the example of hypothermia into the essay?
2. What is hypothermia? How did the author use each paragraph to explain it? What grade would you give this test answer? Why?

The Essay Is Like a Paragraph in Several Ways

If you know how to compose a clear paragraph, you already know much about essay writing. Everything that characterizes a good paragraph characterizes a good essay.

Both are organized to achieve their purposes, explain inferences with proof details, and motivate the reader to react the way the writer wants.

Just as a paragraph is developed with several major and minor supports, an essay uses paragraphs to develop its supporting information.

The main part of an essay is composed of traditional paragraphs. (See Chapter 15.) Usually introductions and conclusions to the essay are different kinds of paragraphs whose purposes are to help the reader stay interested in the topic. (See Chapter 17.)

Both use main-idea sentences. Just as a paragraph uses a topic sentence, the essay uses a thesis statement. The thesis should be an inference and predict the content, the point of view, and structure of the writing for the reader. (See Chapter 14.)

Both essays and paragraphs open with a hook designed to interest the audience. But at the beginning of an essay, the writer can often spend an entire paragraph or two to catch the reader. Both the essay and the paragraph show the reader that the piece is finished. Both must end, not just stop. (See Chapter 17 for a discussion of beginnings and endings.)

Both paragraphs and essays must connect ideas so the reader can follow the writer's thinking. The writer must not only show relationships of ideas within each paragraph but must also link each paragraph to the one before and after it. The essay must show each major shift to a new detail. Both must develop the topic, and both must use emphasis to stress important points. (See Chapter 15 for a discussion of coherence, unity and emphasis.)

Although a typical place for the topic sentence is at the beginning of each paragraph, it can come at the middle or at the end; or it can simply be implied. So, too, can the thesis statement come at the beginning, in the middle, or at the end, or be implied.

COLLABORATIVE LEARNING

1. In your group, answer the questions after each essay.

2. Consider how the essay works. Now that you have read each of the essays in this chapter, discuss and write your answers to these questions:

   a. What is the insight or main idea of each essay?

   b. To explain the insight, what supporting information did each writer use? In each essay, how was all that supporting material organized?

   c. Who is the intended audience for each essay? How do you know?

   d. What do you think each writer wants the audience to get from the piece? In other words, in each essay what was the author's purpose?

   e. Use the lines from the essay to show the writing personality of each writer.

   f. If all the topics, supporting information, audiences, purposes, and organizations are somewhat different in each essay, what then do these essays have in common? (If you can answer this question, you do know what an essay is!)

WRITING TASKS

1. Write an essay following the pattern of one of the writers you read in this chapter. Write a letter like the one to Virginia: choose a current issue that needs explaining and follow the lead of Virginia's letter. Or write a chapter for a travel book about one of your favorite places. Or create an essay answer for a test.

2. Study two or three of your own essays from this class or other classes. How might you use the knowledge gained from this chapter to improve each essay? Revise one essay.

   You can find more information about writing essays in Chapters 24–to the end.

Checklist for Your Essay

Yes	No		
____	____	1.	Do you offer an insight into your topic?
____	____	2.	Do you use both inferences and facts in the paper?
____	____	3.	Do you explain all your inferences?
____	____	4.	Do you write to a specific audience?
____	____	5.	Do you make clear your purpose for writing to your audience?
____	____	6.	Do you write in a voice that matches your topic and purpose?
____	____	7.	Do you organize your paper in a recognizable way?
____	____	8.	Do you link paragraphs and points to the ones before and after?

Chapter Seventeen
Titles, Beginnings, and Endings

Titles, beginnings, and endings have much to do with the success of your writing. Here are strategies for writing each.

TITLES

Movies, books, albums, songs, videos, records—all have titles. Some fit. Some are fun. Some are outrageous.

Has a title ever tempted you to see a movie even if you didn't know much else about it? Have you ever bought a record or video just because of its name? How about a perfume? An aftershave? A breakfast cereal? A drink?

To find a "right" title sometimes takes much thought. (If you usually write a good title, you can skip this section of the chapter.) But if finding a right title is hard work, here are some hints for title writing.

Why Use Titles?

Titles should act like advance salespeople for your pieces. They set the mood, set the tone, prepare your audience. A live TV performance has a warmup before the show begins. For the same reasons, most famous bands performing live have a warm-up band (sometimes several) to get their audiences worked up, receptive. Titles for novels, essays, or movies do the same job. They prepare the audience.

How Do You Create Titles?

1. **Name your subject.**

   Cross-Country Skiing in Michigan
   Gene Splicing
   Resume Writing
   Underwater Photography
   Lady Di's Boys

If people are already interested in the topic, sometimes the name of the subject is enough to make them read further:

2. **Name the subject and your main point.**

   Turnips—How to Grow Them for Profit
   Grow Christmas Trees and Pay Your Way Through College
   Seeing Europe as a College Student
   Differences Between Christ and Buddha

A title that names both the subject and the main point helps your readers see your approach to the topic and decide whether to keep reading. But this approach, like naming the topic, is mundane, quite ordinary. The audience must like the topic already, or the title will not entice them. This kind of title works, however, in many matter-of-fact academic writings. To write this sort of title, find your topic and main point in the thesis.

3. **Name a subject and subtitle; separate them with a colon.**

   Missing: Americans in the Middle-East
   Gold: Found at Sea
   Single-Parent Homes: Today's Challenge to Kids
   Hydrocarbons: Oil and Coal
   1999: The Year of Catastrophes

This type of title is similar to the previous one, but the colon makes it look more sophisticated. Another difference is that the title's wording can play with the reader because the wording keeps the first part somewhat of a mystery until you explain later, after the colon.

4. **Use words that involve people emotionally.**

   America, the Hostage Country
   Your Friends May Be Killers
   Entrepreneurs Abuse College Students
   Step-Parents to Love

This type of title may use words whose very meaning makes people emotional *(hostage, killers, abuse)*. Another kind of word that gets reactions is from current headlines *(hostage, war).* A third kind of word to which people pay attention relates quite closely to their own life situations *(students, college, step-parents, entrepreneurs).*

5. Create contradictions that your paper explains.

Your Food Is Poison
Shoot the Children
Dead Man Walking

The reader wants the contradiction explained. The essay then must clear up the mystery.

6. Ask a question.

Who Shot John F. Kennedy?
Is the United States Losing the Trade War with Japan?
Is a Man Capable of Bearing Children?
Why Get a Degree in the Humanities?

Questions work because readers get curious. In fact, readers may try to answer your question all through the writing. Good.

7. Use sound effects.

Padding Your Pockets with Pounds (alliteration of *p* and assonance in *o* sounds)
Stuff Till I Puff (rhyme of *stuff* and *puff* and consonance in repeated *t*)
Cupid Isn't Stupid (rhyme)

Clever use of sounds grabs your readers. But your paper must live up to the expectation you set up in this title. If you are not equally clever in the rest of the paper, readers may feel cheated.

8. Use an important phrase or line that appears in the paper.

Gag the President
Living by the Pill
Old, Old Time

Titles taken from the body of the text must be intriguing. Later, when the same words reappear in the text, the intriguing phrase must seem appropriate.

9. Play on words.

The Success of Sweet Smells (Title plays on the "sweet smell of success," for an article about perfume)
The Lady Is a Man (Play on "The Lady Is a Tramp")
Eat, Drink, and Die (Play on "Eat, Drink and Be Merry for Tomorrow You Die")

These titles are fun for the readers who recognize the original and the play with words. Such readers want to see how the writer gives the original words new meaning.

Summary

The title can do several things: catch the reader's interest, persuade the reader to read, give the audience something to consider while reading. Some titles seem even more appropriate after the piece is read. Some titles are just good fun.

The writer must be careful to match the mood of the title and the text. Otherwise the audience can be misled. A good title should be interesting and appropriate. If it is interesting, but inappropriate, readers will lose interest fast.

INTRODUCTIONS

Sometimes after watching just the first scene of a movie, you get up and walk around—go to the restroom, talk to your friends, get something to eat. At other movies, though, you sit without moving. Why? What does a film do in the first scene to convince you that the rest will probably be good, too?

Do you have techniques for beginnings? How do you begin an important date? How do you go about asking someone you don't know very well—but would like to know better—to join you?

Writers must answer these same kinds of questions. They have to discover ways to make strangers pay attention. But the approach has to be legitimate. Introductions are not easy.

Why Use Introductions?

Introductions work like titles, although introductions are usually much longer. Both must interest the reader. Both set the tone for the essay: straight talk, humor, technical approach, academic wording, to mention a few. Usually an introduction will identify topics to be covered and predict the author's structure.

How Do You Create Introductions?

1. **Relate your ideas to a contemporary event, ideally one that provokes controversy.**

    On your mark, get set, go! And they are off, not down the 15,000-meter course, but down the halls of college, medical school, internship! Somewhere along the route they get a hurried cup of orange juice or a squirt of Gatorade. Relatives cheer them on. Society waves job offers to them at the final, breathless, ribbon breaking. But that is no way to train an M.D. Doctors should be given time to meet, shake hands, get to know humanity. Until they do, society will get track stars for doctors, but not humanitarians. Medical training must change so it graduates men and women in love with other people and ready to serve humanity.

This introduction relates medical training to running in a 15,000-meter race. It shows that the kind of speed and endurance demanded of a marathon runner ought not to be the criteria by which a medical student is judged. The paper then explains how medical students should be prepared.

2. **Give background information that readers need to know.**

> A buyer looking at houses developed on swampland needs to study important precautions. First, septic tanks are unacceptable in swamps because heavy rains can cause septic tanks to back up waste into homes or yards. Second, the houses must be built up several feet above the streets and roads. If not, rain water may run from the street and swamp into the yard and house. Third, holding ponds must be dug to contain the ever-present swamp water. Fourth, plants and shrubs used in landscaping should be able to withstand water-logged soil and poor drainage. But if all of these conditions are met, the swamp dweller will find natural beauty unmatched anywhere. Nature—animals, birds, flowers, seeds, plants, berries lure the swamp lover to such a home.

The reader should know certain information about swampland homes before purchasing one. But after telling the reader about the precautions, the paper will discuss pleasures of swamp life.

3. **Give reasons for talking about the topic.**

> Vaccinations of small children have almost eliminated certain diseases like whooping cough, small pox, and measles in the United States. But certain children react badly to vaccines. Some die. Parents must know the symptoms to watch for so a child who reacts negatively to a vaccination gets immediate medical attention.

The introduction tells mothers why they need to know the symptoms of adverse reaction to vaccines. The information is so important that without it, some children die.

4. **Begin with an example or an anecdote.**

> The fire blazed in the fireplace. In front of it, the cat stretched out on my feet. The lamps were dimmed low, but light enough for me to see the apples I was peeling for the apple cobbler I was making just for me. I looked around and said to myself, "This isn't bad." At that moment I realized I had finally adjusted to living alone.

The example of a person living contentedly alone sets the mood and tone for the rest of the paper.

5. **Ask questions that readers want answered.**

> "Who owns you? Whom can you trust? Where is money safe?"

This could be a successful beginning for a paper on debts and personal finances, but the paper must answer all three questions.

6. **Begin with an appropriate quote.**

   "A bird in the hand is worth two in the bush," says an old adage. And it is so true. When choosing between a stock that might appreciate and a guaranteed certificate of deposit in a federally insured bank, choose the safe bird in your hand, the guaranteed certificate of deposit.

The quote used here explains that the safe investment is the best investment. Where do you find quotes? You have a great many in your memory. You can quote an expert on your topic, or a poem, a song, a commercial. You can use *Bartlett's Quotations* or the *Dictionary of Quotations*. But select a quote that fits the essay; otherwise, it can mislead your readers.

7. **Define important ideas or words.**

   Combined training is just that—a combination of training horse and rider in dressage, stadium jumping, and cross-country endurance. To succeed at even the training levels of this sport, the rider must dedicate hours of intense work to each discipline. (From "How to Improve Your Eventer: Step by Step" by Charlene Strickland, *Horse Illustrated*. Nov. 85.)

The definition of *combined training* is important because the rest of the piece explains how to train for it. You, too, may need to begin by defining.

8. **Shock your reader with unfamiliar statistics.**

   One of every eleven women will get breast cancer! That person may be you.

This statistic might shock women into reading a paper about breast cancer.

9. **Startle your reader with new ideas or a new way of looking at an old idea.**

   Women should marry only younger men. Today, men die younger than women do, and then women are left alone. If gals married guys at least seven or eight years their junior, women would die first and wouldn't be left to cope alone. Such marriage arrangements could cure society's lonely-widow problem.

Such a cure for the problem is sure to startle some readers.

10. **Move from a general look at an idea to specific thesis.**
    This approach is called the "funnel."

    Migrating tribes ate whatever the land provided. Then agricultural man learned to plant seeds and control his environment so he could live in one place. Today people depend on farmers to produce the crops sold in the supermarket. Yet most people still yearn to grow something of their own. This yearning explains why patio farming of a few vegetables is popular even in the city. No matter what the light conditions, no matter how small the available space, vegetable gardening is possible.

The introduction moves from a general look at food gathering to a specific thesis on vegetable gardening in the city.

11. Explain why you are a believable authority on your subject.

> People who live in the South are different from Northerners. They not only speak differently; they live differently. How do I know? I have lived in each part of the country for at least ten years. To me, the most noticeable contrasts are in religion, education, and work values.

This is an important technique if you are writing from your own personal experience, for the reader deserves some proof that you are a credible speaker on the subject.

12. Stress that the topic is important.

> Buckling a seat belt takes only a few seconds. But those are important seconds because the use of seat belts decreases the number of people killed each year in car accidents. Seat belts also reduce the number of serious personal injuries. And their use can lower insurance rates. For all these important reasons, every driver should wear a seat belt.

To write this kind of introduction, ask yourself why the topic is so important. Your answers can become the introduction.

13. Make a convincing case for the opposition before you destroy it with your own arguments.

> An all-women's college gives women the chance to be leaders, an opportunity they often miss in a coed school. Besides, it lets them meet and relate to other women in situations that no open college offers its females. But most important, all-girls' classes allow women the chance to learn without the mental distractions of men. Sure, these may all be healthy arguments for women's colleges, but in fact, coed universities offer women many more advantages; women should attend them.

The introduction gives three arguments for the all-women's school. But the thesis then states that these arguments are not enough. The paper will show that the opposite position is better for women.

14. Present your opinion very firmly, giving yourself the argumentative edge.

> The American farmer deserves to be treated fairly, treatment he is not receiving from the consumer, the middleman, or the government.

The writer begins immediately by stating that three groups do not treat the farmer fairly. The paper will explain that this contention is true.

15. **Appeal to your readers' vested interests so they will have to agree with your position.**

   Because everyone wants to avoid living out old age in poverty, and because the social security fund may not be there to protect Americans in the next several decades, establishing a retirement fund is vital.

The appeal is to the readers' desire for security. You can appeal to many needs of the audience and show how your topic will satisfy them.

16. **Begin by stating your thesis immediately.**

   Citizen Kane, by Orson Welles, was a technically brilliant movie for its time.

This kind of introduction works well when you have little time to think of an introduction, as when you are taking a timed essay test. Sometimes a poor introduction is worse than starting immediately with the thesis. Avoid this type of introduction when you have more than a class period to write the paper.

17. **Present a problem. Then give the solution in the body of the paper.**

   The number of working women with babies under a year old increased 50 percent, according to a recently released census report. Overall, working mothers with children under five grew from 4.7 million to 6 million. With almost half of all mothers with preschoolers on the job, childcare has become a major concern. (By Burtman, Andrea I. "Who's Minding the Children?" *Working Mother Digest.* 1984.)

The introduction establishes the problem; the rest of the paper gives solutions.

CONCLUSIONS

What makes a good ending? When do you like a song's end? What makes a good ending to a class? How do you know when a party is over? What kind of endings do you like? Endings to books? Endings to relationships? What is the difference between a party with a good ending and one that just fades out?

What Makes a Good Ending?

Effective conclusions are essential to your paper's success. Without them, readers may not know you are finished. Worse, if you do not put your ideas in a perspective, your readers may miss your main point. A good conclusion will round things up so readers have a wonderful sense that you are finished, and if you have done your job, readers will carry the ideas forward themselves, perhaps in a way you have led them. The conclusion, then, must satisfy and stimulate. Do both and you will have done well.

How Do You Create Conclusions?

1. **Make a prediction. (Sometimes the prediction can be dire.)**

    Bulimia will be cured if the nation stops linking thinness to beauty, success, and happiness. Thinness does not always predict these possibilities. Thinness may cause the opposite.

This ending to a paper on bulimia predicted that bulimia could be stopped if American values changed.

2. **Stress the importance of the topic.**

    Over 300,000 victims died of Sudden Infant Death Syndrome (SIDS) last year. That is more than died of AIDS. If SIDS takes this many victims, the nation surely needs to stop it just as it is trying to stop AIDS.

The topic is significant because so many die of Sudden Infant Death Syndrome (SIDS).

3. **Fit the ending and the introduction together.**

    Beginning:

    Children in America are in no better shape today than they were ten years ago, according to the presidential council on physical fitness.

    Ending:

    The case histories of Oscar Doobs and Jim Smith best sum up the contention *that not only are American children no more physically fit today than they were ten years ago,* they have not significantly improved physically in the last thirty years.

The ending refers to the earlier statement about the physical condition of children. Thus, the beginning and ending fit together.

4. **Warn your readers.**

    Don't invest in a career you haven't tried! You could spend years in college preparing for a profession you will hate. You don't want to waste your life, so get involved now in the students' mentor program and find out before you graduate what your chosen career might be like. Afterward may be too late.

The ending warns students that without the mentor program they could graduate and enter a profession they might hate.

5. **Challenge your audience to do or to believe something.**

    Atlantic Beach could be saved if everyone sent old, used Christmas trees to be planted in the frontline sand dunes. Boy Scouts will fix the trees to trap the drifting sand. All you have to do after Christmas is deliver your tree to a local collection point. Do it and help save your bit of the beach.

The challenge is simple: Deliver a Christmas tree to save the beach.

6. **Offer a solution.**

> Deficit spending can be controlled if the Congress raises taxes and if the value of the dollar falls on the international markets. Americans want neither of these solutions. But these are the only answers.
>
> Solutions to the problem of deficit spending: higher taxes and a lower value for the dollar.

If your paper describes a problem, this is the place to offer the solution.

7. **Summarize your main points.**

> Three bills before the state legislature will affect education: the bill to institute merit pay for teachers, the bill to extend the school year to eleven months, and the bill to legalize the selling of marihuana on the school property. None of the three bills has more than a 10 percent chance of passing this session.

Avoid a summary in short papers because readers do not need it; but readers appreciate being reminded of main points in the conclusion of a long paper.

8. **End with a quote.**

> "All's well that ends well," wrote William Shakespeare.

The quote could be an obvious conclusion to a paper. As in the introduction, a fitting quote from an authority on your subject or an apt statement of the issues can be a fine way to end the paper and give it greater significance.

9. **Ask a question.**

Usually concluding questions challenge the reader to think about the topic beyond its treatment in the paper.

> Can you imagine the problems if zoning laws were left up to the owners in each area instead of the zoning council? Who would win? Who would lose? Who should have zoning power?

Following a study of zoning problems, the concluding questions force readers to wonder. Although the conclusion doesn't answer the questions, it helps readers see the implications of the topic.

10. **Close with a story that illustrates your main points.**

> My brother and two of his three children were killed instantly in a head-on automobile collision. A twenty-one-year-old woman, after guzzling beer all afternoon in a local tavern, ran right into them on a two-lane highway. She drove her station wagon around a curve in the wrong lane and straight into my brother's whole family. At the manslaughter trial, three people who had been with the woman all afternoon testified that she'd mixed pot with her beer. Now she sits in

jail instead of college, and disabled, my sister-in-law tries to put her life back together without a husband and her two children. Drunken driving must be stopped!

The dramatic conclusion strongly illustrates the paper's point—drunken driving must be stopped.

11. **Connect your paper to a larger trend, a more general issue, problem, or concern.**

Learning how to use relaxation techniques may free your body from heart attacks. But unless you free your spirit, you shall not be able to relax totally. Spiritual freedom means that you must place all in the hands of a loving God. If He watches that not a bird falls to the ground without His knowledge and concern, He shall surely care for you.

Relaxation is connected to a larger issue: relaxation of the spirit in the hands of a loving God.

Summary

An effective conclusion answers the question "So what?" After you have written your introduction and body paragraphs, ask yourself this question: "I have presented this information to my reader. So what?" Your answer to this question can lead you to a powerful conclusion.

Endings must show the reader that you are finished. Good endings often leave the audience with something to think about or something to do. A major director of Broadway theater said that a good show keeps the audience laughing for two hours and then keeps them up all night thinking. Most of all, endings must satisfy or challenge the reader intellectually or emotionally.

COLLABORATIVE LEARNING

1. To your writing group, take examples of well-written titles, introductions, and conclusions from magazines, newspapers, textbooks. You might take titles of programs from radio or television or titles from songs or movies. Explain why these examples work. Which techniques do these good titles, introductions, and conclusions use?

2. Take one of your essays to your writing group. Ask each person in the group to write a new title, new introduction, and new conclusion for the essay. (Each person might demonstrate different techniques from the chapter.) After all the new parts are written, discuss which techniques seem the most effective for your paper. Rewrite the paper using the best introduction, title, and conclusion

from the group. (Be sure to give the authors credit when you hand in the paper.)

WRITING TASKS: TITLES

1. Name five or so titles of songs, albums, books, movies, TV shows, or plays which are especially good. What makes them work? Which techniques do they use? What names of products now on the market are especially fitting? Why? Find several headlines in the newspaper or in TV news. Which techniques did you discover? Write a report.

2. Use techniques new to your writing style to write several titles for a paper. When you finish, decide which techniques worked best for you. Which techniques fit your writing personality?

WRITING TASKS: INTRODUCTIONS

1. Find several introductions in newspaper or magazine articles. What techniques were used? Which ones made you want to read on? Write your report.

2. Study several introductions to chapters in your textbooks and scholarly journal articles in your major field. What kind of introductions do these authors use? Compare your findings with those of other students. What conclusions can you draw?

3. Write several introductions using different techniques for a paper you are now writing. Which techniques seem to work best?

4. Examine the introductions you have written so far this year. What are some of the techniques you typically use? How successful were they? Explain in writing.

WRITING TASKS: CONCLUSIONS

1. Find examples of conclusions to articles in your favorite magazines. What techniques do you discover? Write a report using examples from the articles.

2. Study the conclusions of several articles related to your major. What kinds of endings did you find? Compare your answers with those of students in other majors. What conclusions can you draw from this comparison? Do people writing in different fields use the same techniques? Why? Why not? Write a report of your discoveries using examples from articles.

3. Using at least three different techniques, write three different endings for one of your papers. After you have written all three conclusions, decide which works best.

4. Study several of your papers to see what techniques you usually use in your own conclusions. How might you change? Write a report.

Checklist for Titles, Introductions, and Conclusions

Yes   *No*

Titles

____ ____ 1. Does your title set the tone for the entire paper?

____ ____ 2. Would your title interest your audience?

____ ____ 3. Do you use one of the techniques discussed in this chapter?

____ ____ 4. Is your title appropriate to your thesis?

Introductions

____ ____ 5. Will the introduction interest your audience?

____ ____ 6. Does the introduction fit the audience?

____ ____ 7. Does the introduction set the mood for the piece?

____ ____ 8. Does the introduction predict the approach or structure of the paper?

____ ____ 9. Does the introduction contain a main-idea sentence?

____ ____ 10. If the introduction lacks a main-idea sentence, have you planned to place it somewhere else in the paper?

____ ____ 11. Have you used one of the techniques explained in this chapter?

Conclusions

____ ____ 12. Does the ending indicate that the piece is finished?

____ ____ 13. Does the ending stimulate the audience to think or do something?

____ ____ 14. Does the ending emotionally satisfy or challenge?

____ ____ 15. Does your conclusion leave the reader feeling "So what?" If it does, you need to revise the ending.

____ ____ 16. Is your ending appropriate to your audience and purpose?

writer's decision five

How Does All This Look When I Write It?
Drafts and Revisions

Introduction

Writing out what you have to say is a start, but only a start—a first draft. This chapter gives you examples and explanations so you can improve your writing in a second draft, a third draft, a fourth—however many it takes.

Do good writers get their pieces right the first time? Usually not. I rewrote the ending to one of my short stories at least eighteen times. But when I finally wrote the eighteenth version, I knew I had it. The ending was right. I guess other readers thought so too, because that short story, after all those drafts, won a first prize.

Chapter 18—Rough Drafts and Revision
> *How to use drafting and revision to your advantage.*

Chapter Eighteen
Rough Drafts and Revision

About forty years ago, when my father asked my mother to marry him and she said yes, he told her he had just bought her a house. He took her to see it. "Let's move in it just the way it is," he said. (These were the days just after World War II.)

"No," said my mother when she saw the house. "We'll have to redo this place to make it livable. The kitchen needs a porcelain sink; the well needs to be brought into the basement from outside so it won't freeze up in winter. And I want a bathroom upstairs next to the bedroom. When we have kids, I don't want to run downstairs everytime I need water!"

My mother got her way. The one-hundred-year-old house was completely renovated before she and my father moved in.

That is revision. We do it to old houses. Writers do it to their writing.

Mistaken Ideas Concerning Revision

Some students do not understand revision. One problem is that they incorrectly assume that short papers don't need to be revised. But few papers of excellent writers come out fine the first time. Other students mistakenly think revision means only correcting spelling, cleaning up punctuation, and repairing grammar. Making such corrections is like changing the wallpaper in a house without renovating.

So if these are incorrect ideas, what is correct?

What Revision Really Is

A good drafter is constantly reworking the ideas, the arrangement of ideas, the basic plan for the project, the arrangement of sentences, the vocabulary, the beginning, ending, examples, comparisons, contrasts, meanings. Good drafters simply experiment until everything affects the audience the way they want.

If you think about drafting as experimenting in all these ways, you won't be tempted to limit your renovations to just grammar, spelling, and mechanics.

There are several main stages to the writing process: brainstorming, writing, cooling, and revising. Drafting might occur in all stages except cooling. Writers jump back and forth from brainstorming to writing to revision as their work and personalities demand. For most writers there is no clean movement from one stage to another. Allowing yourself cooling times to get away from the paper's train of thought is crucial. After a cooling time, you will be able to find weaknesses you would have missed otherwise.

As you revise, you are free to experiment to find what works best. You are not locked into what you said the first or second or even the third time. You can change almost everything if you want. Try alternatives in organization, writer's voices, audiences, purposes, information. Experiment and discover! This process is revision.

Knead your ideas, words, as if they are a huge handful of wet clay or the muscles of an athlete. With the kneading will come inspiration, and after much work, the final product. It is a long way off, but from the pounding, the squishing, the rearranging, comes a piece of pottery that will hold up in the kiln, better muscle tone for the athlete, or writing that will make sense to the readers.

Revising is squishing, squeezing, stretching your ideas until you say precisely what you want to say.

Sometimes during rewriting, something special happens. Writers discover an idea or an image they had not thought of before they said it! This outcome may seem strange, but many authors believe the statement, "How do I know what I think till I see what I say!"

Some Student Revisions

Here are two examples of students' work in several drafting stages. As you watch the papers change and improve, you can see how the revision process works. (Chapter 19 tells you how to polish your paper. It is almost impossible to revise and polish a paper at the same time. So please don't try.)

Life Shift

by Nicole Evans

Draft 1

I packed my sweaters, socks, and favorite stuffed animal. Discarding my old letters and papers, I wiped a tear. Mother, running around nervously, asked if I could use the packing tape yet. I glanced away, began down the stairs and out the door. Walking down the street I remembered sledding last month. I remembered the bonfire at the top of the street and could almost smell burnt marshmallows.

Turning back up the street I stopped at my best friend's house to give her a big hug. She said, "Have a nice life in Florida."

When the writer read her paper to her fellow students, she was quite disappointed because her audience didn't react the way she expected. They didn't get her point. People in her writing group asked her what her feelings and her most dramatic ideas were. She said, "To me it was obvious. But if they had to ask—then I must not have been too clear." So she revised. What makes the second version so much better than the first?

Draft 2

The sweater, socks, and thermal underclothes sank deep into the brown box. They already seemed obsolete, although the weather was still cool in North Carolina. On the top of the box sat my short pants, dresses, and T-shirts. I discarded many old papers and wiped away a tear. Papers I'd written in school, old birthday cards, and notes written by friends sat loosely on top of a pile of trash. Stepping over that trash and across my bed, I waded my way through to the closet. Staring blankly for a moment, I pulled out the last remaining thing—my sled. I hauled the sled down the stairs and out the door, just as I had done many times before. Walking down the street, sled in hand, I remembered the snow, the chill, and the laughter that Sarah and I shared. We had laughed together until our stomachs ached and our eyes watered, warming our insides. I remembered the bonfire at the top of the hill, and could almost smell the burnt marshmallows. I reached my best friend Sarah's house. She answered the door with red eyes and hugged me and my sled. We laughed; I put her sled down in the doorway and we hugged again. She said, "Thanks, Nicole. Have a good life in Florida."

After Nicole wrote this version, she again shared it with students. They wrote personal letters to her, sharing their reactions and making new suggestions. Because all the students now got her main idea, their suggestions became much more specific.

What follows is one letter from a fellow student. Do you agree with the suggestions and Nicole's reactions?

Dear Nicole,
Your writing is smooth. I must admit, had your piece been any longer, I'd probably have cried.

However, some points could be clearer. Stepping across a trash pile is believable, but stepping across a bed seems unrealistic. The ownership of the sled is also a question for the reader. You speak of "your sled" in the second to last sentence. Did you give your sled to Nicole? Here are a few other points. Sara should be identified as your best friend the first time she's mentioned. When you wrote, "Warming our insides," I got the feeling that you want to convey the warmth of friendship; but your sentence seems to say that aching stomachs and watering eyes are necessary to warm one's insides.

If the differences between the first and second are any indication, the third revision will be excellent.

Sincerely,
Linda

Using Linda's suggestions, Nicole revised "Life Shift." In what ways is it improved?

Draft 3

The sweaters, socks, and thermal underclothes sank deep into the brown box. They already seemed obsolete, although the weather was still cool in North Carolina. I emptied my dresser drawers and closet of most of my clothes, filled the box and marked it "storage." In a considerably smaller box, I packed short pants, dresses, and T-shirts, the clothing I would need at my sunny destination. Sorting through the stuff I had accumulated over the years, I discarded many old papers and filed the memories. Papers I'd written in school, old birthday cards, and notes written by friends sat loosely on top of a pile of trash. Stepping over that trash, and around boxes, I waded my way to the closet. Staring blankly for a moment, I pulled out the last remaining thing—my sled. I hauled the sled down the stairs and out the door, just as I had done many times the previous month. Walking down the street, sled in hand, I remembered the snow, the chill, and the laughter that my best friend Sarah and I shared. We had laughed together until our stomachs ached and our eyes watered. We had warmed ourselves from the inside out. I remembered the bonfire at the top of the hill, and could almost smell the burnt marshmallows. I got to Sarah's house, hesitated, then knocked loudly. She answered the door and hugged me and my sled. We laughed; I gave her the sled and we hugged again. Neither of us could speak for a few minutes until Sarah half whispered, "Thanks, Nicole. Have a good life in Florida."

Here is a second student's series of drafts.

Freetown, West Africa

by Susan Leach

Draft 1

Once the ship had docked at Freetown, West Africa, a party of twenty-five schoolgirls disembarked. Each one was the epitome of a tourist complete with sun hat and camera and smelling of insect repellent. Still fresh in our minds was Dakar, the previous port of call, a dignified city with its water fountains and row upon row of well-kept flowers. We had no idea that Freetown would leave us with an unforgettable memory of the poverty-stricken scenes of an underdeveloped, third world country.

The cool, refreshing breeze, our faithful companion during the voyage, now abandoned us. The sweltering heat and humidity made it extremely difficult to catch one's breath, and the desire to pant was overwhelming.

As I rambled by several stalls set up along the quay eyeing the merchandise, I was suddenly aware of a heavy hand on my arm. A "salesman" recognizing a gullible tourist dragged me in front of his stall and with unrelenting insistence exhibited his meagre livelihood. His actions displayed a sense of urgency bordering on desperation. For reasons of self-preservation and compassion (in that order) I came away clutching four wooden elephants which I'm sure will look nice somewhere.

The group gathered together beside a battered, old coach. Our teacher, his forehead glistening with beads of perspiration, motioned us to climb aboard. Reluctantly, we entered the furnace. Gazing through the windows as the coach stuttered down the dirt track, it did not take long for the disconcerting scenes to make an impact. To our astonishment, a woman of about thirty, wearing a simple, patterned, wrap-over skirt interrupted her journey to squat down and relieve herself. She continued on her way.

Everywhere we looked, there seemed to be a puzzlingly high number of children with either lost or deformed limbs. One young boy was suffering as he walked since his mangled left leg was dragging behind him. A young girl, no more than five years old, was scarcely able to handle a small cardboard box because one of her hands was missing. Our guide informed us that many of these children had been born normal and healthy, but their mothers had chosen to inflict physical disabilities on their own offspring at birth to enable them to secure a small income from sympathetic observers.

An overturned cart temporarily brought the bus to a standstill. Within seconds it was swarming with hundreds of children begging us for scraps like newly-hatched chicks demanding to be fed. All around was a mass of hollow eyes belonging to malnutritioned bodies. I singled out one little girl and stared into her huge brown eyes. I searched her face for signs of optimism. I thought I saw a glimmer of hope in those sullen eyes, but it was so brief I'm not sure it had ever existed. All I could see was desperation and doom. Every face transmitted the same message. Disconcertedly, I rummaged through my packed lunch, which minutes earlier had been the subject of protest, to see what I could "spare." I squeezed my pork pie through the window towards the little girl, but before I was able to prevent it, hundreds of tiny hands were snatching at the pie like piranhas devouring human flesh. The little girl didn't even blink; she just accepted her loss as a fact of life. Perhaps tomorrow her small plea would be granted. Perhaps not.

For me, the rest of the day had no relevance. I was filled with guilt. Why is a person denied the right to be happy? Who or what determines who should be in the coach and who should be outside fighting for every morsel of food? The whole group was in a state of shock, their minds unable to comprehend what their eyes registered. We had arrived as naive schoolgirls, and we were leaving with a memory we would never forget.

Before reading further, ask yourself what you would say to the writer to help her improve "Freeport, West Africa."

Do your reactions agree with the following?

- The writer's voice isn't clear. The reader doesn't know who is describing what happened. In the first sentences, the girls are seen from a distance as if someone is watching all of them, but soon the writer shifts to become one of the girls.

- Readers get a summary. Yet, a good writer would add much more information to make readers feel as if they are in Freetown, too. Wouldn't the audience like to see and hear everything that happens to one of the schoolgirls? For example, the dialogue between the girl and the pushy salesman is left up to the reader's imagination. What did he say to make her buy elephants she didn't want? How did he scare her?

- The events should be told in the same tense: past or present.

- Some vocabulary needs changing.

Based on these comments the student wrote more drafts. Here is her final one.

Final Draft

Once the ship had docked at Freetown, West Africa, I stepped off the gangway and joined my party, a group of twenty-five schoolgirls from England between the ages of eleven and fifteen. Each of us was the epitome of a tourist complete with sun hat and camera and smelling of insect repellent. Still fresh in my mind was Dakar, the previous port of call, a dignified city with its water fountains and row upon row of well-kept flowers. Little was I prepared for the drastic contrast of Freetown.

The cool, refreshing breeze, a faithful companion during the voyage, now abandoned us. The sweltering heat and humidity made it extremely difficult to breathe. The desire to pant was overwhelming.

Several stalls were set up on the quay, and as I rambled along eyeing the merchandise, I was suddenly aware of a heavy hand on my arm. A beefy "salesman" recognizing a gullible tourist dragged me to his stall and with unrelenting insistence exhibited his meagre merchandise—carved zebras, tiny giraffes, matching elephant sets, and a few other trinkets I couldn't see on the table behind him.

He pointed to a set of carved elephants. "These good, these good. You like?"

"Yes, they're umm, it's all very nice."

"You buy?"

"I'll come back."

His large fingers, enveloping my arm with disturbing ease, tightened their grip.

"You buy, you buy, yes!"

"All right, all right, I'll buy."

So for reasons of self-preservation and compassion—in that order—I came away clutching four wooden elephants of decreasing size, which I was sure would look nice somewhere.

Finally I assembled with my group beside a shabby, old bus. Our teacher, his forehead glistening with beads of perspiration, motioned us to climb aboard. Reluctantly, I entered the furnace.

Sighs of discontent filled the air. The effort of opening the window and the frustration of realizing its open height was five inches caused yet another sweat droplet to begin its descent down my cheek.

I gazed through the dirty window as the bus stuttered down the dirt track. It did not take long for disconcerting scenes to make an impact. To my astonishment, a woman of about thirty, wearing only a simple, patterned, wrap-over skirt, interrupted her journey to squat down and relieve herself. Then she continued on her way totally oblivious to our stunned eyes watching her every move.

Everywhere I saw a puzzlingly large number of children with either lost or deformed limbs. One boy, three or four years old, suffered as he walked with his mangled left leg dragging behind. A girl, no more than five, could scarcely handle a small cardboard box as the stub at the end of her arm poorly substituted for a hand. Our tour guide in the bus told us that many of these children had been born normal and healthy, but their mothers had inflicted physical disabilities on their own offspring at birth to enable them to secure a small income from sympathetic observers.

An overturned cart of hay temporarily brought the bus to a standstill. Within seconds it was swarming with hundreds of children begging for scraps like newly hatched chicks demanding to be fed. All around was a mass of hollow eyes belonging to malnourished bodies.

I caught sight of one little girl who had been roughly pushed aside in the scurry and stared into her huge brown eyes. I searched her face for signs of optimism. I thought I saw a glimmer of hope in those sullen eyes, but it was so brief I'm not sure it ever existed. All I could see was desperation and doom. Every face transmitted the same message.

Bewildered, I rummaged through my packed lunch to see what I could "spare." I squeezed my hand through the window and held a meat pie toward the little girl, but before I was able to prevent it, hundreds of tiny hands snatched at the pie like piranhas devouring human flesh. The little girl didn't even blink; she just accepted her loss as a fact of life. Perhaps tomorrow her small plea would be granted. Perhaps not.

For me, the rest of the day had no relevance. I was filled with guilt. Why is a person denied the right to be happy? Who or what determines who is in the coach and who is outside fighting for every morsel of food? Shocked, my mind was unable to comprehend what my eyes had registered. I had arrived as a naive schoolgirl, and I would leave with memories I would never forget.

Notice how the student writer improved the paper:

She tells the entire incident in the voice of one of the girls.
She adds new facts, like the girls' ages.
You are with her in the stall with the frightening elephant salesman to hear what happened.
She tells the incident in the past tense and changes some wording.
But the best part of the essay—the ending's reflection upon fate—is kept fairly intact.

Suggestions for Drafting and Revising

A few simple techniques will make your revising easier.

Write on one side of the paper so you can easily cut it apart and tape it together in a new order. Use a scissors and Scotch tape to help you rearrange your paper without recopying it. (Rearranging is easy on the computer!) Experiment.

Write on every other line or double space your typing so you can write between the lines when you revise.

Save your piece on the computer even if you think you don't like it. After a cooling period, you may want part of it.

Save parts you cut out of your piece until you are finished revising. You may decide to use them later.

If you are composing on a computer, make a hard copy periodically so you can see the entire piece, not just the part on your monitor.

Read your paper aloud to someone so you can hear how it sounds. If you cannot find an audience, read your paper into a tape recorder and listen to it as if you were your audience.

When you are ready for the final check for grammar usage, spelling, punctuation, and all mechanics, read your paper one sentence at a time starting with the last sentence. Beginning at the end will force you to look at each sentence in a new light.

Questions to Guide Your Revisions

What should you look for when you revise? Ask yourself questions related to each of the major decisions writers make. These questions should be useful every time you work on a revision.

- *What is your topic?* Do you have only one subject for the paper?
- *What supporting information do you have?* Do you have enough to convince your reader of the points you want to make? What else might you add? Where might you search for more?

- *Who is your intended audience?* How will this audience react to your paper? Why? Do you always keep your audience in mind? In other words, is every example, every idea, every point, every word going to make your audience listen to you? Will you grab your audience? Is there anything your readers might not understand? What needs to be changed for the sake of your audience?

- *What is your paper's purpose?* Does everything in your paper work toward that purpose? Do you ever get distracted from it? What could you change so your effect might be even better?

- *What voice or writing personality are you using to talk to your audience?* Do you keep the same voice all through the writing? If you change, do you have a good reason for changing?

- *What order do you use?* What made you arrange your points the way you did? Is the order the best it can be? What other arrangement might you try?

- *What is your thesis?* Is it an inference, an opinion? Does it predict the main points and structure or summarize the paper? How might you reword the thesis? Did you put it in the best spot so it has an impact on your reader? Where else might you put the thesis?

- *Do your topic sentences clearly explain the paragraphs?* How might you experiment with the topic sentences? By rewording? Adding more information? Placing details in other spots?

- *What technique do you use to begin the paper?* Would you read a paper that begins this way? What other techniques might you try? How could you improve your beginning?

- *What technique do you use to end the paper?* Does your conclusion tell the reader that the paper is finished? What other techniques might you use in the conclusion?

- *Does everything tie together smoothly?* How could you make the paper read so the reader never bumps against a sentence or idea?

- *Do you like your paper?* Will your readers? What could you change so you'd like your own paper even more?

- *How could you publish your paper so your audience could read it?* The reaction of the audience may be your best help in knowing what to revise.

Use these questions on each paper you write until the questions become so much a part of your writing habits that you don't even have to think about them each time you revise. Use them in school, at work, and in your private writing.

More Thoughts on Revising

When you get involved in revision, something quite exhilarating or frightening may happen to you. As you experiment with your paper you will make discoveries. You may be pleased with what you said, never expecting that you even knew you could say what you did. Good writers sometimes have that experience.

At other times, though, when you start to rethink your position, you may put your paper into greater chaos than before you began revising. Don't be afraid to take that risk.

Chaos in learning is often good. Chaos forces one to find a new order, a new meaning. And in the resolution often comes new insight. Have the courage to trust yourself to create meaning from ambiguity and chaos. Sometimes asking the questions to which you have no immediate answer leads to great learning. Writers learn from their own writing.

I used to be a leader for Great Books discussions. We leaders were taught to ask only discussion questions to which we had no answers. The discussion, the searching for answers, led to answers. I encourage you to risk too. Try writing in new ways. Try organization and styles new to you. Newness will make you uncomfortable and unable to predict your end results. But your attempt may help you discover a new way of writing, a new way of handling concepts or ideas that can greatly benefit you.

COLLABORATIVE LEARNING

1. Exchange essays with a member of your group so you can revise an essay written by someone else. Use all the questions from the "Questions for Revising a Paper" given earlier in this chapter. After you have revised the paper, show it to the original author. Explain why you made the revisions. Then have the original author revise the paper again, making whatever revisions seem good. Show both revisions to your instructor.

2. In your group, work together to revise an essay written by one of you for another course. (Make photocopies of the essay, so you each have a copy.) Use all the "Questions to Guide Your Revisions" as you work. When you finish, show the original and the revision to your instructor.

3. With your group, do the Revision Worksheet at the end of this chapter.

4. Read again the "Questions to Guide Your Revision" in this chapter. Then each of you should choose the question that usually gives you the *most trouble* when you write a paper. Explain to your group the reasons why that question causes you problems. Perhaps the group can offer suggestions for easing your difficulties. Next, each group member should chose the question that is usually *easiest* to handle. Again explain your choices to each other.

WRITING TASKS _____

1. Revise one of your own papers using the "Questions for Revising a Paper" as your guide. Begin with the first questions, moving to the others only after you have answered those questions. (It is not a good idea to start with the last questions because your decisions about topic, supporting information, audience, purpose, voice, and organization will affect other issues, such as wording.) Keep revising your paper until you are satisfied with your answers.

2. Do the Revision Worksheet at the end of this chapter.

Checklist for Revising Your Papers

For your checklist, you might use either the "Questions to Guide Your Revision" (earlier in this chapter) or the following:

Yes   *No*

_____ _____ 1. Do you have only one limited subject for the paper?

_____ _____ 2. Do you have enough supporting information to convince your reader of each of your points?

_____ _____ 3. Have you chosen a specific audience?

_____ _____ 4. Does your audience seem appropriate for your topic?

_____ _____ 5. Will *every* example, *every* inference, *every* point, *every* word cause your audience to listen to you?

_____ _____ 6. Is there anything the readers might not understand?

_____ _____ 7. Does everything in your paper work toward your purpose?

_____ _____ 8. What could you change so your effect might be greater?

_____ _____ 9. Do you use a specific writing personality?

_____ _____ 10. Do you keep the same voice all through the writing?

_____ _____ 11. If you change the voice, do you have good reason?

_____ _____ 12. Do you organize your supporting information in a way that is clear to the reader?

_____ _____ 13. Is the order the best?

_____ _____ 14. Is your thesis an inference, an opinion?

_____ _____ 15. Does your thesis predict or summarize your main points and structure of the entire piece?

_____ _____ 16. Did you place your thesis where it has an impact?

_____ _____ 17. Do your topic sentences clearly focus the paragraphs?

_____ _____ 18. Do you use a technique to interest your audience at the beginning of the paper?

_____ _____ 19. Do you use an appropriate technique to end the paper?

_____ _____ 20. Does everything tie together smoothly?

_____ _____ 21. Do you like your paper?

_____ _____ 22. Will your readers like your paper?

_____ _____ 23. Is the paper grammatically correct?

_____ _____ 24. Are all words correctly spelled?

_____ _____ 25. Is your punctuation correct?

Name _____

Section _____

REVISION WORKSHEET _____

To radically revise a paper takes nerve and skill. Sometimes it helps to watch another writer revise. Study Pati Hamilton's original paragraph and her rewrite; then write a letter to Pati (similar to the letter to Nicole found in this chapter).

Original Paragraph

I am so fortunate not to have to wonder what self-improvement is. Self-improvement is within my grasp; however, I have had a great deal of help towards this understanding. During my lifetime, I have had the opportunity to reap the benefits of advice and experience from family members, friends, and peers. I live in a free country where literature is available on any topic I need clarification on. I currently work with a company where one of the primary goals is continuous self-growth. Lastly, higher learning is for everyone.

Rewrite

Do you often wonder why some people are successful? I know I did. As a matter of fact, I was so curious that I began asking those around me what their secret for success was. The replies that I received from these individuals were not surprising, nor were they secrets. In fact, the answer had been staring me in the face for many years. I needed to have the desire to improve upon everything that I set out to do. As I looked around me, I discovered that I had many resources available to me. All I had to do was ask family members, friends, and peers to share their advice and experiences with me. The rest was up to me. As a result, self-improvement is within my grasp.

In your letter to Pati Hamilton:

a. Describe the changes Pati made when she revised her original paragraph.

b. Explain how the changes improved her rewrite.

c. Suggest *specific* recommendations which Pati could use to turn her paragraph into a fine essay.

(Use this page and the next to write your letter.)

Dear Pati Hamilton:

writer's decision six

Do I Say Lightning *or* Lightning Bug?
Putting the Right Word in the Right Spot

Introduction

As you read the title for Writer's Decision Six, do you picture lightning streaks zig-zagging across the sky or one lone, little bug? The right word in the right spot makes a great deal of difference!

Chapter Nineteen

Diction: The Final Touches

It is time to polish, to revise word by word. For some writers, this part of writing is the most fun.

When you write of rain, you want your reader to see and feel the rain, not the color and force of the Indian Rain Maker. So choose the right words to fit snugly together. Influence emotions; don't just state facts. Write powerful images. Create as surely as any craftsman. Doing all this will be exhausting. But somewhere along the way you will discover the truth that lets you say, "Ah-Ha! I've got it!" And readers somewhere will say, "That writer got to me."

Here are specific suggestions to help you.

Surprise Your Reader

Once on every page, surprise your audience. Use a word or comparison or rhythm to bring a smile or anger or delight. Creating surprise isn't easy. But one unexpected word in every 300 invigorates your writing.

COLLABORATIVE LEARNING

Surprise Your Reader

1. Study ten pages of your writing. Together, add at least one surprise to every page. Show your new pages to your instructor.

2. Listen to your favorite instructors or talk show hosts to find several verbal surprises. Share these surprises with your group. .

Be Brief

Mark Twain said, "I would have written you a short letter, but I didn't have time." Make every word work. A word that doesn't work is deadwood. Prune it. Look at your words the way a film director looks at movie footage. To make a movie, a director may shoot one hundred hours of film. But when the footage is edited to make a feature, only two, or, at the most, three hours of the best is left. Prune your sentences ruthlessly.

At this stage, instead of searching for what you can put in your writing, think about what you can remove. For example, I could rewrite this same sentence: *Think not of what to put in your writing, think of what to take out.* Or I could omit more: *Instead of adding words, remove them.*

Take out repetition; change vocabulary if fewer words can make the identical point. Revise sentences. Sometimes you will have to cross out your favorite part: a sentence, an image, even a paragraph. But anything that doesn't help your work must go.

COLLABORATIVE LEARNING

Be Brief

1. With the members of your group, revise the following sentences to cut out wordiness. Example: Whenever I write, I usually keep saying the same thing several times even though I try to say the idea without repeating myself again. (Revised: When I write, I usually repeat myself.)

   a. The girls at Daytona Beach tried to whistle at all the guys on the strip, but whistling was not something they were good at.

   b. Miss California is a very beautiful woman, but she may destroy her sex appeal if she decides to become a mortician.

   c. If students investigate all the possibilities open to them, they can usually find enough money to pay their way through college, but only if they search and use all the resources available to them.

   d. The attached material should help you further your claim to the insurance company. You need to fill out and complete all the enclosed forms. Attach to these forms a copy of the accident report on file in the sheriff's office, a copy of your hospital bills, as well as copies of your doctor's bills, and your account of the time you lost at work. Mail all these to the car insurance company at the address on the enclosed envelope. You will probably receive a check from the insurance company within six months.

2. Cross out all the repetition in five pages of your writing.

Be Clear

To ensure clarity, check all pronouns and their antecedents, use transitions, and depend on action verbs and the active voice.

Check all pronouns to be sure the antecedent is obvious. In the following sentence, we don't know who sprinted: "The store owner saw the suspect as *he* sprinted down the stairs." If this statement were in a police report, you can see the problem: Did the store owner or the suspect run down the stairs? Be especially suspicious of *it* if it is the first word in a sentence.

Use transitions to show relationships between your ideas so no one has to guess at what you mean. You can write: "I saw London. I saw France." But what is the connection? Did you see them even though terrorists threatened to blow up the plane? When did you see them? Did you see only one city in England but the whole country of France? Did you see them both the same summer, or did you make separate trips? Without transitions, the sentences are only singsong nursery rhymes without much meaning. You may want to review transitions in Chapter 15.

Depend on action verbs. Verbs make lean, powerful statements; adjectives and adverbs act like fat, not muscle. "He walked very slowly and hesitatingly across the floor" may mean simply "He stumbled." Say so.

Instead of "to be" verbs, substitute action verbs.

Use the active voice. Make the subject do something. The passive voice usually clutters up a sentence. Notice the difference between the same idea said first in the passive: "I was given a birthday gift by my father" and then in active: "My father gave me a birthday gift." Active voice usually makes a simpler sentence. Here is another example: The memo was sent to everyone who reported to him by the new manager. (passive) The new manager sent the memo to everyone reporting to him. (active)

COLLABORATIVE LEARNING

Be Clear

1. Make all *pronouns* in the following sentences refer to specific antecedents.

   a. The president of the fast-food franchise said that each employee would receive a paid holiday on his birthday.

   b. Whenever the Raiders decide to hire new coaches, they usually choose people who they hope will be assets to the entire management team.

   c. The suspect approached the victim. He says that he was very worried.

   d. The boys pursued the dogs around the corner of 43rd and Sherman Boulevard, down Sherman and around the corner to 44th Street. Later, no one could find them.

e. It is recommended that a store be open at 9:00, not 10:00.

2. Use *action verbs.* In the next examples, take out all the adverbs, and adjectives, and all forms of the verb *to be.* Replace them with action verbs.

   a. We were in the noisy restaurant for a very long, boring time before the waitress finally was there with our cold food.

   b. The manager is the only person in this entire store who is able to O.K. a waiting customer's check.

   c. Outside the registration office is a very unhappy group of freshmen who are requesting with loud voices that they be allowed to sign up for the courses that are already closed.

3. *Use the active voice.* Change these sentences from passive to active.

   a. The pants were returned to the customer service department by the dissatisfied buyer.

   b. After the dessert, the table was cleared by the waiter who expected a 25 percent tip.

   c. Even in the middle of a blizzard, the morning paper was delivered by the conscientious paper carrier.

   d. Although the swimming pool needed to be cleaned and treated, the motel guests were allowed to swim at their own risk.

   e. When the student was convinced by his economics teacher that he was failing economics, his social life was cancelled.

Be Precise

Give examples, facts, statistics instead of vague generalities to clarify your thesis and main points. For example, state the fact, "Fifty-one percent of the infants born each year are female," instead of making the inference, "females lead males in number of births." Write "Ninety-two teenagers heard Horsechild Breakfast play last night" instead of "A lot of kids heard a new-wave band."

Use exact words. If you mean the President of the United States, don't say, "The most important person in the United States." Your readers may not agree that the president is the most important. If you mean that the "boys giggled and primped," say so. You may shock your readers to attention. Check your paper to see that you have explained all important ideas with specifics.

Avoid vague words like factor, element, quality, state, stuff, thing, conditions. These words can have different meanings. In fact, the discriminating reader often interprets such imprecise words as lazy thinking. A careful writer seeks right words and isn't satisfied with substitutes.

See, for example, how the word *factor* in the following sentence can be replaced by actually naming the factors.

> Poor wording: Several factors contributed to the president's re-election.
>
> Better wording: The conservative mood of the country, the high rate of unemployment, and the effective advertising campaign contributed to the president's re-election. (In this revision, specifics replace *the factors*.)

Avoid jargon. Jargon is wording that speaks only to those in the know. One problem with jargon is that it covers up meaning. Try reading some insurance policies. Does a *rider* indicate a loss or gain of benefits?

Study some statements made by public officials. A famous phrase uttered by one such person—"I misspoke myself"—could be restated simply as "I lied." Instead of jargon, use common, ordinary words.

Avoid euphemisms. Euphemisms eliminate unpleasantness by replacing harsh words with words that have softer, vaguer meanings. For example, the hard fact "He died" can be side-stepped by euphemisms like "He passed away," "He went to his reward," "He is no longer with us," "He breathed his last," and "He departed this life."

The problem with euphemisms is that the reader must guess at the writer's precise meaning. In the previous examples, the reader is not told if the person strangled on a piece of chicken bone, if he died peacefully in his sleep, or if his wife poisoned him with insulin. A good writer names the chicken bone if there was one.

So instead of using roundabout words, say exactly what you mean. Euphemisms seldom clarify meaning.

COLLABORATIVE LEARNING

Be Precise

1. Replace all vague information with facts or examples.

   a. Our athletic teams did quite well this past year.

   b. This morning, the stock market report said that the market was moving.

   c. During the last several years, important changes occurred in this state.

2. Change vague words to specific words.

   a. One *element* in the new McDonald's advertising campaign is convincing.

   b. People going on job interviews should find out certain *things* about the companies before they are interviewed.

    c. If *conditions* are met, students can get jobs at the school they are attending.

3. Eliminate the jargon. (The dictionary may help.)

    a. The police picked up the perpetrator.

    b. The enclosed compartment of the vehicle seats six.

    c. The malfunction of the component caused the space challenger to abort its mission.

4. What are the common euphemisms for these words?

    a. Public toilets

    b. Blackheads, pimples, whiteheads

    c. To kill

Choose Words to Suit Your Audience, Purpose, and Tone

Your audience must understand your vocabulary. People speak to infants in baby talk; they surely wouldn't try those same silly words on the president of the college or on a five-year-old. This example is obvious. With your audience in mind, check every word in your piece to make sure it is the right word—neither too elementary nor too sophisticated. Don't insult or bore your reader unless you consciously choose to do so.

Choose words according to the tone and purpose of your work. Words elicit different reactions. What is the difference between a *terrorist* and a *freedom fighter?* A *patriot* and a *double agent?"* Doesn't the name suppose a point of view, an interpretation? Terrorists to Americans can be freedom fighters to their own country.

Not all words have such obvious layers of reaction, yet the name by which you call something or someone will reveal your feeling. Make sure every one of your important vocabulary words is picked for its power. Check your entire paper so every word fits your tone and purpose.

Use technical words only if your audience has the background to understand; otherwise, substitute nontechnical words. Most audiences will be unimpressed by language they cannot understand. Instead of flaunting your technical background, show how knowledgeable you are by clearly explaining difficult ideas.

Avoid slang in formal papers. Slang is a problem because it changes meaning so fast. It is inexact. For a time kids used the word awesome. A car or woman or movie or hairstyle or even a show horse could be *awesome.* But what does awesome mean? In every case, it means something different. Imagine complimenting a woman with the same word a person might use to compliment a horse.

Words must match the mood of the work. If the piece is a love song, all the words must fit the mood. The same is true of a comedy act; the audience expects to laugh and not to weep. If you write satire, don't be literal. In other words, make sure that no words spoil the mood. In this sentence, for example, one word is totally inappropriate: "Todd, a burly kid of about sixteen, weighing at least 209, *nibbled* his four McDonald Big Macs and washed down six large Cokes in less time than his date could eat her one order of french fries." Surely Todd didn't *nibble* his four Big Macs.

COLLABORATIVE LEARNING

Choose Words to Suit Your Audience, Purpose, and Tone

1. Match the words in Column I with the descriptive in Column II to see how words about color can affect you. (You can use items more than once.)

I	II
Baby blue	Office walls in a detention center
Pastel blue	Toddler's blanket
Steel blue	Man's cigar smoke
Sky blue	Fingernails of dead woman
Alligator blue	
Royal blue	

2. Eliminate slang from formal writing. Check your writing and revise all sentences that contain slang. Have someone in your writing group recheck your paper.

3. Match moods. Find the words which destroy the mood in the following sentences. Substitute other words.

   a. Whenever the old timer needed to swear, he shouted, "whoopedaddle" at the top of his lungs, and we kids snorted.

   b. Americans do not respect a president who wishywashes through major decisions.

   c. After orientation, the freshman attacked their first college class in an auditorium that seated at least seven hundred.

   d. The bike trail led through swamps, between sand dunes, and over a piddling hill at least 6,000 feet high.

Take Out Clichés

A *cliché* is a statement that has been used so often it no longer creates any images for the listeners. For example, do you think of a freshly cut beet, red juices glistening, when someone says, "He got red as a beet?" Do you picture that glossy, staining red on a person's cheeks? No? Then *red as a beet* or *beet red* is a cliché. The problem with clichés is that the writer uses them instead of thinking and reaching.

COLLABORATIVE LEARNING

Eliminate Clichés

1. Work as a group to find the clichés in the following paragraph.

    Tonight the Gators meet the Dogs in a head-on collision. No one expects the game to be a piece of cake as the quarterback, a towering hunk, will be reaching for the stars in his last game of his college career. In a televised news conference earlier today, the Gators' coach predicted that this battle will make sports history.

2. Rewrite the paragraph without clichés. Make your version stronger.

3. Check your own papers for clichés. If you find any, eliminate them by saying exactly what you mean, not what other people say. After you rid one paper of clichés, show your writing group your revision. Did you find all your clichés?

Create Comparisons and Images

Martin Luther King moved millions when he said, "I have a dream!" Blacks and whites together chanted, "We shall overcome someday." In the titles of the top forty songs or the albums of your favorite groups, you'll find images. Musicians, song writers, speech writers, poets, advertisers, and politicians whose words are remembered speak with images.

But *images* must match ideas. We have a controversy today because some Americans object to the violent images in the "Star-Spangled Banner." They don't want to sing about rockets, bursting bombs, and war in our national anthem. They want pictures of a peaceful America. They believe that amber fields of grain and the majesty of purple mountains better describe the U.S.A.

Images and comparisons make ideas clearer, help readers understand. Most comparisons associate two things that are different but alike in some extraordinary way. It is the likeness that surprises readers but makes them understand. The most frequently used comparisons are similes and metaphors.

Similes compare two unlike things using the words *as* or *like*. For example, a magazine might rant that "a terrorist is like an angry tarantula." The terrorist, like the tarantula, is obviously dangerous. Here are some other similes:

A woman yelled at her kids, "Stop hanging on me like fleas on a hound dog." (Her kids bothered her as much as fleas frustrated a hound dog.)

"Al Capone, the legendary gangster, was as gentle to his girl friend as a cow to her newborn calf." (Capone's treatment of his girl was like the tender care a newborn receives from its mother, yet the writer doesn't give the outlaw human qualities.)

Metaphors are like similes in that they compare, but they make direct comparisons of two unlike things without using the words *as* or *like*. You have heard the expression, *money burns a hole in some people's pockets,* which means that as soon as some people get money they want to spend it. Here are some other metaphors:

"He built his business on a sinkhole." (Just as sinkholes open up and everything on top of them falls in and sinks, his business has little future.)

"American farm legislation is a million-word dictionary with no alphabetical order." (Understanding farm legislation is as complex as finding a word in a very large dictionary that has no alphabetical order.)

"After the hurricane, we ate sand for a year." (We didn't really eat sand, but the ugly reminders of the hurricane remained an entire year.)

Be consistent. In other words, don't mix your metaphors. Here is a mixed metaphor I actually heard! "When you die you will eat pie in a cloudless sky where everything is coming up roses, little kids wave palm branches and weep no crocodile tears, and everything is A-OK."

Are you confused? So was I! The afterlife described here is bewildering, not comforting.

COLLABORATIVE LEARNING

Create Comparisons and Images

1. Create images:

    a. Make several metaphors about the weather or your school.

    b. Turn the metaphors you just wrote into similes.

2. Find the inconsistencies in these images and revise the sentences.

    a. The new tax laws fingered the rich and fattened the poor.

    b. Water spit up over the sick radiator like bubbles escaping the lid of a pot of boiling spaghetti.

    c. I bombed the test and hibernated for a week.

3. Find some ridiculous images in the newspaper. They will probably be mixed metaphors. Report your findings in writing.

4. Show one of your papers to your writing group. Together, plan at least one simile and one metaphor to add to the paper. How do the new images contribute to the piece?

Develop Rhythm and Harmony

We expect rhythm and harmony in music and paintings, but you can create them in writing, too.

Put rhythm in the ending. Even if you are not a musician or graphic artist, one rhythm is easy to make. If the ending reminds the reader of the beginning, the end gives a sense of completeness, a wholeness. The reader comes full circle and knows the piece is finished. The rhythm is good. Have you ever had the bad experience of reading a magazine, coming to the end of the page, and turning it expecting more of the same article? But the next page started something new. You looked back to see where the article continued and discovered that there wasn't any more. That was not good writing. The author hadn't prepared you for the end. In good writing, you might show the reader that you are finishing by referring to the title or to the thesis or to the introduction. Remind the reader of your first ideas, images, or words. That rhythm in circling back is pleasing.

Match your words with your writing purpose and the occasion. We see a *pig* rooting on a farm, but we call it *pork* on the dining room table. We may milk a *cow*, but we eat *beef* in our hamburgers. So too, you need to harmonize words for your mood.

Choose synonyms. One kind of repetition—using the same vocabulary over and over—bores readers. A word read twice in the same sentence is already dull. Find synonyms in dictionaries and thesauruses.

Vary sentence beginnings. In sentence beginnings beats another kind of rhythm. Just as an identical drum pattern gets boring after a while, so do the same sentence beginnings. Sometimes start with a phrase, sometimes with an independent clause, sometimes with a dependent clause. See if you can avoid *the* or *it* as the first word.

Vary sentence lengths. If all sentences are about the same length, they can get boring. Sometimes make sentences long, sometimes short. Find ways to coordinate and subordinate.

Create parallel structure. This is a marvelous way to create rhythm. Abraham Lincoln, in parallel wording and rhythm, called ours:

a government of the people
> by the people,
> for the people.

Here is another example of parallelism, and with a twist at the end. "Find your sand, unfold your chair, slap on the oil, switch on your radio, whip off your shades, lie back, and sizzle."

Parallel structure pleases your reader's sense of rhythm and emphasizes similar patterns within sentences, within paragraphs, or within an entire essay.

COLLABORATIVE LEARNING

Develop Rhythm and Harmony

1. Create variety in sentence beginnings. Begin the following sentence in three different ways—with a phrase, several independent clauses, and a dependent clause. After you have finished, decide other ways to change the sentence.

    My mother is a victim of Alzheimer's disease. Her personality has changed so much that now she hides important items like her glasses, dentures, shoes, purse, house keys, and even knives in the kitchen and then cannot remember where they are.

2. Vary sentence lengths. Work as a group.

    a. To find out if your sentences are consistently about the same length, and consequently boring, count the number of words in each sentence in one of your essays. When you've finished counting, you should see a huge difference between your numbers—the smallest sentence might hold only three or four words and the longest sentence fifty words or so. If all your sentences seem to be within five or ten words of each other, practice writing other lengths. Shorten sentences by breaking up long ones if you are consistently long. Find ways to coordinate and subordinate ideas if your sentences are consistently skimpy.

    b. For fun, try writing a correctly punctuated, 100-word sentence that makes sense. Then, when you are all through, say the same basic idea in just three words.

3. Put these students' sentences into parallel structure.

    a. It is better to attend college instead of holding a job.

    b. Ferrets can be litter trained and will readily adapt to a diet of cat food.

    c. The fallopian tubes are not open to permit the ovum to pass to the uterus, thereby eliminating the possibility of an egg being fertilized or a woman to conceive.

4. Work as a group to make at least ten sentences parallel in your essays. How does parallel structure enrich your writing?

Be Honest

Write what you know as the person you are, not the person you'd like to be or the person you think might be listened to. Why? If you try to be someone else, your readers will find out so soon you will be stunned. And when they find you out, they will probably ignore you. Why? Dishonest writing almost always sounds dishonest. Use your beliefs, experience, convictions to give your writing honesty, authenticity.

WRITING TASKS

1. Revise one of your pieces of writing using several techniques explained in this chapter. After you finish, explain to your instructor how you revised the paper using the techniques.

2. Using the checklist for this chapter, study another student's piece of writing. After you finish your study, tell the author how to revise the piece using the guidelines from the chapter.

3. Apply one or two techniques you think your writing needs most to all the papers you have written for this course.

Checklist for Diction

Yes   *No*

____ ____ 1. Did you surprise your reader at least once per page?

____ ____ 2. Are you brief?

____ ____   a. Have you avoided useless repetition?

____ ____   b. Have you avoided round about explanations?

____ ____ 3. Are you clear?

____ ____   a. Do all pronouns refer to clear antecedents?

____ ____   b. Do transitions show how paragraphs relate to each other?

____ ____   c. Do transitions show how details relate to each other and to the main points?

____ ____   d. Do action verbs replace unnecessary adjectives and adverbs?

____ ____   e. Does active voice replace the passive voice?

____ ____   f. Do examples, facts, and statistics explain general points?

_____ _____ 4. Are you precise?

    _____ _____ a. Did you avoid vague words?

    _____ _____ b. Did you avoid jargon?

    _____ _____ c. Did you avoid euphemisms?

_____ _____ 5. Did you choose words to match your audience, purpose, and tone?

    _____ _____ a. Will your audience understand all vocabulary?

    _____ _____ b. Did you explain technical terms?

    _____ _____ c. Did you avoid slang in formal papers?

_____ _____ 6. Did you create images?

    _____ _____ a. Do metaphors explain some points?

    _____ _____ b. Do similes explain some points?

    _____ _____ c. Are images consistent?

_____ _____ 7. Did you remove clichés?

_____ _____ 8. Did you use rhythm and harmony?

    _____ _____ a. Is the ending in rhythm with the beginning?

    _____ _____ b. Do synonyms replace repeated vocabulary?

    _____ _____ c. Do you use variety in sentence beginnings?

    _____ _____ d. Do you use different sentence lengths?

    _____ _____ e. Does your parallel structure complement parallel ideas?

_____ _____ 9. Are you honest?

    _____ _____ a. Do you believe your ideas?

    _____ _____ b. Are your sources credible?

    _____ _____ c. Do you like your paper?

Chapter Twenty

A Writer Makes All Six Decisions in "Why I Love Where I Live"

A Pulitzer Prize-winning author, Donald Murray, wrote an entire book, *Write to Learn,* to describe how he created a four-page essay on his grandmother. In his book, Murray explained each of his steps as he wrote that one essay.

I, too, would like to explain how I wrote a short essay called "Why I Love Where I Live" for a local newspaper so you can see how I made each of the six decisions a writer must make as I wrote the article.

At the end of this chapter, you can read the version published by *The Florida Times-Union.*

Writer's Decision I:
What Will I Write About? Finding the Idea

This decision was easy for me. One morning as I opened the newspaper, I saw a new column and this request:

> Write an article for us—no more than two double spaced pages—called "Why I Love Where I Live."

To get a clear idea of what the editor was looking for, I read the first two published entries in the column. Then I was ready to write my own version of "Why I Love Where I Live."

My first decision was made. I had a subject, an idea.

Writer's Decision II:
How Will I Explain My Idea? Gathering the Supporting Information

Once I decided to write that article, I had a much more difficult decision to make. I had to decide what I would say.

In the already published columns, authors told why they liked living in condominiums, why they loved the local beach, or why they loved living near swamps teeming with alligators and rattlesnakes.

But if I were honest with myself, I had to admit that I didn't much like, much less love, my house or my subdivision. I had just moved from the North to the South, and I was homesick. I missed my Northern, two-story home with its wall sconces and leaded-glass windows. I'd exchanged that home with history for a ranch house with no history on a typical, small suburban lot. So I couldn't honestly say that I loved my plain house or my ordinary suburb. I missed the snow, my flowering crab apple tree, the hills, the people. I hated the 100-degree heat. Yet, I was happy to be in Florida and did not regret my decision to move here.

I had to find a different approach to the topic. What others wrote would not work for me.

Then the idea came to me. Instead of searching for reasons for liking my home, I would instead pursue why I enjoy living in the South. My answer to the question "Why I Love Where I Live" would explain what I do like about the South. Please realize, though, that when I made that decision, I wasn't at all sure I'd have enough to say to fill a two-page essay.

To discover what I had to say, I used the method which works best for me when I gather my supporting information; that is, I began to list my ideas.

I began with this *list of supporting information:*

About the South:

I like the *Gone With the Wind* scenery
I like the traditions
I like the literary history
I like the culture

Immediately, I recognized that these items were much too vague. So I started again and tried to list specific details.

My favorite scenes from movies about the South:

Magnolia blossoms, mint juleps, azalea bushes
Debutante balls, wisteria, oaks with moss, border grass, chinaberry trees

In the South I can stop:

Weeding dandelions
Risking dropping six-foot storm windows from the second story in the November wind
Paying $4.50 for four shrimp

In the South it's possible to:

Go to restaurants for "Boiled shrimp—all you can eat"
Treat burns with plants that grow on the patio
Go to the ocean any time

My discoveries:

In this city, lots on water can cost a quarter of a million dollars
The ocean beach is free
We fight foliage the way we fought snow
The grass needs edging
The river is as magnificent as the Mississippi

Changes in my life:

From eating cheese and red meats to eating pecans and seafood
Living in houses without steep roofs
Changing my dread of driving in the blinding snow to dread of blinding rain
Steeling myself for hot humidity, not the cool chill after a late night movie
Enjoying lobster softer, sweeter than Maine lobster
Living with no attics for storage
No freezing cold or snow; but calling the kids in to avoid the afternoon heat
Planting my garden in raised rows

Rewards of Southern living:

No state income tax; therefore, IRS can audit only half as often
Every woman can be Miz without the women's lib label
Leaves change from October until Christmas
Rummage sales every weekend because people have so little storage space

Miracles in the South:

Sand is soil and grows delicious vegetables
St. Augustine creepers are not weeds
Georgia clay is red
Lettuce, peas, onions grow in February
Squash, tomatoes, cucumbers, beans are harvested in May, not August
Roses bloom all year
Azalea bushes turn completely pink

New experiences for me:

Drive-in liquor windows
Freeze warnings: "Take in your plants and pets"
Women dress up without nylons
Barbecue beef can be beef with barbecue on the side
"Hey" means "Hi"
Expressions like "White as a sheet of cotton"
Oyster roasts
Okra prepared like popcorn
Revival tents
Christian music stations
To satisfy my love of antiques, there is St. Augustine, the oldest city in the U.S. just twenty-five miles from my door

Southerners' special spring:

Crocus, tulips, daffodils of North
Dogwood, wisteria, and azalea of South
Peach, plum, apple, citrus, rose smells of West, South, North, East

Realization:

I'll stay here because I'm beginning to feel at home.

By the time I'd written that last line, a surprising thing had happened to me.

I had set out to see what I could honestly say about my new home. I wasn't sure when I started that I liked the South enough to fill up two pages of an essay. But as I wrote, my list grew much longer than I expected. Item by item, I realized that I was accepting the South; in fact, I deeply loved and respected parts of it.

When I'd finished this list—it took several hours—I understood that part of me had accepted my new Southern home. I knew I could legitimately write a long essay to explain that I did indeed "Love Where I Lived." I hadn't expected to end by saying that I felt at home. But I did feel that way. I was delighted!

That's what writing can do for you sometimes. Writing can help you clarify your feelings, your thoughts. And sometimes, as this writing did for me, it can help you work out a kind of reconciliation of ideas or feelings or opinions.

My second decision, choosing supporting information, was settled.

Writer's Decision III:
Who Will Listen? Why? The Audience, Purpose, Voice

AUDIENCE   This decision was made for me, as it will often be made for you. The newspaper's readers would be my audience. The Sunday paper sold a quarter of a million copies regularly throughout Florida.

The audience would be composed of many folks who had lived in the area all their lives, as well as the thousands of people who moved into Florida every year. These transplants might be interested in reading about the South as another transplant (myself) had seen it.

My analysis of audience was correct. The day my article appeared in the newspaper, a DJ from the local radio station (himself a transplant from England) urged his radio audience to read the entire piece because he said it showed what a person who moved here experienced.

PURPOSE In addition to knowing the audience, I had to choose a purpose. That is, I had to decide why I wanted people to read my piece.

I decided that my purpose was very related to my audience. Because so many readers were newcomers to Florida, I wanted them to identify with my point of view. I wanted to make readers remember or understand differences between the North and the South and see the South from the perspective of a newcomer. I, perhaps presumptuously, also hoped that the piece would promote understanding between the long-time and new Floridians. This choice of purpose meant that I could write about only those differences between the North and the South which would not cause anger but create understanding.

VOICE My choice of voice related to this choice of audience and purpose. I would use a conversational tone, a simple vocabulary, and speak as if I were joining someone in the kitchen or on the front porch for morning coffee.

So, briefly, this was my decision three: I would write both to the audience of transplants to Florida who could identify with my point of view and to the long-time Floridians so they might better understand the newcomers.

Writer's Decision IV:
What Is the Best Way to Organize My Ideas for This Audience?

Now I had to decide upon a way to organize all my ideas. I had to develop some plan to help me make all the points I wanted to write; I needed to create a thesis or main idea sentence; I needed to decide on a way to begin and end the piece.

So I thought back to my audience and purpose. I could organize all the items on my lists to please the two kinds of readers in my audiences. This arrangement would give me two parts to the body of the essay.

In one part, I could show how I was learning so much. I'd explain how that very learning helped me accept and like the South. This explanation would satisfy the part of the audience who had always lived in the South and wanted it to be loved. I looked back to my lists of supporting information and found some descriptions of the South that might please this audience:

I'm seeing the nature described in the great Southern novels:

Magnolia blossoms
Chinaberry trees
Azalea bushes
Wild mint for making mint juleps
Great oaks with Spanish moss
White wisteria
Mockingbirds
Swamps and alligators

In part two, for the audience new to Florida, I'd explain the great differences between the North where I'd once lived, and the South where I live now. My essay would be a nostalgic reminder for many of the people who had moved here from other states. So I referred to my lists of supporting information for differences between my old home and my new home. I chose and reorganized these points:

In the South I don't have to:

Weed dandelions
Put up storm windows on the second floor in Nov.
Pay $4.50 for four shrimp
Get audited by the state IRS
Be a woman's libber to be called "Ms"
Go to the drugstore to get medicine for burns
Buy mint

I exchanged:

Cheeses and red meat for pecans and seafood
Fear of blinding snow for fear of blinding rain
Fear of biting cold for fear of heat and sunburn
Basement and attic storage for garage storage
Cool evening air for hot, humid air
Crunchy Maine lobster for soft, sweet lobster
Flat garden rows for humped up rows
"Hi" for "hey"
Drive-ins for food for drive-ins for food and liquor, too
Corn roasts for oyster roasts
Popcorn for okra
"White as a sheet" for "white as a sheet of cotton"
Chill-factor warnings for freeze warnings: "Bring in your plants and pets"
Soil in yard for sand in yard
Soft grass for St. Augustine creepers
October leaf changes for leaf changes October through Christmas

I reread these lists and realized that I had much more to say about my second point than my first. To remedy this inequity, I decided to write my *introduction* to demonstrate my first point: I'm learning so much about the South. When I found the appropriate material, I would try the technique of an anecdote in the introduction.

But I was stuck. I looked over everything I'd written, and not one item seemed to fit into such a beginning for the paper. I got up from my desk and walked around the house trying to find an image that would capture a good deal of my new insight into the South. But nothing struck me. Nothing would work.

Then I walked out to the hot, summer afternoon and sat down on the swing on the shady, front porch. With just a touch, the swing began to move me through the humid, afternoon air. I felt cool. And there I found an opening image. I would use the experience on the front porch swing to begin my piece.

Now I had an idea for the introduction. I had the two main points I wanted to make in the body of the essay. I had the supporting information to develop into the body paragraphs. I was getting organized.

But I still needed a thesis statement and a conclusion. For my thesis, I decided to pull my two main ideas together. I'd say, "I like it here because I'm learning so much about being Southern." This simple sentence would fit the newspaper's theme of "why I like where I live" as well as predict that my article would show what I was learning.

Now I had planned everything but the conclusion. I decided to write the entire piece first and see if an ending came to me as I wrote (endings are usually hard for me to predict before I've written the rest of the essay).

Writer's Decision V:
How Does All This Look When I Write It?
Rough Drafts

Finally, I was ready to write my essay. I laid out my lists, my papers, my plans and began to write. You can see my first draft here. The crossed out words show how I searched for words as I wrote.

Why I Love Where I Live
by Mary Sue Koeppel

Draft 1
Yesterday when it was 95 degrees, ~~I made a discovery.~~ I discovered what every Southerner probably knows: porch swings work like air fans. ~~In fact better than fans. They are free.~~ On that hot afternoon, sitting on the iron laced swing I could, with one little motion of my toes, move the air and feel as if I were being fanned by an elegant Hunter ceiling fan. ~~And all that movement on a swing, Southerners discovered years ago, doesn't cost anything. I understand now why my~~

new Southern home has a swing. Feeling that breeze in that afternoon stillness, I came to understand the place of a swing in my new home—a Southern home.

That is why I like it here. I'm learning so much. You see, Florida, and the South just became my home less than a year ago. Previously, I had lived in the snow country where two winters ago the snow drifts in the alley reached the top of my twenty-foot pine tree. *Snow and ice I understand.* And believe it or not, snow piling high and deep is one of my fondest memories. Thus I didn't expect to like it here. But I do. Let me tell you why.

My neighborhood here is filled with words that speak of southern springs and summers, words from Southern novels like "white magnolia blossoms, chinaberry trees, pink azalea bushes, mint for mint juleps, great oaks, climbing wisteria." Walks during each season have told me of the images that until now a literary artist had to recreate for me.

[This whole paragraph is too stilted! It doesn't create the setting or mood I want. So I try to say the same idea again.]

Perhaps most delightful of all my learning is that I have learned the lore of the Southern spring from all the great Southern literature, wisps of words from Southern novels, the romance, tradition, culture.

[This paragraph, is getting too flowery, so I begin a third time with the same idea. I need to get more specific and say exactly what I mean.]

Words from the great Southern novels live in the spring and summer of my neighborhood. The magnolia tree across the street blossoms white and drops its hard, brown leaves in the wind. The chinaberry tree shades my kitchen window and the azalea bushes turn completely pink to hide even their pale, green leaves. Mint for mint juleps grows wild in my flower beds. Nearby, in Mandarin, the great oaks drip moss and cover whole parts of the road. My neighbors walk along their paths lined with border grass and contemplate their white wisteria.

[Because the writing goes better, I keep to the supporting information on my lists and continue writing.]

I don't have to weed dandelions anymore or risk dropping put up six-foot-tall storm windows on the second story in the burly November wind. Cocktails of four fat shrimp don't cost down $8.50 here.

Here I have learned that It is possible to go to a restaurant with a sign, "Boiled shrimp—all you can eat." If I burn myself, I go to my backyard patio and treat the burn with my own growing plant. If I want mint for fresh mint tea, I just go to the front flower bed and pick fresh mint. And the question, "What will we do this afternoon or evening or weekend?" always has an answer: "Go to the beach."

Your Beaches are open to everyone. But no one in my old hometown would believe that one of your river lots sells for a quarter of a million dollars.

[I cross out words in this last paragraph because I want to be like the readers and do not want to talk about them as "you." Also, the paragraph sounds a bit like a sermon. And I want to avoid preaching.]

The South has taught me many changes. I have exchanged cheeses and red meat for pecans and seafood. I have learned to fear driving in the blinding rain the way I used to fear the blinding snow. I have learned to call the kids inside on hot summer afternoons the way I used to call them in on frostbite cold days. My garage here has had to replace my basement and attic for storage of special treasures. And I have learned to steel myself after an evening in air-conditioning ~~or late-night meetings movie~~ for the wet blanket slap of hot humidity. ~~Not for the late evening's coolness~~

The South, too, has taught me its rewards. Without a state income tax, my possibilities for a tax audit are halved! ~~Here every woman has the title Ms. Miz sounds like Ms. without having to join the woman's liberation movement~~ Here, no woman has to become a woman's libber to win the verbal title Ms. The changing of the leaves lasts from late October through Christmas. In any weekend there is a rummage sale within blocks. And to satisfy my love of antiques, the oldest city in the U.S. sits just 25 miles from my front door.

~~Yes, for all these reasons I like where I live~~

[I'm attempting an ending now and hope that it will be a simple one, a simple return to the title of the piece. But this one-line ending was too abrupt and too short. So I try concluding again.]

But most of all, I like it here in spring. For then the colors and smells of the North and West meet here in the South, and no one can be lonesome. Here are crocus and tulips and daffodils of the North; and dogwood and wisteria, peach, azaleas, and citrus of the South; and the plum and apple and rose blooms that smell of almost anywhere.

[I try to say the same ending again, but in fewer words.]

For ~~then the~~ North and ~~the~~ East, and the West meet here in the South in the glorious smells and colors of spring and no one can be lonesome. ~~For the North and~~ Here are crocus and tulips and daffodils and dogwood, wisteria and azaleas, peach and plum, apple and citrus and roses! Everyone from anywhere ~~else can never be lonesome in those~~ in the states can find a home here.

[The images of the seasons could stand for my hope of experiencing together-ness, just as the swing image had opened the piece.]

I had written all the way through the essay once and felt relieved. The ending had come to me as I'd expected it might. I knew now the shape of the essay—how it would begin and end and how the pieces of the essay would look and fit together. I was pleased so far.

But the first draft was only the beginning. I needed to do a second draft, polish the wording, rearrange some ideas so my points would be clearer, and add some ideas I had not included yet.

Draft 2

To begin this draft, I checked my lists of supporting information to figure out what I'd left out and to decide whether I needed those points.

After careful checking, I realized I had not mentioned several items that could add to the impact of the paper. I had omitted but still wanted to add:

I had exchanged:

hi	for	*hey*
drive-ins for only food and banking	for	drive-ins for liquor, too
barbecued beef	for	beef and barbecue on the side
corn roasts	for	oyster roasts
popcorn	for	okra
"white as a sheet"	for	"white as a sheet of cotton
wind chill factor	for	"bring in your plants and pets"
garden soil	for	garden sand
soft grass	for	tough St. Augustine creepers

I was ready to rewrite the second draft with two main goals: (1) to use the rest of these ideas and (2) to work for a clearer ending.

First, I wrote the paragraph that added the information I had left out of the first draft.

> Before moving here I did not know that "Hey" was not an insult, but could mean "Hi"; that drive-in windows were for liquor, too, not just for fast foods and banking; that women could dress up without wearing nylons; that barbecued beef could be beef with the barbecue on the side; that oyster roasts could be more fun than corn roasts; that okra could taste like popcorn; that in this city with all of its water, a lot on the St. John's River could sell for a quarter of a million dollars. I have heard "white as a sheet" embellished into "white as a sheet of cotton" and the freeze warnings stated as "Bring in your pets and your plants." Sand in the garden is soil; St. Augustine creepers are grass.

[After I proofread the new paragraph, I decided to insert it into the essay above my ending. So it fit right after the paragraph about the tax audits, the Ms. title, the changing of the leaves, rummage sales, and the oldest city in the United States.

Then I looked at my ending. It seemed much too short. I reworded it several more times.]

~~I did not know these things nor did I know that the changing of the leaves could last from late October until Christmas.~~

[I did not like this shorter ending. I returned instead to the theme of learning.]

I did not know that in the beauty of a Jacksonville spring, no one could be ~~I would be no longer~~ lonesome. Here bloom together the crocus, tulip and daffodil of the North and the dogwood and azalea of the South. The fruit trees—peach, plum, apple, orange and the rest of the citrus—perfume even the highways with scents of home. In all this, the roses bloom. I found a home here in the Southern spring just as did the crocus, tulips and daffodils that grew up beside my porch swing.

[This ending was more personal but still did not express my feelings. My ending needed to be more positive and apply to people in the South beyond just Jacksonville. So I tried to simplify the scene more positively. Also, I tried to wind the piece back to the beginning by mentioning the swing. More important, I needed to return to the theme of learning.]

I did not know that I would love it here—here where the Southern spring with the sun and the beach are free and the crocus and tulips and daffodils grow up beside my porch swing, here where the simple experiences other people take for granted teach me to be Southern.

[I was satisfied now that this draft used the pertinent supporting information on my early lists and organized that information to appeal to my audience and achieve my purpose. Now it was time for me to make the last decision.]

Writer's Decision VI: The Right Word

Before I made this last decision, I let my essay cool; I did not look at it for forty-eight hours. After that time, I could read it more objectively because the wording wasn't as familiar to me as it had been right after I'd written it.

During this reading, I had to decide whether the wording was right. Did I say exactly what I meant? Would the essay create the images and feelings I hoped it would? What could I say that might surprise the readers? Would I make them smile and remember what it was like to move here?

During this third revision, while I had these questions in the back of my head, I also had to check for spelling, punctuation, mechanics, grammar, and coherence.

Draft 3

This is a copy of my last draft, the one I sent to the paper for its column called "Why I Love Where I Live." You will note many changes of wording if you compare the early drafts to it.

Why I Love Where I Live

Yesterday on my porch, I discovered something which every Southerner probably knows. Sitting in my iron-laced swing in the flat heat of the 95° summer afternoon, I could, with one small motion of my toes move through the air and create a breeze better than that of any ceiling fan. Feeling that coolness in that hot afternoon, I understood a bit of the place of a porch and a swing in my new home—a Southern home.

That is why I like it here. I'm learning so much. You see, Jacksonville and the South became my home less than a year ago. Previously, in Wisconsin, the snowdrifts in the alley could top my twenty foot pine tree. And believe it or not, snow piling high and deep is one of my fondest memories. So I didn't expect to like it here. But I do. Let me tell you why.

The nature described in the great Southern novels has become the spring and summer of my new neighborhood. The magnolia across the street blossoms white and drops its hard, brown leaves. The chinaberry tree shades my kitchen window, and the azalea bushes turn completely pink. Mint for mint juleps grows wild in my flower beds. Nearby in Mandarin, the great oaks drip moss and cover whole reaches of the road. My neighbors walk between their border grass and contemplate their white wisteria. A mockingbird sings in our tree.

I like it here because I don't have to weed dandelions anymore or risk putting up six foot tall windows on the second story in the burly, November wind. Here, shrimp cocktails made from four, fat shrimp don't cost $8.50. The IRS, without a Florida income tax, can audit me only half as often. And to win the verbal title "Ms.," I don't have to be a woman's libber.

I have exchanged Wisconsin cheeses and red meat for pecans and seafood. I call the kids inside on hot, summer afternoons the way we used to call them inside on frost-biting, cold days. I have learned to fear driving in the blinding rain as I used to fear the blinding snow. I know how to steel myself after an evening movie for the wet-blanket slap of hot humidity. I eat a softer, sweeter lobster and grow vegetables in raised rows. Here the question, "What shall we do this afternoon?" always has an answer: "Go to the beach."

Before moving here, I did not know that "Hey" was not an insult, but could mean "Hi"; that drive-in windows were for liquor, too, not just for fast foods and banking; that women could dress up without wearing nylons; that barbecued beef could be beef with the barbecue on the side; that oyster roasts could be more fun than corn roasts; that okra could taste like popcorn; that in this city with all of its water, a lot on the St. John's River could sell for a quarter of a million dollars.

I have heard "white as a sheet" embellished into "white as a sheet of cotton" and the freeze warning stated as "Bring in your plants and your pets."

Here the sand in the garden is really soil; St. Augustine creepers are grass. And the changing of the leaves in my front yard can last from late October until Christmas.

I did not understand these things before I came, nor did I know that I would love it here—here where the sun and the beach are free and the crocuses and tulips and daffodils grow up beside my porch swing, here where the ordinary experiences other people take for granted teach me to be Southern.

WRITING TASKS

1. Write an essay. Make all the decisions writers must make. Use this chapter as your model as you write.

2. Write an essay in which you describe the ways you make all the decisions writers must make. Use one of your papers as your example.

3. This writing task will challenge you. Write an essay on the topic "Why I Love Where I Live" or "Why I Do Not Love Where I Live." Instead of just writing the essay, think about each step, each decision you make, and record what you are thinking and deciding as you work. In other words, write a description of *how* you are writing the essay *as* you write the essay. You might follow the examples in this chapter and do as I did to explain all the steps I took writing my essay.

   You will accumulate twice as much paper before you are finished because you will not only be writing the essay, but you will be stopping often and commenting on how you are deciding to do what you are doing. Be sure to explain how you make each decision writers make as well as how and why you accomplish each change or addition to your drafts. Hand in both your final draft of the essay as well as all the working papers which describe and show how you create the essay. Why do this extra work? You can learn so much about your own writing style and thought process if you watch yourself work.

assessing your writing

Techniques for Self Assessments and Peer Responses

Introduction

Once you've finished making all the decisions a writer makes, you may wonder how well you've written a piece. These two chapters help you evaluate your success.

Chapter 21—Your Self-Assessment

> *Techniques for doing an assessment of your own work. Learn the questions to ask yourself. Try this self-assessment on each important piece of writing.*

Chapter 22—Techniques for Giving Helpful Peer Responses

> *Specific strategies for peer readers, peer responders, peer editors, and peer tutors. Peers can use these many different ways to help each other improve writing. Some techniques are simple, some more profound.*

Name _____

Section _____

Self-assessment—Long Form _____

1. What are the strengths of your paper?

2. Underline any sections or words that you especially like.

3. What are the weaknesses of your paper?

4. Put a question mark over any part where you are unsure—punctuation, grammar, mechanics, word choice, arrangement of ideas, or anything else you're not sure about. In the margin of your paper, explain your question.

5. How much time did you spend on the paper?

6. Describe the way you went about writing this paper. What, if anything, would you do differently if you could begin again?

7. What will you do to improve your writing next time?

8. How did you try to experiment with this paper? How successful were you? What questions do you have about what you tried?

9. How has your writing changed since the course began?

10. Perhaps you would like more information about some aspect of writing? What would you like to know?

What to Avoid

- Avoid vague, general answers. Statements like "I need to try harder next time" won't help you mature as a writer. Instead, use a specific statement, such as "I wrote only two examples to make my point. Two probably aren't enough to convince my reader. I need to use perhaps five or six."

- Avoid thinking everything is perfect. Almost all writers, no matter how famous or excellent, realize that their writing could be improved. So don't be afraid to point out your own rough spots.

Name _____

Section _____

SELF-ASSESSMENT—SHORT FORM _____

1. What are the strengths of your paper?

2. Underline any sections or words that you especially like.

3. What are the weaknesses of your paper?

4. Put a question mark over any part where you are unsure—punctuation, grammar, mechanics, word choice, arrangement of ideas, or anything else you're not sure about. In the margin of your paper, near the question mark, explain your question.

5. What steps did you take to improve the paper? How successful were you? What questions do you have about what you tried?

6. Describe the way you went about writing this paper.

7. How much time did you spend on the paper?

What to Avoid

- Avoid vague, general answers. Statements like "I need to try harder next time" won't help you mature as a writer. Instead, use a specific statement, such as "I wrote only two examples to make my point. Two probably aren't enough to convince my reader. I need to use perhaps five or six."
- Avoid thinking everything is perfect. Almost all writers, no matter how famous or excellent, realize that their writing could be improved. So don't be afraid to point out your own rough spots.

Chapter Twenty-Two
Techniques for Giving Helpful Peer Responses

Are you the type of shopper who takes a friend along to see how new clothes look before you spend money? Would you buy a used car alone, or would you first get someone else's opinion of it?

What do second opinions have to do with fine writing? Well in writing, too, hearing another opinion often helps you make good choices. Because your peers can help you as you become a better writer, ask for responses from them at any stage of the writing process, from your first decisions about subjects through decisions on your last draft.

This chapter offers many techniques for peer readers, peer editors, and peer tutors. With these strategies, you can help each other improve at any phase of the writing process. So use these techniques whenever you respond to each other's writing.

Why Not Go Alone?

Here are reasons why you ought not to go alone.

- Hearing others respond to your writing will help you build a sense of your audience. You hear how your readers react, what makes them laugh, where they are confused. You won't have to guess at these things. The audience's reaction will guide what you say and how you say it.

- You will receive an assessment of your writing before it is evaluated by the instructor.

- Hearing others' papers and responding to them can often help you recognize your own strengths and weaknesses. Sometimes, by comparing others' papers with your own, you will see what you might do to improve your own writing.

- Being a peer reader gives you some responsibility for others' papers. Because we cannot exist by ourselves, it is important to work with others to learn and improve together.

- Sometimes you will get contradictory advice from your peers. After weighing it, you will have to make the final decision; this will give you practice as evaluator and decision maker.

- You will develop confidence in your ability to follow others' suggestions for improvement. This confidence is important, especially when you agree with the audience's reaction but don't know what to change or how to change what you have written.

- Watching your instructor and other students will teach you how to help others. Use that knowledge as you confer with other students. The plus for you is that you will improve the quality of your own conferences with the instructor.

- You will develop a critical sense of what works and what does not. You will become a more discriminating reader. The end result is that your own writing will improve.

- As a bonus, you will learn new information from your fellow students, especially if your instructor encourages writing about personal interests. The experts in your group can teach you. (From student essays, I've saved hundreds of dollars and learned about ideas I never would have known.)

Clues to Effective Peer Work

In the beginning, you might feel uncomfortable or nervous about your ability to help someone else. One student expressed his feeling, "I feel like the blind leading the blind." Most people feel the same way. Just try your best, be honest, and you will be helpful. Every writer needs feedback from an audience. That is a gift you can offer the writer. Use the following clues every time you respond.

- Never say anything you wouldn't be able to take yourself.

- Be supportive. Encourage rather than discourage.

- Always say what is well done. Even if you must search for it, always make a positive statement.

- Treat other people's ideas reverently. If you are honest, you will realize that letting other people see what one thinks takes much courage. Ideas may be extremely personal or revealing. Sharing your mind is not as simple as sharing a sandwich.

- Make suggestions. Be specific so your fellow student knows exactly what you mean.

- Don't rewrite the other's paper unless your instructor tells you to do so. Your job is to ask questions, point out problems and offer suggestions for change.

- If you know a great deal more than the student whose paper you are editing, be careful not to overwhelm that student with your suggestions. Just point out the most obvious problems. Students learn through encouragement and taking positive steps. Help them.

- You may sometimes know exactly what to point out. Good. At other times you may not be sure. If something seems not quite right, but you cannot say why, at least be honest and tell the writer. Perhaps together you can figure out a solution to the problem.

- Learn from each other.

SUGGESTIONS FOR BEGINNING PEER WORK

Beginning is like holding your nose and jumping into the shocking, cold water. But go ahead because peer responding can be your important tool for learning. Here are many ways to begin. Use these strategies as you *begin* peer work in large or small groups.

Demonstrate Helpful Responses

You might begin by a demonstration of helpful responses in a large group. A student author reads a paper. The entire class listens as the teacher demonstrates helpful responses to the paper as if the student and teacher are having a conference.

Keep a record of the teacher's helpful comments. Observe the leading questions that help the writer know how to improve. Observe techniques that make the student reflect on why certain decisions work and whether those decisions are the best.

Ask the instructor to demonstrate with several students and their papers until the listeners believe that they can manage helpful responding by themselves.

By patterning their own conferences after these conferences, students can learn to hold helpful sessions with each other.

That's Good!

At first, to help students feel comfortable about sharing their papers, all responses from peers can be positive.

One person reads a paper. All the reactions to the paper from peers must be positive. Only if the writer asks for suggestions, may the audience offer them.

How does this approach help students? The positive responses reinforce the good. If something is not mentioned, the writer might assume it does not work. In the beginning, positive reinforcement reduces fears of inexperienced students.

See the Center

A fast reaction to the paper points out the center, the crux of the piece. To use this strategy, the audience reads the paper and then repeats what the paper says, but in just one sentence. The author can read the paper to peers or provide copies.

HINT: That one sentence should point out the main idea or insight, the author's feelings, and the mood of the piece. Write the sentence.

The goal is to find out if the author and the listener agree. If both agree, the paper is on the right track. If they differ, the listeners should tell the author why. The author can use these different reactions to change the paper.

Give a Three-Part Response

This method works well. In a letter or orally, tell the author three points:

1. The best part of the paper

2. The part needing improvement

3. Specific suggestions for improvement

Silent Authors

In a group, one person reads aloud a paper belonging to someone else in the group. A second person keeps notes of the discussion of the paper so the author will have a record later. The author, the third person in the group, simply listens.

By paying close attention to the reading, the author will hear where the reader stumbles because of a problem in the writing and the author can repair the sentences later. Also, the silent author can hear people react to the paper without needing to answer or defend it.

MORE CONFIDENT? TRY THESE PLANS FOR PEER WORK _____

Use these strategies for peer work when you are more confident as a peer responder or if you are ready for more sophisticated responses.

Ask Questions: What Was That?

One person in a group reads his or her own paper.

Before reading, the author describes the intended audience, purpose and writing voice. The listeners should pretend to be that intended audience. As the author reads, any of the listeners may stop the reader anytime with a question to let the writer know when something is unclear. The author does not have to answer the question unless he or she chooses to do so.

Someone in the group keeps a record of all the questions and gives them to the author at the end of the reading.

Write a Letter to the Author

After reading a student's paper, instead of talking, write a letter to the author. Be personal in the letter. Explain how you reacted to the paper and why you reacted that way. Be helpful so the author knows how to rework the piece. Ask questions about parts you don't understand completely. Be supportive. Be as specific as you can. It won't be much help if all you say is, "I liked your paper. I agree with you. Keep up the good work."

After you write the letter, deliver it to the author. If you are there when the author reads your letter, you may wish to talk about the paper.

Ask to see the paper after it is revised. After you read the revision, you may want to write a second letter.

Hear the Author

One author presents the strengths and problems with his or her own paper to the group. This explanation can precede or follow the author's reading of the paper. The group helps the author solve his or her problems.

The Editor Says

Be an editor. Mark up the author's paper with your questions and comments. If possible, write on photo copies of the original.

To be helpful, your comments should be exact and specific. Explain instead of using vague words like *good* or *awkward* or statements like "I don't get this." If you don't get something, explain why you don't get it. If you are confused, say what confuses you. If you need more proof or more examples, say so. To be useful, your comments must be meaningful to the paper's author. Be as helpful as you can.

The following are some variations to use when you edit each other's work. Choose the variation that works best.

- Have several editors in sequence write their comments on the same photo copy, each with different colored ink. Editors then have the benefit of seeing what others thought and adding to the cumulative comments. Each editor should sign the paper in his or her colored ink so the writer knows whom to ask if there are questions.

- Make several copies of the same paper. Have several students edit their own copy of the paper without seeing the reactions of other editors. All the edited copies are returned to the writer who then decides which advice to take.

- Work out an editing chain. After a paper is written, edit it. After the paper is revised, edit it again. Rewrite again; edit it again. Go through the process as often as necessary.

Follow the Author's Directions

If a paper explains how to do something, actually follow the directions it gives. Have the author read the paper aloud and watch you do what it says. If you ask any questions, or if the author sees puzzlement on any of your faces, the author knows that that section of the paper needs revision.

According to a writer of manuals for IBM, IBM videotapes people who are trying to follow directions in their manuals. If people are upset or confused, the writer rewrites the directions in that manual.

Try this approach yourself. If you have access to a video camera, read your paper while the camera films your audience following your directions. It is a marvelous check.

The Narrative—And Then What?

If you have written a narrative, you may want to read it aloud to your audience. Audiences love stories, so if you have told your story well, you will have rapt attention. Try to vary your voice when you have more than one speaker.

Have the audience write down all their questions and comments as you read. They shouldn't interrupt you because that might break the mood. After you have finished, let each listener offer comments and questions.

Often, your story will be perfectly clear to you, but the audience can see places where you need to offer more background or more information. Ask them to tell you what happened. Ask them why a certain action happened. Ask if the beginning got their interest. Did the ending satisfy them? When did they know how the narrative would end?

Reflect on Your Helpfulness as a Peer Tutor

From reflection often comes awareness. So answer these questions after you complete a peer session:

1. Explain the strengths of your partner's paper.

2. Explain the problems in your partner's paper.

3. What specific recommendations did you make to your partner?

4. Which recommendations did your partner find most helpful?

5. Which recommendations did your partner find least helpful?

6. If you were to tutor this same person again, would you change any of your methods? Why?

Reflect on the Results of Your Peer Work

If you reflect on an experience, you often learn more than if you do not reflect. So after you have worked with a fellow student, answer the following questions.

1. What have you learned from your partner's paper that will help you in your own writing? If you learned little, explain why the paper has not been helpful.

2. Have you learned from your partner's instructional explanations? If so, explain. Explain how your partner could improve as your tutor.

Use the Checklist for Peer Readers

Respond to the questions on this checklist *until* you reach the area (topic, supporting information, audience, and so forth) where you judge that the student's paper is having trouble. Answer questions up to and including the troublesome area and then return the paper to the author. After the author's revision, you can use this checklist again.

Sometimes the student author may ask the peer reader to use a certain section of the checklist. Write out your answers to the checklist for the author whose paper you are reading.

Use the entire checklist only if a student's paper has gone through several revisions, or if it is late in the course.

Topic:

_____ 1. What is the writer's topic?

_____ 2. Does the writer stick with the topic? If not, where is the problem?

_____ 3. Is the topic small enough to be developed in the writing space?

_____ 4. What suggestions about the topic would you offer the writer?

Supporting Information:

_____ 5. Is there enough information to convince you?

_____ 6. What other information do you think is needed?

_____ 7. Where might the new information be added?

_____ 8. Are facts present in the paper? Enough? Too many?

_____ 9. Are enough minor inferences which support topic sentences present in the paper?

_____ 10. If the writer uses sources, are these sources given credit?

_____ 11. Make any other suggestions about the supporting information.

Audience, Purpose, Writer's Voice:

_____ 12. Who is the audience?

_____ 13. How might the audience be more noticed?

_____ 14. What is the purpose?

_____ 15. How might the purpose be strengthened?

_____ 16. Describe the writer's voice.

_____ 17. How might the voice be improved?

Organization:

_____ 18. What organizations does the author use?

_____ 19. What might the author do to improve the organization?

_____ 20. What is the main-idea sentence (thesis in a long paper, topic sentence if the piece is a single paragraph)? Is it an inference rather than a fact? Does it clearly point out the content and the structure in the paper? How might it be strengthened?

_____ 21. Does the beginning catch your attention? What else might the author do with the beginning?

_____ 22. Does the ending fit? Were you prepared for it? How could the ending be improved?

_____ 23. What else would you like to see the writer do in the paper?

Revision:

_____ 24. When you compare the rough drafts to each other, what major changes do you see?

_____ 25. If the author made few changes, what else might you recommend?

_____ 26. Sometimes a good idea gets lost in the revision. Do you see any of these lost ideas that you would recommend the author keep in the final paper?

Editing:

_____ 27. Are all the sentences complete sentences? Where are the errors?

_____ 28. Did you find any run-on sentences? Which ones?

_____ 29. What grammatical mistakes need fixing?

_____ 30. Where is the punctuation confusing? Incorrect?

_____ 31. What words are used incorrectly?

_____ 32. What words need to be spelled correctly?

_____ 33. What capitals need to be checked?

Diction:

____ 34. What wording surprised you? Did the surprise work well?

____ 35. Is the author too brief? Too wordy? Where?

____ 36. What images did you find?

____ 37. Is the wording clear? What is unclear?

____ 38. Do the vocabulary and sentence structure match the author's intended voice? Purpose? Audience? Where might there be problems?

____ 39. Which clichés did you find?

____ 40. Did the author use a variety of sentence beginnings?

____ 41. What was the number of words in the longest sentence? The shortest sentence?

____ 42. Did you feel a rhythm as you read the paper? Describe it for the author.

Note on Grading:

Some instructors will give you a grade for your peer responses. Instructors may ask that copies be kept of all the written comments you have made. Here are some ways comments are graded:

- By the peer responder's commitment to help
- By improvement the student made as a helpful editor
- By the thoroughness and perception of the editor's comments
- By the range of comments offered

Part II

Writing Projects

Chapter Twenty-Three

Describe It

Tell your reader how something looks, smells, tastes, feels, and sounds, and you're describing. Some people think this is the easiest way to begin writing because you already have the facts in front of you in the person or scene you want to describe.

Look out any window. Tell what you see, and you are describing. Look anywhere (even into your closet) and say what you see, and you are describing. The hard part is putting the right words on paper so your reader sees or hears or smells or tastes the way you want. Describing well calls for some techniques.

To make your readers see what you see, establish a dominant impression. You might want them to see how the closet is cluttered or how dreary the view from your window is. Everything in your description must contribute to that impression of clutter or dreariness. Because you cannot possibly say everything, you must limit yourself to the details that create that feeling. This limitation gives readers a focus.

Another way to focus is to establish a point from which to see. If you describe the closet, your focus might be what you see from the doorway as you prepare to clean it. Write details you would notice from that viewpoint. If you describe what you see out your window, choose the dreariest point and then relate everything to it. I remember the night a gang burned a car outside my window in Chicago. The next morning, the burned-out Toyota frame would have been a fine place from which to focus the entire dreary scene—empty parking lot with oil stains, newspapers and plastic cups trashed along the curbs, gray brick walls of high-rise buildings on three sides of the parking lot, and no trees or grass or birds.

In most writing, description doesn't exist by itself. Usually a reader wants to know the reason people look or act the way they do. If I wrote about the burned-out car in the ugly parking lot, I'd probably explain why the gang burned the car. Otherwise, many readers wouldn't care about the description.

In the following piece the author doesn't stop with a description of Old Sour Pickle. He uses Pickle to reflect on himself, and by comparing himself to Pickle, describes his relationships with his own boys.

Like Old Sour Pickle

by Robert B. Gentry

Every time I get the urge to roughhouse with my teenage boys I think of "Old Sour Pickle." That's the name we kids teased him with.

"Haw! Haw! Haw!" Sour Pickle'd horselaugh. "Ain't none of you pipsqueaks gonna stay on this here bull!"

Then he'd swagger about in his front yard until he'd get a bunch of us to take him up on his dare. He'd let out another horse laugh, beat his chest with big ham fists, and fall down on all fours—all six-foot five, 260 pounds of him. Soon he was scuffing and kicking and humping around on the ground just like a bull. But have you ever seen a bull with a cigar stuck in his mouth? Well, Old Pickle kept chomping on a smoking butt until it looked as if it'd been mashed in his buck teeth.

Usually I was the first to hit his back, and whoa-uh, I'd be off as fast as I was on. One by one, Old Pickle would shake us kids off like fleas. One time he let eight of us pile on his back. He smelled like a dead cigar. In no time he had us rolling all over the yard.

Pickle was 30 then and had a rock-hard body from construction work. I'm 50 now and in average shape, according to my doctor.

The trouble is, when I start horsing around with my boys, I think I'm Old Sour Pickle. It's my chance to be a boy again. I've been playing bull with my boys since they were tots, but here lately I haven't held up so well. For one thing, I can't shake either boy off. I strain and crawl and my knees get raw. I heave and hump once or twice, then frump! I collapse flat on the floor like a load of sodden pancakes. It finally took fourteen of us kids to flatten Old Sour Pickle. But of course I'm much older and many pounds lighter now than Pickle was then. Excuses! Excuses!

The other day I leaped to another challenge, a water balloon fight. It was Brannon (my youngest) and I against Mark (my oldest) and Tom (Brannon's friend). If I couldn't be Pickle on the ground, I'd be Pickle on the roof. I'd be more mobile and agile.

"To the roof!" I told Brannon. "We'll ambush the clods and turn 'em into drowned dogs." So we threw up a ladder while Mark and Tom were in the backyard counting to 100. Either they cut short their count or I was awfully slow climbing because by the time I got to the top rung of the ladder, I was getting pelted with all kinds of water missiles while Brannon tried vainly to cover me. Up the roof we were trying to regroup when I slipped and almost rolled off the darn thing. Drenched and beaten, I finally climbed down with a big, painful strawberry on my hip.

You'd think I'd had enough, but oh no! Next it was a sock fight. Brannon and I held our own for awhile, until smack! A triple sock wad bashed me in the eye, and I saw stars and fireworks. The pain soon went away and I thought the eye was fine. I thought I could take the kind of blow old Pickle took.

But later I blew my nose, and the eye puffed up like a frog's throat when he's in heat.

"Get me to emergency!" I screamed to my wife. "It's a blood clot going right to my brain!" The trauma team met us at the hospital door. In seconds they found the cause of the puff: air, not blood. The blow had cracked a sinus. My fate would have cracked Pickle up.

And so it goes for this old dad who, like Old Sour Pickle, loves to be a crazy kid again. But I guess I'll just have to be content being young in the head because my body won't retreat one second in time. In fact, with all the aches and pains I've been having lately, I'm beginning to think my body wants to jump ahead and be seventy just as fast as it can. That would put it about as old as Sour Pickle is now, that is if he's still around and not in his grave from playing too much bull.

Besides describing Old Sour Pickle and comparing himself to Pickle, the narrator describes how he handles growing older. So the description does much more than merely tell us what Pickle looked like and how he acted. The writer gives us a reason for reading about Sour Pickle.

Here is another description. Notice how Catherine Bussey wants you to understand more than just the physical description of her main character.

Grandmother Sarah

by Catherine Bussey

"No matter what you say or do, you are creating a lasting memory for some-one." To this day, I have vivid memories of my Grandmother Sarah, who came to live with my family and me when I was ten years old. Most of the families on our long street had a resident, widowed grandmother. But, of course, mine was special.

Physically, Grandmother Sarah may not have been an impressive looking woman, but only to the most casual observer. She was small, five foot two inches tall, and weighed about a hundred pounds. She had snow white hair which she combed back away from her face. She would gather the long strands in her small work-worn hands and twist them into a tight bun at the nape of her neck. The bun would be firmly anchored into place by the tortoise-shell hairpins that she shoved in it at random. Her prominent nose was a handy resting place for her rimless, bifocal glasses, which she was constantly adjusting. Her lips were thin and straight, and it seemed to me that her mouth never got the message from her brain that it was all right to smile. I was not aware that my Grandmother had a severe heart condition (I have not been told yet, nor have I asked) which caused her constant pain. My Mother would speak later of Grandmother's "poor" heart. I never gave a thought, then, to my Grandmother's age. To me, she was ageless.

I was excited by the prospect of getting to know my Grandmother better. The brief visits to her home in the Kentucky mountain area always left me longing for more of her companionship. In her quiet way, she communicated her love for me. She would leave the lamp burning on the table beside the bed because she knew I would be frightened during the night should I happen to awaken and forget where I was and why I was not in my own bed at home. At breakfast each morning, she would heap globs of homemade jam on my biscuit and drown it with the sweet, sticky, delicious mess that oozed into my mouth.

So when she came to live with us, Grandmother Sarah and I had already established our own form of non-verbal exchange of love. She brought into my young life a peace that said, "I want no more from you than you are willing to give; I make no demands on your emotions."

My Mother's words about creating memories, I feel, are true because the memories of Grandmother Sarah are with me every day of my life. I remember her slow saunter, and I even can recall the way her blue eyes seemed to shine with keen interest when we got the mail from our box and handed it to her. She lived for the letters she received from her other daughters.

Grandmother had her stiffness, or, as she called it, "starch in the spine." She was as frugal with words as she was with money. She would never join the rest of the family when we were having one of our many loud debates. She would sit in her rocking chair and move it back and forth in that quiet motion she had that said loudly, "You all are being stupid for no reason, if there can be a reason for being stupid."

When Grandmother Sarah did choose to speak, she had my full attention. After dinner each evening, I had a habit of plopping my school books down on the top of the library table. I would scrape my chair across the hardwood floor and lower my skinny frame onto the seat. All these moves were designed to inform those around me that I would rather be doing anything but what I had to do, namely, my homework. There were usually three or four books in front of me, and I would take my time deciding which subject I would attack first. It was my private war, and I felt each subject was a battle. I could feel my grandmother's eyes on me just as physically as if she had tapped me on the shoulder. "Girl," she said as I looked up, "when you are pondering a problem, write it down. Then list all the reasons you can in favor of a path you want to take toward solving your problem. List all the reasons you can for not walking the path."

"Grandmother Sarah, that will take too much of my time; I am a busy person," I replied with all the aplomb of a ten-year-old. She was asking too much, I thought.

Her reply was simply stated: "Time allotted is strictly your business."

Now, I had not lived ten years without learning that adults did know a few shortcuts in life. So, I reached for my spiral notebook, wrote out my problem, and made the list: "for" and "against," as she had suggested. I was surprised at the ease with which my pencil glided across the page filling it with my thoughts.

Some time later in the week, I realized I was doing my homework without the usual delay tactics. I wanted to write in my notebook before bedtime. I was still following Grandmother's suggested pattern, but I had added my own helpful notations. The month, day and year in the upper right corner would give me a timeframe for a problem. I was not just writing about problems, but I had expanded my daily notations to include observations also. Though I was unaware of it then, my first daily journal was born.

My memories of Grandmother Sarah are helped by the pictures of her in my family album. Her unsmiling face looks back at me from the lifeless photographs. Not so on the pages of my journal. She is alive, and her facial expressions, her movements around the house as she was going about her day are just as keen for me now as they were years ago when she lived with us.

"Like Old Sour Pickle" and "Grandmother Sarah" are descriptions of people. This next essay describes the scene of a car accident from the driver's point of view. If you have ever been in an accident, imagine describing it so others will experience it with you.

The Awakening

by Matt Conklin

It was five in the morning by the time I dropped my friend at his home in the Jacksonville Beach area. I had quite a long drive ahead of me, so being the good friend that he was, he gave me a couple of his beers to keep me entertained on the way home. I cracked opened one of the icy cold beers and began my twenty-five mile drive toward my home in San Marco.

J-Turner-Butler was my chosen route to my house. The long stretch of highway, completely void of traffic, beckoned to me to test the limits of my Honda Civic.

The lights on the road, flying by me in blurred streaks of color, and the monotonous hum of my car's engine put me in a trance. I started to feel extremely tired so I sped up, eager to be asleep in my bed. I rubbed my eyes, finished the beer and pressed on, speeding down the highway. As I drove, I began to feel even more tired; the loud music blaring from my stereo began to fade away, and my eyelids, which seemed to weigh a ton, slowly shut as I drifted off to sleep.

I awoke from my slumber to an explosion of steel intertwining with concrete. My first thought as I awoke was that I had just been hit in the face with a baseball bat.

After a moment of deliriousness, I realized that I had not been hit in the face with a bat, but my face had hit the steering wheel. My tooth had been knocked out; my collar bone felt broken. My instinctual reaction to the pain was to bring my hands to my face. This only caused more pain. My windshield had shattered on impact. The fragments of glass had embedded themselves in every area of my exposed skin. The glass fragments were like miniature razors cutting my face, and, as I touched my face, I pressed these razors deeper, sending waves of pain throughout my body. Thin streams of blood were flowing profusely out of my cheeks and hands, causing me to feel faint.

I wanted to get out of my car, but it had caved in on me, trapping me inside. I sat perfectly still in my self-induced prison. Movement was impossible; my leg was pinned under the collapsed dash. My leg, broken at the knee, was throbbing with pain. I wanted to scream, but there was no one to hear me.

I carefully cleared the blood flowing from my forehead into my eyes and cleared my vision. I was not ready for what I saw. My car's engine had made its way through the car's fire wall and had displaced the center console, forced through by the three-foot-wide concrete telephone pole. As I turned my aching head, I noticed what had made its way out of the car's hatchback and into the front seat: a cooler that had been filled with beer earlier that night. I tried to look outside of my car, but the hood had been pushed up blocking my view through the gaping hole where the windshield used to be, and the only view out of my driver's side window was of the stars which had seemed so promising earlier that evening.

I sat in my car for awhile, awestruck by what happened. I don't know how long I sat there before I began to pass out due to the tremendous pain. As I drifted back off to sleep, I heard the distant sound of sirens from police cars. I sat there silent and still, half unconscious as the tears began to roll down my cheeks. I closed my tear-filled eyes wondering if, when I fell asleep again, I would wake up, or if my eyes would remain shut forever as had so many of my friends' eyes who had died in car accidents caused by drunk driving.

To describe well, show; don't tell. That means, instead of summarizing, list details. Without details, you won't have description. In fact, all good writing gives many, many details. They let your reader overhear and see through your eyes.

COLLABORATIVE LEARNING

1. Discuss "Like Old Sour Pickle." What physical details describe Sour Pickle? What details describe the *I* in the story? How are Old Sour Pickle and the *I*

narrator similar? How are they different? In what ways is this essay describing a man's mortality? After your discussion, record your answers.

2. Discuss "Grandmother Sarah." What details show her to you? What details help you understand the impressions made on the writer? How is the essay more than a description of the grandmother? Record your answers.

3. Discuss "The Awakening." How many meanings can you find for the title? Read aloud at least six descriptive lines that make you see or hear or feel the accident. What is the dominant impression of "The Awakening"?

4. In your writing group, write a description together. To begin, choose something from one of your wallets or purses to describe. Or you might choose a person you all know. Together, make a list of specific facts and details about the subject. At the start, don't worry about the order in your list. Just describe, do not summarize. (*Lovely, kind, handsome, silly* are summary words. Give the facts that make you call the person handsome or silly.) After listing details, decide on the dominant impressions you might emphasize. Organize your list of details so everything points up that impression. Choose and write your description for an appropriate audience, voice, and purpose. Use the worksheets at the end of this chapter to get your group started.

WRITING TASKS

1. You have seen people who remind you of yourself. Describe one such person. If you resemble each other physically, concentrate on the physical similarities. If you parallel each other some other way, focus on that resemblance. You might begin by saying, "So and so reminds me of myself because. . . ." List all the details that emphasize your similarity. Decide on your audience, purpose, and voice. Organize your list of details so it will convince your audience that you are similar. After several drafts, you will probably throw out the first line I gave you and write a paper along the lines of "Like Old Sour Pickle." Use pages 269–270.

2. Describe a special place. Close your eyes and imagine you are there again, or go there. What do you see? hear? smell? taste? feel? Why is the place so special? When you describe the place, make every image reinforce that idea and you'll have a dominant impression your readers will understand. Use pages 271–272.

3. Decide how you might use description in an explanation, a narrative, or an argument to improve a paper which you have already written. Revise the paper placing description where it will work for you.

4. Find a description you have enjoyed reading in a novel, advertisement, news story, essay, or textbook. Explain in writing why that description is so good.

Checklist for Your Description

Yes   *No*

____   ____   1. Did you describe specific facts and details instead of summarizing?

____   ____   2. Did you create a dominant impression, a focus and point of view you want readers to understand?

____   ____   3. After reading your description, can readers close their eyes and replay the entire scene?

Chapter Twenty-Four

Tell a Story

People like good stories. When you remember your life, certain events and people stand out. Special things have happened to you that have happened to no one else in the same way. Some things changed you. Because of all these experiences, you have stories in you.

As you grow close to someone, you want that person to understand you. Often you have to tell why you think or feel the way you do about certain things. The better you can explain, the more the other person will understand and accept.

I remember when I first moved to Florida from the snow country. We had little money. Christmastime came, and we had no snow; it didn't seem like Christmas. But at the least, I wanted a beautiful, fresh Christmas tree. (I thought that one might cost about double what I had paid up North.) Was I shocked to find out that I would have to pay seven or eight times more for the kind of tall, bushy tree I was used to! But even though we had little money, I wanted a real tree and needed to explain to my husband why a tree is important to me (he wanted to skip getting one). So I wrote a story telling of one Christmas tree and one special incident surrounding it. After my husband heard that story, he never again doubted that we needed a Christmas tree—a tall, bushy, natural tree. I had written a personal narrative, a story that helped someone understand me.

One reason to tell a story is to help someone understand you. Another reason is to entertain. Michael Solomon, a student, tells this moving tale that does both.

Out There

by Michael Solomon

"A lot of people go out there," I told my father as I loaded my mountain bike into the back of his pickup. "I just want to ride around."

He put his left hand on the cab of the pickup.

"The ground is so flat that you can ride for hundreds of miles in any direction," I insisted.

He kicked the dirt next to the front tire.

"Come on," I reiterated urgently. "Everyone is riding a bike out on the desert." Perhaps he had the right to be concerned; my grandfather had been lost in the wilds so many times.

We followed I-80 past the rusted copper smelteries and deserted beaches of the Great Salt Lake.

"The only reason people go this way is to get somewhere else," my father grumbled as he adjusted the knob on the radio.

Indeed, the Great Basin, which lies between Salt Lake City and the Sierra Nevada in California, is seldom anyone's destination. The extensive desert valleys of the basin usually provide nothing more than the discomfort and monotony that a traveler must endure in transit. After a few hours of driving, the distinctive lines that mark mountains, dry steam beds, and the delicate desert foliage are reduced to an endless brown haze. Even towns with such colorful names as Wells, Wendover, and Winnemucca are most often remembered as a urinal, a gas pump, and a couple of bucks in quarters swallowed by a one-armed bandit.

I was accustomed to taking off this way. As a child I accompanied my grandfather on his enigmatic excursions across southern Utah. We would drive for hours, eating occasionally from a box of Saltine crackers. Then, unexpectedly, at a point in the road indistinguishable from a thousand other points—without a wayside park or turnoff, not even a tree, stream, canyon, or any other geographical feature that would demand even the slightest investigation—my grandfather would stop, secure the car, and begin a trek up a hill or into a desert swell. He would cut across washes and gullies, avoiding anything that even resembled a trail or path. He made it a point to stand on every big rock and touch every tree. Occasionally he would bend over to collect a twig or a few common pebbles. The only provisions we carried consisted of our box of crackers and a bag of beef jerky.

When I returned home, often days later, my parents always demanded to know where we'd been. My grandfather would mumble vaguely about hills, cliffs, and some sticks he had found. This was never enough to satisfy my parents, however, and they would insist that I respond more specifically. Perplexed, the best answer I could give was, "Out there. We just went out there."

"Here!"

My father pulled to a stop on the shoulder of the road. He left the motor running and helped me lift my bike from the truckbed. As he drove away I could still hear the sugar-soft elevator music coming from his radio. It seemed to intensify the melancholy of the alkaline horizon that lay ahead.

I pushed my bike off the road and into the desert. Immediately I was discouraged by the soft white sand that made pedaling almost impossible. Having lived in Salt Lake City for most of my life, I'd assumed that the terrain would be as hard as the nearby Bonneville Salt Flats, where world speed records were set. I had envisioned an immense flat surface, like a frozen ocean, that would permit me to cycle freely in any direction.

I was not the first to be deceived by the Great Basin. Early settlers, in an effort to find a shortcut to California, were overwhelmed by the difficulties created by the loose sand and scarce water. For pioneers, like the ill-fated Donner party, the struggle across the basin sometimes led to death.

For more than two hours I pushed my bicycle toward the northwest, stopping now and then to empty the sand from my tennis shoes. By noon I'd managed to completely isolate myself from any sign of civilization. I rested for a moment by a mound of dirt and reflected on the harmony and solitude of the desert. Flavored with salt, the wind was almost as palpable as the sand beneath my feet. In the distance a sea gull darted like a white flame along a network of nameless mountains. "This is an incredibly dangerous place," I said to myself.

My grandfather rejected social and political institutions such as roads and paths, not so much because of an innate anarchistic tendency, but out of a genuine curiosity to know what lies in those spaces between the geographic markers that society deems significant. He would often sit on his front porch and contemplate a little outcrop of granite that protrudes from one of the high Wasatch Mountains surrounding Salt Lake City. "Bet nobody's ever been up there; we could be the first ones," he would say with a mysterious twitch in his left eye.

Once, during an attempt to circumvent a slab of quartz-studded rock on a mountain that overlooked the Salt Lake valley, he lost his footing. The fall crushed his leg and left him stranded in a gully full of landslide debris between two enormous rock walls. Since he never told anyone where he was going, it was two days before a rescue team could locate him. Using a helicopter and a complex network of ropes and pulleys, they were able to lift him from the mountain and transport him to the University of Utah Hospital. And as if the fall, the broken limb, and two nights on the mountain were not enough punishment, my grandfather was forced to undergo the humiliating chastisement of a young county deputy: "If you can't stay on the trails, stay at home."

After his fall my grandfather adapted a more subdued system of travel. He began to explore abandoned areas along roads, fences and ditches. He investigated alleys, wandered into construction areas, and even tried to climb into garbage dumpsters. More than once he was reported to the police. He was called a vagrant, an alcoholic, and a peeping Tom. One elderly woman even thought that he was a special agent of the Internal Revenue Service.

Like Don Quixote, who sallied forth not onto the provincial road but rather onto the open Castilian plain, my grandfather found an intense form of freedom as he deviated from the highway. Because this freedom ignores signs, fences, and barriers that are intended to give our movements direction, it's often perceived as a form of subversion. In Don Quixote's case they burned his books. My grandfather was treated differently. One evening my father called the family together. With a few all-encompassing words, he explained and resolved my grandfather's eccentricities. "He's senile," my father told us bluntly.

After two frustrating days of pushing my bicycle across the desert, I stopped under the midday sun. "This is absurd," I said to myself, "I don't even know what I'm trying to do."

I stripped off my clothes, sat down next to a wind-beaten sagebrush, and dug my hand into the dirt. Raising my fist above my head I let a small stream of it fall on my chest and thighs as if to legitimize my existence through some mystical rite.

"Nothing! Nothing!" I cried. "This is absurd, completely absurd." I was about to concede to myself that my father was right—Grandfather was crazy, and maybe I was, too. Then I looked up and noticed a trail of awkward tracks; there was a way back home if I chose to take it.

We don't know the details. Two weeks before we found his body, he must have discovered a manhole left open by a careless city maintenance man. It led to a network of concrete tunnels that form a storm-drainage system. We found him about three miles from home, washed up against an iron grid that prevents refuse from flowing into the canal leading to the Great Salt Lake. His clothes were wet and rotting. And in his pocket, mixed with sand and dirt, I found a few twigs, two stones, and a broken plastic-bottle cap—relics from unknown shrines, souvenirs from places where no one else had ever been.

Discussion Questions

1. Whom do you admire most: the grandfather or the father or the grandson? Why? Whom does the grandson admire more—his grandfather or his father? How do you know?

2. Michael Solomon's story both tells us about himself and entertains us. What did you learn about the narrator and his values? How is the story entertaining?

3. Solomon called his story "Out There." Where is "Out There"? It might be the Great Basin, it might be the outdoors, or "Out There" may be any place away

from civilization, any place off the beaten track. Perhaps "Out There" isn't a place at all, but a symbol for being different, doing the unaccepted, deviating from society's norms. Maybe "Out There" stands for things and ideas to be discovered. Do you have an "Out There"? Where is yours?

4. In a way, this essay fits the moving theme of "young man searches for the meaning of life." Did the narrator find meaning? How do you know? Use the story to explain your ideas.

Reasons for Writing a Personal Story

Why do marriages break up? Why are employees fired? The primary answer to both these questions is often the same: People cannot communicate. Kids often say, "I can't talk to my dad or mom" or "I can't get through to that teacher." The frustration may be expressed in other ways, but each person is saying, "We might talk together, but we don't really communicate."

Levels of Communication

There are several levels on which people communicate: chit-chat, facts, opinions, and feelings. Almost all people can talk on the easy levels of chit-chat and fact. But at the deeper levels, many people have greater difficulty communicating.

Chit-chat. People chit-chat to fill up time with little pleasantries.

Person one says, "Hi, how are you?" (Chit-chat)
Person two says, "I'm fine, and you?" (Chit-chat)

We verbally acknowledge that the other person exists; we expect only the obvious, typical responses that culture labels "polite small talk." This level of conversation reveals little.

Facts. Conversation that offers only factual information doesn't reveal much about the speaker.

"McDonald's restaurants sold over 50 billion hamburgers!" (Fact)
"Last night I saw a movie directed by Oliver Stone." (Fact)

People who are just getting to know each other may ask for such factual information: "Where do you go to school? The answer is a fact: "Piedmont Community College." "Are you married?" Factual answer: "No!" Communicating facts is often unsatisfying because facts reveal only a bit about a person. If you are on a date or meeting someone for the first time and are unhappy about the deadening, uninteresting conversation, try the next level of communication, opinions.

Opinions. Opinions offer insight into beliefs, positions, points of view, and openness to ideas.

"I think that Jane Fonda is one of the best female actors in film." (Opinion)

"Ronald Reagan should never have been elected President of the United States." (Opinion)

Opinions reveal how speakers think. Opinions can be discussed. People who share opinions have a deeper level of interpersonal understanding than those who exchange only factual information.

Feelings. Speaking about feelings demands knowledge of oneself as well as the ability to put that knowledge into words.

"The holidays make me sad because they remind me of how much my mother and stepfather argue." (Feelings)

"I'm afraid to fly in commercial airplanes because I must give control to other people." (Feelings)

When people feel they do not communicate, they usually do not function very well at this level of feelings. People are uncomfortable, and sometimes incapable of, expressing how they feel.

Our society used to tell men not to express their feelings. Men, on the average, die younger than women. Because many men keep their feelings and tensions bottled up, their stress can create negative physical effects.

Communication and the Personal Narrative

In the personal narrative, the writer goes beyond mere fact and opinion to explain the way an experience made the writer or other characters feel. The personal narrative communicates not only an event but also the feelings created by that event and the event's significance. So someone who reads a personal narrative can understand how the event affected the participants.

Elements of the Personal Narrative

In a narrative, a writer works with all the elements of a story: characters, a plot, a setting (where and when something happened), and a theme (the meaning or significance of what happened). Usually, the more powerful the theme, the better the piece might be.

Characters. A good writer creates believable and interesting characters. To make them fascinating, the reader must be able to see what they looked like, hear what they said, see how they acted, and watch little mannerisms that made them different from other human beings.

Plot. The plot, the happening, is often told in chronological order. The plot develops and resolves a conflict. Without a conflict, usually little happens. Plot explains, "What happened?"

Setting. The setting should describe the place and time when the story occurred. Was the event in Milwaukee, at midnight, on the corner of Third Street and North Avenue?

Theme. The theme is the meaning of the story. Usually, if the writer told a good story, it is unnecessary to state the meaning directly, the way it is added in a fable. The point will be clear to readers if they understand how and why the event or setting or characters had such an effect.

Narrator. Someone must tell the tale. This person is the narrator. A narrator can use the first person *I* or can tell the story in the third person using *he, she, they.* If you write in the third person, you can pretend to be omniscient and see inside everyone's mind, or you can decide to tell the tale from only one person's mind as that one person sees it. No matter which narrator you choose, you must be consistent through the entire piece. Make the narrator as honest as possible.

Hints for Writing a Personal Narrative

Writing the personal narrative calls for making all the decisions writers must make. (For a review of these writing decisions, see Chapters 1 through 19.)

The topics that produce the best personal narratives are experiences that changed you or made you look at something or someone differently. For example, in "The Sea Bat," which appears later in this chapter, the student decided to write about his experience in the Navy.

To collect your supporting information, imagine the event from the beginning to end, making notes as you imagine. List the time, place, and the characters. Record all the images, colors, people, dialogue, and sounds. Most important, record how each image, color, person, line of dialogue, and sound made you feel.

For example, here is the first part of the list of facts and feelings remembered by the author of "The Sea Bat."

Facts	Feelings
Age: 17	Inexperience, trusting
Time: twilight	Looking forward to shower
Chipping rust all day	Tired
Statement over the loudspeaker	Curiosity

Choose the audience you want. Decide what you want your readers to take away from the story. Decide who will tell the story and whether the narrator's voice will be formal or informal. The narrator in "The Sea Bat" will be an "I" narrator who tells what he knew as the story happened. The narrator speaks informally to people who should understand an abuse of trust.

Decide on your order. How will you begin? What order will you follow? How will you end? "The Sea Bat" tells the story chronologically.

In one sentence, state your main idea, exactly what you hope to say. You may not use this sentence in your final work, but it will help you clarify your thoughts. In "The

Sea Bat," the narrator says, "I was by nature a trusting child and therefore a natural victim of my 'old salt' shipmates' tricks." Dagdayan uses it to begin a story about trust.

The Sea Bat

by Jose Dagdayan

By virtue of an agreement between the governments of the United States and the Republic of the Philippines, the United States can and does recruit Filipino nationals to serve in the American Navy. Coming from a large and poor family, I was desperately looking for ways to better my life and help my family. So I, a Filipino, for lack of employment and a helping hand, joined the Navy at a very tender age to seek my fortune. I was by nature a trusting child and therefore a natural victim of my "old salt" shipmates' tricks.

It was twilight. The ship was somewhere in the Pacific Ocean slicing the unusually calm water on our way to Hawaii. I had been chipping rust and painting bulkheads all day and was really looking forward to "hitting the hay" early for a much needed rest. As I was about to step into the shower room, suddenly the word was passed over the public announcing system, "Anyone interested in witnessing a rare and very seldom seen denizen of the sea, the sea bat, lay to the fantail immediately." I had never heard of any such bird or animal before, so out of sheer curiosity and perhaps the desire to beat my other shipmates to the scene, I hurried back to my compartment, put on a pair of pants and an undershirt, and promptly made my way to the fantail.

Three men were already there when I arrived. One was holding a net with a long handle while the other had about a two-foot section of rubber hose in his hand. The third appeared to have his eyes glued to something in flight. I looked and squinted to where the observers' eyes were glued, but I could not see anything.

Just about then the observer shouted, "Here it comes again," and made a motion with the net as though he were going to try to catch it. I stepped closer to the side of the ship for a better view, and just as I stooped down, I felt a sharp pain; something hit my behind. As I straightened up to find out who did it, however, my curiosity took control once again when I glimpsed the man with the net still trying to catch whatever that elusive thing was he was trying to catch. And so, like a fool, I bent over again, and wham! I was hit again, only this time much harder than the first and still the cause didn't register. It wasn't until the third whip that it finally dawned on me that I had been made a fool of. By this time, a crowd had gathered and everyone was laughing and having a fantastic time on my account. The lashes I received were far less painful than that embarrassment.

Although the incident happened so many years ago, it was so firmly etched in my mind that the mere sight or sound of anything that vaguely resembles that particular incident, like a bird in flight or a fisherman with a net, triggers something in my memory bank and once again the scene is re-enacted.

Discussion Questions

1. Dagdayan explains a simple event that happens to many new sailors. But somehow the story isn't just about him or sailors; the story shows embarrassment, naivete, hurt, and pain. Most of us have had others hit us with a "rubber hose" even if that hose was not of real rubber. What was the hose in your life? How have others acted to cause you pain and hurt?

2. Notice that the characters are the narrator and the three sailors watching the sea bat. The setting is a ship somewhere in the Pacific Ocean at twilight. The conflict arises when the three sailors test the naivete and curiosity of the young man. Meaning develops as readers see themselves in similar mocking situations as either the embarrasser or the embarrassed. This personal narrative tells a story with more than just action; it shows how the narrator felt about the events, sights, sounds, and people. Make a list of all the specific details in the piece. Notice how many of them evoke emotion.

More Hints for Writing a Personal Narrative

As you write your personal narrative, tell a story that shows how you changed because of something you experienced. Make sure that the experience involves conflict, as most change does.

Start the story as close to the ending as possible. That is, if you want to tell us about the time your dad fell overboard between the boat and the cement dock while you were trying to maneuver the boat and save his life, don't start the story by how you and your dad got up, fixed a huge breakfast, drove to the store for a six pack, drove to the fish camp for bait, put the boat into the water, and so on. Skip all the unimportant events that make for a long, drawn-out story that will bore your audience even before you reach the important part: how you felt responsible for your dad's life.

Communication and the Anecdote

Besides writing a personal narrative you can use a story in an anecdote. An anecdote is a tiny story of only a few lines or a few short paragraphs. Because the story is short, the writer must carefully tell important details. Readers must see everything taking place and understand the point of the story. It is just like a longer narrative in that it uses characters, plot, setting, and theme.

The following anecdote begins an essay on students' legal rights.

Because the college is new, students are not to eat or drink in classrooms. But a woman student brings her cup of coffee into the biology lab every day. The instructor warns her, "No eating or drinking is allowed in the lab." The student ignores the warning. Three days in a row the student ignores the warning. Finally a campus security officer arrives. "You brought coffee into an unauthorized zone. I'm issuing you a moving citation. Pay it or you will not graduate."

Characters are the student, instructor, and security officer. The offender is a woman. The plot is simple. The woman brings coffee into an area where she should not bring it, she is warned, and finally security issues her a citation for a moving violation. The setting is the campus of a new college. The theme is unjust punishment.

In addition to character, plot, setting, and theme, the writer creates dialogue so you hear the words spoken to the student. The narrator who tells the story is uninvolved. Tiny stories like this use chronological order. Events follow in the order in which they happen in real life.

Where You Might Use an Anecdote

An anecdote can begin an essay. A story like the one you just read might make the reader chuckle about the silliness of the penalty or be angry about the seriousness of the punishment. In either case, the story would prepare students for an essay about students' rights. Most people like stories; they usually interest readers. Once the reader is hooked, the beginning job of the writer is over.

Anecdotes also work nicely in endings. A writer can refer to the anecdote in the introduction and come full circle to warn the reader that the piece is ending. More important, an anecdote can show how the story fits the thesis or main points of the essay. A good ending anecdote ties together all the loose ends in the piece and demonstrates the author's points so well that the reader can't forget them. The anecdote at the end need not refer to the beginning. But it must grow out of the ideas in the piece. It cannot be a joke or story just tacked to the end to make people feel good.

Tiny stories also work inside the piece. They might illustrate the author's points. They might change the pace, if the writing is becoming monotonous or tedious. Sometimes, tiny stories clarify points better than long explanations. Best of all, a story adds human interest, humor, or emotions.

The anecdote must illustrate the points the author makes, or it will seem out of place to the reader. In the case of the student caught carrying coffee, the anecdote illustrates the legal problems of students and colleges. It raises important issues a student might address: How should a college punish a student? How should rules be maintained? What are just rules and just punishments? What recourse should be available to a student? You can think of other issues.

When to Avoid Anecdotes

Avoid anecdotes in formal writing. Most readers of formal papers do not expect humorous stories or an appeal to emotions. Also avoid telling tales when you give directions. Usually, stories just get in the way of clear directions.

Avoid using an anecdote as proof. An anecdote merely gives an example or illustrates a point; it doesn't prove anything, no matter how good it is. Also, do not depend on a story to convince your reader. A tale is not an argument. It does not provide evidence.

Where to Find Stories

Most stories should originate with you or your experiences. Otherwise it may be difficult to make up enough details to make the story convincing.

Sometimes, you will research and find stories told by experts on your topic. Don't be afraid to use their stories, provided that you give the authors credit in your piece. When you interview someone about a topic, ask for the stories from the person. Be sure to credit your source in your writing.

COLLABORATIVE LEARNING

1. Answer the Discussion Questions for "Out There."

2. Answer the Discussion Questions for "The Sea Bat."

3. Work together as a group to write a story. Create the plot, characters, setting, and theme. You may want to talk out the story until you all agree on the main points. Then write the story.

4. After you finish writing a personal narrative, take it to your writing group for their peer response. Ask if anything is confusing and needs to be changed. Then revise your work.

5. Take one of your essays to the writing group. With the group, plan an anecdote that might be a good beginning, another that might fit somewhere in the body, and another for an ending. Write out the anecdotes.

WRITING TASKS

1. Write a personal narrative in which you explain an event that you experienced that changed you somehow. Create the entire story, beginning as close to the end as possible. Let the reader feel the punch of your feelings. Write so someone else can understand what changed you. Use both Planning Sheet I and II on pages 285–288 to help you work out the narrative.

2. Add an anecdote to one of your essays in a spot that needs more explanation. Study the anecdote in the essay "Let's Talk" in Chapter 31 as an example of how an anecdote can work.

3. Read three or four articles in popular magazines and several chapters in your textbooks. Notice the anecdotes. Write a report on your findings.

Checklist for a Narrative
(Personal Narrative or Anecdote)

Yes   **No**

____   ____   1. If you created a personal narrative, will the reader understand you better after reading your piece?

____   ____   2. Do you describe the setting—time and place?

____   ____   3. Do you let the reader see your characters' mannerisms, hear them speak, and understand them?

____   ____   4. Do you build the story to a climax?

____   ____   5. Do you create a meaningful theme that your reader will be able to figure out?

____   ____   6. Is your story interesting and clear?

____   ____   7. Did you begin telling the narrative as near the end of the story as possible?

____   ____   8. If you used an anecdote, is it integrated into the essay?

Name _____

Section _____

PERSONAL NARRATIVE _____

Planning Sheet II

(Some students may want to do this Planning Sheet before Planning Sheet I; other students may wish to do it after.)

In a narrative the writer works with elements of story: characters, plot, setting, theme, and a narrator. Use this planning sheet to make decisions about how you will use each of these in your personal narrative.

Remember that fine personal narratives are often about an event which somehow changed you or made you see things differently.

Characters: Who are the important people in your story? Describe what they look like and how they act.

Setting: Where and when does your story take place? Describe the place(s) and time(s).

Plot: What happens in your story? What is the conflict? Use this space to chart your plot. (Remember that good stories often begin close to the ending.)

Theme: What is the point, the theme, the meaning of your story? (If you are telling the story so people will understand you better, think about what you want your readers to understand by the time they finish the story.)

Narrator: Who will tell your story?

Peer Reviewer _____

Title of Essay _____

Author of Essay _____

PEER EVALUATION—NARRATION _____

Questions by Susan Slavicz

1. What incident did the writer describe?

2. Circle any forms of the verb "to be" used in the paper (is, was, were, are, has been, might have been). Underline the active verbs.

3. Write three sentences from the narrative which use specific, colorful language which allows the reader to "see" or "hear" what is happening.

4. What one single impression stands out in this paper? If there is not one, how might you suggest that the writer work towards this?

5. How is the essay organized—what is the plot outline?

6. From whose point of view is the paper written?

7. What is the setting of the narrative? Write a sentence from the narrative which tells the time or describes the place.

8. What do *you* think is the main idea of the narrative?

9. Copy a sentence that you particularly liked.

10. Does the paper have a beginning paragraph that lets you know the topic and direction of the paper? Explain.

11. Does the paper have a concluding paragraph that seems to draw the various ideas in the paper together? Explain.

Chapter Twenty-Five

Explain with Examples

You know how to use examples.

Who are rich Americans? To answer, you would give examples; you might name Ronald Reagan, George Bush, Ted Kennedy, Jacquelyn Onassis, Madonna.

What types of business hire college students part time? You might answer: fast-food places, retail stores, childcare facilities, gas stations, restaurants. You'd offer examples.

Which fast-food chains hire college kids? You could name McDonald's, Burger King, Wendy's, Hardee's, Arby's, and others. These are examples.

At graduation, what would you say to a high school graduate? Roger Rosenblatt answered that question for his son in a marvelous *Time Magazine* essay. Note his examples as you read.

Speech for a High School Graduate

by Roger Rosenblatt

Others will exhort you to take risks, to be yourself, never to look back or lose your faith. Not I. If the truth be told, I do not want you to take risks. Oh, maybe a selected few to preserve your self-esteem, but not the killing kind of risk, nothing netless. As for being yourself, that's fine, as long as you are happy with yourself. Otherwise, be someone else. You'll find your way; most everyone does. Never to look back? I'd say look back quite often. If you don't look back, you won't know it was you who smashed the china. Never lose faith? Of course you will. People lose their faith.

So what truth can I give you, my college-boy-to-be, on your way out? You'd think I would be able to produce *something*. Words are supposed to spill from writers' minds like shrimp, especially on momentous occasions like graduation, weddings, funerals; we do it all. Instead, I reach in my desk for some verbal pocket watch to wrap up for you in tissue paper, and come up blank. Too dazed or polite, you stare at my face the way Telemachus must have stared on the beach at Ithaca, searching for Ulysses among the sailors.

Should I offer you wishes? Poets have done that for their children from time to time. In *Frost at Midnight* Coleridge wishes his son Hartley a life surrounded by nature. I could wish the same for you, though I have less trust in nature's benevolence. Still, Mary McCarthy said something interesting in an interview recently: that "our perception of the world and our values stem absolutely from the possibility of some reasonably true perception of nature—which is gradually disappearing and will soon become impossible." That could be so. Myself, I like watching the ocean.

Yeats wished for his girl a sense of ceremony and tradition in *A Prayer for My Daughter*. I'd repeat that wish for you, as long as you did not turn into a snob, like Yeats. In *This Side of Truth*, Dylan Thomas, probably hoping to protect himself, wished that his son Llewelyn would hold all judgments in abeyance. "Each truth," he wrote, "each lie, dies in unjudging love." That I will not wish for you. Have your love and judgment too.

If not wishes, how about aphorisms? Everyone can use an aphorism. I wish I could remember one, something especially Delphic or brilliant from *The Consolation of Philosophy*, the *Bhagavad Gita*, the *Koran*. Charlie Chan said: "Evidence like nose on an anteater." Does that count? Russians are better at such things. Once in my earshot Lillian Hellman observed, "A crazy person is crazy all the time." I have frequently found that valuable, particularly when in the company of a crazy person who is, for the moment, lucid. Confucius said: "Filial piety is the constant requirement of Heaven." That seems to me an excellent aphorism.

What would you say to purely tactical advice? Over the years I picked up several emotional maneuvers that might serve you well as contingency plans. When lonely, for example, read murder mysteries: I find them soothing. When angry, choose solitude. When lovesick, do push ups, run a mile or two, or step out with the boys: I don't know why that helps, but it does. When bored, see the movie *Bringing Up Baby*. When in despair, dress to the nines. I often wear a white shirt to work when I want to pit elegance against the fates. You might try that. (Do you own a white shirt?) When glum, call home.

Or should I present you with a parable? You've probably heard the ones about the good Samaritan and the Prodigal Son. No matter. Neither parable applies to you. You were born a good Samaritan and prodigality has never been one of your problems. Frankly, I do not know a work of moral fiction that could improve your character, for it has always seemed to your mother and me (admittedly prejudiced but not blind) that your character never needed much improving. I have not known anyone more fair-minded, more considerate, more able to swallow disappointment. Not from me did you get these things. Why should I expect to give you something special now?

Unless, as in the old days, you would like a story. This is a true one (I can swear to it), about a father and a son in a playground twelve years ago, in the spring, around noon. The boy was five. He had a basketball, which he dribbled off his toes half the time, and which he kept shooting at the hoop—underhand, both hands, straining to reach the rim. The father sat on a bench and watched. The boy kept at it. Then some bigger boys sauntered over, snatched the ball away and shot around, leaving the five-year-old watching too.

Gearing up for the rescue, the father asked his son if he wanted him to retrieve the ball. The boy said, "No. I think I can handle it." Which he did, simply by standing among the others patiently, occasionally catching the ball and passing it to one of them, until one of them eventually passed it to him. That's all there is to that story. The five-year-old continued to play ball, and his father sat in the sun. Goodbye, my boy.

Notice how Rosenblatt begins with examples of what others might say to a high school graduate. "Others will exhort you to take risks, to be yourself, never to look back or lose your faith. Not I." He goes on trying to figure out what he should tell his son. He wonders, "Should I offer you wishes?" He gives his son some of the wishes poets made for their kids. Then he wonders if he should offer aphorisms, and he gives examples of aphorisms. He thinks next about tactical advice. So he gives examples of tactics, like what to do when lonely, angry, lovesick, bored, in despair, or glum. Rosenblatt wonders whether to offer a parable. But he talks himself out of that one. Finally he tells a story, an example of what the young son did once with a basketball. And there he ends because he knows his boy will be O.K.

It's a wonderful essay from a Dad who is proud of his son.

What Examples Do

Examples explain points. I might say, "My life is very hectic." You don't really know what I mean until I give examples: "Since this last weekend, I lost my job, broke up with my best friend, had my car towed into the repair shop, and received a notice from my bank that my checking account is overdrawn." These examples explain what I mean by "My life is hectic."

A vivid example works like a picture. If you overhear someone say, "The neighborhood is dangerous," you may not see the picture until you hear the examples. If the speaker explains that in the last two months there have been two murders, a rape, break-ins into thirteen apartments, four fires set by arsonists, and six cars stolen all in a three block area, you'll see what she means by "The neighborhood is dangerous."

Examples show instances or cases. Often a magazine story about a major news event will follow the story of just one person involved. From that one person's story, the reader is supposed to see what it's like for the rest of the people in the situation. For example, the farm problem can be illustrated by the story of one farm family's problems. Or the street gang problem can be told by following one gang member through one day or one week. The reader understands more about the plight of farmers or street gangs after reading the detailed example of one member.

What Examples Do Not Do

Examples prove little. You cannot argue that something is true on the basis of one or even several examples. If you try to prove something with examples, the opposition can usually point to exceptions that will justify a conclusion different from yours. Even if you provide a great many examples, they will not offer enough evidence to prove an argument because examples just show how some cases are.

For example, a scrutiny of one welfare family may explain one family's problems. The author can say that other families are like this one, and perhaps readers will understand families on welfare a little better. But because all families on welfare are not in the same kind of trouble, the example doesn't prove what it is like for all welfare families. So the example only clarifies or illustrates the problems faced by some people.

There is a simple reason why examples do not prove. Lists of examples are usually incomplete. Remember how this chapter began? You could give examples of some rich people, but you wouldn't be able to list all rich people in the United States. You might name some places that hire college students for part-time jobs, but the list would probably be incomplete if you worked on it for years.

What Kinds of Examples Work Best?

Although good, clear examples are powerful, they won't help you unless they are typical (ordinary), relevant, and specific.

Examples Should Be Typical

Examples should be typical (usual, ordinary). In other words, you should not pull out a far-fetched or unusual example.

Suppose you want to explain that taking care of a swimming pool is simple and takes little time. Here are a typical and a nontypical example.

Typical example (ordinary, usual): Taking care of a pool is simple. You need to test the water and put in chemicals every week or so. Then sweep the top every day and the sides once or twice a month. Doing all this for a pool takes about fifteen minutes a day.

Nontypical example (unusual): Some rich people hire a pool caretaker whose total job is to keep up the pool. So taking care of the pool is simple.

Suppose you want to explain how the people in your dorm are causing your life to be miserable.

Typical example: On my floor, one of the women plays her pipe organ records twenty hours a day so loudly that I can hear them even through ear plugs; another woman cooks every day but never offers me even a taste; a third knocks on my door at least four or five times a day to borrow something or just to talk about her love life. (Usual happenings)

Nontypical example: Last year, one of the women threw a birthday party for herself, and it lasted thirty-six hours (Exceptional case)

Examples should be typical so they explain, rather than contradict, your point. Typical examples don't allow anyone to say, "But that's an exceptional case!"

Examples Should Be Relevant

Examples should be relevant (related to the issues the author discusses.) The irrelevant example is off the point.

Suppose you list new responsibilities of the eighteen-year-old high school graduate. Here are relevant and irrelevant examples of what you might say.

Relevant example: The eighteen-year-old is beginning a life in which society holds him or her responsible for actions. At eighteen, men must register for the draft or be denied financial aid to college. Men and women are treated like adults in criminal court and are allowed to negotiate and sign loans and other documents.

Irrelevant example: In Texas, kids younger than eighteen can be sentenced to death row.

Kids on death row who are not yet eighteen are irrelevant to the issue of the adult responsibilities of eighteen-year-olds. Irrelevant examples should be left out of your essay.

Examples Should Be Specific

Examples should be so specific (detailed) that the reader sees exactly what the author means. An unspecific example lacks clear details or precision. Suppose you are writing about how difficult it is to pronounce, or even name, the ingredients in prepackaged iced tea. Here are specific and nonspecific examples to support that point.

Specific example: In fruit iced teas, some ingredients are difficult to pronounce: maltodextrin, aspartame, magnesium oxide, and phenylalanine.

Nonspecific example: Packaged iced tea often contains numerous ingredients that most people cannot name or pronounce.

In the nonspecific example, the reader doesn't know whether to agree, because the example doesn't explain. If ingredients in the tea are named and the reader cannot pronounce them, it's easy to agree with the writer.

Suppose you write home to ask for money for the next school term. You might give specific or nonspecific examples of how you would spend the money.

Specific example: Next term I will need to pay for tuition, books, lab fees, supplies, board and room, car insurance, car payments, and gas.

Nonspecific example: Next term I'm going to need a lot of money to pay all my expenses here at college.

The specific example names the expenses; the nonspecific example never names them. Certainly, specific examples are more convincing and interesting to read.

Good Writers Use Many Examples

Sometimes you can stack up many examples to explain your point. Nine or ten examples will usually show what you mean better than just two or three because a group of examples shows many sides of your point and their scope is larger. If you can point out how sixteen people got rich following your plan, you are more convincing than if you say how two people became rich on your plan. A doctor who has only one successful open-heart surgery is not as convincing as the surgeon who can list a hundred examples of healthy open-heart surgery patients.

In "Speech for a High School Graduate" earlier in this chapter, Rosenblatt offers his son many examples of wisdom spoken to high school graduates; but the dad tells the son that not all advice is worthwhile: He lists the kinds of things not to be believed; then he tries wishes, aphorisms, tactical advice, and concludes with a personal anecdote.

Examples in Student Essays

In this essay "Excuse Me, Do You Speak English?" student Kris Janin offers many examples of misleading words and phrases in the English language.

Excuse Me, Do You Speak English?

by Kris Janin

Have you ever wondered why you drive on parkways but park on driveways? If you were raised speaking the English language, you may tend to take for granted the ease with which you use it to communicate. But misleading words and phrases could make English very difficult to learn as a second language.

Perhaps you should imagine trying to teach English to someone who is completely unfamiliar with it. You could start with something simple such as the word for the number one. "One" sounds as if it should be spelled beginning with the letter "W", but there is no "W" to be seen. Why? There's a "W" in why. After "one" comes "two," and there is a "W" that is apparently not needed. The confusion has begun, and it will only get worse.

As you progress with your imaginary student, you'll have to explain why "good wood" rhymes but "good food" doesn't. And don't forget to point out that "some" and "numb," which look nothing alike, are pronounced almost identically. Good luck with "tomb," "comb," and "bomb."

Some words and phrases can paint strange pictures in the mind. Will you need a swimsuit to get into a car pool? You may think that this is strange, but I won't eat Bird's Eye brand foods, because I don't want my meal staring back at me. The phrase "hung jury" can stimulate images too bizarre to talk about.

If you've ever flown *on* a plane, then you have more guts than I do. This doesn't mean that your intestinal tract is larger than mine, but most people prefer to ride *inside* the plane. Have you ever heard the news that two planes almost slammed into each other; then you can say that they nearly missed. And hog futures can be a good investment, even though hogs have no future. Becoming bacon is not a career. Aren't you happy that you already understand this language called English?

Paramedics carry an injured person on a litter. You may be shocked to see so much litter on the roadside. Your cat had a litter of six. It's good that they are trained to poop in their litter. If you would like a cat for a pet, don't look for one in a cathouse. You can right a wrong or write a paper. You can't buy love, but you can make love. Thirty-love, Chris Evert serving. It's good that your meals aren't served at ninety M.P.H. You would probably starve before ever "catching a bite." Intelligent people are often referred to as being bright. It's a shame that you can't adjust your television's I.Q. with the brightness control.

If you told these jokes to someone who did not speak English, the humor would probably be lost in the translation. So the next time you hear a person from a foreign country speaking "broken English" perhaps you should listen with understanding and praise instead of disdain. Then browse through a thesaurus and feel lucky that you already comprehend one of the most difficult languages in the world.

In this essay, the humorous approach is fun to read. Examples of misleading words and phrases are typical, relevant, and specific. Many examples illustrate that English is difficult to learn as a second language.

Examples

Where do examples come from? Finding examples sometimes means looking hard at an experience and seeing just what is there. Read "Astonished at the Sights" to see how A.J. Witt uses several examples to show his reactions to New York City. A.J.'s early draft of the introduction just said the kids were playing ball in a place that looked bad. I asked him to give specific examples of how bad that place was. He said the kids played around dead dogs!

Here is his revised introduction and the entire essay.

Astonished by the Sights

by A.J. Witt

In a small sandlot, somewhere in the Bronx, in New York City, eight kids ranging in age from six to twelve, played stick ball. The field had trash spread throughout it, and three or four dead dogs lay right in the middle of the playing area. I could not see the bases for the trash and the little grass that was there, but when one of the kids hit the ball and began running to first base, he had to leap over one of the dead dogs to get to first base. I could hardly believe my own eyes. I had never witnessed anything this dramatic before. New York City reminded me of how lucky I was to have all the things that I had.

I was astonished by the sights. There was an energetic man who came up to our car at a red light and asked if we would pay him to wash our windshield while we sat at the red light. This was his way of making money to survive. Other homeless people just sat on the sidewalk in their tattered clothes in front of run-down buildings watching the cars go by. I saw a business man in a three piece suit come out of Burger King eating a hamburger; apparently he didn't like the sandwich so he threw about half of it away into a trash can. Not but two seconds after the remainder of the sandwich had been tossed into the trash can, a homeless man dashed to it and dug out the half eaten sandwich. When he pulled it out, his eyes got as big as half-dollar coins. Then an immense smile came to his face. Happily, the man started eating the hamburger. Ironically this took place in front of a fruit stand. At the stand an old lady picked up an enormous vine of grapes to purchase; as she picked up the vine, a plump grape fell off and rolled about five feet away. The happy man who was devouring his prized hamburger dashed for the grape, picked it up, and anxiously popped it into his mouth.

Ever since that trip to New York City, I have always been more thankful for the things that I used to take for granted. Now when I see a piece on television about the homeless or people not having anything to eat, I see in my mind the expression on the man's face when he found the half eaten hamburger.

To write a paragraph using many examples, writers like Rosenblatt and Witt often use a main-idea sentence and several examples that explain the main point. A conclusion ties the examples back to the topic sentence. Or the examples may come first, with the writer uniting them all later in the main-idea sentence.

Tests

Using many examples is not limited to papers written for composition courses. Tests may ask you to give examples. When they do, give as many examples as you can, but explain each example so the teacher knows you know what you mean. These sample test questions ask for examples:

- Explain at least three ways by which the mother may be responsible for the brain damage of an unborn fetus. (To answer this test question, you would give three or more examples of ways mothers might harm the unborn fetus.)

- People who are against a state income tax use several arguments. What are these arguments, and how would you answer each of them? (To answer this question, you would first name several examples of arguments against a state income tax and then respond to each example.)

- Advertising is partially responsible for the state of our country's morals. Defend or disagree with this statement by explaining at least three advertising campaigns that uphold or question traditional moral beliefs. (To answer this test question, you would first have to decide whether you agree with the first statement. Then you would have to find three examples of ad campaigns and use them to explain your position.)

Writers May Use One Long (Extended) Example

Instead of using many examples, writers sometimes use just one long example all through the paragraph or essay. This technique works especially well for case studies or when the writer must explain a point in detail. Here is an extended example, an answer to the test question, "Give an example of yellow journalism you found in today's mass media."

Because the mass media in the United States is sometimes motivated by a desire to make money at the expense of truth, it can be guilty of yellow journalism. Yesterday, while waiting in a grocery checkout line I read a powerful example of such yellow journalism.	topic sentence
The headlines read, "Boy Born Speaking English Sentences." According to the article, a baby boy was born last week in Trinidad with the astounding ability to communicate with his mother and father in full English sentences. The mother, who never attended school, told the reporter, "My son speaks better English than our doctor!" The boy's father could not speak any English but said through an interpreter that the boy was a miracle. According to the doctor who delivered the baby,	Extended example of yellow journalism in story of baby born speaking English

the boy could recite the first lines of the
most popular song in Trinidad. The boy himself
was never quoted because the article said he
was being kept in seclusion pending an
investigation by the government.

    The talking baby is a good example of how
the yellow journalist appeals to a reader's
naive curiosity. The headlines and entire
article play up the strange, the unique, the   conclusion
sensational. The boy himself could not be
observed. Obviously, the baby's ability to
communicate is a fraud.

This answer to the test question is one extended example. It summarizes and explains why one case is an example of yellow journalism.

COLLABORATIVE LEARNING

1. Look through your textbooks. Find a paragraph, or several paragraphs, in which the author uses many examples to explain a point. Also, find an extended example that makes a point or explains an issue. Show these examples to your writing class.

2. In your writing group, practice thinking with examples. To do this, first decide on a topic. (You might choose one from the list of sample topics in this chapter.) Then choose an audience and a purpose for writing to that audience about that topic. Finally, list at least five examples you might use to explain that topic to that audience. (Some examples will probably be on the tip of your tongue. To make sure you don't forget any, you might cluster, list, do tree branching, or ask questions until you have many examples.) The following is an extended example that illustrates how you might work out this exercise.

    Topic: Services needed in the college library
    Audience: The librarians or administration
    Purpose: To explain how the library might better serve
    Examples of services the library might offer:
    The library might:
    Remain open several more hours each night
    Give free computer time to students doing research
    Offer free typing for the physically handicapped
    Hire another reference librarian
    Reduce fines on overdue books
    Have a free return day every month for overdue books

Keep textbooks for each course on reserve

Now it is your turn to make examples explain your points.

3. Show your understanding of the issues in the essay "Speech for a High School Graduate" presented early in this chapter. Write out your answers to at least four of these questions:

    a. What is a netless risk? Have you ever taken such a risk?

    b. What might Rosenblatt be alluding to when he says, "I reach . . . for some verbal pocket watch to wrap up for you . . ."? When do people usually receive watches? What does a watch represent?

    c. Who was Telemachus? Why would he search for Ulysses? Who might have been the Telemachus at your high school graduation?

    d. What did Dylan Thomas wish from his boy? Why?

    e. What is an aphorism? Which of Rosenblatt's examples of aphorisms means the most to you? Why?

    f. What are the *Consolation of Philosophy,* the *Bhagavad Gita,* and the *Koran*? Why would these be mentioned at a graduation ceremony?

    g. Who are Charlie Chan, Lillian Hellman, and Confucius?

4. Find at least ten examples in "Excuse Me, Do You Speak English?" and record your examples on the Examples Worksheet at the end of this chapter.

Writing Tasks

1. Write a formal essay in which you use many examples to explain something. Use the Multiple Examples Planning Sheet. Or write an essay in which you depend on one or two long examples to make your point. (Use your own topic or choose one from the list on the next page.) When you have finished, be sure that each example is clear, typical, specific, and relevant. Use as your models the essays "Excuse Me, Do You Speak English?" "Astonished by the Sights," and "Speech for a High School Graduate."

2. Check essay tests you have written for other courses to find questions that asked for examples. Reread your answers. Did you make use of the ideas in this chapter? What could you improve? Rewrite one of your test answers and show it to your instructor. (You might check for similar questions in review sections of your texts or papers distributed by instructors.)

Sample Topics

Excuses	Stress	Heroes
Football injuries	Modern fairy tales	Glass ceilings
Romantic music	Stupidity	Bad dates
Problems on the job	Today's myths	Gangs
Nonalcoholic drinks	Billboard pollution	Poverty
Successful people	Outdated thinking	Stubbornness
Ways to cheat	Good jokes	Unfair laws

Ways to deal with certain groups (teachers or police or waiters)
Decisions you've been proud to make or decisions you've regretted

Checklist for Using Examples

Yes **No**

1. Do your examples explain your points?

2. Are all your examples specific?

3. Is each of your examples relevant?

4. Are your examples typical?

5. Do you use enough examples to be convincing?

6. Do all your examples fit your audience and purpose?

7. Do you arrange your examples in an effective order?

8. Do you use transitions to show how your examples fit together and explain your main ideas?

Name _____

Section _____

EXAMPLES WORKSHEET _____

A. Find at least ten examples in "Excuse Me, Do You Speak English?"

    1.

    2.

    3.

    4.

    5.

    6.

    7.

    8.

    9.

   10.

B. In "Astonished by the Sights" a student reacted to New York City with examples of sights that astonished him.

   1. List at least five specific details the writer pointed out which let you see the sandlot and its activity.

   2. What specific words did the student writer use to help you see the homeless man?

     The sandwich?

     The grape?

   3. List some words or descriptions which Witt wrote that move you.

Peer Reviewer_____

Title of Essay_____

Author of Essay _____

PEER EVALUATION EXAMPLE _____

Questions by Susan Slavicz

1. Write the paper's thesis.

2. What characteristic/s does the writer write about?

3. Give three specific examples used in the paper to support the thesis.

4. Circle the transitional words in the paper.

5. Underline the "to be" verbs.

6. Put a star by your favorite image.

7. Discuss what you might do now if this paper were yours. Be specific. (Write this answer.)

8. Discuss the paper with the writer.

Chapter Twenty-Six
Explain with Direction/Process

How does a student apply for a loan?
How is a bill developed and passed by the U.S. Congress?
How does someone get to your house from the college?
What happened during math class?
How did the Japanese survive the bombing of their cities?
How is food digested by the human body?

Thinking about a process is not new for you. You ask questions like these or find them on tests. Even as a child, you learned how to follow directions and tie a shoelace, eat from a fork, wash your hair, order from a menu, play ball, and keep score.

Giving directions seems easier than following directions. Doesn't it seem easier to tell someone how to do a writing assignment than actually to compose the paper? Have you ever stopped at a gas station for directions, listened carefully, driven a little farther, and then had to stop again to get clearer directions? Giving clear, accurate, specific, easy-to-follow directions and explanations is an art. It is a difficult art.

People waste time, money, energy, and good will every year because they do not get clear directions or they themselves do not think out a process clearly.

But there is a second type of process paper. Sometimes you won't give detailed directions which you expect your audience to be able to follow. Instead you will perform a more difficult process—you will *explain how something is done but which is so complicated or difficult that you will not expect the reader to do the process.*

Finally there is a third type of process paper that explains *not how* to do something, but *explains rather what happened.* All of these are types of process papers; the giving of step-by-step directions, though, is the most often practiced.

Three Different Ways to Explain and Write Process Essays

You might be asked to do three kinds of thinking and writing about process in college.

1. *Sometimes you give directions and expect a listener to follow the directions to get the results you predict.* You might give directions to a place or directions on how to do something. If you give directions to the nearest shopping mall, the reader hopes to follow the directions and get to the mall. If you tell how to make butter cream fudge, the reader expects to follow your directions and turn out the fudge. Giving and/or following directions requires creating and following detailed, clear, step-by-step directions.

2. You can *explain how something is done, but not expect the listener to do anything except understand.* If, for example, you tell how people used to thatch the roofs of houses, the listener may learn how to thatch, but won't expect to go thatch a roof. You may describe the process used for building a dam across a major river like the Mississippi, but you don't expect anyone to build a dam after listening to you. In the same way, you might say how food is digested in the human body, how lung cancer develops, or how a police dog learns to find drugs. In this kind of writing, the listener understands the process without expecting to do it. On essay tests, you might be asked to explain such a process.

3. You may *describe an event or recreate* an event in a step-by-step description. Since the event is already past, your listener can participate only through you. You might be asked to explain what happened in a math class to a fellow student who missed it. Events like the Super Bowl and the World Series are described so people who couldn't attend learn what happened. Good writing helps listeners see and feel an event after the fact.

1. HINTS FOR GIVING DIRECTIONS

Choose a Topic

To describe how to do something, you must know the subject well enough to be complete and accurate. An audience appreciates hints that only an expert would know. If you do not know the subject well, and you must write about it, then do your homework before you write.

Collect Supporting Information

You can collect your information in many ways, such as doing the process, imagining, or making a flow chart.

Do the Process. Write down each step as you perform it

Imagine. One method that works for many writers is imagining yourself actually doing the process. Imagine the *equipment* and *materials* you'll need to complete the task and name them. Imagine the *skills* or background knowledge needed to do the task and name them. Imagine doing each step in the task. Be sure to name all the steps in *chronological order.* Mention *optional steps,* if there are some. Indicate the *trouble spots.*

Make a Flow Chart. Instead of imagining and listing, make a flow chart and show each step on the chart. Use arrows to indicate how the parts relate.

Draw. Draw pictures of the process.

Videotape. Videotape someone doing the process; then watch the video as you write to make sure you include all information.

Write to Your Audience

Avoid writing directions that are clear only to the people who already know or understand the process. If a person already knows, an explanation just wastes time.

If the audience has any questions as it reads, you need to provide more explanations because a clearly explained process leaves no questions in the reader's mind. The reader should have to make no inferences, no guesses.

Be accurate. If you mean a stoplight, don't say stop sign. Making your audience guess your meaning is unfair.

Take nothing for granted. I remember sulking over a skirt pattern and saying to my grandmother, "I can't follow these directions." She took one look at my pathetic attempt to sew a zipper and said, "You have to turn the material inside out before you sew that seam." The directions had not said to turn the material inside out. Those directions were no good because they were clear only to someone who didn't need them.

Choose Your Voice

Be simple. Good writers explain complicated ideas in simple terms. Explain *every* term the reader might not know. Sound as if you know what you are doing. Make your reader trust you because your voice is sincere.

Use the second person *(you)* to give directions. Use action verbs *(grind, separate, cut, divide)* to tell the reader what to do.

Organize Your Supporting Information

After you decide your purpose, you can choose your organization.

Here is the simple way to organize and give directions. You might develop your own variations, but this is the traditional formula that works for verbal demonstrations or written directions.

Introduction:

- Explain when, where, and how these directions might be used.
- Include any special preparation (skills, background, equipment, and materials) the audience ought to have before beginning the project.
- In just one sentence, state all the steps of the process. This one sentence (the hardest part of all) will be your thesis in an essay or your topic sentence in a paragraph.

Body of the Essay:

- Break the entire process into small, manageable steps.
- Explain each step in clear detail so the reader knows exactly what to do and how to do it.
- Use chronological order so your audience doesn't get mixed up about what to do first, second, and so on.
- Explain how each step is related to the steps before and after it.
- Define all the terms the audience may not know.
- As you give the steps, warn your readers just before you come to problem spots. Explain how to avoid the problem.
- Most important, emphasize all the most vital points. Until readers are comfortable with the directions, they might not know an important point from a less important one.

Conclusion:

- Sum up the main steps for your audience.
- Point out the significance of the process.
- If appropriate, show that the process might be adapted to other situations. If you explain how to apply for a student loan, you might show how these same procedures can be used to apply for a scholarship. Audiences find such commentary valuable.

Introduction and "How to Write a Personal Letter"

EXAMPLE **Essay: Giving Directions**

In "How to Write a Personal Letter," Garrison Keillor tells how to do a process—write a letter. His folksy, easy style and simple directions give technical advice as well as emotional support. Keillor is an essayist and the humorist of the radio show "Prairie Home Companion."

How to Write a Personal Letter

Garrison Keillor

We shy persons need to write a letter now and then, or else we'll dry up and blow away. It's true. And I speak as one who loves to reach for the phone and talk. The telephone is to shyness what Hawaii is to February, it's a way out of the woods. And yet: a letter is better.

Such a sweet gift—a piece of handmade writing, in an envelope that is not a bill, sitting in our friend's path when she trudges home from a long day spent among wahoos and savages, a day our words will help repair. They don't need to be immortal, just sincere. She can read them twice and again tomorrow: You're someone *I care about, Corinne, and think of often, and every time I do, you make me smile.*

We need to write, otherwise nobody will know who we are. They will have only a vague impression of us as A Nice Person, because, frankly, we don't shine at conversation, we lack the confidence to thrust our faces forward and say, "Hi, I'm Heather Hooten, let me tell you about my week." Mostly we say, "Uh-huh" and "Oh really." People smile and look over our shoulder, looking for someone else to talk to.

So a shy person sits down and writes a letter. To be known by another person—to meet and talk freely on the page—to be close despite distance. To escape from anonymity and be our own sweet selves and express the music of our souls.

We want our dear Aunt Eleanor to know that we have fallen in love, that we quit our job, that we're moving to New York, and we want to say a few things that might not get said in casual conversation: *Thank you for what you've meant to me. I am very happy right now.*

The first step in writing letters is to get over the guilt of not writing. You don't "owe" anybody a letter. Letters are a gift. The burning shame you feel when you see unanswered mail makes it harder to pick up a pen and makes for a cheerless letter when you finally do. *I feel bad about not writing, but I've been so busy,* etc. Skip this. Few letters are obligatory, and they are *Thanks for the wonderful gift and I am terribly sorry to hear about George's death.* Write these promptly if you want to keep your friends. Don't worry about others, except love letters, of course. When your true love writes *Dear Light of My Life, Joy of My Heart,* some response is called for.

Some of the best letters are tossed off in a burst of inspiration, so keep your writing stuff in one place where you can sit down for a few minutes and—*Dear Roy, I am in the middle of an essay but thought I'd drop you a line. Hi to your sweetie too*—dash off a note to a pal. Envelopes, stamps, address book, everything in a drawer so you can write fast when the pen is hot.

A blank white 8" x 11" sheet can look as big as Montana if the pen's not so hot—try a smaller page and write boldly. Get a pen that makes a sensuous line, get a comfortable typewriter, a friendly word processor—whichever feels easy to the hand.

Sit for a few minutes with the blank sheet of paper in front of you, and let your friend come to mind. Remember the last time you saw each other and how your friend looked and what you said and what perhaps was unsaid between you; when your friend becomes real to you, start to write.

Write the salutation—*Dear You*—and take a deep breath and plunge in. A simple declarative sentence will do, followed by another and another. As if you were talking to us. Don't think about grammar, don't think about style, just give us your news. Where did you go, who did you see, what did they say, what do you think?

If you don't know where to begin, start with the present: *I'm sitting at the kitchen table on a rainy Saturday morning. Everyone is gone and the house is quiet.* Let the letter drift along. The toughest letter to crank out is one that is meant to impress, as we all know from writing job applications; if it's hard work to slip off a letter to a friend, maybe you're trying too hard to be terrific. A letter is only a report to someone who already likes you for reasons other than your brilliance. Take it easy.

Don't worry about form. It's not a term paper. When you come to the end of one episode, just start a new paragraph. You can go from a few lines about the sad state of rock 'n' roll to the fight with your mother and your fond memories of Mexico to the kitchen sink and what's in it. The more you write, the easier it gets, and when you have a True Friend to write to, a soul sibling, then it's like driving a car; you just press on the gas.

Don't tear up the page and start over when you write a bad line—try to write your way out of it. Make mistakes and plunge on. Let the letter cook along and let yourself be bold. Outrage, confusion, love—whatever is in your mind, let it find a way to the page. Writing is a means of discovery, always, and when you come to the end and write *Yours ever* or *Hugs and Kisses,* you'll know something you didn't when you wrote *Dear Pal.*

Probably your friend will put your letter away, and it'll be read again a few years from now—and it will improve with age.

And forty years from now, your friend's grandkids will dig it out of the attic and read it, a sweet and precious relic of the ancient Eighties that gives them a sudden clear glimpse of the world we oldtimers knew. You will have then created an object of art. Your simple lines about where you went, who you saw, what they said, will speak to those children and they will feel in their hearts the humanity of our times.

You can't pick up a phone and call the future and tell them about times. You have to pick up a piece of paper.

2. HINTS FOR DESCRIBING HOW SOMETHING COMPLICATED IS DONE _____

This is another type of process paper. Instead of giving step-by-step directions which you expect your reader to do, in this type of paper you expect your reader to understand a complicated process, but not do it. For example, if you explain how an atom is split, you shouldn't expect your audience to go split an atom after reading your paper. In such a paper, your purpose is to help the reader appreciate the splitting. Or, if you explain how to take a Black Belt test for a Martial Art, you shouldn't expect your readers to go take the test or pass it.

A few variations make this kind of paper easy to write (but different from the step-by-step process paper).

Introduction:

- Interest your audience in the process.
- Show why it is important and might be used.
- In just one sentence, state how the process is done. (This sentence will be your thesis statement.)

Body:

- Break the process into small, manageable parts.
- Explain each step in detail.
- Be as clear as possible; use examples to explain.
- Define terms the reader might not know.
- Show how each step is related to the steps before and after.

Conclusion:

- Sum up the main points.
- Emphasize the significance of the process.
- Explain other ways these same principles are applied. If you told how oil is drilled in the North Sea, you might offer variations for other parts of the world such as drilling in the Gulf of Mexico or off the coast of Alaska.

Example

In the following essay, Brad Anderson explains the rigorous test he went through when he became a Black Belt. But this essay is not a step-by-step process paper. Brad wants his readers to understand the process, but he doesn't expect most of his readers to take the test.

The Fighting Arts

by Brad Anderson

Since beginning my martial arts career, I've been punched, kicked, thrown, stabbed, and generally abused more times than I care to remember. I split my eye open with a sectional staff, a Kung-foo weapon. Most of my knuckles have been broken practicing with nunchucks, wooden swords, or by breaking boards. But I am currently a second degree Black Belt.

My test to become a Black Belt is a testament to the extremes some people will go in their endeavors to become martial artists.

Imagine yourself lying on a bed of three inch nails. Then picture someone setting ten full size concrete patio slabs on your stomach, while a two hundred pound weightlifter waits to swing a ten pound sledgehammer onto the pile of rock sitting on top of you. After two punishing blows from the sledgehammer, the pile of rock crumbles.

Minutes after the bed of nails ordeal, I'm lying on the ground. Looking up at the driver of the van, preparing myself physically and mentally, I give him the signal to drive over me.

"Do it!" I yell. The motor roars, my guts squish inside my body, and then it's over. I hop up, seeing stars, but otherwise physically unhurt after being run over by a full sized Chevrolet van.

Still dirty from being run over, I'm standing over a five gallon bucket with water and concrete bricks in it. My right arm has an eighth inch stainless steel rod piercing the skin behind the elbow. I bend over the bucket. My instructor wraps a rope on the bucket over the rod sticking through my arm. The test is to pick up the pail of water and bricks off of the ground and spin around twice with the bucket hanging from the spike in my arm. After completing these rigorous tests, I then fought with my instructor's instructor for two minutes.

Passing this test would not have been possible without years of training and practice. It took me four years of hard work to prepare myself for that Black Belt test.

Certainly after reading this essay, most people won't run out to take the Black Belt test. This essay intends to explain how the test is given and what the student must do to pass. Readers can appreciate and perhaps shake their heads in admiration or awe.

3. Hints for Writing the Third Type of Process Paper— Recreating an Event

The third kind of process essay records an event and answers the question: "What happened? Rather than giving directions as did Garrison Keillor in "How to Write a Personal Essay," or describing how something complicated is performed as did Brad Anderson in "The Fighting Arts," in this type of paper you describe an event. The event is over, but you make the reader see, hear, smell, touch, taste, and most importantly, understand the significance of the event. This paper seems like the personal narrative, but the experience described is not personal.

Introduction:

- Set the stage. You might describe the scene, characters, and the occasion.
- Set the mood with your images and wording.
- Give background the audience may need to understand the event and its significance.

Body:

- Recreate the event from start to finish. If you interrupt the chronological time order, be sure the reader knows.
- Describe the event in such detail that the reader can see the colors, people, and animals and know what went on. Show what happened. Don't just summarize.
- Record dialogue if it will help the reader hear what is happening. Record all the other sounds, too.
- Describe the smells if they will help the reader understand.
- Make the reader feel the emotions that you and/or others felt.

Conclusion:

- Show how the event ended.
- Stress the event's importance.
- Set the mood so the reader must be affected by the way the event turned out.

Example

The following is the moving Pulitzer Prize-winning account of how the first unknown soldier was laid to rest on Nov. 11, 1921. This unknown soldier of World War I was later joined in Arlington National Cemetery by unknown soldiers of World War II, the Korean War, and the Vietnam War.

For his essay, "He was home, the unknown, to sleep forever," the Associated Press awarded Kirke L. Simpson the first byline by a news service writer. As you read, imagine yourself at the ceremony.

He was home, the unknown, to sleep forever among his own

by Kirke L. Simpson

Under the wide and starry skies of his own homeland, America's unknown dead from France sleeps tonight, a soldier home from the wars.

Alone, he lies in the narrow cell of stone that guards his body; but his soul has entered into the spirit that is America. Wherever liberty is held close in men's hearts, the honor and the glory and the pledge of high endeavor poured out over this nameless one of fame will be told and sung by Americans for all time.

Scrolled across the marble arch of the memorial raised to American soldier and sailor dead, everywhere, which stands like a monument behind his tomb, runs this legend: "We here highly resolve that these dead shall not have died in vain."

The words were spoken by the martyred Lincoln over the dead at Gettysburg. And today with voice strong with determination and ringing with deep emotion, another president echoed that high resolve over the coffin of the soldier who died for the flag in France.

Great men in the world's affairs heard that high purpose reiterated by the man who stands at the head of the American people. Tomorrow they will gather in the city that stands almost in the shadow of the new American shrine of liberty dedicated today. They will talk of peace; and of the curbing of the havoc of war.

They will speak of the war in France that robbed this soldier of life and name and brought death to comrades of all nations by the hundreds of thousands. And in their ears when they meet must ring President Harding's declaration today beside that flag-wrapped, honor-laden bier:

"There must be, there shall be, the commanding voice of a conscious civilization against armed warfare."

All day long the nation poured out its heart in pride and glory for the nameless American. Before the first crash of the gun roared its knell for the dead from the shadow of the Washington monument, the people who claim him as their own were trooping out to do him honor. They lined the long road from the Capitol to the hillside where he sleeps tonight; they flowed like a tide over the slopes about his burial place. They choked the bridges that lead across the river to the fields of the brave, in which he is the last comer.

Soldiers, sailors and marines—all played their part in the thrilling spectacle as the cortege rolled along. And just behind the casket, with its faded French flowers on the draped flag, walked the president, the chosen leader of a hundred million, in whose name he was chief mourner at his bier. Beside him strode the man under whom the fallen hero had lived and died in France, General Pershing, wearing only the single medal of victory that every American soldier might wear as his only decoration.

Behind came the carriage in which rode Woodrow Wilson, also stricken down by infirmities as he served in the highest place of the nation, just as the humble private riding in such state ahead had gone down before a shell or bullet. For that dead man's sake, the former president had put aside his dread of seeming to parade his physical weakness and risked health, perhaps life, to appear among the mourners for the fallen.

After President Harding and most of the high dignitaries of the government had turned aside at the White House, the procession, headed by its solid blocks of soldiery and the battalions of sailor comrades, moved on with Pershing for the long road to the tomb.

Ahead, the white marble of the amphitheater gleamed through the trees. People in thousands were moving about the great circle. Down below the platform placed for the casket, in a stone vault, lay wreaths and garlands. Above the platform gathered men whose names ring through history—Briand, Foch, Beatty, Balfour, Jacques, Diaz and others—in a brilliant array of place and power. They were followed by notables from all countries gathered here for tomorrow's conference and by some of the older figures in American life too old to walk beside the funeral train.

At the arch where the choir waited the heroic dead, comrades lifted his casket down and, followed by the generals and the admirals who had walked beside him from the Capitol, he was carried to the place of honor. Ahead moved the white robed singers, chanting solemnly. Carefully the casket was placed above the banked flowers, and the Marine Band played sacred melodies until the moment the President and Mrs. Harding stepped to their places beside the casket.

Mr. Harding showed strong emotion as his lips formed the last words of the address. He paused, then with raised hand and head bowed, went on in the measured, rolling periods of the Lord's Prayer. The response that came back to him from the thousands he faced, from the other thousands out over the slopes beyond, arose like a chant.

Then the foreign officers who stand highest among the soldiers or sailors of their flags came one by one to the bier to place gold and jeweled emblems for the brave above the breast of the sleeper. Already, as the great prayer ended, the president had set the American seal of admiration for the valiant, the nation's love for brave deeds and the courage that defies death, upon the casket. Side by side he laid the Medal of Honor and the Distinguished Service Cross.

The casket, with its weight of honors, was lowered into the crypt. A rocking blast of gunfire rang from the woods. The glittering circle of bayonets stiffened to a salute to the dead. Again the guns shouted their message of honor and farewell. Again they boomed out: A loyal comrade was being laid to his last, long rest.

High and clear and true in the echoes of the guns, a bugle lifted the old, old notes of taps, the lullaby for the living soldier, in death his requiem. Long ago some forgotten soldier poet caught its meaning clear and set it down that soldiers everywhere might know its message as they sing to rest:

"Fades the light;
"and afar
"goeth day, cometh night,
"and a star
"leadeth all, speedth all,
"to their rest."
The guns roared out again in the national salute. He was home, the unknown,
to sleep forever among his own.

COLLABORATIVE LEARNING

1. In your writing group, explain how you felt after reading "He was home, the unknown, to sleep forever." After discussion, write your answers.

   How do you think the writer wanted you to respond? What were your clues? Why did the author refer to Lincoln? What mood does the writer create with words like *martyred, cell, scrolled, chant, prayer,* and *requiem?*

   How does the writer relate the burial of the unknown soldier to the larger issues of war and peace?

   How might a war veteran respond to the essay?

   How does the writer fulfill the guidelines for recreating an event? What extras make this piece worthy of one of the highest writing awards in the United States?

2. What is the difference between Kirke L. Simpson's writing and the writing by the members of your writing group? Let each person in the group explain at least three differences in his or her writing. How is your writing similar? Explain your differences and similarities in a letter to your instructor. If your writing group concludes that all members say about the same thing, write one letter. Otherwise, write separate ones. Use examples from "He was home, the unknown, to sleep forever" to clarify your points.

3. Bring a set of directions for your writing group to follow in class—for example, directions for tying a scarf or a knot; assembling a toy; cleaning something like jewelry, brass, silver; filling out a form; or using the personal computer. These directions should be written by someone not in your class.

   Follow the directions in your writing group. Any time the group has to interpret the directions or make a guess, decide how to improve the directions. Rewrite the directions. Share the original directions and your revision with your instructor.

4. In your writing group, practice clear directions.

   a. Choose a topic you can test in the classroom. Think of your own topic or use one of these:

   How to make a paper cup
   How to get from the class to another place on campus
   How to eat spaghetti
   How to draw a specific design
   How to fold a napkin
   How to tie a square knot or any other kind of knot

   b. Follow the organizational plan for giving directions found earlier in the chapter.

   c. After you finish, enlist someone to try your directions. If you are asked questions, or if the person tries to do the same step several times, your directions have problems.

   d. Revise the directions until they are unambiguous (clear).

   e. Turn in all your drafts and your revised, wonderfully clear directions to your instructor.

5. In a text for another course, find a description of a process. You might find how food is digested, a film is edited, a product is marketed, or something is made or destroyed. Take the description of the process to your writing group. Discuss how well it fulfills the guidelines for such writing. Did the group have difficulty understanding? Why? Who is the intended audience for this writer? What was well done?
   Write a letter to the author(s) and describe your responses.

6. With your group, recreate an experience so your readers know what the experience was like even though they were not with you. To do this, remember an event you all shared—a guest lecture, homecoming, a class experience, a tragedy, a good time. If you can find nothing you all share, have an experience together. All of you might attend the same event together, see the same movie, eat the same kind of cafeteria food, or walk through the corridors or parking lot of the school. If activities are impractical, write about the first time you worked together.
   Follow all the directions for writing a description of an event. Turn in one essay from the group to your instructor. After finishing the essay, each person should write a memo explaining how he or she helped write the essay.

WRITING TASKS

1. Find the worst set of directions you can. In a paragraph to the author of the directions, explain why they are so poor. Revise the directions until they are clear. Hand in the poor directions, your paragraph to the author, and your revised directions.

2. Write a short note, no longer than a paragraph, to someone important to you, giving directions on how to do something. (Possible topics: How to wash your favorite sweater, wax your car, operate your stereo, pack your suitcase, check your apartment or home while you are gone, water your plants.) Use the guidelines in the chapter and all the decisions writers make.

3. Practice writing clear directions for something you can test. For example, tell how to do something on your job, at home, for a hobby, or a craft. Make the situation as real as possible. Follow the hints for writing directions and do the Planning Sheets on pages 324–325. Turn in all your drafts and your clear directions to your instructor.

4. Explain some experience that happened to you when you tried to give or follow directions and failed. Here are two stories to start your thinking.

    Joe worked for a construction company, redoing old houses during the summer. Once he discussed whether to buy a new front door or redo the old door. The foreman told him to use the old door. As Joe was leaving the job to buy more paint, the doorbell rang. The foreman yelled, "Get the door." Joe did. He bought a new door! The boss meant, "Answer the door!"

    A woman mailed a sound tape to her male friend. Her directions to him said, "Play song number two. It tells you how I feel." So the friend listened to "Breaking Up is Easy." Only later did the woman find out that she hadn't specified the side of the tape. Her friend was supposed to hear "Everlasting Love."

5. Describe an event so well that your readers experience it even though they were not there. To do this, follow the hints in the chapter and the leadership of the piece "He was home, the unknown, to sleep forever."

6. Look over review questions at the end of chapters in any of your texts, review sheets provided by instructors, and essay questions on your old tests to find questions that ask you to describe a process. In an essay, answer one of these questions using the guidelines in this chapter. When you have finished, ask the appropriate professor to read your essay and react to it. If you do not feel free to ask the professor, ask another student in the course to read the paper and make suggestions. Revise the paper.

CHECKLIST FOR EXPLAINING WITH DIRECTIONS/PROCESS _____

Yes   *No*

If you are giving directions:

____ ____   1. Did you explain when, where, and how these directions might be used?

____ ____   2. Did you list the necessary equipment and materials?

____ ____   3. Did you list the skills and background required to accomplish the task?

____ ____   4. Did you explain all unfamiliar terms?

____ ____   5. Did you break the process into manageable steps?

____ ____   6. Did you arrange all the steps in chronological order?

____ ____   7. Did you explain how each step related to steps before and after it?

____ ____   8. Did you name trouble spots?

____ ____   9. Did you stress important points?

____ ____   10. Did you suggest other ways to apply this process?

____ ____   11. Did someone test your directions?

If you are describing a process, but do not expect the reader to perform the process:

____ ____   12. Did you interest the audience in the process?

____ ____   13. Did you show why the process is important?

____ ____   14. Did you explain who uses the process?

____ ____   15. Did you describe each part of the process?

____ ____   16. Did you define all unfamiliar terms?

If you are describing an event you witnessed:

____ ____   17. Did you recreate the event so well that readers experience it even though they were not there?

____ ____   18. Did you write for your audience?

____ ____   19. Did you describe the colors, smells, sounds, people, scene, mood, feelings, dialogue, action, emotions?

____ ____   20. Did you create a mood?

____ ____   21. Did you keep to chronological order or have a good reason for not following it?

Name _____

Section _____

DESCRIBING A PROCESS: PLANNING SHEET _____

1. Which process will you describe?

2. Why is the process important or interesting?

3. Who might want to understand the process? Why?

4. What terms do you need to explain or define for your audience?

5. What are the major parts of this process? Use more sheets if you need them.

6. What is your thesis for your paper?

Name _____

Section _____

GIVING DIRECTIONS: PLANNING SHEET _____

1. Topic: _____
2. Audience: _____
3. Purpose: _____

Needed items: List the items or material which the reader will need.

Flow chart: Make a flow chart showing each step in the process. Use more sheets if you need them.

Name _____

Section _____

PROCESS: WRITE A LETTER _____

"We need to write, otherwise nobody will know who we are," says Garrison Keillor in his essay in this chapter. So first read his essay. Then write a letter to the class to let us get to know you. The easiest way to write the letter is to use Keillor's process: describe where you are; tell us what you are thinking and be bold; tell us what is important to you. Let the letter flow along without trying to impress anyone, because the letter to impress is, Keillor says, the hardest letter to write. Just picture the class and then write to us, your friends. "Writing is a means of discovery," Keillor writes. We want to discover you, and you will discover something about yourself as you write. (Write your letter here.)

Dear _____

Chapter Twenty-Seven

Explain by Comparing and Contrasting

If you are going to buy a shirt, sweater, or pair of shoes, do you purchase the first ones that you see? I doubt it. You do comparison shopping. You probably check the label, price, and quality of the goods, comparing until you find the best fit, best value, the right style, and the right color.

Perhaps you don't like to shop. Yet you do compare and contrast. You decide which person to date or which person to marry, which job offer to take, which place to live. You even decide where to eat and what to wear. Anytime you choose to go out with one person instead of another or to take one course rather than another, you are comparing or contrasting.

Comparison and Contrast Defined

In a comparison, you find similarities. A comparison shows how something is like something else. You can compare two or more of almost anything: objects, ideas, people, events. How was last year's homecoming like this year's? How is my stepfather like my own dad? What do I like about both sweaters? How was the fighting during the Civil War like the battles of the War of 1812?

In a contrast, you find differences. These differences can be between people, cultures, ideas, things, events. How was this year's homecoming different from last year's? How is my stepfather unlike my own dad? Which of these sweaters is the best buy? How were the naval battles of the Civil War different from those during the War of 1812?

Notice that all these examples compare two items in the same logical groups: two men, two wars, two events, two countries.

Why Compare or Contrast?

The most obvious reason is to clarify or explain how something is like something else, how it is different, or how it has changed. You might explain to your mom how your stepdad is like your own dad because you simply want her to understand your point of view. In many of your essay tests, teachers will ask you to explain with comparisons or contrasts so they will know you understand the subject matter. To compare and contrast effectively, you have to know both your subjects better than if you simply described each one alone.

Another reason for thinking with comparisons and contrasts is to help make a decision among several alternatives. If you must choose between two jobs or several cars and can't be immediately decisive, it may help to compare ways these two jobs or cars are alike and contrast ways they are different. After you finish, you can look at the most important differences and then make your choice.

A third purpose for writing comparisons and contrasts is to use familiar things to explain unfamiliar things. For example, you might compare a grass snake with a pigmy rattlesnake for someone who knows grass snakes but has never seen a pigmy rattler. Or you might compare someone you are setting up to go on a blind date with someone that date already knows.

A Comparison and Contrast
"Grant and Lee: a Study in Contrasts"

Read the following essay by Bruce Catton, an eminent historian of the Civil War. Catton points out obvious similarities between the great Civil War Generals—Grant and Lee. But most of Catton's essay is about contrasts. Both generals represent conflicting traditions. Yet both men, the conclusion states, were quite alike.

Grant and Lee: A Study in Contrasts

by Bruce Catton

When Ulysses S. Grant and Robert E. Lee met in the parlor of a modest house at Appomattox Court House, Virginia, on April 9, 1865 to work out the terms for the surrender of Lee's Army of Northern Virginia, a great chapter in American life came to a close, and a great new chapter began.

These men were bringing the Civil War to its virtual finish. To be sure, other armies had yet to surrender, and for a few days the fugitive Confederate government would struggle desperately and vainly, trying to find some way to go on living now that its chief support was gone. But in effect it was all over when Grant and Lee signed the papers. And the little room where they wrote out the terms was the scene of one of the poignant, dramatic contrasts in American history.

They were two strong men, these oddly different generals, and they represented the strengths of two conflicting currents that, through them, had come into final collision.

Back of Robert E. Lee was the notion that the old aristocratic concept might somehow survive and be dominant in American life.

Lee was tidewater Virginia, and in his background were family, culture, and tradition . . . the age of chivalry transplanted to a New World which was making its own legends and its own myths. He embodied a way of life that had come down through the age of Knighthood and the English country squire. America was a land that was beginning all over again, dedicated to nothing much more complicated than the rather hazy belief that all men had equal rights, and should have an equal chance in the world. In such a land Lee stood for the feeling that it was somehow of advantage to human society to have a pronounced inequality in the social structure. There should be a leisure class, backed by ownership of land; in turn, society itself should be keyed to the land as the chief source of wealth and influence. It would bring forth (according to this ideal) a class of men with a strong sense of obligation to the community; men who lived not to gain advantage for themselves, but to meet the solemn obligations which had been laid on them by the very fact that they were privileged. From them the country would get its leadership; to them it could look for the higher values—of thought, of conduct, of personal deportment—to give it strength and virtue.

Lee embodied the noblest elements of this aristocratic ideal. Through him, the landed nobility justified itself. For four years, the Southern states had fought a desperate war to uphold the ideals for which Lee stood. In the end, it almost seemed as if the Confederacy fought for Lee; as if he himself was the Confederacy . . . the best thing that the way of life for which the Confederacy stood could ever have to offer. He had passed into legend before Appomattox. Thousands of tired, underfed, poorly clothed Confederate soldiers, long-since past the simple enthusiasm of the early days of the struggle, somehow considered Lee the symbol of everything for which they had been willing to die. But they could not quite put this feeling into words. If the Lost Cause, sanctified by so much heroism and so many deaths, had a living justification, its justification was General Lee.

Grant, the son of a tanner on the Western frontier, was everything Lee was not. He had come up the hard way, and embodied nothing in particular except the eternal toughness and sinewy fiber of the men who grew up beyond the mountains. He was one of a body of men who owed reverence and obeisance to no one, who were self-reliant to a fault, who cared hardly anything for the past but who had a sharp eye for the future.

These frontier men were the precise opposites of the tidewater aristocrats. Back of them, in the great surge that had taken people over the Alleghenies and into the opening Western country, there was a deep, implicit dissatisfaction with a past that had settled into grooves. They stood for democracy, not from any reasoned conclusion about the proper ordering of human society, but simply because they had grown up in the middle of democracy and knew how it worked. Their society might have privileges, but they would be privileges each man had won for himself. Forms and patterns meant nothing. No man was born to anything, except perhaps to a chance to show how far he could rise. Life was competition.

Yet along with this feeling had come a deep sense of belonging to a national community. The Westerner who developed a farm, opened a shop or set up in business as a trader, could hope to prosper only as his own community prospered—and his community ran from the Atlantic to the Pacific and from Canada down to Mexico. If the land was settled, with towns and highways and accessible markets, he could better himself. He was his fate in terms of the nation's own destiny. As its horizons expanded, so did his. He had, in other words, an acute dollars-and-cents stake in the continued growth and development of his country.

And that, perhaps, is where the contrast between Grant and Lee becomes most striking. The Virginia aristocrat, inevitably, saw himself in relation to his own region. He lived in a static society which could endure almost anything except change. Instinctively, his first loyalty would go to the locality in which that society existed. He would fight to the limit of endurance to defend it, because in defending it he was defending everything that gave his own life its deepest meaning.

The Westerner, on the other hand, would fight with an equal tenacity for the broader concept of society. He fought so because everything he lived by was tied to growth, expansion, and a constantly widening horizon. What he lived by would survive or fall with the nation itself. He could not possibly stand by unmoved in the face of an attempt to destroy the Union. He would combat it with everything he had, because he could only see it as an effort to cut the ground out from under his feet.

So Grant and Lee were in complete contrast, representing two diametrically opposed elements in American life. Grant was the modern man emerging; beyond him, ready to come on the stage, was the great age of steel and machinery, of crowded cities and a restless, burgeoning vitality. Lee might have ridden down from the old age of chivalry, lance in hand, silken banner fluttering over his head. Each man was the perfect champion of his cause, drawing both his strengths and his weaknesses from the people he led.

Yet it was not all contrast, after all. Different as they were—in background, in personality, in underlying aspiration—these two great soldiers had much in common. Under everything else, they were marvelous fighters. Furthermore, their fighting qualities were really very much alike.

Each man had, to begin with, the great virtue of utter tenacity and fidelity. Grant fought his way down the Mississippi Valley in spite of acute personal discouragement and profound military handicaps. Lee hung on in the trenches at Petersburg after hope itself had died. In each man there was an indomitable quality . . . the born fighter's refusal to give up as long as he can still remain on his feet and lift his two fists.

Daring and resourcefulness they had, too; the ability to think faster and move faster than the enemy. These were the qualities which gave Lee the dazzling campaigns of Second Manassas and Chancellorsville and won Vicksburg for Grant.

Lastly, and perhaps greatest of all, there was the ability, at the end, to turn quickly from war to peace once the fighting was over. Out of the way these two men behaved at Appomattox came the possibility of a peace of reconciliation. It was a possibility not wholly realized, in the years to come, but which did, in the end, help the two sections to become one nation again . . . after a war whose bitterness might have seemed to make such a reunion wholly impossible. No part of either man's life became him more than the part he played in their brief meeting in the McLean house at Appomattox. Their behaviour put all succeeding generations of Americans in their debt. Two great Americans, Grant and Lee—very different, yet under everything very much alike. Their encounter at Appomattox was one of the great moments of American history.

In what ways are the two generals similar? How are they different? How are their traditions similar? How are the traditions different? What makes both men great?

How To Do Comparisons and Contrasts

When a teacher finally told me the easy ways to contrast and compare two things, I wondered at all the time I had lost trying to invent my own method. Perhaps you have already discovered a good procedure. If not, let me explain some simple ways you might organize a comparison or contrast.

Finding the Basis for
Your Comparison or Contrast

The basis for your comparison is the fundamental information that makes your comparison or contrast. You will understand this easily by looking at the chart on the next page. At the top of the first column, note the label for the first item being compared: "Community college." Note the label "Similarities" on the middle column. Note the label on the third column for the other item being compared: "University."

A second set of three columns below looks just like the ones above except for the middle label—"Differences."

Students who forget the middle column have a hard time working out the basis of their comparisons. A writer always must gather supporting information for a paper, and the charts are a good way to do this for the comparison and contrast thinking. Use this information to find a reason or point for the comparison/contrast paper.

Writing the Main-Idea Sentence

Your main-idea sentence usually points out the basis of the comparison. To decide on a suitable thesis for a paper on this subject, study the information in the chart. Which school do you think is better for someone who has been a B-student in high school even though he studies almost every night?

A working thesis might sound like this: "Even though both the community college and the local university offer students an advanced education, since the community college offers extra academic help through Learning Centers, free tutors, conferences with degreed instructors, and smaller classes, it would be a better choice for a student having difficulty maintaining high grades." You may not use this exact wording in your final work, but stating your thesis this way will certainly help you organize and write the

Collecting Supporting Information for a Comparison or Contrast

Community College	Similarities	University
12 hours	Average load	12 hours
45 hours of General Education	Requirements	45 hours of General Education
Degree	Goal	Degree
Classrooms, library, gym	Basic facilities	Classrooms, library, gym
	Differences	
15–55 students	Class size	40–800 students
Teachers with degrees	Qualification of teachers	Graduate Assistants for basic courses
Basketball, golf	Popular sports	Football, basketball, golf, tennis
30 choices	Clubs	90 choices
Free tutors, learning centers for most subjects, and conferences with instructors	Assistance with instruction	Conferences with instructors
$40	Cost per credit	$100
High school diploma	Entrance requirements	1,000 on SAT
AA, AS	Degrees available	BA, BS, MA, MS, PhD, EDD

paper. Naming the points you are going to cover will help you keep them in mind as you write.

The final thesis might say, "Even though both the community college and the local university offer students an advanced education, since the community college offers a variety of extra academic help, it would be a better choice for a student having difficulty maintaining high grades."

Stressing the Significance of Similarities or Differences

Remember that a fine paper points out the significance of the similarities or differences you mention. That is, you need a purpose—a reason—for your comparison/contrast. Otherwise, your paper has no point, and after reading it, your audience is apt to say, "So what?" You might point out differences so readers see that one car is superior to another and would be a better purchase. Or you might show how one team differs from another and ought to be supported. Perhaps you show that Alzheimer's disease is more dangerous than AIDS, and consequently, more federal money ought to be spent on its cure than on a cure for AIDS. The important point is to give your readers a reason for your comparison or contrast.

Organizing Your Supporting Information in the Paper

There are different ways you can organize your comparison or contrast.

Point by Point:

One, you can begin with the points in the middle column of your chart and show how each of the two subjects being compared reacts to that point. Using the middle column of the previous chart, you might say, "Both community colleges and universities' requirements in general education are the same—forty-five hours." You would then explain. Or if you were talking about differences, you could use a middle point to begin, "Class size varies from small classes of 15 to 55 students at the community college to large classes of 40 to 800 in the undergraduate programs of the university." Then you would explain. Gradually, you would work through all the points on the middle column.

Block by Block:

Two, you can talk about all the points in your first column first and then talk about points in the third column later. In this kind of block first discuss all the community college's points: average student load, requirements, class size, faculty, popular sports, clubs, assistance with instruction, cost entrance requirements, and so forth, and then after you finish with the community college, go on to discuss the same ideas about the university. Notice how you would use the middle column to guide you through the identical ideas for each block. Readers will find the comparison easier to follow if they find the same order of main points in discussions of both the community college and then the university. Be consistent.

Creating Your Drafts

After you have gathered all your supporting information and organized it in columns, after you've recognized an audience and purpose, and after you've decided how you will organize the paper, you're probably ready to create your drafts. You might choose among several patterns people use to write a comparison or contrast:

- Point by Point: Patterns that make many points about both subjects within one paragraph (Many points about both the community college and university)
- Block by Block (Half Paragraphs): Paragraphs divided into halves so each of the two subjects receives half of the paragraph (half the paragraph on the community college and half on the university)
- Block by Block (Entire Paragraphs): Entire paragraphs written about each subject (paragraphs about only the university and paragraphs about only the community college)

Point by Point

Patterns that make many points about both subjects within one paragraph work well if you don't have much to say about each salient point. Just write a sentence or two about each point. Notice how Blair Robertson, a Canadian student, does this as he makes several observations about both Canada and the United States in each body paragraph of his essay:

Canada and the United States

by Blair Robertson

Canada and the United States share a border for more than five thousand miles; thus it has been assumed that they are almost identical countries. But, while Canada and the United States are quite similar, the differences in geography and the personalities of the people are the major differences that distinguish one country from the other.

There are major differences in the geographical makeups of *Canada and the United States.* Both countries are large, but they make use of their land much differently. *Canada's* total area is 3,851,809 square miles and is the second largest country in the world while the *Unites States* has an area of 3,615,122 square miles. Because of *Canada's* harsh climate and rugged terrain, most of the country is forced to live in the southern areas. Therefore, only about one-third of the country has been developed. The *United States,* on the other hand, has a much more suitable climate for living. Even the northern parts of the country are warmer than most of the southern regions of *Canada*. Because of the agreeable weather, the people are able to settle in almost all areas of the country and thus make better use of the land. The weather is also the major reason why the *United States* has a larger population. *Canada* has a population of 23,000,000 while the *United States*, despite having a smaller area, has a population of 240,000,000. The differences in population not only make the U.S. wealthy and powerful, they also have a tremendous effect on the personalities of both peoples.

The general personality of the people in *Canada* does, in fact, differ quite a bit from the people in the *U.S.* Because of their smaller population, *Canadians* often seem to have an inferiority complex. It is true, however, that many *Canadians* think their country is the best, but they also seem to be overwhelmed by the power and wealth of the country directly to the south. *Americans* know that their country is a world power, and because of this, they have a great sense of pride. Their patriotism is so great that many *Americans* never think about any other country because they are wrapped up in their own. In sociological terms, *Americans* are ethnocentric, meaning they think their own culture or nation is superior to all others. Another difference of personality is the degree of aggressiveness of the two countries. While *Canadians* are relatively passive because of their small population and lack of military power, *Americans* always seem anxious to fight for their country. This aggressiveness is related to the immense spirit and pride in their country and their belief in the *"American Way"* of doing things. *Canadians*, too, have pride in their country but they take pride in the freedom and beauty of the nation rather than in their military prowess. These differences of personality contribute to the uniqueness of each nation and give each a character and tone. [Italics added.]

The similarities between Canada and the United States, would, at first glance, make one assume that the two countries are almost identical. However, this is not the case. The great differences in the geography and the personality of the people make each country different in its own way. Although Canada and the United States are close neighbors and good friends, it is quite fortunate that they have been able to remain different, one from another.

Block by Block (Half Paragraphs)

Another arrangement divides paragraphs in half. This way, one half of the paragraph can be about the first subject, the second half about the second. The following is a sample paragraph that uses this pattern.

We two students are quite alike. At twenty, my life's goal is to help people who suffer economic or social calamities. While attending college, I live at the Hillside Apartment Complex and do at least thirty hours of social work there a week. I am a serious person with a serious outlook on life; practical jokes seem a waste of time. The future seems important, but I feel anxious about it since I can do nothing to stop a cosmic annihilation. [The paragraph changes here.] My writing partner, who is also twenty, is like me in many ways. His goal is the same as mine—to help people, but he intends to be a medical doctor and concentrate on assistance through holistic medicine rather than social work. He, too, lives in an apartment, the Springfield Apartments, only one mile from me. My partner thinks it is cruel to play practical jokes like dumping water, pulling out chairs, or hiding purses on folks. Like me, he is afraid of the planet's future because he has so little control over it.

Block by Block (Whole Paragraphs)

In the third pattern, you might write an entire paragraph (or several paragraphs) about one of your subjects before you write an entire paragraph about your other subject. For example, Mark Twain uses one entire paragraph to describe how he saw the great Mississippi *before* he became a riverboat pilot. In his entire second paragraph, Twain contrasts the way he sees the Mississippi *after* he became a riverboat pilot. Notice how Twain refers to the same points (sunset, log, etc.) in each paragraph.

Two Ways of Seeing a River
by Mark Twain

Now when I mastered the language of this water and had come to know every trifling feature that bordered the great river as familiarly as I knew the letters of the alphabet, I had made a valuable acquisition. But I had lost something, too. I had lost something which could never be restored to me while I lived. All the grace, the beauty, the poetry, had gone out of the majestic river! I still kept in mind a certain wonderful sunset which I witnessed when steamboating was new to me. A broad expanse of the river was turned to blood; in the middle distance that red hue brightened into gold, through which a solitary log came floating, black and conspicuous; in one place a long, slanting mark lay sparkling upon the water; in another the surface was broken by boiling, tumbling rings that were as many-tinted as an opal; where the ruddy flush was faintest was a smooth spot that was covered with graceful circles and radiating lines, ever so delicately traced; the shore on our left was densely wooded, and the somber shadow that fell from this forest was broken in one place by a long, ruffled trail that shone like silver; and high above the forest wall a clean-stemmed dead tree waved a single leafy bough that glowed like a flame in the unobstructed splendor that was flowing from the sun. There were graceful curves, reflected images, woody heights, soft distances, and over the whole scene, far and near, the dissolving lights drifted steadily, enriching it every passing moment with new marvels of coloring.

I stood like one bewitched. I drank it in, in a speechless rapture. The world was new to me and I had never seen anything like this at home. But as I have said, a day came when I began to ease from noting the glories and the charms which the moon and the sun and the twilight wrought upon the river's face; another day came when I ceased altogether to note them. Then, if the sunset scene had been repeated, I should have looked upon it without rapture and should have commented upon it inwardly after this fashion: "This sun means that we are going to have wind tomorrow; that floating log means that the river is rising, small thanks to it; that slanting mark on the water refers to a bluff reef which is going to kill somebody's steamboat one of these nights, if it keeps on stretching out like that; those tumbling 'boils' show a dissolving bar and a changing channel there; the lines and circles in the slick water over yonder are a warning that troublesome place is shoaling up dangerously; that silver streak in the shadow of the forest is the 'break' from a new snag and he has located himself in the very best place he could have found to fish for steamboats; that tall dead tree, with a single living branch, is not going to last long, and then how is a body ever going to get through this blind place at night without the friendly old landmark?"

No, the romance and beauty were all gone from the river. All the value any feature of it had for me now was the amount of usefulness it could furnish toward compassing the safe piloting of a steamboat.

Other essays in this text make use of more than one kind of technique for comparing and contrasting. Read "Why I Love Where I Live," at the end of Chapter 20, to see how I compare and contrast living in the North and South. In the essay, "Old Sour Pickle," the writer compares Sour Pickle to himself. Good writers often use a combination of different techniques for writing comparisons and contrasts. Work out a chart to help you think through your own comparison and contrast. Such a chart will help you decide on the techniques to use. Try the point by point if you have many small points to make. Try the longer block by block methods if your comparisons or contrasts are complicated and need explaining. Whichever methods you choose, remember that you are showing readers a comparison and/or a contrast for a reason. Your reason must keep the reader from saying: "So what?" Please your readers; give them a reason for reading.

COLLABORATIVE LEARNING

1. For practice, analyze the information used in a comparison/contrast essay. (Study the sample chart in this chapter and then use the chart at the end of the chapter.) Fill in the columns with the information that the writers used in *one* of the following three essays in this chapter: a. "Grant and Lee: A Study in Contrasts," or b. "Canada and the U.S.," or c. "Two Ways of Seeing a River."

2. Read the completed essay "Why I Love Where I Live" in Chapter 20 and make a chart of the comparisons and the contrasts. (Use the chart at the end of this chapter.)

3. This exercise will help you practice thinking in comparisons and contrasts. In your writing group, draw a chart containing a set of three columns for comparison and three for contrast. On the chart, put all the supporting information an audience would need to make a decision about one of the choices listed here. Be sure to choose your audience and your purpose for writing. Do this for at least three of these topics:

    Whether to buy an American or foreign car
    Whether to listen to music on records or CDs
    Whether to invest in stocks or bonds
    Whether to live in an apartment or a dorm
    Whether to enlist in the armed forces or not
    Whether to have a family or not
    Whether to be a conservative or a liberal
    Whether to be a Democrat or a Republican
    Whether to be a vegetarian or a flesh eater
    Whether to work for financial or another type of success

4. Identify ads that use comparison or contrast to tempt you to choose one product over another. What makes these ads successful or unsuccessful? Write a report of your findings.

WRITING TASKS

1. Write an essay in which you compare or contrast, or both, to explain your ideas or to lead someone to a choice. As you write, be sure to make each of the decisions writers make. If you do not want to use your own topic, choose one from the list given here. Pick a topic that benefits you; perhaps review for a course or help yourself make a decision about something you must do or buy.

    Use the chart at the end of this chapter. Fill in each column until you have covered all the points you think have a bearing on your decision. It is better to have more information than you might use. What conclusions do you reach when you look at your finished chart? These conclusions can become your purpose or main idea for the paper.

    Be sure you always have a reason for telling your reader about the topics you choose. You don't want your reader to say "So what!" after reading what you've written. Instead, clarify something or help the reader make a choice.

Two supervisors   Two athletes   Two teachers   Two jobs
Two parents   Two families   Two writers   Two cars
Two movies   Two poems   Two short stories   Two novels
Two churches or two different beliefs or different values
Two musicians or two performers or two experiments or two results
Two events, such as two birthdays or weddings or births or deaths
A person before and after or now and then
Two different parts of the country

2. Just for an experiment, write a comparison that is heavily slanted toward one view rather than another. Choose words and images and examples to make your slanting work. Make all the same decisions as you would in any writing task.

Checklist for Comparisons/Contrasts

Yes   *No*

____   ____   1. Did you compare/contrast two things in the same logical group?

____   ____   2. Did you compare/contrast for a significant reason?

____   ____   3. Did you develop more than obvious points of comparison?

____   ____   4. Did you give specific examples to explain each point of the comparison/contrast?

____   ____   5. Are the organization and purpose clear to the readers?

____   ____   6. Did you write so readers are never confused?

____   ____   7. Do you use transitions that inform the reader of your movement from one point to another?

____   ____   8. Did you eliminate all grammatical and usage problems?

Name _____

Section _____

Comparison/Contrast Planning Sheet _____

You might find it helpful to complete this page either before or after working out a chart (as on the next page) for your own comparison/contrast topics.

Two topics to be compared/contrasted:

Audience:

Purpose (the reason for making your comparison/contrast):

Main points you will use to compare/contrast: (These points are found in the middle column of a comparison/contrast chart.)

Thesis:

Name _____

Section _____

COMPARISON/CONTRAST CHART PLANNING SHEET _____

Use your own topic or devise the chart for either *Lee and Grant,* or *Canada and the United States,* or *Two Ways of Seeing a River* (all three essays in this chapter), or *Why I Love Where I Live* (Chapter 20).

	Similarities	

	Differences	

Peer Reviewer _____

Title of Essay _____

Author of Essay _____

PEER EVALUATION—COMPARISON/CONTRAST _____

Questions by Susan Slavicz

Answer the following questions from another student's paper.

1. What are the two broad subjects discussed in the paper?

2. Within these two, what common characteristics are examined? Is the primary emphasis on comparing or contrasting?

3. How is the paper structured?

4. Give a specific example or detail for each of the paper's main assertions; e.g., Grant's background: "Grant, the son of a tanner on the Western frontier . . . had come up the hard way and embodied nothing in particular except the eternal toughness and sinewy fiber of the men who grew up beyond the mountains."

5. Circle all "to be" verbs: "is", "was", "are", "were".

6. Write the paper's thesis.

7. Underline all transitional phrases.

8. Chart the paper's main ideas.

Chapter Twenty-Eight

Explain with Definitions

What is it?
A falling star?
A UFO?
A satellite burning up as it hits the atmosphere?
Just an airplane?
A poltergeist?

We ask "What is it?" many times in our lives because we want to know the answer. We want to learn. We want our curiosity satisfied.

A definition explains what something is. A definition answers the question, "What is it?"

Some definitions are harder to give than others. If a child asks, "What is love?" we might have a hard time explaining because there are so many kinds of love: love of spouse, love of country, love of one's own children, platonic love. Is each of these loves the same? Of course not.

Other definitions are easier to explain. What is a square knot? People as different as a lobster seaman or a scarf designer could say what that is and show how to tie one.

We make decisions based on our understanding of terms. Do you buy pure orange juice or pure orange juice from concentrate or orange juice from pure concentrate? What do these terms mean?

Sometimes we say we cannot get any answers. Often that means that the person with whom we must deal cannot give us a straight definition.

Why Should You Know How to Define?

Knowing how to define accurately can be to your advantage. Think of the many tests you have taken that asked you for a definition. Obviously, knowing how to define can help you do better academically.

Another use for the definition is in explaining. A definition is often the first step in an explanation. First you tell what something is; then you might give examples of it, compare or contrast it with something else the listener knows, or perhaps give the story behind it. At times, you will have to define words or ideas your listener doesn't understand so the rest of what you say makes sense.

We use definitions to make decisions. Suppose you want to buy some life insurance, but the sales agent wants to know if you want *whole life* or *term* or *universal life*. Until you understand the definition of each kind of insurance, as well as the benefits and drawbacks of each, it is hard to decide on the right kind of insurance. Without clear definitions, you might make a decision that you'll regret later.

Good salespeople define simply and clearly. This is especially true when the product they sell is complicated or made up of several parts. Good teachers define clearly. You know what they are talking about.

Some court cases depend on definitions of terms. For example, a state might define an alligator as a fish. You might argue whether an alligator is really a fish. But if you work with alligators, and fish receive special monetary benefits from the state, you would want an alligator to be defined as a fish. You can think of other issues that rest on definitions.

How do Writers Use Definitions?

Read the following essay by Lance Morrow. His essay first appeared in *Time Magazine.*

In One Ear, In the Other

by Lance Morrow

If everyone's life is a movie, every life may need a musical sound track: a heroic overall theme (like *Lawrence of Arabia* or *Star Wars*) and the various mood pieces to accompany the separate moments—romance, sorrow, shopping. There might be a bright reveille on waking, a theme to shower by, music for orange juice and coffee, bustling big-city notes, perhaps (like those in 1950s New York office-girl sagas such as *The Best of Everything*), by which to go to work. Winning an important contract might call forth *Chariots of Fire.* The approach of one's personal Great White Shark would be announced by an ominous sawing of cellos.

It could be done. The technology exists. An aural implant, perhaps a pulse monitor so that the music would follow the body's beat. . . .

On second thought, it is a revolting idea. But at least the permeating noise would be customized. As things stand now, the brain is assaulted by an indiscriminate aerosol of sound that comes out of a can and spreads like a virus. Canned music is a sort of Legionnaire's disease seeping through the world's hotels: a Lawrence Welkish synthetic, a dense cloud of inanimate noodling. It drifts from elevator to lobby, from lobby to dining room and coffee shop, thence even to the men's room, then jumps from hotel to hotel, from city to city, from country to country, until no corner of the earth is safe from this blight of the sprightly, a technique of musical leveling that can make any music—the Beatles, Simon and Garfunkel, Mozart, 2 Live Crew, the Soviet anthem—sound like *Raindrops Keep Falling on My Head.*

Enlil, the Mesopotamian god of the atmosphere, sent down a flood upon the world because of "the intolerable uproar of mankind." Unwanted noise for some reason provokes irrational fantasies of revenge: either submit to noise or annihilate the source. If Enlil were still in office, not a square centimeter of the earth would be dry. The only sound would be a gentle global lapping of waves.

Noise performs its function in nature: as a warning, for example, or a cry of pain, or as an aural accounting of reality (those are footsteps that you hear approaching, that is the surf, that is your boss). Noise by definition ought to be random, as life is random. If noise is programmed, deliberate, even institutionalized, it had better have a good reason. It had better be Bach.

Noise is often a form of stupidity and an invasion of the mind. Nature left the side gates to the brain (the ears) incautiously open. Any passing Visigothic mob of decibels can come swarming in, marauding, overturning thoughts, wrecking the civilization.

An infant's cry of distress is so pitched by nature that its urgency cannot be ignored. Thus life is served, the baby is fed. But certain other noises that cannot be ignored (the whooping car alarm, the political campaign) lead to madness, homicide or, in most of us, an exhausted disgust. The poor battered ear grows accustomed to the occupying armies.

If noise assaulted a different sense, say, the sense of smell, then people would race from the room at the smell of jackhammers, boom boxes and certain long stretches of Wagner. Somehow the human nose has kept a comparative purity of response; it remains a proud, indignant organ. The ears, however, are defeated territory.

Canned music settles over the mind like a terrible exhalation of "air fresheners." Noise becomes sinister when it ceases to be episode and becomes environment. When someone carries a loud radio onto a bus, what you have is an individual committing an aggression against his surroundings. But canned music is an assault of the surroundings against the individual. The environment itself commits the aggression and does so ironically in the guise of universal inoffensiveness.

A funny effect: the raunch of rock 'n' roll comes to sound like the Church Lady. The Rolling Stones' *I Can't Get No Satisfaction: dum dum dum dum . . . dum dum*

dum dum. Thus does detoxified music become most toxic, a lemon-scent, pine-suffused fallout.

In Japan, WALK signs at intersections have been programmed to tinkle *Comin' Through the Rye* or other tunes for pedestrians as they cross the street. The effect is charming, at least to a stranger, because it is unexpected, a silly cross-cultural grace note, a line of sunlight. But canned, environmental, globally permeating noise fills no human need. Somehow it has achieved a life of its own. The world's hotel managers should pull the plug, to universal applause. Then everyone in the lobbies of the world could appreciate the subsequent sound of one hand clapping.

What Is a Logical Definition?

A definition is usually made up of two things: a category and distinguishing characteristics.

A category. This means you put whatever you are defining into a larger category. Ask yourself, "The thing I'm defining is a kind of what?" If you are defining a desk, you might say that a desk is a kind of furniture. If you are defining a pencil, you might say a pencil is a kind of writing tool. A dog is a kind of domesticated animal. Crack is a kind of drug. Cocaine is a kind of drug. Canned music is a kind of noise.

Distinguishing characteristics. Ask yourself, "How is this [whatever you are defining] different from all the other things in that same category? What makes it different from all the others in the same group?" When you answer, you will be giving the distinguishing characteristics. For example, a school desk is a kind of furniture that is distinguished from other furniture because a school desk has these characteristics:

> It is used primarily for writing.
> It has a hard, flat surface that can be used for writing.
> It usually contains a storage space.
> It usually has four legs that touch the floor.
> Students usually sit to use the writing surface.

Certainly after you describe this, the reader will see that the school desk is a kind of furniture that cannot be confused with other furniture like a sofa, or a movable bar, or a kitchen stool.

In summary, long definitions, like the explanation of canned music, give the reader the category (the kind of _____) as well as all the distinguishing marks (how it is different from all other things in that category).

Strategies for Working Out Long Definitions

To write a long definition of something, state the category it belongs to and its distinguishing characteristics. Then add whatever else will make the explanation clear. Your long definition of something might include some or all of the following:

A description	What not to expect
Its uses	What it is not
Its effects	Types or kinds
Its causes	Examples of it
Reasons for or against it	When it might be used
Symptoms or markings	What it is like (comparisons)
Cures or solutions	What it is different from (contrasts)
How it acts	Historical meaning
What to expect of it	Anything else that will help you explain what it is

How do you know how many of these points to include in a definition? You have to decide based on your audience and your purpose. If you are to give a simple definition, you give only the category and distinguishing characteristics. On the other hand, a thorough definition might give all of the above points. But your best test is to fit your explanation to your purpose. If you know why you are defining for your special audience, you can decide which of these points your audience needs to know. For this reason, it is vital to know your audience and your purpose.

If your audience is drug users and your purpose is to explain how to get treatment, you would write a paper entirely different from the one you would write for an audience of parents who need to know if their children might be using the stuff.

Writers write for real audiences and for reasons that make sense to that audience. Otherwise the reader wouldn't keep reading. So depending on the audience and the purpose, the writer decides what to say, how much to say, and how to say it. This explanation of how to write a definition is only to help you write one when you decide that your audience wants or needs a definition.

Synonyms in Definitions

Synonyms, terms that mean the same as the term you are defining, offer short definitions. But because each word of our language usually means something slightly different, it is important to choose appropriate synonyms. A synonym will help you define as long as your readers understand one of your terms—either the one you are defining or its synonym. In sentences like the following, a synonym can explain your meaning quite easily.

The man was intoxicated, drunk.
Yesterday the optometrist, my eye doctor, told me I was a good candidate for permanent contact lenses.

If you use a synonym the reader does not know, the synonym is useless as a definition. For this reason, keep your audience in mind and choose synonyms to fit your readers.

Defining by Negation

You might define by explaining what something is not. This technique works well if you think the reader might confuse your term with something else or if you want another way to clarify what you mean. You might say, for example, that a chiropractor might not be a medical doctor. Or you could say that a pond is not a lake. A surrogate mother is not the adopting parent.

The Most Difficult of all Definitions

If you want a challenge, try explaining something you cannot see, or hear, or touch, or taste, or smell. If you cannot handle it with your five senses, you are in the realm of the abstract.

Ideas, which are abstract, are difficult to define. What is love? What is a traitor? What is evil? What is goodness?

You can define abstract ideas in the ways described earlier: by putting the term into a category, describing its distinguishing characteristics in that category, and giving synonyms for it. Yet, after you are finished doing this with an abstract word, your readers may still be left with questions.

So what else do you do? You show the idea in action. If you are defining a traitor, you don't just tell what a traitor is by category and characteristics; you show the reader a traitor in action. But one example of traitorous activity won't be enough because not every traitor acts the same way. And to complicate the problem, a traitor to some people is a hero to others. So you need to give many different examples of the traitor in action so the reader can see what you mean by *traitor*.

You may also want to limit your definition to just some situations. You might have heard a speaker say, "For the purpose of this speech, we will limit *taxation* to just . . ." or "I will not speak of all forms of love, only of mother love." Use a statement to show your readers that you will talk about only one interpretation or one definition.

Defining abstract terms can be a challenge, but an interesting challenge, as can be seen in the following sample papers.

What Is a Scapegoat?

by Patricia Hawkins

Common interpretation of the word "scapegoat" implies any person who shoulders the blame for another. However, this secular definition has lost sight of the original roots, which originated in religious ritual. In ancient Jerusalem, the people presented the Jewish high priest with two goats on the day of atonement. One goat represented the Hebrew God, Jehovah, and was killed as a sacrificial offering. The second goat represented the evil spirit, Azazel, and was called the "scape-

goat." During the ritual, the priest laid his hands upon the scapegoat and confessed the sins of the people of Jerusalem. Afterwards, the scapegoat was sent
into the wilderness as a symbol that all confessed sins were forgiven. An insight
into the background of the word makes one appreciate "scapegoat," though the
tradition behind the definition ceased long ago.

See "Collaborative Learning" later in this chapter for discussion questions on "What
Is a Scapegoat?" and the next essay, "The Living Will."

The Living Will

by Suzanne M. Packard

The Living Will is a signed, dated, and witnessed document which allows people
to state in advance their wishes regarding the use of life-sustaining procedures.
To the Living Will, they can also add provisions which appoint someone else to
direct care if they cannot do so. (This person is called an "attorney-in-fact.") The
beauty of the Living Will is that it pays attention to the wishes of the individual.
Signers of the Living Will can prohibit certain life-sustaining treatments such as
CPR, incubation for feeding, or a mechanical respirator if they do not wish these
to prolong life mechanically.

The purpose of the Living Will is stated in the document itself, "If at such a
time the situation should arise in which there is no reasonable expectation of my
recovery from extreme physical or mental disability, I direct that I be allowed to
die and not be kept alive by medications, artificial means or 'heroic measures.' I
do, however, ask that medication be mercifully administered to me to alleviate
suffering even though this may shorten my remaining life."

The Living Will was developed in 1968 by a group called Concern for Dying.
The concept is much the same now as it was then, though the will is revised
periodically to reflect changes in the legal climate and the growing patients' rights
movement. Almost half the states in the nation have some form of legislation
making the Living Will document legally binding under certain circumstances.
Many legal advisors feel that the Living Will is enforceable because it is an asser-
tion of the right to self determination of one's body and the constitutional right to
privacy. But to be legal, the Living Will must be signed by two adults who are not
related by blood to the person making the will and who are not designated as
"attorney-in-fact." These two signatures provide proof of execution, meaning that
the signature of the Living Will was witnessed and that the Living Will was not
made under duress. If the witnesses are heirs of the estate, or related to the
maker of the will, a conflict of interest may arise and cause problems in the execution of the Living Will. If an "attorney-in-fact" is appointed in the will, the document must be notarized.

In the article that follows, notice how the writer, scholars, and various heads of government struggle with a definition. As you read, think of other words that are also difficult to define.

'Terrorism'—a term notoriously difficult to pin down

by Rushworth M. Kidder

Just exactly what *is* "terrorism"?

Following the American bombing of Libya, the word is being bandied about on all sides. The United States and its allies refer to the regime of Col. Muammar Qaddafi as "terrorist," while Libya and its friends describe the U.S. action as "terrorism."

In fact, the term is notoriously difficult to pin down.

"The great difficulty when you get into [discussions of terrorism is that] right away you run into problems with definitions," notes Noel Koch, a specialist in terrorism at the U.S. Defense Department.

Last summer, when Vice-President George Bush convened his Task Force on Combating Terrorism, the group spent a number of days simply trying to agree on a definition. The final report notes that "terrorism is a phenomenon easier to describe than to define."

The problem, terrorism experts say, is that the term shifts according to one's viewpoint. The United Nations has struggled long and hard over the problem, since it is often said that "one man's terrorist is another man's freedom fighter." Terrorism, a pejorative term, is often described by those who favor it as "paramilitary action," as "resistance to occupation," or as part of a "war of national liberation."

Nevertheless, experts on terrorism interviewed recently in the U.S., Europe, and the Middle East agree on some common elements.

"The crucial element," says Prof. Paul Wilkinson of the University of Aberdeen, Scotland, "is the deliberate attempt to create fear, intensive fear, in order to coerce the wider target into giving in to what the terrorist wants."

Prof. Eytan Gilboa of Hebrew University in Jerusalem notes that "we have to make a distinction between the accidental killing of innocent civilians and an official deliberate policy of hurting civilians."

He notes that civilians are often killed both in guerrilla warfare and in terrorism. "The question is if you do it by accident or if you do it on purpose," he says. "In my understanding of it, terrorism means that you do it on purpose."

British scholar Brian Crozier calls attention to different forms of terrorism. "There's disruptive terrorism," he says, and "there's theatrical terrorism to draw attention to the cause. And there is a very important form of terrorism which is nearly always overlooked, and that's what I call coercive terrorism: Terrorism against the terrorists' own side."

In that category, for example, come the numerous bombings and assassinations carried out by various Palestinian groups against one another.

Other scholars emphasize that terrorism needs both a political motive and an audience. The motives underlying common crime are more often individual rather than political. And common crime usually involves only two parties (the criminal and the victim), whereas terrorism, which seeks to amplify and spread fear, has three: the victim, the criminal, and the audience, usually reached through the news media.

Other terms commonly used in discussions of terrorism include:

State-sponsored terrorism. This term is applied when an established government supports the activities of terrorist organizations. It is usually reserved for cases in which the sponsoring nation uses the terrorists to further its own policy goals beyond the territory in which the terrorism occurs. Libya, Syria, and Iran are generally recognized as major state sponsors of terrorism, although some experts believe much of the funding and support for international terrorism can be traced to the Soviet Union and its East bloc allies.

State terror. This term covers acts of violence and intimidation perpetuated not by small groups of clandestine terrorists but by the military and political apparatus of the state itself. Nazi Germany practiced state terror, as do many communist countries. The term is open to broad interpretation: Palestinians on the Israeli-occupied West Bank accuse Israel of practicing state terror, and Libya accuses the U.S. of the same thing.

Selected U.S. definitions of terrorism.

Department of Defense, 1983

"The unlawful use or threatened use of force or violence by a revolutionary organization against individuals or property with the intention of coercing or intimidating governments or societies, often for political or ideological purposes."

FBI, 1983

"The unlawful use of force or violence against persons or property to intimidate or coerce a government, the civilian population, or any segment thereof, in furtherance of political or social objectives."

State Department, 1984

"Premeditated, politically motivated violence perpetrated against noncombatant targets by subnational groups or clandestine state agents."

Department of Justice, 1984

"Violent criminal conduct apparently intended:

To intimidate or coerce a civilian population.

To influence the conduct of a government by intimidation or coercion.

To affect the conduct of a government by assassination or kidnapping."

The Vice-President's Task Force on Combating Terrorism, 1986

"The unlawful use or threat of violence against persons or property to further political or social objectives. It is usually intended to intimidate or coerce a government, individuals, or groups or to modify their behavior or policies."

COLLABORATIVE LEARNING

1. Reread the definition called "What is a Scapegoat?" earlier in this chapter. After you finish, discuss these questions and write your answers.

   a. Today, what is a scapegoat?

   b. Who have been some scapegoats of the twentieth century?

   c. Who is the audience for this paragraph?

   d. What strategies for writing the long definition did you find used here?

   e. How does the writer of this definition use an approach completely different from that of the writer defining *crack*?

   f. What other questions do you have about scapegoats? How could the answers to your questions be used in a longer definition?

2. Reread the essay by Suzanne Packard earlier in this chapter and together answer the following questions.

   a. Which strategies for writing a long definition did Suzanne Packard use? Support your answers with examples from her definition.

   b. If you were writing a longer paper about the Living Will, what other questions, besides those already in the definition, should you answer?

   c. Do you think that hospitals, doctors, or families should honor a Living Will when someone that has made out such a will is dying? What benefits do you see? What problems do you see? After you answer these questions, think about how answering these questions might make an even longer paper about the Living Will.

3. In your writing group, practice thinking with the long definition. To do this follow these steps:

   a. Choose a term to define, something you would like to explain, such as *bass guitar, root canal, mechanical heart, rock music* or *wrap-around mortgage.* Or choose a term you wish someone else had understood like *AIDS, women's rights, mutual fund, stock option,* or *politically incorrect.*

   b. Decide on an audience who could benefit by knowing the definition of the term.

   c. Decide why that audience would need or want to know that term.

   d. Decide on the information to include in your definition for that audience. (Refer to the points that might be included in a long definition.)

Repeat steps a through d with several terms until your group has a feeling for creating long definitions.

4. In the *Oxford English Dictionary* find interesting definitions and histories of one or two words. (A copy of the dictionary will be in a library.) Summarize the histories for the writing group.

5. With your group, write a note to a dentist, doctor, recruiter, or someone else asking for a definition of something. For example, you might ask a dentist about a crown for a tooth. What is a crown? Is it different from a cap? Why should a tooth be crowned instead of filled? When should a tooth be crowned? How much does a crown cost? How is the crown put on? What is the crown made of? How long should it last? Do you see that these questions are vital to a patient who needs a crown? (During your lifetime, you will ask for many definitions from professionals, and you will be asked to give definitions, too. So it is helpful to know the thinking that results in a fine definition.)

6. Find exam questions that call for a definition. A question might include many points, only one of which might ask for a definition. (For example, a journalism test item might say: "Yellow journalism reflected the values of the nineteenth-century immigrant. To agree or disagree with this statement, give a definition of *yellow journalism* and explain how it reflected the attitudes and prejudices of the times.") Take samples of questions that ask for definitions to your writing group. Discuss how to organize answers to these questions. Show your test questions to your writing instructor.

WRITING TASKS

1. Write a letter to someone important to you—a teacher, friend, or anyone else. In the letter, define something you would like that person to understand. You might explain an illness that you have, define the career that you want, or define some aspect of a sport you play, to name a few possible topics. As you write the letter, be sure to make all the decisions writers must make.

2. Write an essay in which you use a definition to explain what you mean. Make all the decisions writers must make.

   Topic: Choose your own topic or let one of the ideas listed here suggest a topic:

Nightmare	Acid rain	Antique
Ugliness	Yankee	Disability
Westerner	Stereotype	Just wage
Friendship	Weed	Welfare

Shotgun	Laser	Epidemic
A kind of music	A specific musical instrument	

A term used in sport, fashion, education, science, business, religion

Supporting Information: Gather all the information that you might use in a long definition.

a. Put the term into a large category by asking yourself, "This is a kind of what?"

b. Find all the distinguishing characteristics of your topic. Add whatever else will make the explanation clear. Include any, or all, of the following:

Physical description	Uses
Effects	Causes
Reasons for or against	Symptoms or markings
How it acts or works	What to expect
What not to expect	Types or kinds
Examples	Historical meaning
Cures or remedies or preventive measures	Advantages/disadvantages
What it is like (comparisons)	People involved
What is different from (contrasts)	When it occurs
Anything else that will help you explain what it is	Solutions

Audience: Decide on the audience for whom you are defining.

Purpose: Remind yourself of the reasons why you want your audience to know this definition.

Voice: Decide on the writer's personality, which you will use.

Organization: Look over all your supporting information and decide how you will organize it to have the greatest effect on your audience.

Thesis: Write a main-idea sentence to guide your writing of the paper.

Drafting: Write your paper to see how it looks and then rearrange it until your definition suits your audience.

Revision: Study each word and sentence to be sure it matches the audience, the writing personality and the writing occasion.

3. Write an essay in which you define a term that is difficult to pin down. Following the pattern of "'Terrorism'—a term notoriously difficult to pin down." Research to find various meanings groups and/or experts give the term. Be sure to explain why the term is difficult to define and relate it to a present-day

controversy. Possible topics: men's rights, women's rights, humanism, funda-mentalist, liberal, chauvinistic, patriotism, equality.

Checklist for a Long Definition

Yes   *No*

____   ____   1. Did you put the word you are defining into a larger category?

____   ____   2. Did you say how it was different from everything else in the same category?

____   ____   3. Did you have a specific audience for your paper?

____   ____   4. Did you have a reason for writing to that audience?

____   ____   5. Did you use different kinds of supporting information to satisfy your audience and achieve your purpose?

____   ____   6. Did you organize the paper so you accomplished your purpose and affected the audience the way you wanted to affect it?

____   ____   7. Did you rewrite until every word is your best choice?

____   ____   8. Do you like your paper?

Name _____

Section _____

START-UP WORK SHEET FOR A DEFINITION PAPER

Topic:

Audience:

Purpose:

Category: Put your subject into a larger category by asking yourself, "This is a kind of _____?" (In the example of the long essay in this chapter CANNED MUSIC was called a kind of NOISE.)

Distinguishing Characteristics: Below, explain the distinguishing characteristics which fit your topic. Not all will be appropriate, so fill out those which you might use in your paper. (Gather more information than you need so you can choose the best information to use.)

1. Physical description

2. Its effects

3. Its causes

4. How it acts or works

5. What to expect of it

6. What not to expect of it

7. Examples

8. Cures or remedies or preventive measures

9. What is it like (comparisons)

10. What is it different from (contrasts)

11. Uses

12. Reasons for it (or against it)

13. Symptoms or markings

14. Types or kinds

15. Historical meaning

16. Advantages or disadvantages

17. Who is involved

18. When it occurs

19. Cures or solutions (if needed)

20. What it is not (to prevent a mix-up from something else)

21. Anything else that will help you explain what it is

Choose the most important of these items (1–21) to use in your long definition paper; then place an asterisk next to the seven or eight items you think you will use.

Peer Reviewer _____

Title of Essay _____

Author of Essay _____

Peer Evaluation Definition Paper _____

Questions by Susan Slavicz

1. What is the writer defining?

2. Write the paper's thesis.

3. Give five concrete examples from the paper which illustrate the author's points.

4. This paper should be organized around the thesis. Briefly tell how the writer uses supports or furthers the main points.

Chapter Twenty-Nine
Explain with Causes and/or Effects

Which caused which? Did rivers spring up because great cities were there? Or did the earliest cities develop where the rivers ran? If you were an ancient thinker, you might reason that the rivers grew up wherever there were large cities. Today we smile at that analysis.

Causes

Why is your hair the color it is today?
Why are you eyes their color?
Why are you in school?
Why did you eat what you ate for breakfast?

The answers to all these questions are causes. Your mom and dad (causes) gave you your natural hair color (effect) and eye color (effect) through your genes. Maybe your hair is different today (effect) because you changed (cause) it or because the sun bleached (cause) it. You are in school (effect) because you or someone else decided that you would be in school (causes). You ate what you ate today (effect) because you or someone else fixed it or because you enjoyed the taste or because you had nothing else around (causes).

A *cause* is the reason something is the way it is or the reason something happens. A cause answers the question, "What made this happen?"

Effects

What will be the result of your attending all your classes and doing all your homework?
What will happen if you eat 3,000 calories every day for an entire year?
What would be the effect of a 200-mile-an-hour tornado?

The answers to these questions are effects. Well, if you attend class faithfully (cause), you will not be penalized for poor attendance (effect); if you eat 3,000 calories daily for a year (cause), you may put on extra weight (effect); the tornado will damage any structure (effect) it hits directly (cause).

An *effect* is a result. It answers, "What happened, or happens, because of that?" "What happened, or happens, as a result?"

Why Think about Causes and Effects?

We often want to know why something happened or why something is the way it is. Why is there political turmoil in the Middle East? What is causing the fighting in Ireland? Why did the United States become a democratic country? Why do people wear animal fur? What is the effect of war toys on kids? Why date the person you are dating? Knowing the answers to questions like these makes us better informed and more conscious of our personal decisions.

If we think about the reasons behind something, we are less apt to be buffeted by them. Studying causes and effects lets us be in control. If you find out that a certain kind of perfume causes your sneezing, you can choose not to wear it any more and stop the sneezing. If you find out that you are depressed on your birthday because you're unhappy with what you've done with your life, you can choose to change and won't have to be depressed any more. If you don't figure out why you are depressed, you'll probably keep suffering.

We want to know causes and effects in serious social situations. Do casual contact, exchange of blood, and kissing cause AIDS? If we know the causes, society can take precautions to avoid the disease. Hysteria can be prevented.

What are some effects of AIDS? What are the physical effects of the disease? What does it do to the families of those who have the disease? What are effects of AIDS on whole school systems, labor laws, testing and privacy? As you can see, sometimes knowing causes and effects is vital to life.

In less serious situations, we want to know the causes of everyday problems. Why does the car not start? Why did the shower stop up? Why does the toilet not flush? Why did tuition go up? Why are my taxes higher? Why do I smell mildew?

We also want to know effects. If I vote for the Democrat for president, will my taxes go up? If I vote for the Republican for mayor, will my taxes go up? If I have a degree in computer science, will I be happy with the career choices that degree offers? If I become a teacher, will I be satisfied with my salary?

Writing about Causes and Effects

Writing about causes and effects may be simple in some situations. If you explain why you bought a black Labrador for your pet instead of a Maine Coon cat, most people will not get upset with your analysis. You have your own personal reasons.

At other times, writing about cause and effect can be much more complicated, especially if you write of human behavior. It is difficult to figure out human motives. Why did your friend not telephone? Why did your teacher seem so grumpy today? Why did your mother give you a pink shirt for your birthday? Your ability to figure out other people's reasons depends on their willingness to tell you the truth. Maybe your friend didn't call because he forgot but is ashamed to tell you, so he gave you another excuse. Maybe he is trying to break off your relationship and wants you to get the hint. It is harder to figure out human behaviors than causes for physical things like why the key broke in the lock.

Many subjects, particularly in the social sciences, are difficult to handle. If you treat controversial subjects like abortion, AIDS, politics, or criminal punishment, readers may not agree with your analysis of problems. If you state that aborting a fetus is not murder because the fetus is not a human being or that women who do abort are free to make decisions for their own bodies, some readers may disagree. These kinds of analyses are hard to handle because people do not agree about human behavior, attitudes, moral positions, and beliefs.

Guidelines for Writing about Causes and Effects

The following are some guidelines that will help you as you learn the art of writing an analysis (giving causes or effects) of controversial issues and human behavior.

Usually, more than one cause or effect is behind a significant situation or event. There might be several causes for a person's being fired from a job. One cause will not explain child abuse or drug addiction or vandalism. Usually there is more than just one effect, too. What would be the effects of your not finishing college? What are the effects of the weapons race? A writer must handle several causes and effects.

If you say an event has only one cause, you have to check it out by making sure that there are no other possible causes and that, whenever you have that cause, the same effect always follows. If you say the car wouldn't start because the battery was dead, check it out. If you put a fresh battery in the car and the car starts, you know that the battery was the problem. If you put that dead battery in another car and that car won't start, you have another check.

Just because something happens first doesn't mean that it causes the next thing to happen. If you see a black cat and then have a nightmare, it is silly to think that the cat caused the nightmare. Suppose you fell down some steps and hit your head and then got a headache; it doesn't necessarily mean that falling and hitting your head caused the headache. Maybe you have a brain tumor that is causing you to fall down and giving you the headache.

Some issues have important causes and effects as well as less important ones. If you are pressed for space, treat the important ones in your paper. (You can't give all the reasons why the mothers-in-law in America have a bad name, but you can give some reasons.) Sometimes, though, you can't leave out anything because if you do, you distort the truth. This point is especially true if you are giving the causes behind an accident or a scientific experiment. If you say that the car went out of control due to icy road conditions and don't mention that the driver was drunk, you haven't told all the causes of the accident.

Because it's sometimes impossible to treat all the causes or effects of human behavior, acknowledge those you don't discuss. Tell your reader that there are more causes or effects for important social issues, but that your paper is limited to just the ones you name. If you don't, your reader will accuse you of treating only part of the issue or of prejudice. For example, you know there are many causes of child abuse, but you might limit your paper to reasons parents who were abused abuse their own children.

Acknowledge the authorities you researched.

Warn your readers with qualifiers like "It seems that . . ." and "According to what is known now . . . " It is difficult to be absolutely sure when you try to establish causes or effects. Qualifiers let readers know you are being careful, and this will make them more apt to take you seriously.

Some Sample Papers Analyzed

The first of the two student papers presented here, "Salad Days," explains a personal event and the effects it had on the writer.

Salad Days

by Ruth Ware

I recall walking to a Seven-Eleven with my sister Toni. I can remember passing the flower shop and the slew of office establishments. I remember the rust color sidewalk, red brick walls, and the Marlboro advertisements on the windows of the store.

This particular day it was 100 in the shade, I was five, and Toni had come with me to buy something cool to drink. I, though, had something else in mind. I was going to pilfer something, and I wasn't going to be discovered.

As the two of us strode into the store, I saw that the layout was perfect for my intentions. The counter sat at the center of the aisles that projected out from it like rays from the sun.

After I was certain Toni was on the other side of the room, I squatted down at the end of the candy aisle to make sure no one saw me. I noisily opened and shoved a piece of red-hot gum into my mouth. Hastily, I trotted after my sister who had already gone out the door. The gum was much too large for my mouth, but I had no idea that it was obvious.

Toni turned around and inquired, "What's in your mouth?"

I muffled, "Nothing," and shook my head. My eyes were tearing because the gum was so hot.

Again she demanded to know what I had in my mouth. Once more I shook my head and muffled.

But she discovered the gum and later told my mother what I had done.

Putting both of us in the car, mother backtracked to the store. I cried all the way there. Mother forced me to walk up to the tall lady at the counter and tell her I was sorry as I paid the penny I owed her. I thought I might have to go to jail. I had not contemplated what might happen if I were caught.

This experience embarrassed and humiliated me greatly. I don't intend ever again to play the part of the thief.

"My salad days,
When green in judgement" [Shakespeare] are over!

Questions

1. What are several causes and effects in the piece?

2. What are some long-term effects of the mother's reaction?

3. This writer relates a personal experience about stealing and punishment. How might you develop an impersonal paper on the effects of stealing?

Charting Causes and Effects

Below is a flow chart of causes and effects made by the writer of "Salad Days." You can work out a similar chart to show causes and effects for any paper you write. Such a chart helps you think out many points which you might otherwise miss.

Why I Will Never Steal

Because

I stole once as a child and
it was a bad experience.

Immediate Result

I was caught, and it embarrassed
and humiliated me terribly.

Other Immediate Results

After I was caught, I was made
to apologize for what I had done.

Long-Range Results

I have no desire to steal again.

More Long-Range Results

I will get an education and
make a living the honest way.

More Long-Range Results

I will pursue my life in a respectable
manner and earn confidence.

What Is the Overall Result of this Experience?

I'm not even tempted to steal again!

Example

"Tournament: Killer of Hundreds of Billfish" treats a less personal issue. The writer
explains cause and effects to make you believe his point. Notice how the writer uses
some of the guidelines given earlier for a convincing cause-and-effect paper.

Tournament: Killer of Hundreds of Billfish

by Doug Keech

Three out of every four blue marlin and every white marlin and all sailfish
caught during the Daytona Beach Striking Fish Tournament over the past eight
years have been killed. The killing of these fish has had a substantial effect on the
fishing in the whole Daytona area. If the tournament were to be made a release
tournament, hundreds of fish would be saved each year.

A release tournament differs from a kill tournament in that every fish is given a certain amount of points, due to its estimated weight. The fish does not have to be killed and brought into the weigh station. When a boat hooks up with, say a 350 pound blue marlin, the boat calls a committee boat which comes alongside and verifies the catch.

To release a fish, the angler brings the fish boatside and the mate or some other crew member grabs the wire and removes the hook. Some boats just grab the leader and cut the hook, leaving it in the fish's mouth. The hook will rust out or be wiggled out by the fish.

Before releasing the fish, the sailors use a sharp, spearlike pole to tag the fish with a special tag from the tournament. This tag contains information on the fish, like its estimated weight and the location where it was caught. If someone else at a later date catches the fish, he sends the tag to either the tournament committee or the state fish and game commission. Here the dates, location of the catches and weights of the fish are plotted. Thus the tags make possible knowledge about the migratory and eating habits of the fish.

Since the Daytona tournament started in 1979, the charter fishing in Daytona has slowed down substantially. The summer before the tournament, seventy-nine sailfish were caught; last year only fifty-one were caught, the most since 1979. But not only has the sailfish population declined, so has the blue and white marlin population.

If the fishing in the Daytona area is to rebound and again flourish, its anglers will have to show some conservation. A giant step in that conservation would be to make the kill tournaments release tournaments and keep the fish alive.

Questions

1. The writer hopes for what effects from tournaments that release instead of kill fish? How does he support this hope? Do you believe him?

2. What does the writer think is the cause of fewer sailfish and marlin being caught in the kill tournaments? Do you think that is the only cause of the lower tournament kill?

3. What does the writer do well? How might the writer have strengthened his paper?

4. The writer chose the voice of a concerned captain of a charter fishing boat. Do you hear that voice speak in the essay?

Tumbling from Causes to Effects

Causes have effects. Those effects often become causes themselves. Then those effects-turned-causes have effects that, in turn, become causes. This process keeps repeating.

If causes and effects keep tumbling, how do you get a hold on them? One of the great joys of being a writer is that writing gives you control. You, the writer, decide where you will stop the tumbling from causes to effects to causes to effects. You put a box around part of the world and you say, "I will study just that much!" You put order on the square about which you are writing. That's what it means to be a writer: to make sense out of some of the random points of life. You can decide where you want to start and where to stop. You decide how big your box in your writing will be.

And if you can control just a part of life by making sense of it in your writing, you are apt to be able to control more of yourself in life outside of writing. This is one of the effects of being a writer. You learn how to put meaning on the chaos you find in life. You learn how to think about it in different ways. You learn how to control it. Then it cannot control you! If you know what this control means, you are on your way to being a good writer.

Essay to Study

Notice how S. I. Hayakawa controlled and gave meaning to this experience in his life.

The Value of Unoriginal Remarks

by S. I. Hayakawa

An incident in my own experience illustrates how necessary it sometimes is to give people the opportunity to agree. Early in 1942, a few weeks after the beginning of the war and at a time when rumors of Japanese spies were still widely current, I had to wait two or three hours in a railroad station in Oshkosh, Wisconsin, a city in which I was a stranger. I became aware as time went on that the other people waiting in the station were staring at me suspiciously and feeling uneasy about my presence. One couple with a small child were staring with special uneasiness and whispering to each other. I therefore took occasion to remark to the husband that it was too bad that the train should be late on so cold a night. The man agreed. I went on to remark that it must be especially difficult to travel with a small child in winter when train schedules were so uncertain. Again the husband agreed. I then asked the child's age and remarked that the child looked very big and strong for his age. Again agreement—this time with a slight smile. The tension was relaxing.

After two or three more exchanges, the man asked, "I hope you don't mind my bringing it up, but you're Japanese, aren't you? Do you think the Japs have any chance of winning this war?"

"Well," I replied, "your guess is as good as mine. I don't know any more than I read in the papers. (This was true.) But the way I figure it, I don't see how the Japanese, with their lack of coal and steel and oil and their limited industrial capacity, can ever beat a powerfully industrialized nation like the United States."

My remark was admittedly neither original nor well informed. Hundreds of radio commentators and editorial writers were saying exactly the same thing during those weeks. But just because they were, the remark sounded familiar and was on the right side, so that it was easy to agree with. The man agreed at once, with what seemed like genuine relief. How much the wall of suspicion had broken down was indicated by his next question. "Say, I hope your folks aren't over there while the war is going on."

"Yes, they are. My father and mother and two young sisters are over there."

"Do you ever hear from them?"

"How can I?"

"Do you mean you won't be able to see them or hear from them till after the war is over?" Both he and his wife looked troubled and sympathetic.

There was more to the conversation, but the result was that within ten minutes after it had begun they had invited me to visit them in their city and have dinner with them in their home. And the other people in the station, seeing me in conversation with people who didn't look suspicious, ceased to pay any attention to me and went back to reading their papers and staring at the ceiling.

Questions

1. What is the cause of the prejudice?

2. What is the effect of the unoriginal remarks?

3. Do you agree with Hayakawa that one way to rid prejudice is to show how alike we all are? How can unoriginal remarks have that affect?

COLLABORATIVE LEARNING

1. In your writing group, think about causes and effects. For each of the situations listed, decide on several causes. (Ask, "Why is this so? Why did it happen?") Then decide on several effects of the situation. (Ask, "What happens as a result of this?")

   For example, one cause for eating purple cotton candy might be that the candy maker handed it to you free. Another reason might be that you like the taste of grape cotton candy. An effect of eating the candy is that your teeth and tongue turn purple for several hours afterward. Another effect might be that you get ill and resolve never to eat purple cotton candy again. Enjoy and use your imagination. Find several causes and effects for each topic below.

Causes		Effects
?	Eating purple cotton candy	?
?	Wearing braces on teeth	?
?	"A" grades	?
?	Getting a raise at work	?
?	Teen pregnancy	?
?	Spring break	?
?	Fasting	?
?	Arguing with a sales clerk	?
?	Chewing tobacco	?
?	Suicides	?

2. Just for fun, to practice thinking with causes and effects, try this.

Ask your partner why he or she is wearing something or doing something. Each time your partner answers with an explanation, ask "why" again. For example, your partner might be wearing a gold necklace.

> You ask, "Why are you wearing the gold necklace?"
> Your partner may answer, "My girl friend gave it to me."
> You ask, "Why did she give it to you?"
> Answer: "Because she likes me."
> You ask, "Why does she like you?"
> Answer: "Because we enjoy the same things."
> You ask, "Why do you like the same things?"

Keep this chain going as long as you want.

You can reverse the game and try playing with effects. Begin by asking your partner, "What if . . . ?" You might use a job or grades or a car to begin to ask, "What if?" Here is an example of how you might interact with a partner.

> You ask, "What if, after college, you get the job you want?"
> Your partner may answer, "Then I'll be a lawyer in my uncle's firm."
> You ask, "And then what might happen?"
> Answer: "I'll have to work fourteen hours a day to keep up with my cousin Tom."
> You ask, "And then what might happen?"

Keep asking "And then what might happen." until you want to stop. Answers to that question will probably be effects. For variety, you could each write your questions and answers and keep exchanging papers until you have a chain of at least five to eight questions and answers. Can you keep the chain going even further?

3. Discuss the questions found after the essays called "Salad Days," "Tournament: Killer of Hundreds of Billfish," and "The Value of Unoriginal Remarks" earlier in this chapter. After you've answered the questions, write a report of your responses.

4. Sort out the causes and the effects in the following story. Notice how the causes create effects that immediately become causes themselves. With your group, make a diagram to see the causes and effects at work.

> At breakfast, I read in a newspaper ad that the book shelves I'd been wanting were reduced $50 if the buyer picked them up and put them together. So as soon as the store opened, I rushed to buy the unassembled shelves. While I paid the bill, two men lugged the heavy packing crate containing shelves and hardware out of the store and lashed it into my trunk. Since the new book shelves were seven feet high, the crate stuck out of the trunk by over a yard. I carefully drove the ten miles home.
>
> When I finally jumped out of the car to see how the shelves had survived the trip, I saw that they looked fine, but the rear bumper of my car was dangling almost to the road.
>
> The men had tied the heavy crate to the bumper! As I'd stopped and started at traffic lights, the two hundred pounds of shelving had broken loose the entire back bumper. True, the bumper was a bit rusty, but it might have lasted several years without the strain of the shelving tied to it.
>
> The next day, an auto-parts dealer told me that parts and labor to install a new bumper would cost $800! Well, the car was worth little more than that, so I decided to get a new car instead of a new bumper!
>
> Now I have to make monthly car payments all because I tried to save $50 on new bookshelves.

WRITING TASKS

1. Write a letter (or an essay if you think that might be more effective for your audience) in which you explain causes behind something important to you. It's vital that your audience understand your situation. Make up your own situation or use one of the following:

Why you deserve a raise (to your boss)
What caused you to get a traffic ticket (to your insurance agent or the department of motor vehicles)
Why you didn't keep an appointment (to your teacher or friend)
What caused your auto accident (to your insurance agent)
Why you need more cash (to your parents or spouse or loan officer)
Why you need to move out (to your parents or your roommates)

Before you write, choose the persons to whom you will write as well as the purpose. Then explain the causes of the situation as clearly as you can. Revise to make your explanation appropriate to your audience and purpose. Use the Planning Sheet at the end of the chapter.

2. Have you ever had a childhood experience that you will never forget? What happened to you? Explain your experience as cause and effect so someone who doesn't know you very well will understand how you were affected. Before you write the paper, you might make a flow chart of causes and effects similar to the one made by the student writer of "Salad Days" to show how your experience affected you.

3. Analyze a situation or a problem or a solution by discussing its causes or effects or both. To write your analysis, make each of the decisions writers must make.

   For your *subject*, choose a situation, problem, or solution you want to explain or analyze from the point of view of causes or effects. You might elaborate on one of the topics in Writing Task 1, choose a topic from the following list, or pick your own subject. Limit your points so you can control them in your paper. Complete the Planning for the Cause and Effect Paper at the end of this chapter.

smoking	gravity	cancer
teenage gangs	unhappy children	parasites
saturated fat in fast foods	the price of oil	rumors
stock market moves	terrorists	fertilizers
skipping class	gene splicing	garbage
falling in love	racial tension	acid rain
belief in an afterlife	housing projects	potholes

4. In texts for other courses, find several discussions of causes and/or effects. Photocopy these discussions and then, for each, write a paragraph in which you explain how convincingly the author handled the subject. (History, natural sciences, social sciences, and technology offer many possible interpretations of causes and effects.)

Checklist for Explaining with Causes and Effects

Yes   *No*

____ ____ 1. Do you explain all the causes or effects of something? If you omit some, do you warn your readers?

____ ____ 2. Is your explanation of causes or effects convincing?

____ ____ 3. If you've used other people's ideas, do you give credit to your sources?

____ ____ 4. Do you use enough supporting information to be believed?

____ ____ 5. Do you write for your audience throughout the paper?

____ ____ 6. Do you remember your purpose throughout the paper?

____ ____ 7. Do you use a writer's voice that fits your audience?

____ ____ 8. Do you follow the guidelines for writing about causes and effects found in this chapter?

____ ____ 9. Did you organize the paper into an order that makes good sense to readers?

Name _____

Section _____

WORKSHEET—CAUSE AND EFFECTS _____

Read the essay "Tournament: Killer of Hundreds of Billfish" in this chapter. Use the space below to answer the four questions asked after the essay. As you answer these questions, you may realize how difficult it is for the writer to identify or isolate causes and/or effects.

Name _____

Section _____

PLANNING FOR THE CAUSE AND EFFECT PAPER _____

Topic:

Audience:

Purpose:

After you choose your topic, plan a flow chart to collect some ideas about your topic which you can use in this kind of paper. Use the chart on the next page.

Flow Chart for Causes/Effects

Topic: _____

Because: (fill in these blanks)   **Long-Range Results:**

Immediate Result: **More Long-Range Results:**

Another Immediate Result: **More Long-Range Results:**

What Is the Overall Result of this Experience?

Peer Reviewer_____

Title of Essay_____

Author of Essay _____

PEER EVALUATION—CAUSE AND EFFECT _____

Questions by Susan Slavicz

1. Does the writer deal with the causes or effects of the topic?

2. What is the subject being discussed?

3. What is the paper's thesis? Give three examples the writer uses in this paper to support the thesis.

4. Who might be most interested in reading this paper? Is the writer's tone consistent with this audience throughout the paper?

5. List the primary divisions this writer uses for the organization of the paper.

6. Circle the transitions used in the paper.

7. What information would you like for the writer of this paper to include that he or she did not?

Chapter Thirty
Reflect and Comment

Thinking human beings often reflect on the events they see around them. They ponder the way people act and their motivations. They wonder about the way things are and how they might be. They ask questions.

Why Do Bad Things Happen to Good People? is the title of a book that tries to explain the problem of evil. Why do good people seem to suffer and other people lead lives with little pain? Why does one person get sick? Why do people die young? *The Book of Job* raises some of these same questions.

We wonder if our generation is worse or better than the one before it. Even the ancient Greeks thought their new generations had problems.

We look at our values and our morals and our ethics. *Time Magazine* in the late 1980s spent pages asking questions about America's ethics.

Look at the medical and scientific problems raised by our new technology. What should we do about these issues? Should *every* scientist be allowed to do whatever is possible?

How do you live the good life? What is it? These are questions to start you thinking about issues on your own.

What Is a Reflective Paper?

A *reflective paper* muses about questions, wonders, ponders, asks about problems, dilemmas, issues and human nature itself. Such a paper offers the writer an opportunity to read what other people think and a chance to reflect and comment.

How Does One Write a Reflective Paper?

This type of paper usually offers a reflection on an issue or question or problem. Along with the reflection, the writer may offer a critical commentary or a point of view about the issue. Both the reflection and the commentary may happen simultaneously in the paper. *A writer begins with an issue or puzzle about life and writes reflections on it through a story, or an incident or a character sketch, or a description, or a group of examples.*

The writer of "Football as a Religion," which appears later in this chapter, comments scathingly on how some people react to sports. Football could stand for all sports and the fan, John Doe, described in the essay, could stand for all sports fanatics. Through a description of the fan and his love of football, the writer suggests his attitude toward such fanaticism.

An author who feels sad that some people know little geography or have little sense of cultures other than their own might reflect on the problem with examples he or she knows. The sad tone would match the reflection.

Usually, the choice of *vocabulary*, *sentence structure*, *examples*, *voice* of the writer or speaker, and the *mood that* is set in the piece *tell how the author feels.* Sometimes the writer builds to a climax so the ending gives the readers a punch.

To write this type of paper, make all the decisions that writers make. Good ideas for this type of writing often develop from your journal entries.

The following are some examples of the reflective paper.

War Games and Wanton Boys Who Went to Church

by Robert B. Gentry

It was 1947 and Little League had not yet come to Knoxville. No adults used us as vicarious stars, and no coaches defeated us with the winning syndrome. We were free to get dirty and disorganized, to wander around the woods at will. No parents bothered us there unless we missed meals; then they came yelling for us or sent some goody-goody girl to threaten us with dire warnings. We had lots of time and space to climb trees and run up and down hills, to pick berries and catch crawdads or loaf away the day by a slow meandering stream.

But, nature could get boring. So could games like mud hockey and rolly bat. Roughhousing was fun but not nearly exciting enough. We hungered for something much more dynamic, something proud and exhilarating, something with awesome power and profound guts. We craved the total risk, the ultimate edge. There was only one thing that could give us the fantastic thrill of glorious victory: WAR.

We'd choose up sides and start growling at each other. "We're the Americans and you're the Japs!" "Baloney! We're the Americans and you're the Nazis!" The argument always got heated, but it never got settled; each side would go storming off, calling itself the good guys and the other side a bunch of devils.

For defensive positions we'd dig elaborate trenches and throw up shaky tree houses. Our attack plans consisted of all kinds of complicated strategies and tactics, but these usually went awry when the battle began. Our "offensive" really amounted to a lot of wild charging and yelling things like, "Take this, you dirty kraut!" as we pumped away with our trusty Red Ryder b-b guns or tossed hedge-apple grenades with bulldog firecrackers in 'em.

Oh, we'd get cuts and bumps, but I don't recall anyone getting seriously hurt. We survived this mischief because we'd cover ourselves with all kinds of make-shift protection. My dad's WWI helmet and gas mask gave me excellent head cover. One chubby kid clanked around in some ancient armor his grandpa had given him. We called him "Fat Armor." He trudged so slowly everyone got a nice potshot at him, but he didn't give a durn because the pellets would just ping off him. We'd try to stop him with stones and grenades, but they'd bounce off him too. He just kept on coming like Frankenstein's monster, plodding and clanging and roaring inside that armor with the visor down, his troops crouched behind him in single file, using him for cover as if he were some huge tank. We finally got wise and started pelting 'em from the flanks, but that didn't stop Fat Armor. He still broke through our front line, flailing the air and scattering us all over the place because nobody wanted to get hit by his iron hands. Unfortunately, some of us did feel his wrath in big welts and bruises.

Then one day Fat Armor got his. It zinged through the small slit in his visor. He threw off his helmet screaming "Times out! Times out!" The pellet hadn't pierced the flesh, but he had a nasty welt on his face, like a wasp sting. That's exactly what he told his mother he had—a wasp sting—and she kept him in for three days. After that we made a rule that you couldn't shoot anybody above the chest or in the "privates." But the rump was fair game. When several kids went home with "bee stings" to the butt, the parents made a rule that we couldn't skinny-dip in the creek anymore. But we did anyway.

For body armor I wore a thick canvas tent over an old poncho I'd gotten from Army Surplus. Although these were fine defenses against pellets and firecrackers, they made me sweat like a hog. They were also good against stingers when we went raiding yellow-jacket holes. Those poor jackets! We used to take fiendish delight in zapping them. Whenever I hear the line in Shakespeare's *Lear*, I think of those bee raids: "we are to the gods as flies are to wanton boys; they kill us for their spite."

Yes, we wanton boys killed ants and bees and spiders and flies for the sheer fun of it. And we rationalized this slaughter the way adults do. For instance, once we were resting after a bee raid. We sprawled out on the ground bloating ourselves with "big oranges" and "moon pies." The soft drinks had coated our lips and tongues a fiery orange and we looked like clowns. We were elated that not one of us had gotten stung in the attack.

Then in dead seriousness one boy said, "These attacks are a whole lot of fun because we're doing God and the grown-ups a great big favor. These yellow-belly bees are just like the Japs; they've got to be wiped out so the woods'll be safe to play in. It'll make America a lot stronger too." Another boy said, "If your parents give you any guff, tell 'em the Bible says we're supposed to multiply and subdue the earth, which includes killing the stinger bees, so we're right on target with the Good Book." Everybody thought this was a good idea except one kid who didn't know what subdue meant. But after he was told, he thought it was the best possible thing we could tell parents because every one of them was a devout church-goer, and of course we were too.

In this piece, based on one of his journal entries, Robert Gentry looks at the impact of war on the games and minds of boys right after World War II. Notice that the writing moves from war as a fun game to war as a serious state of mind that children and adults rationalize, even on religious grounds.

Gentry doesn't say, "Oh, isn't it terrible that kids grow up with the killing urge!" Instead, he shows children gorging themselves on junk food as they brag about destroying bees, which they compare to slaughtering Japanese. The darkly comic irony speaks for itself. The value judgments are left up to the reader.

Football as a Religion

by Juvenal Jones

Football's the Number 1 Grade A Sacred Bull in the country. It's not a sport; it's a razzle-dazzle religion. If it weren't, people wouldn't idolize players and coaches, they wouldn't call them things like SPEED DEMON, FANTASTIC SUPERSTAR, COACHING WIZARD and PIGSKIN WONDER. They wouldn't carve their names and records on monuments, they wouldn't build big statues of them, and they wouldn't enshrine them in halls of fame. If football weren't the most SENSATIONAL RELIGION in U.S. history, if it weren't richer than most churches, you wouldn't have all those Monday-morning quarterbacks preaching about it as if it were life and death, players and coaches wouldn't be making the big loot some evangelists rake in, football stars wouldn't be getting fat deals in films and TV, and the whole religion wouldn't be hauling in enough bucks to cure cancer in a year.

If football weren't something he fervently believed in, John Doe wouldn't sit glued to the tube and watch it day and night. When the big game's on, five derricks couldn't pull him out of that chair. Football's got him under a supernatural spell, and everything else he tunes completely out.

At work he's a faceless number, a small nut in a giant machine that's run by a vague, modular management; to his wife he's a fat oaf that ignores her and robs her of her feminine potential; to junior he's the stingy-dull-reactionary-oppressive-not-with-it-over-30 drag who's causing all the war and misery in the world.

But when the big game's on and he's slouched in front of the tube, feeding his gaping face beer and junk food, his big belly stuck up in the air nearly blocking his view, he's in seventh heaven.

He fights no crowds; he battles no traffic. He just pushes a button and miracle of miracles: the whole stadium flashes into his den in living color. He moves not a muscle. He sits right on his dead rump, gets all the action he wants, and is a hero to boot.

He can be a Coach Crunch or a Bear Brawn and call the moves of his troops as they romp up and down the battlefield trying to stomp the enemy. He can be a Joe Jock or a Clod Clunk and hurl a 90-yard TD bomb—something he's longed to do since he was a water boy on the junior-high team.

And like a war god in a lazy-boy recliner, he gets all kinds of violence. He gets loads of organized violence by the pile full. He loves to see those lines tear into each other. He thrills to hear that leather pop and those helmets smack. He has a living ball when 4600 pounds of meat and bone all fall down in a wild orgy of heads smashing into butts and more butts butting heads and cleats digging into backs and elbows and fists jamming groins while John Doe's leaping up and down like some guy in a Dionysian frenzy yelling his head off for the home team because it's fourth down and one to go—then next play HUP! the quarterback shoves it into the fullback's gut who rams off tackle's rump ripping knees and stomping heads and split end's nose—the blood spurting through face mask weaving and staggering blind to sideline full of gals in red-hot pants cheering and shaking and cartwheeling—the whole crowd drunk and roaring. "Hit 'em a lick! Hit 'em a lick! Harder! Harder!"

In this article from *The Rise of the Hump House* by Juvenal Jones, a satiric character comments on America's passion for football. The exaggeration throughout the piece and the distorted usage at the end of it are literary devices that convey the writer's view of football as crass, gaudy, sensual, and brutal.

The Maine Mystique

by Martin Dibner

It never matters where I stop the car. A gas pump in West Virginia. A motel outside Albuquerque. A scenic turnout near the Continental Divide. They see the yellow license plate from Maine. Time stops.

"Main, eh?" A faraway dreamy look. Always that dreamy look.

Maine grabs them. The idea of Maine. Reasons vary. It may recall a New England visit years ago. "Got as far as Boston. Never did make it into Maine. Wanted to, real bad. But some day—" Or:

"Maine, eh? I was stationed in Presque Isle [or Portland or Brunswick or Kittery] during the last mess [Vietnam or Korea or World War II]. Ate lobster till it came out of my ears. Listen, if I was to go back—"

Or he's never been to Maine. He read about it in *Field & Stream* and *Sports Afield* and *Reader's Digest*. "Me and the missus has it figured out to get us to Maine, see? We got this little café up for sale. Don't look like much but bein' right here on the highway and all . . . and get us one o' them campers, see—?" That dreamy look. "We'll make it, hear? Me and the missus, some day."

Some day. He's eighty now.

In Arizona they ask about the moose. In Iowa about the corn. In Idaho about the you-know-what. In Georgia they want to know about the birds.

"No quail, mister? Hennery? You heah that? 'Scheah Maine feller jes sayad they ain't no quail shootin wheah he come fum. Partridge? Never heah tell o' no partridge roun about'cheah . . .''

A North Michigan deer poacher who pumps gas for a sideline studies the Maine tag and scratches his stubble of jaw. "Vacationland? That mean nobody has got to work?"

They were there once or read about it and nurse the dream. They cling to the dream from childhood, when tales of Maine's virgin forests and clear blue lakes stirred the spirit of adventure locked in young American hearts. Rockbound coast. Thoreau. Winslow Homer. Evangeline. Logging camps. The river run.

The virgin forests are gone now. Few lakes are clear and blue. Yet the mystique clings. People want Maine to be as they dream it must be or as they remember it. Man seeks freedom from monotony as much as he does freedom from pressure and Maine is the last best thing we have to the natural state. Contentment and fulfillment and serenity, ingredients of that curious American word, happiness.

I realize it when I stop somewhere and see that dreamy look. It needs no words. I know what the man is saying. I drive away gassed-up, oil-checked, blessed by a stranger. The direction I'm going doesn't matter. For me all roads lead to Maine.

COLLABORATIVE LEARNING

1. Complete the annotated reading sheet (see the end of chapter) for "War Games and Wanton Boys Who Went to Church."

2. Discuss the essay, "War Games and Wanton Boys Who Went to Church" in your writing group.

   a. What are some well-written lines in the essay? Read the lines aloud.

   b. What values, by implication, does the author hold up for critical comment?

    c. Describe the voice of the writer and give lines from the essay that prove your description.

    d. Show how the author moves from war seen as a game to war as a serious state of mind that children and adults rationalize.

    e. Write a summary of your discussion.

3. Study "Football as a Religion" in your writing group.

    a. Read your favorite or well-written lines aloud.

    b. How would you describe the John Does, the sports fans, that you know?

    c. This essay obviously exaggerates. Give some examples. What is the purpose of the exaggeration?

    d. What color does the author use? Why use that color?

    e. How does the voice in this article compare with the writer's voice in "War Games and Wanton Boys Who Went to Church"?

    f. What values does this author question?

    g. Write a summary of your discussion.

4. Discuss the "Maine Mystique."

    a. According to this essay, what intrigues people about Maine?

    b. Maine might be a symbol for the dreams and hopes within each individual. Although these dreams and hopes may never become real, they are fresh, clear signs of beauty and contentment that would probably be marred if the place they represented were actually seen. Do you agree with this statement? Why?

    c. Martin Dibner says, "All roads lead to Maine." What might he mean? Imagine several different meanings, if you can.

    d. What does this essay imply about those who do not live in Maine? Give examples from the essay to support your view.

Writing Task

1. Write your reflections about an issue, a problem, an ethical question, a value, or an irritation. Make all the decisions writers make. This is your opportunity to tell people how you see a problem or an issue.

Choose a Subject. To begin, decide on an issue, a question, a problem, a puzzlement, or a value about which you have strong feelings or a strong opinion. Because you will provide a critical commentary or offer a point of view about the issue along with your reflection, you might write out how you stand on your subject before you begin the paper.

Gather Supporting Information. A writer usually begins with an issue or puzzle about life and writes his reflections on it through a story, an incident, a character sketch, a description, or a group of examples. So think about an incident, a person, examples, or a situation that would show how you think and feel about the issue. Then gather details (list, cluster, tree-branch, or free-write) until you have many specific details to use to persuade your readers to agree with you.

Choose Your Audience, Purpose, and Voice. Decide who should know, or be influenced by, your reflection. Decide why you want this audience to listen to you. Finally decide the voice of the writer for your piece. This is a good paper with which to try satire or scathing criticism.

Organize Your Supporting Information so it will have the effect you desire on your audience. If you are to tell a story, organize so the reader must reach the same conclusion you reach. If you describe, choose to emphasize details that will force your reader to respond the way you wish. You might want to reread the two sample essays in this chapter and Chapters 23 (on descriptions) and 24 (on narratives) and 25 (on examples).

Write and Rewrite Your Drafts. Rewrite until you like the paper because it says just what you wish.

Revise. Check for mechanics, usage, and grammar. Finally, put the best word in the best spot. Try a variety of vocabulary words until you match the tone of the paper with *every* word.

Topics to use, if you wish

Superbowl mania	The lottery
Sex outside marriage	Latch-key kids
Terrorism	Dating rules
Women's or men's liberation	Business ethics
Suffering of the innocent	Poverty
Unwed fathers	Dishonesty
Censorship	The homeless
Sentences for crimes	Unfairness of birth
Selfishness of people	Power-grabbing

Checklist for Reflective Paper

Yes   *No*

____   ____   1. Do you feel strongly about your topic?

____   ____   2. Do you use a story, character sketch, examples, statistics, facts, to make your points?

____   ____   3. Does your writer's voice match your commentary on the issue?

____   ____   4. Does your writing build to an impact that forces your readers to reach the same conclusions you do?

____   ____   5. If you told a story, did you begin as close to the ending of the story as possible?

____   ____   6. Did you do more than simply summarize your position on a topic?

____   ____   7. If you told a story, did you use dialogue? Setting? A narrator?

____   ____   8. Did you describe your position so well that your readers must agree with you?

____   ____   9. If you wrote a character sketch, did you describe your characters doing something important for your reflection on an issue?

Name _____

Section _____

REFLECT AND COMMENT REPORT SHEET _____

1. Summarize your answers to the questions about "War Games and Wanton Boys Who Went to Church" in Collaborative Learning 1.

2. Summarize your answers to the questions about "Football as a Religion" in Collaborative Learning 3.

3. Summarize your answers to the questions about "The Maine Mystique" in Collaborative Learning 4.

Name _____

Section _____

REFLECT AND COMMENT WORKSHEET _____

Annotate Your Reading

One of the best ways to study an article or a short story is to annotate each paragraph or each section. For this exercise, ask three questions of each paragraph:

    a. What is the main idea of the paragraph and how does the writer support the main idea?

    b. What is my personal response to the ideas in this paragraph?

    c. What questions do I have after reading this paragraph? Your questions might be about vocabulary, or the meaning, or anything else about the paragraph.

Here is my own annotation for the first paragraph of the essay called "War Games and Wanton Boys Who Went to Church."

    1. a. Main idea—In Knoxville, in the late '40s, children were allowed to play without much interference or supervision of parents.

         Supports—No little league, no coaches, kids played in trees, wandered around woods, picked berries, got dirty, caught crawdads.

      b. Personal Response—It must have been great to be a kid then and to have so much freedom.

      c. Question—What is a crawdad?

Now it is your turn. Annotate the next paragraphs of the essay, "War Games and Wanton Boys Who Went to Church."

    2. a. Main Idea—

        Supports—

      b. Personal Response—

    c. Questions—

3. a. Main Idea—

        Supports—

    b. Personal Response—

    c. Questions—

4. a. Main Idea—

        Supports—

    b. Personal Response—

    c. Questions—

5. a. Main Idea—

Supports—

   b. Personal Response—

   c. Questions—

6. a. Main Idea—

Supports—

   b. Personal Response—

   c. Questions—

7. a. Main Idea—

Supports—

   b. Personal Response—

   c. Questions—

8. a. Main Idea—

    Supports—

    b. Personal Response—

    c. Questions—

9. a. Main Idea—

    Supports—

    b. Personal Response—

    c. Questions—

Peer Reviewer_____

Title of Essay_____

Author of Essay _____

PEER EVALUATION—REFLECT AND COMMENT _____

Questions by Susan Slavicz

1. What is the writer's thesis?

2. How long is the introduction (sentences)? What does the introduction do to engage the reader's interest (give a personal experience, define the topic)?

3. How would you describe the writer's voice (sad, happy, reflective)? How did you arrive at your answer?

4. After reading this paper, tell the writer one piece of information that you would still like to have.

5. Tell the writer one part of the paper that you really liked.

6. Underline all the action verbs in the paper.

7. Circle all the transitions in the paper.

8. After reading this paper, do you have more ideas for your own reflective paper? Explain.

Chapter Thirty-One
Write Summaries

Professors often use the word *summary*—or words that mean *summary*—in their assignments:

> "Prepare a *summary* of the chapter for next class."
> "*Summarize* the two articles; compare the conclusions in each article with the conclusions we reached during class discussions."
> "Write a *precis* of the article."
> "Do an *abstract* of the article."
> "After writing a *synopsis* of the plot, critique the [play, film, novel, or short story]."
> "*Condense* the reports into one page of recommendations."
> "Write an *annotated bibliography* of [whatever topic]."

Each of these assignments asks for a summary—asks the student to read what another author has written and understand the work so completely as to be able to precisely restate what the author said, but in the student's own words.

Many college assignments ask you to produce this restatement of the author's work before doing something else to the work—evaluating it, for example, or commenting on some aspect of it. This chapter, however, simply concentrates on how to do the summary well.

What Is a Summary?

A summary is a shortened version of a longer piece. It leaves out such unimportant details such as examples or asides but keeps all the main ideas of the original work. A summary retains the thought patterns of the original piece in order to show how the original author thinks and reaches his or her own conclusions. To summarize well, you must precisely restate an author's ideas in your own words; but your version, because it treats only main points, should be shorter than the original.

Why Know How to Summarize?

Summarizing is one of the most crucial skills college students can learn. But it is more than a survival skill needed in college. You will also use it on most jobs and in your daily life.

As a student, you take notes of lectures, recording just the important ideas and skipping less important ones because you cannot write as fast as a lecturer can speak. If you cannot summarize, you mix up details and examples with main points and conclusions and write a hodgepodge of information in your notes.

As a writer, you show your ability to summarize on essay tests and in various kinds of assignments. To write a good research paper, for instance, you might need to summarize dozens of other works.

As a good reader, you know the difference between main points and explanations of main points. To study, you are able to pick out main points and summarize.

As a consumer, you want to pick out important points made by salespeople and politicians and sort out irrelevant ideas, unimportant issues, and unsupported conclusions.

Employees should be able to summarize customers' requests, clients' opinions, business information, reports, conferences, meetings, and other pertinent materials for their supervisors or fellow employees.

HOW TO WRITE A SUMMARY

Writing a summary takes several specific skills. If you master each of the skills explained here, you will summarize well.

1 – Understand Your Assignment

Make sure you understand your assignment and know exactly what to do. Sometimes you may be asked simply to summarize. Other times you might be given more specific directions, such as "Condense the main points into one paragraph and evaluate" or "Write a critique of" or "First summarize the three articles and then react to" something. Be sure you do exactly as you are asked. If you are to summarize only a part of an article or book, rather than the whole thing, make sure you summarize only that part. If you are in doubt about the requirements of your assignment, ask your instructor.

How long should your summary be? Length depends on the assignment. Usually a summary is about one-half to one-fourth the length of the original although some summaries might be shorter. For example, as part of a written critique, you might summarize a two-hour play in one paragraph. But you might need several paragraphs to summarize William Faulkner's Nobel Prize Acceptance Speech, even though it is only four paragraphs, because the great author had already pared his speech to essentials.

2 – Describe the Author's Background and the Specifics of the Publication

In a summary, give as much background on the author as might be useful to your audience. If the article or book you are summarizing does not give the author's background, consult various library resources, such as the appropriate *Who's Who*.

Also in your summary, be sure to state such publication facts as where, when, and by whom the piece of writing was published. You can find most of these facts in the front of a book or magazine.

3 – Write for Your Audience, Not Yourself

Keep in mind the audience who will read your summary. To write for your readers, you will have to determine what you can assume your audience already knows and what you must explain. Ask yourself questions like these: What background does my audience have? What can I take for granted? What do I have to explain? How much do I have to explain?

When you write a summary, you need to fulfill your audience's expectations: The audience assumes that you will treat the author's ideas fairly, that you will give only an overview of the piece, that you will identify your source so they can read the original or other materials by the same author, and that you will summarize only ideas from the source and not add your personal ideas or reactions.

4 – Find and Keep the Main Ideas of the Original Piece

When preparing to write your summary, study the original source in great detail. To begin this study, read your material until you understand it. Usually, it is good to find and underline all the main points the author makes. In the margins, write comments to yourself about the structure of the piece. That's right, mark up the pages unless the piece belongs to the library or someone else; if it does, make photocopies and mark up the copies.

If you'd like more help with understanding a piece and discovering its main points, try following these suggestions:

Find the thesis statement. One of the short cuts to understanding a piece of writing involves locating the thesis and letting it be your guide to the paper. (Reread Chapter 14 if you have questions about finding a thesis.) After you find the thesis, locate all the sentences that explain the thesis or refer to it. If you cannot find a thesis, these next suggestions may be helpful.

Study the title. Although some titles are written just for fun or to catch a reader's eye, most are serious guides to the piece. If the title is serious, turn it into a question.

Then read the entire paper to see how it answers the question. Such questions and answers may lead you to the author's main ideas.

Search the conclusion for the author's main ideas. An author might summarize main points in a conclusion. But even if the conclusion is not a summary, its structure may still provide leads to the organization and main ideas of the piece. For example, if the conclusion states a solution to a problem, the work probably dealt with the problem that needed a solution. If the conclusion gives an answer, the work might have raised a question. If the ending explains effects, the work may consider causes of those effects. (Reread Chapter 13 if you need to review types of organizations.)

Find all topic sentences because they should support and explain the author's main ideas. Topic sentences might be in the beginnings, middles, or ends of paragraphs. (Review the discussion of main-idea sentences in Chapter 14 if you have questions.)

5 – Eliminate Unimportant Ideas

After you identify the main ideas, cross out all unimportant details. An idea is unimportant if it adds nothing to the meaning of a sentence or a paragraph. Keep facts, statistics, quotes, descriptions, adjectives, and adverbs only if they add new meaning.

In the paragraph that follows, unimportant ideas are underlined. They will be eliminated in a summary. In this paragraph, the topic sentence is the first sentence.

> *Free-lance writers often have a difficult time making a living as writers.* In fact, the average salary is about $6,000 a year. Can you imagine living on $6,000? Most free-lance writers take part-time jobs like pumping gas, working in restaurants, retail selling, and working on assembly lines to supplement their incomes. Other writers find well-paying jobs in professions connected to writing. Reporters for newspapers, teachers, ministers, and public relations officers are often free-lance writers who hope to write a best seller.

Even if you identify most of a work as unimportant, the meaning must still be left untouched in the part you identify as important. A summary using all the original wording would look like this:

> "Free-lance writers often have a difficult time making a living as writers. In fact, the average salary is about $6,000 a year. . . . Most free-lance writers take part-time jobs . . . to supplement their incomes . . . or find well-paying jobs in professions connected to writing. . . ."

6 – Paraphrase the Author's Words

A paraphrase restates the author's meaning in your own words and in your own sentence structure. Paraphrases convince your readers that you have totally understood and digested the original writing. In a good paraphrase, *add no new ideas, change no ideas,* and *omit no ideas.*

Use synonyms for the original wording, *rearrange the sentence structure,* and *keep the same tone or feeling.* How do you do all this?

- **Use synonyms.** First substitute your own words for the author's words. Using a simple vocabulary that adds nothing, changes nothing, and omits nothing is a good idea. Try pretending you are telling a brother or a roommate what you have just read.

The following examples demonstrate how you can begin to paraphrase using synonyms.

"Free-lance writers often have a difficult time making a living as writers" might become this with *synonyms: Independent writers usually cannot survive financially on their earnings.*

"In fact, the average salary is about $6,000 a year" might become *Their average pay is only $6,000 annually.*

"Most free-lance writers take part-time jobs to supplement their incomes" might become *Independent authors usually depend on income from part-time work.*

"Other writers find well-paying jobs in professions connected to writing" might become *Others opt for adequate salaries in related careers.*

- **Rearrange each reworded sentence.** Use in your new sentence an order of ideas that is different from that in the original sentence. For example, if the author started with a subject, you might change the sentence so it begins with the object. Or begin with a verb.

The following are examples of how sentences can be reordered to good effect.

"Independent writers usually cannot survive financially on their earnings" can be reordered to say *Surviving on their earnings is difficult for independent writers.*

"Their average pay is only $6,000 annually" can be reordered to say *Six thousand dollars is their average annual pay.*

"Independent authors usually depend on income from part-time work" can be reordered to say *Part-time work usually supplements their incomes.*

"Others opt for adequate salaries in related careers" can be reordered to say *Full time jobs in related careers supplement authors' incomes.*

7 – Keep the Same Tone

Even though you use your own words and sentence structure, be careful not to change the tone. If the original used a formal voice, so must you. If the original was sarcastic, keep the same sarcastic tone. Many writers will be formal, so it is easy to match their tone. (Notice the similar tones in the reordered sentences you just read.)

8 – Follow the Same Thought Pattern and Organization as in the Original

The following suggestions may be especially useful when you summarize a work longer than a paragraph.

- Decide which paragraphs make up the introduction, body, and conclusion of the original. In your summary, keep the same ideas in your introduction, body and conclusion.

- Find signal words (transitions) that show how the author moves from one idea to the next. (See the discussion of paragraphs in Chapter 15 for a review of transitions.) Terms like *first, second, last, on the other hand, more difficult, but, maybe,* and *perhaps* signal the author's organization of ideas. Pronouns, too, show how the author relates points. In your summary, follow the same thought patterns as the author by using transitions and pronouns to predict the structure of the piece and to explain how ideas relate to other ideas. Notice that in the paragraph that follows the italicized signal words give clues to the author's structure and relationships of ideas.

  Example: Free-lance writers *often* have a difficult time making a living as writers. *In fact,* the average salary is about $6,000 a year. Can you imaging living on $6,000? *Most* free-lance writers take part-time jobs *like* pumping gas, working in restaurants, retail selling, and working on assembly lines to supplement their income. *Other* writers find well-paying jobs in professions connected to writing. Reporters for newspapers, teachers, ministers, and public relation officers are often free-lance writers who hope to write a best seller.

  Often implies that many, but not all freelancers have a difficult time. *In fact* clues that the next sentence will explain the sentence just before. *Most* again qualifies the number of free-lance writers. *Like* hints that examples follow. *Other* says that a different group is now discussed.

- Use the same order of ideas in your summary as the author used. This order means you cannot begin the way the author ended. Nor can you rearrange main points to your own liking.

- Treat similar parts of the work in similar ways in your summary. If the original gives three reasons, with about equal space for each, you ought to summarize those three reasons in an equal way, that is, in three sentences or three clauses or three phrases. You cannot give one reason a sentence and shorten other reasons to phrases because you would be changing the author's emphasis.

An Essay and Its Summary

Read the following excerpt from the book *Oswald Jacoby on Poker* by the legendary poker player Oswald Jacoby.

Once you have read the piece, study the summary of it. Notice that even though the summary is much shorter than the original, it includes the main points of the original, follows the same order as the original, omits the details and examples Jacoby used to explain the three types of players, devotes an approximately proportionate amount of space to each of the three classes of poker players, credits the author and the original source, is written for an audience and not for the writer, and paraphrases Jacoby but keeps his informative tone.

Oswald Jacoby on Poker

by Oswald Jacoby

Thesis { . . . the expert [poker player] is a psychologist. He is continually studying the other players to see, first, if they have any telltale habits, and second, if there are any situations in which they act automatically.

Main Ideas and Supports { In connection with general habits, I divide poker players into three classes

(a) the ingenuous player,

(b) the tricky, or coffee-housing player,

(c) the unreadable player.

Support I **The ingenuous player** When the ingenuous player looks worried, he probably is worried.

examples { When he takes a long time to bet, he probably doesn't think much of his hand.

When he bets quickly, he fancies his hand.

When he bluffs, he looks a little guilty, and when he really has a good hand, you can see him mentally wishing to be called.

This ingenuousness, incidentally, is seldom found in veteran players. A player of this type usually quits poker at an early stage on account of his "bad luck."

Support II **The tricky or coffee-housing player** At least ninety percent of all poker players fall into this category.

examples { The tricky player has a great tendency to act just opposite of the way he really feels. Thus with a very good hand, he trembles a little as he bets, while with a poor hand, he fairly exudes confidence. Of course, he may be triple-crossing, but year-in and year-out I have played in a great many games, and have found that at least two times out of three when another player makes a special effort to look confident, he has nothing, while when he tries to look nervous, he is loaded.

examples { There is one mild little coffee-housing habit that practically never fails to act as a giveaway.

That is showing too much nonchalance. For instance, it is my turn to bet, and as I am about to put my chips in the pot, one of the other players casually lights a cigarette. Experience tells me that this casual player is at least going to call me, and is very likely to raise me if I bet.

Accordingly, if I do see that sign, unless my hand is really very good, I refuse to bet for him and simply check.

Support III **The unreadable player** This particular individual is, of course, the hardest opponent of all.

comparisons Invariably, he knows all the rules of correct play, but departs from all of them on occasion. Unlike the ingenuous player, who acts the way he feels, or the coffee-house, who acts the way he doesn't feel, this player has no consistency.

Accordingly, the fact that he exudes confidence or looks nervous gives no clue to the nature of his hand.

Summary of Oswald Jacoby on Poker: In the excerpt of his book, *Oswald Jacoby on Poker,* Jacoby says that the adroit player studies other poker players to find their revealing habits and actions. Using such behaviors, Jacoby, a legendary poker player himself, groups players into three categories: ingenuous, tricky, and unreadable.

Ingenuous players, he says, usually respond the way they feel. They do not last long as poker players and blame "bad luck."

Ninety percent of poker players are tricky, coffee-housing players. These players' actions belie their feelings. But over-nonchalance almost always gives them away.

The most difficult player to beat is the unreadable player. He understands the game, but he acts inconsistently.

A Second Essay and Summary

Read the following article about the cartoon Doonesbury. Then read the summary of the article by Emma Marx. Decide how well Marx fulfilled the strategies for writing a summary; use the checklist at the end of this chapter to guide you.

Newspaper standards dictate that Doonesbury will take the week off

by Art Frederickson

Doonesbury fans are in for a week of aggravation. And so are those of us who will get complaints from them because their favorite comic strip will not appear in *The Florida Times-Union* next week due to subject matter the newspaper considers inappropriate. Garry Trudeau, who draws the Doonesbury strip, is known for his willingness to satirize any subject. In April 1986, the strip included a listing of individuals accused of leaving the Reagan administration under ethical clouds. One name should not have appeared, the syndicate sent out a retraction and we dropped the strip for the remainder of that sequence. Doonesbury fans howled.

In September, Trudeau teed off on Pat Robertson and the evangelist's presidential ambitions. That strip was withheld from publication when Trudeau made strong references to God and Christ. Again, strong fan reaction.

Trudeau has unlimbered his guns again, this time aiming initially at Oral Roberts and that evangelist's claim he will die if he doesn't get $4.5 million in contributions for his medical school. However, Trudeau quickly turns his guns from Roberts to God in a manner the newspaper's management feels will outrage more readers than it will amuse.

The cries of "censorship" from Doonesbury fans are as predictable as the days of the week. In the previous instances, they angrily but unrealistically insisted that readers should be allowed to decide what they want to see and read. However, this point of view will not stand the glare of either logic or practice.

James L. Whyte, vice president and general manager of *The Times Union* and the *Jacksonville Journal*, points out that "as publisher of these newspapers, we have a responsibility for everything that is published. Some people have the notion that we have an obligation to publish everything that comes along."

A newspaper can't publish everything it receives, he said. "It's a damned-if-you-do-and-damned-if-you-don't situation. We pass judgment every day on what to publish. We don't run every opinion column, we don't run all pictures that are taken and we don't publish all news stories that are presented to us. We have subjective standards as well as objective standards—and the same thing is true with everyone who reads our newspapers."

William E. Sweisgood, editor of the editorial page of *The Times-Union*, agreed. "We have certain standards. We have to have them."

A recent example of such judgments was the decision not to publish three of the four photos sent by The Associated Press on the public suicide of the state treasurer of Pennsylvania. It was felt they would be offensive to the vast majority of our readers. Undoubtedly, there were readers who felt we should have printed these pictures, but we exercised the judgment we felt was responsible.

Any newspaper receives hundreds of thousands of words and scores of various illustrations each day. Probably 10 percent see the light of print. Someone must decide what is published and what is not. It is a selection process that is far from as easy as it appears and requires considerable experience and knowledge of current events. It is the winnowing part of the process we call editing. Those who feel they have been denied something often claim it is censorship. This is the kind of semantical debate that is as endless as it is pointless.

This process involves several criteria. In the instances in which it is a valid consideration, one of these is community receptiveness to the subject matter. In this case, the reaction to a satirizing of God is not likely to be well received in a community such as Jacksonville. The bottom line, as Whyte put it, is a balancing of the wrath of Doonesbury fans "against what the publishers of the newspaper have set as their standards and against what the publishers believe to be their responsibility to the community. No matter what decisions are made, there will be those who disagree."

Summary: Doonesbury

by Emma Marx

According to Art Fredrickson, reader advocate for the *Florida Times-Union,* the Doonesbury cartoon will not run the week of February 1 in the *Florida Times-Union* because the newspaper judged the content of the cartoon inappropriate.

The paper has made the decision to withhold Doonesbury twice before: after Doonesbury incorrectly named a person from the Reagan administration as leaving "under unethical clouds" and when Doonesbury satirized evangelist Pat Robertson's presidential ambitions.

In the present controversy, Doonesbury satirizes Oral Roberts's plea for $4.5 million so God would not call Roberts home. Fredrickson says the newspaper judged that Trudeau "turns his guns from Roberts to God." Readers, the paper judged, would not find the strip funny.

Fredrickson says that in the past Doonesbury fans cried censorship and argued that readers should have the right to decide what to read. The newspaper calls this argument illogical and impractical for several reasons.

James L. Whyte, vice-president and general manager of the paper, is quoted as saying that publishers are responsible for what they publish and that no newspaper can publish everything it receives, although some readers mistakenly think a newspaper is obligated to publish everything.

William E. Sweisgood, editor of the editorial page of the same newspaper, agrees with Whyte. He says that editors call the process of selecting material that meets the paper's standards "editing." People who feel they "have been denied something often claim . . . censorship."

According to Fredrickson, the editing process in the Doonesbury case takes into account the community, which will not be receptive to "satirizing God." Whyte summarizes that the anger of the Doonesbury readers must be weighed against the publisher's standards and the publisher's responsibility to the community. Whatever the publisher's decision, Whyte predicts that people will disagree.

Steps for Writing a Summary

Follow these steps if you write a summary.

1. Know precisely what your assignment asks you to do.

2. Give credit to your author and the specifics of publication.

3. Write for your audience, not yourself.

4. Select main ideas from the work.

5. Eliminate all unimportant details from your summary.

6. Paraphrase all important ideas in your own words.

7. Keep the same tone.

8. Follow the thought patterns and organization of the original.

COLLABORATIVE LEARNING

1. A summary should be written for an audience. In writing, explain how the following summary ignores the expectations of an audience.

    > In *Of Men and Angels,* the author gives a good interpretation of what is happening in the Christian fundamentalist movements today. One of the main characters tries to tell other characters how to live their lives her way. In the end, the character gets her deserved reward. If you're like me, you will agree with the author's views about religion.

2. Practice paraphrasing each of the next sentences by first rewriting it with synonyms and then rearranging your reworded sentence. Be sure to keep the tone the same.

    a. His prejudices include persons who drink too much, practice dishonesty, and handle their money permissively.

    b. As far as social status is concerned, I'm at the bottom: I do not own a checkbook, I eat frogs, I never dated a Miss America.

    c. In collaborative learning, sometimes called "learning in a group," challenge is certainly a key element. But challenge is not defined as competition or bombardment of each other's value judgments. That kind of challenge can be stifling and defeating to other students. Challenge offered in the spirit of cooperation, sharing, and mutual respect can move learning forward.

    d. If given the proper tools and motivation, most college students have the ability to evaluate and grade their own work.

    e. When quality circles first started in Japan, they consisted of eight to ten members who met once a week to study and discuss improvement of their company's product or the workplace. These meetings were held with a supervisor to solve on-the-job problems and to brainstorm new ideas. The quality circle has as its foundation the idea that those who feel the impact of a decision ought to be involved in making it.

Pick Article –

3. In a summary, you should treat equal parts of the work equally. Read the short essay that follows and test yourself to see if you can a) first summarize the facts about the three writers in three equal sentences and then b) summarize the facts in three equal parts of one sentence. Keep the order the same as that of the original.

    > Black writers have made important contributions to American culture. Take the examples of Alice Walker, James Weldon Johnson, and Zora Neale Hurston.
    >
    > Alice Walker won the Pulitzer Prize for Literature in 1982 with *The Color Purple*. Steven Spielberg turned that novel into a movie that provoked commentary by blacks all across America.
    >
    > James Weldon Johnson, who wrote during the 1920s, is remembered as a vital contributor to the Harlem Renaissance. Among his poems and novels is the work most people know. The poem tells the story of creation as if God were a lonely God who made the world to give himself company. Many students, black and white, memorized that poem, "The Creation." Johnson is best remembered for his mastery of sound and imagery.
    >
    > Probably the award for the greatest American novel by a black would go to Zora Neale Hurston's *Their Eyes Were Watching God*. Some critics call her the finest black novelist of all time. Although almost forgotten for years, her writing is making a comeback through readers and critics of feminist and black literature.

WRITING TASKS

1. For a difficult challenge, summarize William Faulkner's Nobel Prize Acceptance Speech. Because Faulkner is such a fine writer, you may need to look up vocabulary which is new to you and discuss the images he creates before you try to resay in your own words what he has said. For example, Faulkner ends with the statement that "the poet's voice need not merely be the record of man, it can be one of the props, the pillars to help him *endure* and *prevail*." Before you can resay what Faulkner says, you need to know what a prop is, that the image of the pillar here is one of a support, and more important, that the words *endure* and *prevail* each have different meanings. But the speech is definitely worth your study.

On Receiving the Nobel Prize

by William Faulkner

I feel that this award was not made to me as a man, but to my work—a life's work in the agony and sweat of the human spirit, not for glory and least of all for profit, but to create out of the materials of the human spirit something which did not exist before. So this award is only mine in trust. It will not be difficult to find a dedication for the money part of it commensurate with the purpose and significance of its origin. But I would like to do the same with the acclaim too, by using this moment as a pinnacle from which I might be listened to by the young men and women already dedicated to the same anguish and travail, among whom is already that one who will some day stand here where I am standing.

Our tragedy today is a general and universal physical fear so long sustained by now that we can even bear it. There are no longer problems of the spirit. There is only the question: When will I be blown up? Because of this, the young man or woman writing today has forgotten the problems of the human heart in conflict with itself which alone can make good writing because only that is worth writing about, worth the agony and the sweat.

He must learn them again. He must teach himself that the basest of all things is to be afraid: and, teaching himself that, forget it forever, leaving no room in his workshop for anything but the old verities and truths of the heart, the old universal truths lacking which any story is ephemeral and doomed—love and honor and pity and pride and compassion and sacrifice. Until he does so, he labors under a curse. He writes not of love but of lust, of defeats in which nobody loses anything of value, of victories without hope, and worst of all, without pity or compassion. His griefs grieve on no universal bones. He writes not of the heart but of the glands.

Until he relearns these things, he will write as though he stood among and watched the end of man. I decline to accept the end of man. It is easy enough to say that man is immortal simply because he will endure: that when the last ding-dong of doom has clanged and faded from the last worthless rock hanging tideless in the last red and dying evening, that even then there will still be one more sound: that of his puny inexhaustible voice, still talking. I refuse to accept this. I believe that man will not merely endure: he will prevail. He is immortal, not because he alone among creatures has an inexhaustible voice, but because he has a soul, a spirit capable of compassion and sacrifice and endurance. The poet's, the writer's duty is to write about these things. It is his privilege to help man endure by lifting his heart, by reminding him of the courage and honor and hope and pride and compassion and pity and sacrifice which have been the glory of his past. The poet's voice need not merely be the record of man, it can be one of the props, the pillars to help him endure and prevail.

2. Summarize the article "Let's Talk" for someone important in your own life. Follow each of the strategies explained in the chapter and use the checklist on your final copy. (This essay first appeared in *Single Parent*.) Record your summary on the "Summary Worksheet" at the end of this chapter.

"Let's Talk!"

by Mary Sue Koeppel, M.A.

My newly divorced friend, Peter, called me late one night. "You're supposed to know how to talk to people. Tell me straight. Do you think I can't talk to my boys?"

"What makes you wonder that?" I asked. "Something must have happened?" (I'd heard him talk to his kids on the phone, spent whole afternoons with all of them. I did know a little about how he talked to his boys.)

Peter said, "I just had another bad call from my ex-wife. She told me to stop calling my kids. She said I made Brian and Tim so nervous that they were in a cold sweat when they got off the phone after talking to me." Peter sounded hurt and confused. "She doesn't want me talking to them. She says I don't know how to talk to them. She never said that when we were still married. *What am I doing to them?*"

In my work with single parents I have found that Peter's problem was not uncommon. He was trying very hard to stay in contact with his six and eight-year-old sons who lived with their mother. Consequently, he'd frequently phone the boys and try to talk to them. But, according to Peter, talking to them was very difficult. He would ask the boys questions and they would answer. The conversations I'd heard had gone like this:

"Hi, Brian. How are you?" asked Peter.

"Fine."

"Did you go to school today?"

"Yes," said Brian.

"Did you have fun?"

"Yes."

"Well, did you play T-ball?" asked Peter.

"Yes."

"After school, too? Did you practice T-ball after school?"

"Yes."

"Can't you say anything else but 'yes'?" Peter asks.

By now the father is casting around in his mind for new topics of conversation. He wants to hold Brian on the phone as long as he can; he wants to get his boy talking to him. But the boy isn't cooperating. He's polite in answering all his Dad's questions, but he's offering nothing. Finally, after several more minutes of this kind of conversation, Peter and Brian hang up. Peter is frustrated. He had continued to push his son to answer questions even though he was aware that the boy was upset by a conversation which sounded like an interrogation.

But Peter's frustration was born because he didn't know how else to get his son talking. He'd ask a question, the boy would answer yes or no politely. That was all. How could he get his son talking without interrogating?

So Peter and I talked that night on the phone about a basic communication technique. Peter is an educated man, a successful business man, but he hadn't heard of the difference between an open and a closed question.

Closed questions are those which call for "yes" or "no" answers. They close off the conversation because they ask for only a simple word in answer; they ask for no explanation, no modification of thought. All of Peter's questions to his son were these closed questions. His son could answer with a yes or no.

Open-ended questions, on the other hand, can be answered only with longer answers. They call for explanation, analysis, or observation. To answer an open question, the responder may have to give details, clarify, or express his feelings.

Notice the difference between the questions in these examples:

Father: "Did you play T-ball after school?" *(Closed question: the answer is yes or no.)*

Father: "What did you and your friends do after school tonight?" *(Open question: the answer calls for an explanation, not a simple yes or no.)*

"Are you happy?" *(Closed)*

"How were you feeling when you guys won 31–17?" *(Open)*

"Did you practice T-ball tonight?" *(Closed)*

"When you practice T-ball, what kinds of things does the coach tell your team?" *(Open)*

Certainly the second question in each of these sets asks for more information than a simple "yes" or "no" and is more likely to get a conversation going.

People who use these open-ended questions must, however, be sincerely interested in the other's response. If the answer to the question is ignored or responded to in such a way that the answerer feels put down, defensive, or manipulated, he will close up and answer in as few words as possible.

However, if the sincerely interested questioner asks open-ended questions and receives the answers with interest and sincerity, the answers will begin to flow smoothly and the conversation will begin to have life of its own.

This simple little distinction between open and closed questions has many ramifications. It applies to talking to anyone in any situation. Often, for example, the conversation that seems to begin and stop, and begin again and stop again, may have this same problem. For example, you meet someone; you like him or her, but the conversation just stumbles along no matter how many questions are asked, how many starts you make. Maybe part of the problem lies in the type of question being asked. Ask open-ended questions, and you are likely to talk on and on. Dinner table conversation between members of the family may be susceptible to the same problems. So can the time a parent spends with his kids immediately after school or work.

Parents who truly want to know their children, dates who are eager to learn about each other, and friends who wish to share more deeply can develop skills that cause a conversation to take off by itself. Such conversations can surprise and delight you. They lead to areas you could not have opened by yourself because the closed question you ask can only concern things about which you already know enough to ask.

The open question can take you to whole new areas, to subjects and feelings you, the questioner, could never have foreseen, areas limited only by your imagination and the person to whom you speak.

Checklist for a Summary

Yes   *No*

____ ____ 1. Did you follow all instructions for your assignment?

____ ____ 2. Did you identify your original source in your summary?

____ ____ 3. Did you give the author's background?

____ ____ 4. Did you remember the needs of your audience?

____ ____ 5. Did you keep the same main points as in the original?

____ ____ 6. Did you resist the temptation to add new information?

____ ____ 7. Did you resist the temptation to change information?

____ ____ 8. Did you retain all important ideas?

____ ____ 9. Did you omit examples and unimportant details?

____ ____ 10. Did you paraphrase by using synonyms and rearranging the structure of the original sentences?

____ ____ 11. Is your summary shorter than the original?

____ ____ 12. Did you include transitional words?

____ ____ 13. Did you keep the organization and thought patterns of the original work?

Name _____

Section _____

SUMMARY CHAPTER_____

More Practice Paraphrasing

Paraphrase the following. Be sure to use synonyms for all main words, rearrange each reworded sentence, and keep the same tone or feeling. Yet, change no ideas, add no ideas, omit no ideas. This paraphrasing skill is hard to master, but worth the effort for writers.

1. As corporations have experienced stiffer competition and slower growth, they have pressed employees to work longer days.

2. Cost-cutting layoffs by businesses reduced professional and managerial ranks, leaving fewer people to get jobs done.

3. The growing scarcity of leisure, dearth of family time, and horrors of commuting all point to the need to resume an old but long-ignored discussion on the merits of the thirty-hour or even the four-day work week.

4. How long can America remain a world-class power if we constantly emphasize social skills and physical prowess over academic achievement and intellectual ability?

5. No one resents questions from people who honestly want answers to their honest questions.

6. I intend to live long enough that I can watch each of my video tapes from beginning to end.

7. To use dialogue effectively in essay writing, you must have an ear for the way other people talk and the ability to recreate it accurately.

8. A clear sentence is no accident. Very few sentences come out right the first time, or even the third time.

9. A sentence about my job? My job consists mainly of doing the things that other people do not want to do!

10. Products and services are moving around the world in ever greater quantities at ever greater speeds. But at the same time people are demanding more direct participation at the local level in decisions that affect their futures.

Name _____

Section _____

SUMMARY WORKSHEET _____

Read the essay "Let's Talk" in this chapter. Then summarize the essay by following each of the "Steps for Writing a Summary" (pages 408–09) in the chapter. Try to summarize so succinctly that you fit your entire summary on this page.

Summary:

Read the essay "Once More to the Lake" by E. B. White in Chapter 16, or "America Needs Its Nerds" by Leonid Fridman in Chapter 33, or "On Receiving the Nobel Prize" by William Faulkner in this chapter, or the paragraph "Is It Worth It?" on page 165. Summarize *one* of these pieces following the "Steps for Writing a Summary" given in this chapter. Think and study until you can fit your entire summary in this space.

Summary:

Chapter Thirty-Two

Write Critiques

You get asked questions:

> How was the movie?
> Did you enjoy the art exhibit?
> Should we join the health club?
> Who is the finest economics professor on campus?
> Why was Dickens a great novelist?
> How well does *The Good War, an Oral History* by Studs Terkel reflect the social mood of the period it covers?

To answer any of these questions, you have to evaluate, to offer a bit of a critique. Critiquing is part of life: We get evaluated on our jobs, graded in courses, chosen as friends. We constantly choose—where to spend our money, which film is worth seeing, which car to buy, which major to study. If we make such decisions consciously, based on evidence rather than on our own prejudices, we are critiquing. An assignment to write a book review is an assignment to write a critique.

What Is a Critique?

Put simply, critiquing means judging something against the standards set for that something by someone knowledgeable in that area. For example, in a critique of a potato salad, a person who knows food judges one specific potato salad against the characteristics of good potato salad. A critique of *Halloween VII*, a horror movie, judges it by the standards set for fine horror movie. A critique of a specific novel, *The Color Purple*, evaluates the novel according to the standards of good fiction.

A *critique* explains what the writer or maker has attempted, it evaluates that attempt, and it offers evidence to justify the evaluation. The evidence must be sufficient to enable the reader of the critique also to judge or evaluate the piece being critiqued.

Writers often analyze literature: plays, short stories, novels, poems, biography, history. But other subjects can also be reviewed: performances in theater, film, radio, TV, or recordings. Other subjects, too, like food, cars, products, and job performance can be evaluated.

What Does Writing a Critique Involve?

Writing a critique involves knowing the piece. A reviewer must carefully study the piece to understand the work. It may mean reading the novel or biography several times, driving the car in a variety of conditions, or eating at the restaurant more than once.

Writing a critique involves knowing the standards by which such a work is usually judged. For example, a reviewer uses certain criteria for evaluating clay sculptures and somewhat different standards for critiquing pen-and-ink drawings. Car buffs have specific standards for sports cars in the $80,000 price range and other standards for touring bicycles. There are points by which trial lawyers are judged. You would laugh if someone tried to judge major league baseball pitchers, narrative poems, and college libraries by the same standards.

More important, *a critique must make clear the standards by which it is judging.* A critique must judge by standards, not just by personal or subjective reactions; saying "I liked it" or "I didn't like it" is not enough. The reviewer who says the work is good or poor must support that judgement with enough evidence to convince readers.

As you study different sciences, arts, and the humanities, you will learn the different standards by which each subject judges. Professors will explain these standards and help you apply them. So this chapter will not try to explain all the various standards you might use in your critique. To find standards to use, I recommend that you consult experts in whatever field you are critiquing. Read or interview to find the standards to apply.

Writing a critique involves making a judgment. Besides offering standards, a critique must judge. It evaluates how well something measures up to the standards set for its category. For example, a critique might show how one clay piece measures up to the standards for realistic clay sculptures. Another critique might explain how "The Barn Burning" measures up to the standards for good short stories. *A Confederacy of Dunces* would be judged against the standards for a satiric novel.

Obviously making critical judgments takes knowledge because the reviewer must know and understand two things: the piece itself and the standards by which pieces like it are judged. The more knowledgeable the reviewer, usually the more convincing the review. If the reviewer lacks background about either the work or the standards by which such works are judged, the review may suffer from bias or unfairness.

Writing a critique involves writing for an audience. Keep your audience in mind as you evaluate because the audience will help you decide what to say and how to say it. For example, if you review a horror film for a film course, your purpose might be simply to evaluate it as a piece of art. But if you were reviewing for student government to help decide the list of free movies to offer during the coming semester, your evaluation might conclude whether or not a certain film is a waste of the student council's money. In each case, you must use evidence to support your conclusions.

MAIN PARTS OF A WRITTEN CRITIQUE

Readers expect to find certain ingredients in a critique. If some are missing, an audience feels cheated. Readers expect a short summary, facts about the background of the work and its creator, an explanation of the criteria on which the evaluation will be based, the evaluation itself, and a conclusion. Each of these main parts is explained here in more detail. The novel *The Color Purple,* which won the Pulitzer Prize for Literature in 1982 and is found in most libraries, is the example used for planning a critique.

1. Short Summary

Before writing a critique of anything, the writer needs to describe it or summarize it for those who may not know it or may have forgotten it. Another reason for including the summary is so the writer can refer to it later during the evaluation.

The summary should be no longer than a paragraph or two. Plays, short stories, poems, novels, autobiographies, biographies, histories—nonfiction and fiction—all must be summarized in a paragraph or two. Tell the name of the piece, the author, the main point or theme, and the supporting points. Refer to the discussion of summaries in Chapter 31 if you need help.

If you review something not written, like a piece of sculpture, a kind of tire, a stereo system, a pen-and-ink drawing, or a supervisor in retail sales, you must describe the thing or person to the audience. Tell what it is, who made it, and pertinent facts about it. Make your description specific so the reader sees exactly what you are evaluating. Again, a paragraph or two of summary is enough. One of the weaknesses of beginning writers is evident if they spend more time summarizing than evaluating.

The following is a brief summary of the novel *The Color Purple.* Notice that the writer tells you what *The Color Purple* is (novel) and who wrote it (Alice Walker) and summarizes the main events about the character (Celie) and theme (awakening of every woman to self-worth and triumph over adversity) in one paragraph.

Example:
The novel *The Color Purple* by Alice Walker chronicles the life of the main character, Celie, from age fourteen until well into middle age. Celie is a black woman whose ugly experiences early in life make her dependent on her husband. In the beginning of the novel her self-image

is extremely low. Gradually, however, through her friendship with another woman character, Shug, she awakens as a woman and person. The entire story, told in letters, reveals the growth of a mature, lively, sensitive woman. Although the events are Celie's, the story might be about the awakening of every woman to self-worth and triumph over adversity.

2. Facts about the Background of the Work and Its Creator

Give facts about your source so your readers can go to the original if they choose.

If you're critiquing a written work, you need to give the publishing facts—title, author, publisher, date of publication and the edition you used.

If the piece you're studying is not written, give other background. For a piece of artwork, state the name of the artist, the place the artwork is displayed, the year it was created, the medium used, and anything else the reader needs to know to credit the right source. For a person, you might give pertinent information such as name, age, career, and relevant family connections. For a movie or video, name the director, producer, editor, actors, distributor, date of release, and film company.

If appropriate, tell something about the creator of the work—the author, artist, designer. Give enough information so the reader of your critique understands the maker's background. If you are unsure about the creator, check the *Who's Who* in your library. Or ask someone knowledgeable in the field. If you are judging a dish at a local restaurant, you may need to consult a waiter or the chef to find out background.

Example: The following facts should be included in an essay which critiques the novel *The Color Purple*:

Facts about the book:
The Color Purple, by Alice Walker, First Washington Square Press Printing 1983 Edition, 1982 Copyright

Facts about the author:
Alice Walker, who received a Pulitzer Prize for *The Color Purple,* also wrote a book of essays called *In Search of Our Mothers' Gardens*, several volumes of poetry, two collections of short stories, several novels, and a biography of Langston Hughes. Born in Georgia, she now lives in California.

3. Criteria the Writer Will Use to Evaluate

In a critique, state the criteria by which you will judge the work. You may have to do research to find what experts say. For example, to critique a summary, you could use the criteria given in the previous chapter. To critique a Maine Coon as a show cat, you'll have to use the criteria for that breed. Go to your library and read reviews by the experts in the field to find their criteria. You might also do interviews to find the criteria. If you want to know the standards for judging a good real estate salesperson, you might interview several owners of real estate businesses to see what their criteria are. Just make sure that the people are true experts in their fields.

You must state the sources for the criteria you use in your paper. Experts' opinions give credibility to your evaluation. Using experts' criteria will also stop you from reacting personally, that is, just giving your own opinions based on your subjective point of view. And finally, stating your sources offers readers the chance to learn more by researching the same or similar sources.

The following criteria could be used to measure strengths and weaknesses in a novel or a short story.

Examples:

Theme—Is the point the author makes. The point is often about human nature and what it means to be a human being.

Characters—Have believable motivations for their actions and are fully rounded; readers empathize with them.

Setting—Is made up of the time and place. Time is believable and accurate and places are clear and fit the characters who move in them; if the story is fantasy, the setting must be real enough to cause readers to suspend disbelief.

Plot—Is the action. Plot must be believable for characters in those settings with those motivations. Plot works to a climax and ends letting the audience feel a sense of completion; if no completion is given, the reader understands why.

Point of View—Is held by the teller of the story, omniscient or limited, and is appropriate.

Diction—The wording matches the characters, setting, action, and theme.

Tone—Is the author's attitude toward the subject and it fits the work.

4. Evaluation of the Piece

To evaluate, the writer matches the experts' criteria to the piece being studied. The writer must show how well the work fulfills each standard. The writer should quote or refer to specific spots of the piece to explain how the piece meets the criteria.

Each standard should be applied and critiqued separately unless the writer wants a short evaluation or unless two points can be explained by the same information.

In the notes that follow, the writer matches the standards for a good novel against *The Color Purple*.

Examples:

Standard: The theme is the author's point. Often the point offers an understanding of human nature and what it means to be a human being.

The Color Purple graphically shows how a black woman, Celie, grows up with little self-worth but gradually learns to be a sensitive, warm, loving, fulfilled human being. Readers see both what destroys and what builds self-worth in the main character, Celie, who represents all women.

Standard: The *characters* have believable motivations for their actions and are fully rounded; readers empathize with them.

Celie, after being raped, her children sold, her sister lost, is understandably fragile. But Shug, the wild, independent woman, loves her and teaches Celie through acceptance and patience that she is worth love and care. Men in the novel fare worse. It is as hard for the reader as it is for Celie and Shug to accept the evil and indifference of the male characters: the man Celie called father and her husband.

Standard: The *setting* is based on time that is believable and accurate and places that are clear and fit the characters who move in them.

The setting in Africa is less vivid than the American setting because the African scene comes only in letters to Celie from her sister, Nettie. So it is understandably sketchy. Because the rest of the story is told through the eyes of Celie as she writes letters to God and her sister Nettie, the setting is hers to make accurate. Most times, the reader is fully aware of what Celie wishes to explain but must accept the limitations of the letter to God who supposedly doesn't need much detail about the settings.

Standard: The *plot* is believable for characters in those settings and with those motivations. It works to a climax and ends letting the audience feel a sense of completion; if no completion is given, the reader understands why.

In *The Color Purple*, the reader must fit together pieces of the plot. Some events must be figured out as Celie herself figures them out: the reader and Celie discover together what happened to her children. Other events the reader understands only after Celie mentions them in several letters to God. (Why does Nettie finally run away? Who is Shug Avery?) By the end of the novel, the reader is satisfied that Celie will be O.K. She has her family around her. She has reached mature answers to man's important questions: "Why us need love. Why us suffer. Why us black."

Standard: The *point of view* is the teller of the story. The choice must be appropriate.

The point of view in this book is certainly Celie's. The story is told through her letters to God and her sister Nettie's letters to her. Although Nettie writes letters to Celie, the reader sees them only when Celie finds and reads the letters herself. Everything is thus seen through the eyes of the main character.

Standard: The *diction* matches the characters, setting, action, and theme.

In the early letters the diction matches the uneducated writer. But as Celie matures, the letters that tell the story, mature. Here is one of her first statements, "Two of his sister come to visit. They dress all up. Celie, they say. One thing is for sure, You keep a clean house."

Standard: The *tone*, the author's attitude toward the subject, fits the work.

In *The Color Purple*, Alice Walker, a feminist, creates a young woman men put down, but who, when given the chance through Shug, becomes a warm, independent feminist herself.

Certainly the author respects her subject, as she creates a woman who matures into independence—a woman who asks the basic question every human must ask, "Why?" No matter what Celie's experiences, Walker treats them with reverence and respect.

5. Conclusion about the Work

The writer states an opinion about the work based on how well the work meets the standards for that kind of work. The conclusion is the writer's final chance to evaluate the piece, so a thorough conclusion will probably restate the reviewer's main points as evidence for the final judgment.

The example that follows is the writer's conclusion for the critique of *The Color Purple.*

Example:

The Color Purple is a fine novel because it meets the major standards of a novel. It develops a universal theme, that of a woman gradually coming to know herself and her answers to questions every mature person asks about life. It traces the development of a main character from age fourteen and limited self-worth to the emergent maturity of a sensitive woman. Rounded characters, involved plot, a story told in the first person through letters, a sympathetic tone, believable settings, and tuneful diction distinctly state a universal theme that all human beings, whatever their race, can read.

Storm Warnings

1. Notice that the essay which critiques *The Color Purple* still needs to be written. The examples only explain and collect the kinds of information writers need.

2. If you criticize problems or deficiencies in the piece, be sure your remarks are not satiric or sarcastic. Biting language may be humorous, but it does not show a reverence for evaluation. Another kind of voice to avoid is one that is showy or ostentatious. Because this is an academic assignment, use a formal voice.

Steps for Writing a Critique

Follow these steps as you write a critique:

A. Decide on the piece you will evaluate.

B. Study the work carefully. If you are critiquing a book, be sure to study the title, thesis, main points, and conclusion. Read the preface and introduction to find the author's purpose and audience. If you are evaluating an activity, do it several times under different conditions: Eat in the same restaurant, drive the same car, shave with the same razor. If the piece is an object, study the painting or drawing, or whatever, until you understand it.

C. Write an essay which uses all five parts of the critique.

    1. Look up background on the maker or writer of the piece you will critique.

    2. Summarize or describe the piece.

    3. Find experts who tell you the criteria to use to evaluate that type of work. Read critics (for example, in the *Book Review Digest, Film Review Digest,* and *Restaurant Reviewer*) to learn their standards. You may have to search the reviews closely because critics often blend their criteria into their evaluative statements.

    4. Evaluate the piece using the standards of the experts. Acknowledge your expert sources as you write. Use examples from the work.

    5. Draw your own conclusions about overall values of the piece. Be sure to support your evaluation and conclusion with quotes or descriptions from the work itself. Otherwise, you will merely offer your opinion without sufficient evidence to persuade your readers to agree with you.

Example of Critiques

Read Linda Moore's critique of James Clavell's book *The Children's Story* and the critique of "Once More to the Lake" by Sarah Giles. Notice how well both writers combine all the elements of a fine critique. (Numbers indicate pages from their sources.)

The Challenge of The Children's Story

by Linda Moore

    The Children's Story is a novelette written by James Clavell, whose other books include *King Rat, Noble House,* and *Shogun.* Clavell was born in Sydney, Australia in 1924 and came to the United States in 1955. He did not become a citizen, however, until 1963 (*Who's Who 599*), the same year *The Children's Story* was written. In a personal note at the end of the book, Clavell explains that it was his young daughter who inspired the story. She had come home from school one day reciting the Pledge of Allegiance but had not been taught what the words meant. "It was then," Clavell writes, "that I realized how completely vulnerable my child's mind was—any mind for that matter—under controlled circumstances." Clavell illustrates the devastating potential of his realization in *The Children's Story*. In a country that has just been conquered by a totalitarian state, a classroom of seven-year-old children are introduced to the "New Teacher," who skillfully turns them against their country, their parents, and God.

    The beginning of the story introduces the children's teacher, Miss Worden. She is described as having "gray hair," a "lined face," and "well worn clothes." The fact that Miss Worden had never married is also disclosed. The reader is effectively guided into the thoughts and feelings of the main characters by what Sylvan Barnet of Tufts University terms a third-person "omniscient narrator" (88). The narrator reveals that Miss Worden was afraid, not just for herself, but mostly for the children. She understood how willing the children were to accept any knowledge given to them.

Johnny is introduced as one of the children in the classroom. Of everyone in the room, Johnny is the only one who is not afraid. His father had warned him not to be consumed with fear, so Johnny has allowed his emotions to take the form of hatred instead—hatred for the strangers that have taken over his country.

When the New Teacher enters the classroom to dismiss Miss Worden, much to the children's surprise she is "young" and "beautiful." Her uniform is "neat and clean." It is noteworthy that, in a book review for the *Library Journal*, Joyce Smothers criticized Clavell's description of Miss Worden as a "stereotyped 'old maiden lady'" (2148). Sylvan Barnet, however, recognizes that characters in a story can be used to define each other, through their similarities or their differences (101). This is exactly what Clavell has accomplished by introducing the New Teacher, clearly in sharp contrast to the old one.

The story begins by telling the time of day: "It was two minutes to nine" in the morning. The significance of this statement will not be realized until the conclusion of story. The old teacher, Miss Worden, is dismissed. The New Teacher immediately begins to win over the children. She impresses them with a song and surprises them by already knowing all the children's names. She then allows them to begin their Pledge of Allegiance. When they had barely begun, she interrupts them to question its meaning. Discovering that the children have not been taught its meaning, she easily convinces them—with the exception of Johnny—of how silly it is to say that a flag is more important than people. Johnny challenges her further than any of the other children by telling her that even so, it is still their flag and they always pledge to it. The New Teacher resolves Johnny's argument by agreeing that it is indeed a fine flag; therefore wouldn't it be nice if they could all have a little piece of it? The flag is then cut into pieces and the flagpole is discarded.

As the story continues, the New Teacher, in similar fashion, convinces all the students—even Johnny—that their parents have had some wrong thoughts that need to be corrected and that God does not answer prayers, only people can. The New Teacher is successful; Johnny is resolved to work hard to learn the new ways and the New Teacher is content with a feeling of accomplishment. The climax is reached when the New Teacher looks at her watch and the reader is again told the time: "It was 9:23."

The Children's Story is presented in a very believable fashion. Clavell has developed his characters, setting, and atmosphere in a style supportive of his theme. Throughout the story, the characters are presented consistently. Everything the

New Teacher does is compared to what Miss Worden used to do and is always different and more exciting. For example, when Miss Worden left the room crying, some of the children cried, too. To calm them, the New Teacher sat on the floor and began to sing. "The children stopped crying because Miss Worden never, never sang to them and certainly never sat on the floor, which is the best place to sit, as everyone in the class knew." Also, Johnny is the one student in the class who does not want to be reassured by the New Teacher. He repeatedly questions her, taxing her talents to win him over. The fact that Johnny is resistant and some-what prepared by his father lends credence to the story.

Clavell's choice of the classroom as the setting for his story is an important one. As Sylvan Barnet points out, the setting is the key element of the atmo-sphere. The setting provides "the background against which we see the charac-ters and the happenings" (78). A child's classroom is familiar to most any reader. The innocence of young children and their willingness to learn are brought to the mind of the reader and create a perfect backdrop for *The Children's Story*.

The atmosphere is further developed by the writing style. *The Children's Story* is written in the informal style of a child's book. To have written the story any other way would have contradicted the simplicity of the characters and the set-ting. The title of the book serves as a reminder to the reader, however, that *"The" Children's Story* is not just "a" children's story.

Although written simply, *The Children's Story* is very provocative. In *Best Sell-ers*, critic R. V. Williams notes that Clavell leaves "the reader uncomfortably thought-ful about severe current social ills and parental irresponsibility in the intellectual development of their children. *The Children's Story* details the possible conse-quences of that neglect" (128). The book does not, however, provide us with any clear-cut answers. In his personal note, Clavell himself says that *The Children's Story* "keeps asking . . . questions. Questions like 'what's the use of 'I pledge allegiance' without understanding?' Like 'Why is it so easy to direct thoughts and implant others?' Like 'What is freedom and why is it so hard to explain?'"

In his story of what could possibly take place in twenty-five short minutes, Clavell has attempted to raise the reader's consciousness. A child's mind is a pre-cious resource that needs to be cultivated with care. It is the responsibility of parents, as well as teachers, to educate children as to the meanings of the ideas they wish the children to accept. Without a moral foundation to stand firmly upon, children are sent into the harsh storms of reality naked and vulnerable. In *The Children's Story*, Clavell's theme should be viewed, not just as one of questions raised and left unanswered, but as a challenge—a challenge to always seek new and better methods of preparing children to master the world in which they live, rather than letting their world master them.

Bibliography

Barnet, Sylvan. *A Short Guide to Writing about Literature*. 3rd ed. Boston: Little, Brown and Company, Inc., 1975.

Clavell, James. *The Children's Story*. New York. Delacorte Press, 1981. (Note: *The Children's Story* has no page numbers.)

Smothers, Joyce. "Clavell, James. 'The Children's Story.'" *Library Journal*, 106 (1981), 2148.

Who's Who in America. 43rd ed. Chicago: Marquis Who's Who, Inc., 1984, 599.

Williams, R. V. "Fiction: 'The Children's Story.'" *Best Sellers*, 41 (October 1981), 243–44. Rpt. in *Contemporary Literary* Criticism. Ed. Jean C. Stine. Detroit: Gale Research Co., 1983, 128.

The Unforgettable Journey: "Once More to the Lake"*

by Sarah Giles

"Once More to the Lake" is a narrative essay written in 1941 for E. B. White's monthly column in *Harper's Magazine*. White, who lived from 1899 to 1985, was also an imaginative children's author, with books such as *Charlotte's Web* and *Stuart Little* to his credit. In 1938, White and his family moved to the Maine coast and remained there for the next five years; it was during this period that he began to write the column for *Harper's Magazine* where "Once More to the Lake" made its debut.

The essay opens with a brief account of how a family vacation at a lake in Maine during White's childhood became an annual tradition; this sets the stage for the rest of the piece, which takes the reader on a journey back to that lake as White describes how he returns there with his son years later. Dozens of little things—a scent, a trail, a dragonfly—ignite old memories, and soon White feels an eerie reversal of roles during this vacation with his son: "I began to sustain the illusion that he was I, and therefore, by simple transposition, I was my father" (200).

By closely interweaving memories with the present, White effectively conveys his illusion that no time has elapsed between the vacations of his youth and the one he is on now. One moment he is recalling fond memories of everything from steamboats to doughnuts; the next, he and his son are stepping into a convenience store to buy some soda. The store triggers a fresh onslaught of memories, and White returns to the past once more (205).

These memories, generously sprinkled with descriptions of the lake and its surroundings, also serve to create an intricately detailed setting. White uses his

---

*You can read the entire essay by E.B. White in Chapter 16 "Understanding the Essay," pages 173–78.

clear, uncomplicated style to construct lingering images such as this one: "In the shallows, the dark, water-soaked twigs, smooth and old, were undulating in clusters on the bottom against the clean ribbed sand, and the track of the mussel was plain" (202). But the setting of this piece isn't merely a backdrop against which the action will take place; rather, it plays a crucial and central role in the story. Editors Marlies Danziger and W. Stacy Johnson explain that the setting often directly affects the action and character (27). Such is the case here, where the setting of the lake conjures up old memories for White, determines the things White and his son do, and even becomes a haunting reminder of White's mortality.

It is interesting to note that White's son, the one other significant character in this essay, remains both nameless and faceless. This calculated omission of the son's defining characteristics enhances White's paradoxical realization that while he is obviously the father on this trip, he sees himself in his son as the boy virtually re-enacts scenes from White's past vacations. The result is a disorienting identity confusion, evident in statements such as "I felt dizzy and didn't know which rod I was at the end of" (202) and "I had trouble making out which was I, the one walking at my side, or the one walking in my pants" (205). White's dilemma would not be as credible if the boy were described in detail, because then the reader would have had no difficulty distinguishing White from his son. The boy's anonymity contributes greatly to the sense of jumbled identities.

Ironically, the sense of timelessness and continuity portrayed throughout the essay is disrupted at the very end by White's stark realization that death is no longer a distant shadow but an immanent reality. While the meaning is revealed not so much with subtleness as with suddenness, the tone of the entire piece deftly prepares the reader for the irony of the final sentence and at the same time alludes to the ultimate theme. Tone, as defined by editors William Watt and Robert Bradford in *An E. B. White Reader*, is "a blend of the writer's attitudes towards both his subject and his reader" (30). Watt and Bradford continue to point out that the best way to discern the tone of a piece is to examine the author's word choice. White's word choice suggests a nostalgic tone: "You remember one thing, and that suddenly reminds you of another thing. I guess I remembered clearest of all the early mornings, when the lake was cool and motionless, remembered how the bedroom smelled of the lumber it was made of and of the wet woods whose scent entered through the screen" (201).

In the midst of all of this reminiscing, however, lurks the revelation that not everything has remained the same through the years. White notices that a certain trail by the lake has disappeared, and later notes with some consternation that the boats on the lake now have noisy outboard motors. These changes symbolize the passage of time and foreshadow the final sentence where, as he watches his son pull on a wet swimsuit, White reaches an epiphany: "As he buckled the swollen belt suddenly my groin felt the chill of death" (206). The subtle changes displayed in this ostensibly immutable lake make White painfully aware that time marches ever onward and will eventually affect everything in its path . . . including White himself.

This essay is crafted in the eloquent yet uncomplicated style that has made White one of the most beloved authors of the twentieth century; he skillfully integrates memories, setting, and character into a powerful statement concerning one of the most formidable elements of human existence: mortality. Watt and Bradford contend that he combines "the accurate observation of the reporter and the rare insight of the poet" in this narrative by meandering along a carefully laid trail of memories, waiting to deliver the punch until the very end (285). Thus the readers are not only lavished with vivid impressions of a rustic scene, but are also dealt an abrupt jolt that will provoke them to consider the swiftness of life and the inevitability of death.

Works Cited

Danziger, Marlies K., and W. Stacy Johnson. *An Introduction to Literary Criticism.* Boston: D.C. Heath and Company, 1961.

Watt, William W., and Robert Bradford, eds. *An E.B. White Reader.* New York: Harper and Row, 1966.

White, E.B. "Once More to the Lake." *Harper's Magazine* (1941). Rpt. in *The Essay: Old and New.* Eds. Edward P.J. Corbett and Sheryl L. Finkle. Englewood Cliffs: Prentice Hall, 1993. 200–206.

COLLECTIVE LEARNING

1. In your writing group, discuss "The Challenge of *The Children's Story.*" Figure out how Linda Moore's review follows the scheme for a critique. Find her summary, the background facts she offers about the novelette and Clavell, the criteria she used for evaluating the book, her evaluation, and her conclusion. A hint: Moore, a student, often skillfully combines parts of her summary, criteria, and evaluation into the same paragraph. After you locate each of these parts of the critique, decide how she supports her conclusions. On the basis of Linda's review, would you want to give *The Children's Story* to someone you know to read? Why or why not? Write your conclusions in a report.

2. Read E. B. White's original essay, "Once More to the Lake," which is printed in Chapter 16. After you read his essay, read aloud some of your favorite lines. Then reread what Sarah Giles, a student, said about White's essay in her critique.

   a. In your group, study each of her paragraphs separately; paraphrase the points which Giles makes in each paragraph.

    b. After you have finished, ask each other, "If you reread White's essay in 25 years, might his effect on you be different? Why?"

    c. What might be some reasons why White's essay is popular and often anthologized?

Give your instructor a summary of your discussion.

3. As a group, practice critical evaluation.

    a. Choose a topic you all agree to evaluate. The topic might be one homecoming float, your school song, your school desk or chair, a good hot-fudge sundae, a good pizza, a careful hunter, an effective mayor, a personal computer, a software package, a specific athlete, a school team, or anything else you choose.

    b. Decide on an audience for your critique. Whom do you want to listen to your evaluation?

    c. Make a list of the standards by which your topic would be judged. For example, if you choose to critique a homecoming float, name all the standards by which you judge a winning homecoming float, or if you name a basketball center, decide the standards by which a fine center is judged.

    d. Use your standards to evaluate. After class, you might go as a group to a local restaurant and order a pizza or a piece of apple pie in order to judge it. Or look at a homecoming float so you can judge it. Or go to a football or basketball game and judge one of the plays or the entire game. If you don't want to travel, just sit at your school desks and evaluate them.

    e. Write your critique. Then ask other writers to evaluate your critique according to the standards of this chapter.

4. Bring several critiques from newspapers or magazines to discuss in your writing group. You might look in entertainment sections for reviews of movies, records, concerts, art gallery openings, and books; in the food or entertainment sections for restaurant critiques; or in the sports pages for critiques of games or players. You can learn much about writing by studying other reviewers at work. Pick some of the most interesting reviews and talk about them. How did a review try to make you accept its point of view? Did the reviews follow the suggestions given in this chapter? What extras did you find in some reviews? What was left out? Would you trust any of these reviewers' opinions? Why? As a group, in writing, critique one review. Show both the review and your critique of it to your instructor.

WRITING TASKS

1. Write a critique of a nonfiction book. To do this critique, follow the major decisions that all writers must make.

   Decision I. Choose the book to critique. This book might be required for one of your courses, or it might be a book you have already read because the topic interests you. Read the book.

   Decision II. Gather supporting information for your critique. To do this, follow the suggestions made in this chapter. You will need information to write all the MAIN PARTS OF A WRITTEN CRITIQUE: (a) the summary, (b) the facts about the author and work, (c) the criteria for measuring strengths and weaknesses, (d) the evaluation, and (e) the conclusion. You will probably need to research the standards by which the particular book should be judged. In other words, the standards for autobiographies, biographies, scientific reports, histories, and so on, will be different.

   Decision III. Decide on your audience, purpose, and voice.

   Decision IV. Decide how you will organize all your information so your audience will reach the conclusions you reach.

   Decision V. Write your drafts. Keep revising until you know you will make your audience take notice and fulfill your purpose.

   Decision VI. Polish your paper by using the techniques in Chapter 19.

2. Write a critique of a novel or short story. Evaluate the fiction using the same standards as those used for the novel *The Color Purple* critiqued earlier in this chapter. As you write your critique, make all the decisions writers must make. (These decisions are summarized just above in Writing Task 1.)

3. Critique a film, an art piece, a play, CD, performance, specific car, or restaurant. Again, as you write, make all the decisions writers make, as summarized in Writing Task 1.

4. Critique something that has not performed for you as well as you expected it might or something that performed quite well. You might critique your car, a razor, a home permanent, a computer software program, or a membership, to name a few. As you write your evaluation, make all the decisions writers must make.

Checklist for a Critique

Yes   No

____   ____   1. Did you summarize the work or describe it before you evaluated it?

____   ____   2. Did you give relevant background about the author or creator?

____   ____   3. Did you give background information about the work so readers could find it themselves?

____   ____   4. Did you state the criteria by which you judged?

____   ____   5. Did you use the experts' criteria to evaluate the work?

____   ____   6. Did you give credit to the experts for their criteria?

____   ____   7. Did you use quotes or references to the actual piece to support your opinions?

____   ____   8. Did you use an appropriate writing voice?

____   ____   9. Did you keep your audience and purpose in mind?

____   ____ 10. In your conclusion, did you explain the overall value of the piece?

Name _____

Section _____

WRITING A CRITIQUE WORKSHEET _____

Read the remarkably short, short story "Ernest Wilson's Plea Bargain" and then write a critique of it. The "Steps for Writing a Critique" will remind you of the process to follow. You may want to concentrate on the *plot* (what happened), the *characters* and their motivations, the *setting*, the *theme*, and the *language or tone* of the story.

Facts about the Author: Heather Wishik lives in the Northeast and writes and publishes poetry and fiction.

Facts about the Work: First published in *Kalliope*, Volume 13, Number 3, page 63.

Ernest Wilson's Plea Bargain

by Heather Wishick

It was the year after selling the grocery, and they were splitting time, Vermont and Florida, a camper down there, a trailer here. The first spring back north and Helena came up sickly, trouble swallowing. She didn't say much at first. Always was close mouthed, poor thing.

I saw her, you know, just before. I had eggs, so many I didn't know what to do. I'd heard she was doing poorly so I made a custard and took it up to the trailer. She was rocking on the porch, midmorning and her dishes undone.

He was mowing and grumbling, grumbling and mowing.

I asked if I'd better do up the kitchen but she said no, she'd get to it. Looked scared. Said he'd be at her if she let me help. Gobbled the custard right there on the porch and handed back the dish. Said she hadn't eaten in a couple of days, nothing would go down.

Seems he'd of eaten the custard if she tried to save it. Didn't believe she was sick, told her to stop her faking, he hadn't retired to play nursemaid. I tell you she shook when she stood to see me out.

Next day it was, he called the sheriff. They found her in the rocker, strangled. And now everyone's calling him poor Ernest, confused, his brother says, ever since Pearl Harbor. His brother says he just needs therapy. More likely he'd been beating her ever since Pearl Harbor and she never told.

Now you see there in the paper where he's made a deal with the judge. Probation. Shame on them. Wish she had told. I would of. I hope.

Write your critique on the next page.

Chapter Thirty-Three

Write an Argument

In everyday speech the word *argument* often means a quarrel, an altercation, a bout of name-calling, or a disagreement. You might say, for example, "The neighbors are having a terrible argument; they're yelling obscene names at each other and pushing and shoving." Or a military officer might tolerate no disagreement from a subordinate: "Don't argue with me, soldier! Do it the Army way."

In English courses, however, and in subjects like philosophy and the law, *argument* means that you can use convincing reasons and logic to show that your position is true or likely to be true and opposing views are not.

Two purposes of argument are persuasion and defense. For instance, you may think your grade on an essay test is too low. You therefore develop a logical argument to show that you answered a particular question thoroughly and according to the teacher's criteria. Your aim is to *persuade* the teacher to raise your grade. But the teacher may hold firm in his or her evaluation of your answer and, through careful logic, *defend* the grading as fair.

A third purpose of argument is to *attack* a position which you think is misleading, false, unfair, or evil but not give your own alternative. For example, you might attack the governor's proposed tax increase to solve the state's financial crisis without proposing a solution of your own.

To Develop Your Argument

Choose a workable subject. Be sure that you're interested in the topic, believe in it, and are knowledgeable about it. Also, be sure to limit the topic so you can handle it in the time or space available to you. (Reread the discussions of choosing and limiting a topic in Chapters 1 through 5 if you need help.)

Ask a controlling question. A good question is unbiased. Such a question allows you to investigate all sides of an argument before you decide upon the side of the argument to defend. In other words, unbiased position questions allow you to keep an open mind as you investigate your topic. If you choose to argue a point of view before you find out facts or investigate the other side, you might be tempted to ignore arguments of the opposition which you don't like or think are unimportant. Students often change their minds after they finish their investigations into controversial topics.

Here are some examples of unbiased, controlling questions:

Should the federal government establish a law to forbid the sale of handguns? (Your open question allows you to find out about the issue of handgun sales before taking a side.)

Should the legal drinking age be lowered to 18?

Would the consumption of less meat make a positive contribution to the environment?

Should a free college education be provided to all college students who maintain a GPA of B or higher?

For more information about a question that will lead to a good topic to argue, reread *Chapter 5, Questioning*. Remember that informative questions do not lead to argument papers because these questions are usually answered with fact. *Who kicked the most field goals in the NFL last season?* is an informative question. The answer is a fact and is therefore hard to argue. So choose a topic and draw up a position question about the topic. Use words like "should," "would," "is," "are," "does," "ought." Then, with an open mind, collect your evidence.

Gather good evidence. Find the facts and figures that can be verified and used to support your argument. An important fact that you might wish to include in an argument for stricter firearms legislation is that "over 25,000 Americans die each year because of shootings, accidents, suicides, and murders caused by guns," according to Senator Edward Kennedy. Or if you want to argue that the legal drinking age should be left at twenty-one, you could use factual evidence (statistics, for example) to show that teenage drinking has been a significant factor in crime, traffic fatalities, or other misfortunes.

To build solid arguments around such topics as gun control and the legal drinking age, you may need to consult materials in the library to locate factual information. You may also be able to get relevant facts from government or private sources, like police and health agencies.

You may also want to use informed opinions of experts as part of your evidence. An informed opinion would be that of a psychologist whose research and publications on teenage drinking have received high ratings from other authorities on teen-age problems. Remember: informed opinions are best when supported with facts.

Be fair to the other side. If you cannot or will not understand the opposing side's view, if you think you are completely right and your opponent is all wrong, or if you detest your opponent as a person, then you are severely lacking in objectivity. Without objectivity, you probably won't be able to argue effectively.

Being fair in an argument means that you calmly acknowledge your opponent's major points, and you concede any truths that your opponent may demonstrate. For example, in his argument for tougher gun control laws, Edward Kennedy concedes that there is probably truth in the opposing view that "lawless people . . . will not feel obliged to abide by gun-control restrictions."

Take a stand. Your stand in an argument is your position. Your position can be stated in a thesis sentence. If you asked a controlling question and then gathered evidence, your answer to your question becomes your thesis. Here are two argumentative positions stated as theses:

> Stricter laws controlling handguns are the most direct way to reduce the deaths and injuries caused by these guns. (The thesis answers the question: should the government establish a law to forbid the sale of handguns?)
> The legal drinking age in this state should be raised from nineteen to twenty-one. (This thesis is the answer to the question: should the drinking age be lowered to eighteen?)

Look for holes in the other side's position. A hole in an argument may be a lack of supporting details, insufficient evidence, an incomplete rebuttal, an irrelevancy, a fallacy, or some other lapse in reasoning (to identify all the ways an argument can fail is probably an impossible task). If you find holes in your opponent's position, point them out. Your explanation of these holes and your presentation of strong evidence against your opponent's thesis form a *refutation* of your opponent.

In the following imaginary conflict between student and teacher, do you see any holes in the student's argument? In the teacher's position?

Student: It just doesn't seem fair.

Teacher: What's unfair?

Student: I took good notes and reread the assignments. Some of them I read twice. I underlined the important things in the book; I even double-underlined the points you stressed in class. Yet all I got on this test is a C+.

Teacher: I appreciate your study efforts. But a course in history, or any course for that matter, just must include more than what is discussed in class. Now take the Second Reform Bill: it's certainly important and. . . .

Student: This question on the Second Reform Bill cost me twelve points! If the Second Reform Bill's so important, why didn't you cover it in class?

Teacher: Look, we meet three hours a week. I can't possibly lecture on every topic from the French Revolution to the present. I have to be selective in my teaching.

Student: Well, I have to be selective in my studying. I'm taking five courses. I'm working twenty-five hours a week.

Teacher: Look, I'm not going to say how many students I'm teaching or how much I'm moonlighting on the side. My one point here is that you're responsible for reading that text.

Student: I read it, I told you. I can't master everything I read.

Teacher: I am not going to spoonfeed you by testing only what we cover in class. You know, a very real test of education is how much you can learn on your own, how well you can deal with the unexpected.

Lawton Green, my colleague who teaches philosophy, found holes in both arguments. According to Professor Green:

The student implies that his grade should be higher because of the amount of his preparation effort. The classroom is probably not the place for evaluating persons according to their effort, but rather according to their performance. The teacher could have said so.

The student also implies that all important portions of the subject should be covered in class. The teacher replies that he hasn't time to cover all portions.

The teacher's response here is an incomplete rebuttal. It doesn't indicate why he failed to alert students to the fact that he considered the Reform Bill so important as to include it on the test, even though limited time prevented its presentation in class.

The student emphasizes his combined academic and other work load. I take that to be, not an appeal to pity, but an explanation of his selectivity. Of course teachers and students have to be selective because of the immensity of the subject. So the explanation is superfluous. The teacher's implied response, that he too has overextended himself, is quite irrelevant to the issue at hand.

The student's reading of his text only once or twice could be challenged as insufficient but isn't.

Beware of fallacies. A *fallacy* is a faulty inference occurring within an argument. Thus a fallacy involves reasoning that fails to satisfy the conditions of valid argument. Some fallacies are very obvious, whereas others are hard to detect. Here are some common fallacies which you should avoid in your arguments and watch for in opposing arguments.

1. *Sweeping generalization.* According to Morris Engel, this fallacy occurs when "a general rule is applied to a specific case to which the rule is not applicable because of special features of that case." This fallacy often uses words like "always," "everybody," "nobody," "no one," "all," "every," "none." Instead of these general words which allow no exceptions, use words which do allow exceptions: "most," "almost," "frequently," "often," "many," "usually."

   Example: Since jogging is always healthy exercise, Frank Jones should jog more. It will be good for his asthma. (Asthma sufferers do not always benefit from jogging or exercise so the general rule cannot be applied.)

2. *Snob appeal.* This fallacy often appears in advertising. An ad may try to persuade you to buy a certain product because a movie star or a famous athlete claims to use the product. Similarly, someone may try to persuade you to accept a certain view or to join a particular organization because it's what "the movers and shakers, the people in the know" do.

Example: When you join our club and follow our exercise program, you will be joining the real athletes in this community.

3. *Begging the question.* This fallacy is reasoning in a circle. It begins by assuming that something is true and then concludes with the same assumption.

    Examples: The present administration is weary and incompetent, for it is fatigued and unable to act effectively.

    The cement cracked where it came apart.

4. *Either-or fallacy.* An either-or argument takes an issue and allows only two alternatives for it. In this fallacy, there are more than two options. Grades, for example, do not automatically spell success or failure in a job or career. Some very successful business people did poorly in school or dropped out, and many notable achievers in the arts and professions never finished college.

    Examples: Either you make good grades in college or you'll be a flop in the job market. America—love it or leave it. Either you are with me or against me.

5. *Irrelevant conclusion.* This fallacy results when a conclusion does not logically follow from a premise.

    Example: He is a renowned author and will be a perfect choice for the new teaching post at the college. (The assumption here is that since the person is a skilled writer, he will be a good teacher, a conclusion that does not follow; expert writing doesn't guarantee expert teaching.)

6. *Appeal to Authority.* This fallacy uses authority without offering reasons why the authority offers his or her position. Thus, the reader has only the conclusion.

    Example: We need more federal loans for college students. The president said so himself yesterday. (In this example the president doesn't explain why college students need more federal loans. The assumption is that his word—authority—is enough.)

Use deductive and inductive reasoning. An argument can be deductive or inductive. Both kinds of argument contain premises or propositions. When you argue deductively, your premises are so related to your conclusion that it is impossible for you to have true premises unless your conclusion is also true. As Irving Copi has defined it, a deductive argument is "one whose conclusion is claimed to follow from its premises with absolute necessity, this necessity not being a matter of degree and not depending in any way upon whatever else may be the case." For example,

If automobile insurance rates increase as much as twenty percent, I will have to give up my car.
The state insurance commission will deregulate auto rates on January 1, and insurance companies have announced a twenty-five percent rate increase effective on that date.
Therefore I will have to give up my car.

In contrast, when you argue inductively, you present, in Copi's words, an argument "whose conclusion is claimed to follow from its premises only with probability, this probability being a matter of degree and dependent upon what else may be the case." (*Introduction to Logic*, 6th ed., MacMillan, 1982) For example,

> Mary liked the first three movies in which Rob Lowe starred.
> I did also.
> Mary has seen Lowe's fourth movie and likes it.
> Thus, when I get around to seeing it, I will probably like it too.

The inductive method has been extremely productive in modern science, and lawyers, educators, as well as other professionals, frequently rely on it.

Structure your argument well. Although not every argument has to follow a strict, definite form, the conventional essay has proven to be an effective way to arrange both oral and written arguments. An outline of this form looks like this:

Introduction: • Introduce the problem or issue.
            • State your thesis clearly.
            • Make sure your introduction leads directly and logically to your thesis statement.
Body: • Give background, history, or necessary definitions.
            • Support your thesis with sound logic and convincing, specific detail.
            • State the other side's major points.
            • Refute arguments of the other side by explaining any holes or fallacies in your opponent's reasoning.
Conclusion: • If your argument is long and involved, sum up its major points.
            • Restate your thesis.
            • Stress your main idea in a closing statement that is forceful and very convincing.

Example: It is time to study a full argument. Read William F. Buckley's "Cancer Patients Need Access to Pain-Relieving Drug" to see how he applies the principles of argument to this subject. Do you agree with his position? Why? Why not?

Cancer Patients Need Access to Pain-Relieving Drug

by William F. Buckley

The movement to ease the awful pain of some deaths from cancer is showing signs of life. Not inconceivably, the present Congress could make the decisive move: to permit doctors, administering to terminally ill patients who have failed to respond to lesser drugs, to give injections of heroin.

It has been a very long fight, and Judith Quattlebaum of Washington has led it, unflaggingly. It was more than 10 years ago that she undertook to organize a committee to bring to the attention of Congress, which passes laws regulating the use of drugs, the plight of Americans who suffer great pain of the kind that could be alleviated by such injections of heroin as are routinely administered in Great Britain to those who are certain to die.

What Mrs. Quattlebaum keeps running into is a) a part of the medical establishment that against all reasonable evidence persists in insisting that a combination of lesser drugs will accomplish the same pain abatement (there are plenty of doctors on the other side, and the British experience is now long, and conclusive); and b) more important, those in Congress who succumb to the argument that to authorize heroin in the hospitals would be to flood the streets with this dangerous drug, augmenting the incidence of drug addiction.

But the data have been carefully accumulated, and the Committee on the Treatment of Intractable Pain has in hand data difficult to contend with. If every milligram of heroin that is proposed be legally authorized to hospitals tending to cancer patients were stolen from the hospital safes at 2 o'clock in the afternoon and made instantly available to street peddlers of illegal heroin, the result would be to augment the existing supply of illegal drugs by between 2 percent and 4 percent.

Since there is little likelihood that 1,000 hospitals would coordinate the circumstances for such an operation, more difficult than the Normandy landing, what we see is a threat of no consequence.

And then the most important figure of all. Since 1980, when the committee came close to winning congressional approval, 8,000 persons per year have died of cancer of that excruciatingly painful variety that might have been sharply mitigated if only Congress had acted.

The good news this season has been the activity of Sen. Daniel Inouye, who is the principal Senate sponsor of the heroin bill. He is joined by a number of senators across the ideological spectrum. Sen. Dennis DeConcini has been very active. Add Sens. John Melcher, Quentin Burdick, Ted Stevens, Thad Cochrane, Donald Riegle, Carl Levin, John Warner, Nancy Kassenbaum, James McClure, Patrick Leahy—and, most recently, Robert Dole.

The principal opponent of the measure is Rep. Charles Rangel of Harlem, a man of great charm and persuasion who is, however, a fundamentalist on the drug problem. If heroin is bad, Rangel reasons, then why would Congress authorize its use? Well, Congress authorizes the use of napalm, and every day in every hospital, tools—and drugs—are used that, misused, would cause trouble, sometimes death. But Rangel does not own Congress, and much turns on the position taken, as yet unstated, by the president. . . .

Sen. Edward Kennedy, as chairman of the Committee on Labor and Human Resources, presides over that committee that normally would hear testimony for and against the proposed measure. He has told his colleagues that he is too busy to undertake to examine the proposed bill during this session. But congressional tradition holds that at least one committee of Congress should hear testimony and the House Subcommittee on Health and the Environment—which reports to the Committee on Energy and Commerce—heard such testimony.

It would be altogether conventional for the Senate to waive its own hearings, accept those of the other house and move directly to a vote on the floor.

Kennedy, who often speaks of the unnecessary cruelties of life, ought to react to the principal problem, which is: every day's delay means 25 deaths in unnecessary pain. The whole of Congress should be alerted to this point. It is responsible to pass the bill—or to vote it down. What is not responsible is simply to dither away another month, year, decade, letting the agony of the hopeless subsidize congressional torpor.

Buckley uses this simple structure for his argument:

Introduction:

1. The proposal: that Congress should pass a bill "to permit doctors, administering to terminally ill patients who have failed to respond to lesser drugs, to give injections of heroin"

2. A brief history of the proposed bill and Judith Quattlebaum's struggle to get heroin treatment approved.

Body of his argument:

3. Opponents' positions: lesser drugs will accomplish pain abatement and also heroin will flood the streets

4. Refutation of opposing views: data showing that medical use of other drugs will not abate all pain, and heroin will not flood streets.

5. Positive features of the proposal: its main benefit and its important backers in Congress

6. Refutation of Representative Charles Rangel's argument

Conclusion:

7. Closing statements: appeal to Congress to act responsibly now and pass the bill

Example: "America Needs Its Nerds," a charming essay by Leonid Fridman, uses a simple argument. He begins with a challenge, "There is something very wrong with a system of values in a society that has only derogatory terms like nerd and geek for the intellectually curious and academically serious." The essay then defines the negative word, "geek." (A good way to begin an argument is to define your terms so the reader understands the terms the same way you do.) After defining terms and stating how ludicrous the name "geek" is, the writer gives examples of how anti-intellectualism is rampant in prestigious institutions and in U.S. elementary and high schools.

Then Fridman states, "Enough is enough." Here is the turning point of the essay. Now the writer makes his case for fighting the anti-intellectual values of our society. His arguments include a contrast of educational values between the U.S. and East Asia and another contrast between the prestige and salaries of the best of U.S. professors and those of those overpaid ballplayers. Each comparison makes the reader wince because the comparisons are so true.

The writer reaches his major argument: how can America continue to compete in the technological race or remain a political and cultural force if we "emphasize social skills and physical prowess over academic achievement and intellectual ability"? Fridman says we import our intellectuals now. He states that spending more money on schools is no solution unless we change the attitude toward learning and reward and value good students and faculty.

Finally he ends his essay with a threat: "If we are to succeed as a society in the 21st century," we must change. He emphatically tells the reader what must change. Then in the last sentence, he returns to his title and the first sentence, but he maintains his threat, "And until the words 'nerd' and 'geek' become terms of approbation, not derision, we do not stand a chance."

America Needs Its Nerds

by Leonid Fridman

There is something very wrong with the system of values in a society that has only derogatory terms like nerd and geek for the intellectually curious and academically serious.

A geek, according to *Webster's New World Dictionary,* is a street performer who shocks the public by biting off heads of live chickens. It is a telling fact about our language and our culture that someone dedicated to pursuit of knowledge is compared to a freak biting the head off a live chicken.

Even at a prestigious academic institution like Harvard, anti-intellectualism is rampant: Many students are ashamed to admit, even to their friends, how much they study. Although most students try to keep up their grades, there is but a minority of undergraduates for whom pursuing knowledge is the top priority during their years at Harvard. Nerds are ostracized while athletes are idolized.

The same thing happens in U.S. elementary and high schools. Children who prefer to read books rather than play football, prefer to build model airplanes rather than get wasted at parties with their classmates, become social outcasts. Ostracized for their intelligence and refusal to conform to society's anti-intellectual values, many are deprived of a chance to learn adequate social skills and acquire good communication tools.

Enough is enough.

Nerds and geeks must stop being ashamed of who they are. It is high time to face the persecutors who haunt the bright kid with thick glasses from kindergarten to the grave. For America's sake, the anti-intellectual values that pervade our society must be fought.

There are very few countries in the world where anti-intellectualism runs as high in popular culture as it does in the U.S. In most industrialized nations, not least of all our economic rivals in East Asia, a kid who studies hard is lauded and held up as an example to other students.

In many parts of the world, university professorships are the most prestigious and materially rewarding positions. But not in America, where average professional ballplayers are much more respected and better paid than faculty members of the best universities.

How can a country where typical parents are ashamed of their daughter studying mathematics instead of going dancing, or of their son reading Weber while his friends play baseball, be expected to compete in the technology race with Japan or remain a leading political and cultural force in Europe? How long can America remain a world-class power if we constantly emphasize social skills and physical prowess over academic achievement and intellectual ability?

Do we really expect to stay afloat largely by importing our scientists and intellectuals from abroad, as we have done for a major portion of this century, without making an effort to also cultivate a pro-intellectual culture at home? Even if we have the political will to spend substantially more money on education than we do now, do we think we can improve our schools if we deride our studious pupils and debase their impoverished teachers?

Our fault lies not so much with our economy or with our politics as within ourselves, our values and our image of a good life. America's culture has not adapted to the demands of our times, to the economic realities that demand a highly educated workforce and innovative intelligent leadership.

If we are to succeed as a society in the 21st century, we had better shed our anti-intellectualism and imbue in our children the vision that a good life is impossible without stretching one's mind and pursuing knowledge to the full extent of one's abilities.

And until the words "nerd and "geek" become terms of approbation and not derision, we do not stand a chance.

Fridman uses this structure for his argument:

Introduction:

1. Thesis: "There is something very wrong with the system of values in a society that has only derogatory terms like 'nerd' and 'geek' for the intellectually curious and academically serious."

2. Definition of terms: "A geek, according to *Webster's New World Dictionary* is a street performer who shocks the public by biting off heads of live chickens."

Body of the Essay:

1. Examples of anti-intellectualism—Harvard, high school, elementary schools

2. Reasons why anti-intellectual values must be fought:

    a. Value of education in East Asia

    b. Prestige and material rewards of professors in countries outside the U.S.

3. Threats

    a. America will lose the race in technology

    b. America will no longer be a world class power

    c. America will no longer be a political and cultural force in Europe

    d. More money spent on education will not solve problems unless we value intellectual prowess more than social skills

Conclusion:

1. Solution to the problem: "American culture must adapt to demands of our times, to the economic realities that demand a highly educated workforce and innovative, intelligent leadership."

2. Return to title and thesis: "Until the words 'nerd' and 'geek' become terms of approbation and not derision, we do not stand a chance."

Notice how Fridman's argument is similar in structure to Buckley's argument.

Example: A third example of the argument is "Eat Less Meat; Save the Planet" by John Robbins. Early in his essay Robbins asks his readers to "Consider how many precious resources are squandered to produce the feedlot beef that goes into hamburger—and how this wanton waste affects our health and well being." The paper argues that a great number of precious resources are squandered and that all this waste causes dangerous health problems for people. In brief, his entire essay offers only reasons why we should eat less meat. What follows is an example of a "Reasons Why" argument.

Eat Less Meat; Save the Planet

by John Robbins

There is one very simple step to take if you aim to live a long and healthy life: Eat less meat.

The benefits are more dramatic than you have probably imagined. By eating less meat, for instance, you can help stave off sun-induced cancers, which will be epidemic if the ozone layer continues to be depleted at current rates. You can also make water safer for drinking, reduce world hunger, protect the tropical rain forests and guard virgin land from the ravages of oil drilling, not to mention lower your cholesterol and risk of heart disease.

All this just by ordering a plate of pasta instead of a hamburger.

Consider how many precious resources are squandered to produce the feedlot beef that goes into a hamburger—and how this wanton waste affects our health and well-being:

Every year, 8,000 square miles of Latin American rain forests are cleared for cattle grazing. That translates to 55 square feet to produce a quarter pound of beef.

The environmental consequences of this destruction are disastrous. Scientists report that 1,000 species become extinct every year because of deforestation, impoverishing the earth's biological diversity. Another threat comes from carbon dioxide. Whenever forests are burned, not only is carbon dioxide spewed into the atmosphere, but carbon-storing trees are lost. This process fuels the life-threatening greenhouse effect—the ominous buildup of gases that trap heat in the atmosphere, raising global temperatures and killing off food crops. . . .

Cattle churn out greenhouse gases, too. Their intestines generate more methane than almost any other single source. One chemist estimates that the world's cattle emit up to 100 million tons of methane into the atmosphere each year. Synthetic nitrogen fertilizers, used primarily to grow cattle feed, release enormous amounts of nitrous oxide, another greenhouse gas.

Meat production also increases the amount of chlorofluorocarbons (CFCs) released into the atmosphere. These chemicals are used in refrigeration, which meats, unlike grains and other foodstuffs, require. The Styrofoam containers that fast-food hamburger chains use also contain enormous amounts of CFCs. CFCs accelerate the greenhouse effect and break down the ozone layer, the natural filter that protects us from ultraviolet rays. Skin cancer induced by excessive exposure to these rays is already increasing dramatically.

The U.S. Department of Agriculture keeps tabs on just how much the meat-production industry costs us in terms of natural resources here at home. Cattle are responsible for nine times as much organic waste-water pollution as the entire American population. Livestock production is directly responsible for 85 percent of topsoil erosion, seriously jeopardizing future crops. And while it takes only 25 gallons of water to produce a pound of wheat, it takes 2,500 gallons to produce a pound of meat.

Our craving for meat ever increases our demand for foreign oil. We burn 22 times more fossil fuel—used for transporting cattle, operating slaughterhouses, etc.—to produce a pound of protein from meat than we do to produce a pound of protein from wheat. Eating less meat, then, would reduce the necessity of drilling for oil in environmentally sensitive areas like Alaska.

Our meat-based diet also exacts an enormous human toll. If Americans were to eat just two meatless meals a week, they would free up land to grow enough grain to feed the starving children of the world. Livestock consume 80 percent of the corn and 95 percent of the oats eaten in this country. Overall, it takes 12 to 16 pounds of grain to produce one pound of feedlot beef.

One of the first investigations into a grain-for-meat trade-off was born of necessity. During World War I, the Danish government was forced to institute rationing. Instead of grain being fed to livestock, it was given directly to people—in effect, a mass experiment in vegetarianism. The results, reported after the war in the *Journal of the American Medical Association*, flabbergasted scientists. In Copenhagen, the death rate from disease during the period was 34 percent lower than it had been for the preceding 18 years.

For healthy, well-nourished people today, cutting back on meat may be a matter of life and death, too. Research shows that people who eat less meat and more whole grains, fresh vegetables and a fruit cut their odds of heart disease and cancer. They also have lower rates of osteoporosis, diabetes, ulcers and stroke. In short, they live longer.

Eating less meat, then, provides us with a chance to help ourselves and our environment, making the world a healthier place to live for centuries to come.

John Robbins is the founder of Concerned Citizens of Planet Earth and author of *Diet for a New America*.

Compare this argument with that of William F. Buckley's "Cancer Patients Need Access to Pain-Relieving Drugs." Which argument is easier to follow? Which is easier to agree with? Why? As you read the essays, what did you learn about arguing?

The Mock Argument

So far we have been talking about the straight argument in which you say exactly what you mean and try to refute the other side with clear, convincing evidence. Another persuasive tool you can use is the mock argument. In the *mock argument*, the writer often employs irony. With *irony* you say one thing and mean another. When you use irony and mockery to ridicule opposing views, you are writing *satire*.

Satire does not depend on strict logic and is not a reliable method in straight, formal argument. Satire often rouses emotions through exaggeration, humor, wit, or shock effect. A satire that has all these qualities is "A Modest Proposal" by Jonathan Swift. It's also an excellent example of a mock argument in essay form.

Written in 1729, "A Modest Proposal" grew out of Swift's first-hand observation of the awful poverty and brutality that plagued the Irish people. The satire shows Swift's profound indignation over England's oppression of Ireland, and to a lesser extent it satirizes certain ills of the Irish themselves. Major excerpts from the work follow.

A Modest Proposal

by Jonathan Swift

It is a melancholy object to those who walk through this great town or travel in the country, when they see the streets, the roads, and cabin doors, crowded with beggars of the female-sex, followed by three, four, or six children, all in rags and importuning every passenger for an alms. These mothers, instead of being able to work for their honest livelihood, are forced to employ all their time in strolling to beg sustenance for their helpless infants, who, as they grow up, either turn thieves for want of work, or leave their dear native country to fight for the Pretender in Spain, or sell themselves to the Barbadoes.

I think it is agreed by all parties that this prodigious number of children in the arms, or on the backs, or at the heels of their mothers, and frequently of their fathers, is in the present deplorable state of the kingdom a very great additional grievance; and therefore whoever could find out a fair, cheap, and easy method of making these children sound, useful members of the commonwealth would deserve so well of the public as to have his statue set up for a preserver of the nation. . . .

There is likewise another great advantage to my scheme, that it will prevent those voluntary abortions, and that horrid practice of women murdering their bastard children, alas, too frequent among us, sacrificing the poor innocent babes, I doubt, more to avoid the expense than the shame, which would move tears and pity in the most savage and inhuman breast.

The number of souls in this kingdom being usually reckoned one million and a half, of these I calculate there may be about two hundred thousand couples whose wives are breeders; from which number I subtract thirty thousand couples who are able to maintain their own children, although I apprehend there cannot be so many under the present distresses of the kingdom; but this being granted, there will remain an hundred and seventy thousand breeders. I again subtract fifty thousand for those women who miscarry, or whose children die by accident or disease within the year. There only remain an hundred and twenty thousand children of poor parents annually born. The question therefore is, how this number shall be reared and provided for, which, as I have already said, under the present situation of affairs, is utterly impossible by all the methods hitherto proposed. For we can neither employ them in handicraft or agriculture; we neither build houses (I mean in the country) nor cultivate land. They can very seldom pick up a livelihood by stealing till they arrive at six years old, except where they are of towardly parts; although I confess they learn the rudiments much earlier, during which time they can however be looked upon only as probationers, as I have been informed by a principal gentleman in the county of Cavan, who protested to me that he never knew above one or two instances under the age of six, even in a part of the kingdom so renowned for the quickest proficiency in that art.

I am assured by our merchants that a boy or a girl before twelve years old is no salable commodity; and even when they come to this age they will not yield above three pounds, or three pounds and half a crown at most on the Exchange; which cannot turn to account either to the parents or the kingdom, the charge of nutriment and rags having been at least four times that value.

I shall now therefore humbly propose my own thoughts, which I hope will not be liable to the least objection.

I have been assured by a very knowing American of my acquaintance in London, that a young healthy child well nursed is at a year old a most delicious, nourishing, and wholesome food, whether stewed, roasted, baked, or boiled; and I make no doubt that it will equally serve in a fricassee or a ragout.

I do therefore humbly offer it to public consideration that of the hundred and twenty thousand children, already computed, twenty thousand may be reserved for breed, whereof only one fourth part to be males, which is more than we allow to sheep, black cattle, or swine; and my reason is that these children are seldom the fruits of marriage, a circumstance not much regarded by our savages, therefore one male will be sufficient to serve four females. That the remaining hundred thousand may at a year old be offered in sale to the persons of quality and fortune through the kingdom, always advising the mother to let them suck plentifully in the last month, so as to render them plump and fat for a good table. A child will make two dishes at an entertainment for friends; and when the family dines alone, the fore or hind quarter will make a reasonable dish, and seasoned with a little pepper or salt will be very good boiled on the fourth day, especially in winter.

I have reckoned upon a medium that a child just born will weigh twelve pounds, and in a solar year if tolerably nursed increaseth to twenty-eight pounds.

I grant this food will be somewhat dear, and therefore very popular for landlords, who, as they have already devoured most of the parents, seem to have the best title to the children.

Infant's flesh will be in season throughout the year, but more plentiful in March, and a little before and after. For we are told by a grave author, an eminent French physician, that fish being a prolific diet, there are more children born in Roman Catholic countries about nine months after Lent than at any other season; therefore, reckoning a year after Lent, the markets will be more glutted than usual, because the number of popish infants is at least three to one in this kingdom; and therefore it will have one other collateral advantage, by lessening the number of Papists among us.

I have already computed the charge of nursing a beggar's child (in which list I reckon all cottagers, laborers, and four fifths of the farmers) to be about two shillings per annum, rags included; and I believe no gentleman would repine to give ten shillings for the carcass of a good fat child, which, as I have said, will make four dishes of excellent nutritive meat, when he hath only some particular friend or his own family to dine with him. Thus the squire will learn to be a good landlord, and grow popular among the tenants; the mother will have eight shillings net profit, and be fit for work till she produces another child.

Those who are more thrifty (as I must confess the times require) may flay the carcass; the skin of which artificially dressed will make admirable gloves for ladies, and summer boots for fine gentlemen.

As to our city of Dublin, shambles may be appointed for this purpose in the most convenient parts of it, and butchers we may be assured will not be wanting; although I rather recommend buying the children alive, and dressing them hot from the knife as we do roasting pigs. . . .

I think the advantages by the proposal which I have made are obvious and many, as well as of the highest importance.

For first, as I have already observed, it would greatly lessen the number of Papists, with whom we are yearly overrun, being the principal breeders of the nation as well as our most dangerous enemies; and who stay at home on purpose to deliver the kingdom to the Pretender, hoping to take their advantage by the absence of so many good Protestants, who have chosen rather to leave their country than to stay at home and pay tithes against their conscience to an Episcopal curate.

Secondly, the poorer tenants will have something valuable of their own, which by law may be made liable to distress, and help to pay their landlord's rent, their corn and cattle being already seized and money a thing unknown.

Thirdly, whereas the maintenance of a hundred thousand children, from two years old and upwards, cannot be computed at less than ten shillings a piece per annum, the nation's stock will be thereby increased fifty thousand pounds per annum, besides the profit of a new dish introduced to the tables of all gentlemen of fortune in the kingdom who have any refinement in taste. And the money will circulate among ourselves, the goods being entirely of our own growth and manufacture.

Fourthly, the constant breeders, besides the gain of eight shillings sterling per annum by the sale of their children, will be rid of the charge of maintaining them after the first year.

Fifthly, this food will likewise bring great custom to taverns, where the vintners will certainly be so prudent as to procure the best receipts for dressing it to perfection, and consequently have their houses frequented by all the fine gentlemen, who justly value themselves upon their knowledge in good eating; and a skillful cook, who understands how to oblige his guests, will contrive to make it as expensive as they please.

Sixthly, this would be a great inducement to marriage, which all wise nations have either encouraged by rewards or enforced by laws and penalties. It would increase the care and tenderness of mothers toward their children, when they were sure of a settlement for life to the poor babies, provided in some sort by the public, to their annual profit instead of expense. We should see an honest emulation among the married women, which of them could bring the fattest child to the market. Men would become as fond of their wives during the time of their pregnancy as they are now of their mares in foal, their cows in calf, or sows when they are ready to farrow; nor offer to beat or kick them (as is too frequent a practice) for fear of a miscarriage.

Many other advantages might be enumerated. For instance, the addition of some thousand carcasses in our exportation of barreled beef, the propagation of swine's flesh, and improvement in the art of making good bacon, so much wanted among us by the great destruction of pigs, too frequent at our tables, which are no way comparable in taste or magnificence to a well-grown, fat, yearling child, which roasted whole will make a considerable figure at a lord mayor's feast or any other public entertainment. But this and many others I omit, being studious of brevity.

Supposing that one thousand families in this city would be constant customers for infants' flesh, besides others who might have it at merry meetings, particularly weddings and christenings, I compute that Dublin would take off annually about twenty thousand carcasses, and the rest of the kingdom (where probably they will be sold somewhat cheaper) the remaining eighty thousand.

I can think of no one objection that will possibly be raised against this proposal, unless it should be urged that the number of people will be thereby much lessened in the kingdom. This I freely own, and it was indeed one principal design in offering it to the world. I desire the reader will observe, that I calculate my remedy for this one individual kingdom of Ireland and for no other that ever was, is, or I think ever can be upon earth. Therefore let no man talk to me of other expedients: of taxing our absentees at five shillings a pound: of using neither clothes nor household furniture except what is of our own growth and manufacture: of utterly rejecting the materials and instruments that promote foreign luxury: of curing the expensiveness of pride, vanity, idleness, and gaming in our women: of introducing a vein of parsimony, prudence, and temperance: of learning to love our country, in the want of which we differ even from Laplanders and the inhabitants of Topinamboo: of quitting our animosities and factions, nor acting any longer like the Jews, who were murdering one another at the very moment their city was taken: of being a little cautious not to sell our country and conscience for nothing: of teaching landlords to have at least one degree of mercy toward their tenants: lastly, of putting a spirit of honesty, industry, and skill into our shopkeepers; who, if a resolution could now be taken to buy only our native goods, would immediately unite to cheat and exact upon us in the price, the measure, and the goodness, nor could ever yet be brought to make one fair proposal of just dealing, though often and earnestly invited to it.

Therefore I repeat, let no man talk to me of these and the like expedients, till he hath at least some glimpse of hope that there will ever be some hearty and sincere attempt to put them in practice.

But as to myself, having been wearied out for many years with offering vain, idle, visionary thoughts, and at length utterly despairing of success, I fortunately fell upon this proposal, which, as it is wholly new, so it hath something solid and real, of no expense and little trouble, full in our own power, and whereby we can incur no danger in disobliging England. For this kind of commodity will not bear exportation, the flesh being of too tender a consistence to admit a long continuance in salt, although perhaps I could name a country which would be glad to eat up our whole nation without it.

After all, I am not so violently bent upon my own opinion as to eject any offer proposed by wise men, which shall be found equally innocent, cheap, easy, and effectual. But before something of that kind shall be advanced in contradiction to my scheme, and offering a better, I desire the author or authors will be pleased maturely to consider two points. First, as things now stand, how they will be able to find food and raiment for an hundred thousand useless mouths and backs. And secondly, there being a round million of creatures in human figure throughout this kingdom, whose sole subsistence put into a common stock would leave them in debt two millions of pounds sterling, adding those who are beggars by profession to the bulk of farmers, cottagers, and laborers, with their wives and children who are beggars in effect; I desire those politicians who dislike my overture, and may perhaps be so bold to attempt an answer, that they will first ask the parents of these mortals whether they would not at this day think it a great happiness to have been sold for food at a year old in the manner I prescribe, and thereby have avoided such a perpetual scene of misfortunes as they have since gone through by the oppression of landlords, the impossibility of paying rent without money or trade, the want of common sustenance, with neither house nor clothes to cover them from the inclemencies of the weather, and the most inevitable prospect of entailing the like or greater miseries upon their breed forever.

I profess, in the sincerity of my heart, that I have not the least personal interest in endeavoring to promote this necessary work, having no other motive than the public good of my country, by advancing our trade, providing for infants, relieving the poor, and giving some pleasure to the rich. I have no children by which I can propose to get a single penny; the youngest being nine years old, and my wife past childbearing.

We cannot know exactly what Swift had in mind when he wrote this provocative essay. We have to interpret his meaning and use examples from the work to support our opinions.

I interpret the satire this way. To advance his irony, Swift invents a fictional character and has him develop a grotesque, inhuman scheme to rid Ireland of its poverty. This character is a proposer who claims to have the best interests of the Irish in mind. What he proposes has the appearance of logic but is grossly absurd. Notice that Swift has the proposer use the essay form: introduction, body, and conclusion. Swift also makes the proposer structure the scheme like a straight argument, as this outline of the proposer's major points shows.

1. Statement of the problem

2. Explanation of the problem and introduction of the proposal

3. Discussion of the proposal in detail

4. Explanation of the proposal's benefits

5. Refutation of opposing views

6. Closing statement in which the proposer disclaims any personal profit motive and appeals to the public good

The character of the proposer, then, functions as a kind of literary puppet, and Swift, the author, is like a puppeteer pulling his character's ridiculous strings. Another way of interpreting the proposer is that he appears as a mask for Swift. Through his mask, Swift says one thing and means another.

We infer Swift's real intentions from the way he lets the proposer talk. Swift seems to be saying that the terrible conditions in Ireland have resulted from social and moral ills which need to be exposed and corrected. The targets of his satire include corrupt authorities in Ireland and England, selfish aristocrats, greedy landlords and businessmen, Papists, decadent partygoers, wastrels, thieves, and those who abuse and brutalize children. All of these targets and others are mentioned or implied through the essay.

Moreover, in a brilliant stroke of irony in a paragraph late in the essay, Swift makes the proposer argue against what really ought to be done to help Ireland (and the world) become a far better place. (This paragraph begins with "I can think of no one objection that will possibly be raised against this proposal. . . .") The virtues and common sense we see the proposer condemning in this paragraph are the values that Swift, the moralist, ironically upholds.

COLLABORATIVE LEARNING

1. Look for problems in arguments in letters to the editor, television commentaries, editorials, political speeches, ads, and other sources. Take your favorite examples to class and discuss them with your writing group. Have the group select the most blatant problem and the most subtle one. Justify your choices in writing.

2. Write a group argument. The group decides on a good topic. Then one person writes the introduction, including an explanation of the problem and a thesis statement. Another person gathers evidence to support the thesis, another puts this evidence in written form using inductive and deductive reasoning, and still another refutes opposing arguments and writes the closing statement.

3. Look at arguments in this chapter. The group selects the best argument and the worst one. Justify these choices in writing.

WRITING TASKS

1. Write a letter to the editor of your local paper on a topic about which you feel particularly strong. In your letter use the techniques of straight argument.

2. Write an essay of argument. Introduce the problem or issue. Define terms your readers may need to know and offer background or history your readers should know in order to understand the issues. Make sure your introduction leads directly and logically to your thesis statement. In the body, develop sound evidence and reasoning to support your thesis. State the other side's major points and refute them by explaining any holes or fallacies in your opponent's reasoning. If your argument is long and involved, sum up its major points in the conclusion. Stress your main idea in a closing statement that is forceful and very convincing.

3. Write a letter to our congressional representative or someone important to you. In the letter, take a stand on a particular issue. Use the essay form.

4. Using an ironical mask and the structure of a straight argument, write your own modest proposal satirizing something about which you are disturbed. Use as your model Swift's "A Modest Proposal."

5. Attend a trial at your local courthouse and summarize one of the attorney's arguments. Point out any examples of inductive and deductive logic in this argument. If you were the attorney in this case, would you have argued any differently? Why?

Sample Topics

Should the government maintain its present affirmative action policies or should the policies be changed?
Should Americans be offered a national health insurance?
Should the state sponsor a lottery?
Should smoking be banned in all public places?
Should some illegal drugs be legalized?
Should women serve in military combat units?
Should the English language be gender neutral?
Should English be the official language of the U.S.A.?
Should high schools offer students free condoms?
Should sex education courses be offered in elementary schools?

Name _____

Section _____

ARGUMENT/FALLACIES WORKSHEET _____

See if you can create six slogans for some product or idea; each slogan or statement should use one of the six major fallacies. If you can create the fallacies yourself, you can be quite aware of their use by the advertising or political arms of the media.

EXAMPLE: Product = *Nike Air Jordans*

Sweeping generalization: My new Nike Air Jordans keep my feet from hurting, so all of you can stop your feet from aching by buying Nike Air Jordans, too.

Snob appeal: Michael Jordan swears by Nike Air.

Begging the question (reasoning in a circle): The superb fit of these Nike Airs makes them very comfortable.

Either-or fallacy: Either you wear Nike Airs or you are a nobody on the court.

Irrelevant conclusion: Jordan's Nike Airs make him a great athlete.

Appeal to an authority in a different field: Wall Street traders recommend wearing Nike Airs during lunch breaks because they support your feet better than most footgear.

Your turn:
Product or Idea: _____
Sweeping generalization:

Snob appeal:

Begging the question (reasoning in a circle):

Either-or fallacy:

Irrelevant conclusion:

Appeal to an authority in a different field:

Chapter Thirty-Four

Master Essay Tests

One good way to introduce this chapter is to tell ＾ ＿out a history test I had many years ago. It consisted of one question that M＾ ＿nstead, my teacher, wrote on the chalkboard:

> Explain at least two main causes an＾ major social ramifications of the American Civil War.

Here is a close approx＾ ＿n of how I tried to plan my answer to the question. At first I griped and rambl＾ ＿ny mind: "Unfair! We had only one day to prepare for this test." But then I fa＾ ＿e question and said to myself:

> I know th＾ ＿s of the Civil War. No problem there. But what on earth does *ramifications* mean＾ ＿e it's a fort or defensive line or something. Better ask Mrs. Winstead. But nobody's ＾ ＿er anything. I don't want to go up to her desk and look stupid. I'll just work on the ＿ses first and then on the social part. I know what *social* means so if I describe Southern society during the war, I should be pretty close on the second part. Here goes.

The next day when I got my test back, I was shocked to see a 65 on it. I had received 50 points on the first part of my answer but only 15 on the second part. My Southern-society strategy had not worked very well. Actually my score was one of the higher grades in the room, and when Mrs. Winstead announced that she was counting this as a practice exam, I was greatly relieved.

I did poorly on this test because I did not fully understand the question. I was too shy to ask the teacher to clarify the meaning of a key word and tried to answer the second part of the question by ignoring what I did not understand. Thus my faulty planning led to an answer which was faulty.

As I once did, many students today find essay tests difficult and do not use sound strategies when they take these exams. If you are one of these students, this chapter is designed to increase your understanding of essay questions and to give you suggestions on how to write good essay answers.

Different Kinds of Essay Tests

Essay tests vary widely as to kind and length. They may be the short-answer kind; that is, each question can be answered in a few sentences or a short paragraph. Or they may contain questions which require longer responses of several paragraphs or even pages. Further, these tests may be the open-book or closed-book type; they may be written in class or out of class. The in-class essay is really a first draft written under pressure of a time limit (often 50 minutes); therefore, it cannot be a polished piece of writing. The take-home exam, however, may be written several times before it becomes a finished product. Usually this test is evaluated more strictly as to form and content.

Whether you take your essay test in class or out of class, you don't have free choice of subject. The instructor chooses the subject for you and puts it in the form of one or more questions. You may or may not have a choice of questions to answer on an essay test. But in any case, one key to doing well on this exam is to understand as much as you can about essay questions.

Understanding What Essay Questions Ask

Most essay questions are designed to test your knowledge of specific subject matter, as do the following:

- Trace a bite of food through your digestive system. List the organs of the digestive tract in order that the food passes through them. Also indicate in proper order the accessory glands and organs the food would not pass through but which aid in the digestive process. (A question in biology)

- Compare and contrast operant conditioning with classical conditioning. (A question in psychology)

- Summarize the plot of Hawthorne's "Young Goodman Brown." Be sure to give the major events of the story in the exact order in which they occur. (A question in literature)

The questions here ask you to recall and order factual information. In other words, the teachers use them as tools to see how well you have committed certain important points to memory and how well you can organize these facts into clear, concise answers.

Other essay questions, however, are more complex. The following question, for example, asks you to interpret the symbols in a famous Greek work, compare its ideas with your own views, and then take an argumentative stand:

- Explain the meaning of the cave and the light in Plato's "Allegory of the Cave." How do Plato's ideas in this allegory compare and/or contrast with your own ideas on the nature of reality? Do you agree with Plato? Why or why not? (A question in humanities or philosophy)

To answer some questions like the next one you have to use your imagination and recast certain situations:

- Imagine yourself first as the Southern battlefield commander and then as the Northern field commander at the Battle of Gettysburg. Discuss how you would conduct the battle from these two perspectives. Explain your reasons for the strategic and tactical decisions you make. (A question in military history)

The following question requires that you recognize facts and draw reasonable conclusions form them:

- Identify three inferences you have made recently and explain the facts which prompted you to make these inferences. (A question in logic)

To write effective answers to the preceding three essay questions, you have to be more than a good memorizer and organizer. You must be able to write answers that reflect your skill in critical thinking.

Critical thinking is the ability to make sense out of the world. This kind of thinking helps you distinguish between right and wrong, develop sound values, find and understand information, relate to people, solve problems, and work toward goals. Critical thinking relies on facts. It may use theories, but it also needs common sense, imagination, and feeling to develop fully.

Understanding How Essay Questions Are Structured

An essay question may contain one or more parts. This next question asks for a description and stresses five features about Lee and Grant.

- Describe Generals Lee and Grant at Appomattox. In your description, include information about their *appearance, dress, mannerisms, attitudes,* and *conversation.*

The teacher has constructed the question this way because he or she wants you to be sure to mention certain facts about the generals in your description. The question is carefully worded to help you organize these facts in a clear, concise order. Note that it begins with nonverbal descriptors such as *appearance* and *dress* and ends with the verbal descriptor *conversation.* Thus the question can help you write an answer that proceeds from the outer man (the way each general looks) to the inner man (the way each one thinks and feels as suggested by his attitudes and talk).

On the other hand, some questions are open-ended and give you considerable latitude in answering. Such are the *prompt* questions which appear in some English skills exams. These questions are not written in complete sentences. They present their subjects in very general frameworks and prompt you to create your own specific topics and write about them. The following question, for instance, is designed to test your ability to write clear, correct, and thoughtful essays:

> One of the best or worst experiences a college student can have.

Notice that the question contains a *category* (experience), a *class* (best or worse experiences) and a *characteristic* (a college student can have) that differentiates this college experience from other experiences the person might have. To answer this question you would have to explain your own best or worst experience, like getting a final grade of 'A' in a very tough course or waiting in a college registration line for six hours.

Understanding How Essay Questions Are Worded

The wording of an essay question is a very important indication of what the teacher expects in your answer.

Before you start to write, you should read the question carefully and make sure you understand every word in it. Pay particularly close attention to key words in the questions.

I call these key words buzz words. *Buzz words* often signal how you are to answer the question and what kind of information you should include. Here are some typical buzz verbs and the meanings which teachers usually intend when they use these verbs in their essay questions. Notice that for each verb there is a sample essay question in parentheses which shows how the verb is used.

Buzz Verb	**Meaning and Sample Test Question**
affect	Influence; bring about a change in (How did France's aid to the American revolutionaries affect the outcome of the Revolutionary War?)
analyze	Divide into component parts and show the relation of each part to the other parts or to the whole (Analyze acquired immune deficiency syndrome [AIDS] with emphasis on possible causes of the disease, early symptoms of it, and its major effects in the advanced stage.)
classify	Organize according to a class or category (Classify the ways you and several of your friends or acquaintances study for exams.)
compare	Give the similarities and/or the differences (Compare at least two major advertising techniques of two corporations that produce the same product.)

contrast	Show the differences (Contrast the concept of nirvana in Buddhism with the idea of the mystical experience in Christianity.)
define	Determine the meaning, qualities, or significance of (Define what you mean by an excellent teacher.)
describe	Explain the features, properties, or qualities of (Describe some typical symptoms of myocardial infarction, the medical term for heart attack.)
discuss	Examine a subject or topic carefully (Discuss some advantages and disadvantages of the multinational corporation.)
evaluate	Judge carefully; determine the value or worth of something by applying standards to it (Using precise moral, ethical, and business standards, evaluate the practice of insider-trading in the stock markets.)
exemplify	Show or illustrate by examples and details (Define good sportsmanship and exemplify it in some of the games you play and/or watch.)
identify	Establish the identity of; ascertain the origin, nature, or distinctive characteristics of (Identify these characters from Shakespeare: Ophelia, Goneril, Desdemona, and Titania.)
illustrate	Clarify by examples, details or comparisons (Illustrate some changes in clothing styles for young men or young women during the last five years.)
interpret	Explain the meaning or significance of (Interpret this passage from Ecclesiastes in the Bible: "All is vanity!")
justify	Demonstrate or prove to be right or valid (React to this statement argumentatively: "The registration system at this college works to the advantage of the student." Justify your argument with facts and relevant details.)
signify	Make known; serve as a sign of (How did the emperor Constantine signify his tolerance of Christianity during the early years of his reign?)
summarize	Restate briefly; condense a subject to its essential points (Summarize the essential points of John F. Kennedy's inaugural address.)

These buzz verbs may have noun forms that frequently appear in essay questions: *analysis, definition, description, evaluation, interpretation,* and *summary.*

The following buzz nouns are also quite common in test questions:

Buzz Noun	**Meaning and Sample Test Question**
cause	Something that produces an effect; a reason (Explain two major causes of the War of 1812.)
characteristic	A distinguishing feature (Explain an important characteristic of supply-side economics.)
content	(1) Subject matter of a book or literary work (How does Jefferson arrange the content of the "Declaration of Independence"?); (2) meaning or significance of a literary or artistic work (Explain the content of the poem "The Waste Land" by T. S. Eliot.); (3) something contained inside a receptacle (What are some of the typical contents of leaking containers of hazardous wastes?); (4) proportion or amount of specified material contained, present, or yielded (The chemical content of acid raid is different from the environmental substances which caused the acid condition. Explain.)
effect	Result; impression; power to produce a result; way in which something acts upon something (What effect[s] do the grading policies at your school have on you as a learner?)
factor	Something that contributes to a result, process, or accomplishment (What factors contribute to the high productivity of the salt marshes in Duval County?)
form	Shape and structure of something as distinguished from its content or substance (Explain the statement, "The basic embryonic form in all vertebrate animals consists of five tubes.")
parallel	Something that closely resembles something else; a comparison indicating likeness; (Point out parallels between some of the stories in *The Tales of Ancient Egypt* and some stories in the Bible.)

Criteria for Writing Good Answers to Essay Questions

An important step to writing well on essay tests is learning the standards by which essay questions are graded.

A good answer meets the following criteria:

- *It gives only what the question calls for* and does not introduce irrelevant information.
- *It contains accurate statements.*
- *It is well organized and is careful to follow the exact order* or sequence of the question; for instance, if the question has several parts, the answer addresses part one first, part two second, and so on.
- *It contains specific examples* to support its general statements.
- *It is emphatic;* that is, its general points and specific details are directly pertinent to the buzz words in the question.
- *It follows the proper rules of documentation and gives credit to any sources it uses,* including the textbook. (*Note:* Students writing in class under the pressure of time and without the aid of books and notes may not be able to comply fully with this standard. But they should make every effort to give credit to the sources they use.)
- *It clearly distinguishes between the student's own views and those of authorities from whom the student borrows.*
- *It is clear and concise* in its wording.
- *It is grammatically correct.*

Example: Now using the standards just stated, let's evaluate answers to two essay questions. Here is the first question with key words underlined (it is based on a question in *Culture and Values* by Cunningham and Reich, Volume 2, 1982):

Define *religious ecstasy.* Do you see any examples of religious ecstasy in the world today? If so, explain these examples. If not, why do you think religious ecstasy is missing today?

The answer to this question (the kind you might write for a take-home test) follows:

The movie *Agnes of God* is an example of how religious ecstasy manifests itself in our world and brings up the question of whether we benefit from our unfamiliarity with it.

Agnes, a nun, is being brought before a jury on charges of murder. A court psychologist is assigned to the case to provide the court with a psychological profile of Agnes. In the course of her research, the psychologist discovers that Agnes is repressing a traumatic childhood. Her fanatical mother had not only sexually and physically abused her but also instilled in her the belief that she was essentially evil and, to be forgiven for her sins, she must lead a religious life dedicated to serving God.

During her initiation at the convent, Agnes leads a life of self-denial and begins to have unexplainable experiences. She sings hymns in a voice not her own and occasionally bleeds from the palms of her hands as Christ did when being crucified. Due to her innocence, Agnes believes that her conception of a child is a result of another mystical experience and that she is being punished again. This time she reacts by releasing her pent-up frustrations and hatred toward what she thinks is an unmerciful God and killing her baby at its birth.

The psychologist finds it difficult to make a final assessment but is being pressured by the state, which in turn is being pressured by the church. The state, not wanting to prosecute a nun, wishes to conform to the church's desires to release Agnes and return her to the convent to avoid unwanted publicity. On the other hand, the psychologist feels that it is the state's moral obligation to give Agnes's psychological well-being priority over what is essentially a political issue.

The end of the movie leaves me wondering whether society benefits from our unfamiliarity with this type of experience.

In earlier times, these experiences were the focus of many artists and writers such as Gian Lorenzo Bernini and Richard Crashaw. These artists used the lives of Teresa of Avila and John of the Cross as themes for their sculpture and poetry respectively. I feel that society's lack of faith in one another and of the unfamiliar deprives us of a greater understanding of each other and the driving forces behind a great many.

This answer is not successful because it does not deal with the entire question. The question asked for a *definition of religious ecstasy.* None is given. The question *also* asked for examples or an explanation of why religious ecstasy is missing today. But the answer gives merely one example by summarizing a film. The last sentence of the answer is particularly troublesome in its faulty wording and lack of clarity.

Example: Now consider this next question and answer, part of a take home test. Identify the buzz word in the question. Then read the answer.

For what reason might an authoritarian or totalitarian culture find expressionist art a threat and suppress it?

A totalitarian culture would probably find expressionist art enough of a threat to suppress it for several reasons. For one thing, totalitarianism requires unquestioning obedience to authority. To dominate a culture, a dictator must completely control it. Expressionism, on the other hand, relies on personal freedom. Often concerned with the subconscious and the inner person, the expressionist must be free to range widely in art and life, to probe, to exaggerate, even to distort reality. The flexibility of the artist and the rigidity of the dictator produce a sharp conflict which often results in the dictator suppressing the artist.

Tsarist Russia, for example, oppressed the great writer Fyodor Dostoyevsky, himself a forerunner of twentieth-century expressionism. In his famous letter on Soviet censorship, Alexander Solzhenitsyn says that Dostoyevsky was imprisoned in Siberia for belonging to a socialist discussion group which the tsar considered dangerous and subversive. Solzhenitsyn also lists in the letter many later writers who were persecuted by the Stalin regime; among these were authors like Maximilian Voloshin (x-xii) who were strongly influenced by literary expressionism.

Further, some expressionistic art has as its major theme social protest, and thus totalitarian regimes would see it as a threat. George Grosz's drawing *Fit for Active Service* (1918), for instance, makes a mockery of a military examining station in Germany during World War I. The doctor in the drawing is examining a standing skeleton and announcing that it is ready for military service (*Culture and Values*, 2:375). This work hammers home the brutality and waste of war and would no doubt be despised by a dictator like Hitler bent on using patriotism as a force to spur a nation to war. In fact, Hitler attacked all German art of the early twentieth century (including expressionism), calling it impotent and a disgrace to German cultural traditions (261). By 1933, he was actively suppressing the modern art he had condemned earlier in *Mein Kampf.*

Unfortunately, totalitarian attacks on expressionism and other forms of modern art did not die with Hitler and Stalin. Throughout the world today, many leftist and rightist regimes are infamous for dragging artists and intellectuals off in the middle of the night to prisons or to be executed. Even in the United States there are growing numbers of people who fervently believe that the imagination should be bounded to the narrow confines of their own rigid dogmas and creeds. In the name of religion, these authoritarians try to deny students access to artists like Kafka, Kandinsky, and Pollock. But these reactionaries are fighting a losing battle. Great art will withstand their attacks.

Works Used:
Cunningham, Lawrence and John Reich. *Culture and Values: A Survey of the Western Humanities.* 2 vols. New York: Holt Rinehart and Winston, 1982.
Hitler, Adolf. *Mein Kampf.* Trans. Ralph Manheim. Boston: Houghton Mifflin, 1971.
Solzhenitsyn, Alexander. "Letter to the fourth National Congress of Soviet Writers." Reprinted as part of the introduction of Solzhenitsyn's *One Day in the Life of Ivan Denisovich.* New York: Bantam, 1978.

Notice how much better this answer is than the one about religious ecstasy. In the opening sentence, the writer repeats the buzz word (reason) of the question (a good way to begin an essay answer). Then the writer directly addresses the matter of expressionism vs. dictatorship. The answer is written well and organized adequately, and it clearly distinguishes between the writer's views and those of sources. Note the sources within the answer and the bibliography at the end of it. Of course, a student writing this answer in class under timed conditions would not be able to document with citations and bibliography.

COLLABORATIVE LEARNING

1. Find several of your answers to essay test questions. These answers might be for this course or another. Study your answers to see how closely you followed the suggestions in this chapter. What did you do well? What could you improve? Take these essay answers to your writing group and share them. Explain to the group the ways in which you followed the hints in the chapter and the ways that your answers might be improved. Revise one essay answer.

2. Study the answer on expressionism and totalitarianism. Could the answer be improved in any way? Would it be stronger with more specific examples? The last paragraph is quite general and opinionated. Is it fully convincing? If so, why? If not, how would you rewrite it to make it more convincing?

469

3. Take to class five or more essay questions you might have to answer for other classes. Analyze each question by answering the following:

   a. What exactly does each question ask you to do?

   b. How is each question structured? What are the parts? What should you do first? Second? Third?

   c. What are the buzz words in the question? What do these buzz words expect you to do?

WRITING TASKS

1. From your own experience and/or with the help of outside sources, write your own answer to the question on religious ecstasy discussed in this chapter.

2. To prepare for essay exams, make up questions your teachers might give you. Then practice answering these questions using the suggestions given in this chapter.

Checklist for Answering Essay Tests

Yes	No		
____	____	1.	Did you identify the buzz word(s) in the test question?
____	____	2.	Did you use the buzz word(s) in your answer?
____	____	3.	Did you answer only what the question asked?
____	____	4.	Is your information accurate?
____	____	5.	Do you follow the sequence of the test question in your answer?
____	____	6.	Do you offer specific examples that explain your general statements?
____	____	7.	Do you give credit to your sources if you used sources?
____	____	8.	Do you distinguish between your views and those you borrow from authorities?

Final Note

And so we reach the end of our time together. After all the work you've done—reading the text, conferring with your instructor, collaborating with others, and writing by yourself—you should be a better writer now than you were before you opened this book or began a writing course.

But learning to write well is lifetime job. Malcolm Cowley, a famous author who practiced his writing craft into his eighties, told my colleague, Kevin Bezner, that he, Cowley, was still learning to write at eighty.

A writer is never finished learning about writing. A piece of writing is never finished; it can always be improved, no matter who wrote it.

I hope you learned enough to be comfortable as a writer. But I also hope you've learned enough to be able to improve your writing all through your educational career and beyond.

Do write and tell me how you do!

organization and, 205
and peer response, 256
suggestions for, 203–205
what it is, 197–198
Rhythm, developing, 222–223
Rosenblatt, Roger, 291–193

S

Satire, 449
Senses, in description, 317
Setting
in critique, 424
in personal narrative, 278
Sherill, Donna, 144
Similarities, significance of, 334–335
Similes, 221
Simpson, Kirke, 318
Slang, 218
Small, Virginia, 143
Snob appeal, 440
Solomon, Michael, 274–276
Solution, as conclusion, 189
Source, reporting, 87
Spatial order, 137, 140–141
Specificity, of examples, 295
Standards
for critique, 423
knowing those used to judge a work,
420
Statistics, as introduction, 186
Steps, breaking process into, 310
Story
as conclusion, 190
to entertain, 273
to further understanding, 273
reasons for writing, 276
Structure
of argument, 442
in critique, 424
Students, and essays, 179
Subject
choosing for argument, 437
practice in narrowing, 9–10
as title, 181–182

Summary
as conclusion, 190
in critique, 421
and essay, 404
example of, 404–408
how to write, 400
Supporting information
arranging in logical order, 162–164
collecting when writing about process,
310
for comparison or contrast, 334
deciding on appropriate, 160
in essay, 179
gathering, 86
interviewing to find, 69–70
organizing, 311, 335
and peer response, 256
predicting, 151–152
and revision, 204
strategies for collecting, 48
ways to arrange, 137–147
where to find, 47
Surprise, using diction to, 213
Swift, Jonathan, 450
Synonyms, 222, 403
in definition, 351

T

Tape recorder, using during interview, 72
Tests, nature of essay, 462
Theme
in critique, 423
in personal narrative, 278
Thesis, 149
as introduction, 187
and revision, 204
Thesis statement, 179
in essay,
finding, 401
Thinking process, 63
Three-part response, 252
Time order, 137, 138
Title
studying, 401